OXFORD THEORETICAL PERSPECTIVES IN LAW

Series Editor

ALEXANDER TSESIS

Professor and D'Alemberte Chair in Constitutional Law, Florida State University College of Law

Due Process as American Democracy
Martin H. Redish

OXFORD THEORETICAL PERSPECTIVES IN LAW

The *Oxford Theoretical Perspectives in Law* series publishes works that explore a diversity of topics pertinent to jurisprudence, statutory review, constitutional principles, substantive entitlements, procedural justice, legal history, and policymaking. The series is committed to intellectual diversity.

Books in this series parse, critique, expand, and elaborate theoretical approaches to broad ranges of legal topics. Authors' works explain the principles, priorities, sensibilities, perspectives, traditions, or social conditions that drive evolution of law. Authors write of how sovereignty, wealth, connection, privilege, culture, and popular discourse influence legal concepts, rules of decision, procedural justice, and substantive fairness. The series further examines how law impacts sociology, politics, traditions, and culture and, in turn, how they impact precedents, policy priorities, administrative tactics, separation of powers, and representative governance.

Oxford Theoretical Perspectives in Law offers a forum for pursuit of contested matters in legal theory that impact contemporary society. Approaches range from empirical, to normative, to positivist. The basic concept may be said to articulate core, rule of law principles in subjects that range from constitutional law to property law.

Authors in the series advance fields of knowledge by elaborating, parsing, analyzing, and criticizing text, history, norms, doctrines, and structure. They thereby provide readers with substantive and structural frameworks to be used in research and teaching. Comprehensive studies enable authors and readers to explore challenges facing a variety of current affairs. A dive into legal theory, ultimately and perhaps idealistically, seeks to evaluate and effectuate fairness and justice.

DUE PROCESS AS AMERICAN DEMOCRACY

MARTIN H. REDISH

Louis and Harriet Ancel Professor of Law and Public Policy
Northwestern University Pritzker School of Law

OXFORD
UNIVERSITY PRESS

Oxford University Press is a department of the University of Oxford. It furthers the University's objective of excellence in research, scholarship, and education by publishing worldwide. Oxford is a registered trade mark of Oxford University Press in the UK and certain other countries.

Published in the United States of America by Oxford University Press
198 Madison Avenue, New York, NY 10016, United States of America.

© Martin H. Redish 2024

All rights reserved. No part of this publication may be reproduced, stored in a retrieval system, or transmitted, in any form or by any means, without the prior permission in writing of Oxford University Press, or as expressly permitted by law, by license, or under terms agreed with the appropriate reproduction rights organization. Inquiries concerning reproduction outside the scope of the above should be sent to the Rights Department, Oxford University Press, at the address above.

You must not circulate this work in any other form
and you must impose this same condition on any acquirer.

Library of Congress Cataloging-in-Publication Data
Names: Redish, Martin H., author.
Title: Due process as American democracy / Martin H. Redish.
Description: New York : Oxford University Press, 2024. |
Series: Theoretical perspectives in law series |
Includes bibliographical references and index. |
Provided by publisher.
Identifiers: LCCN 2023050059 | ISBN 9780197747414 (hardback) |
ISBN 9780197747438 (epub) | ISBN 9780197747421 (updf) | ISBN 9780197747445 (online)
Subjects: LCSH: Due process of law—United States. |
Democracy—United States.
Classification: LCC KF4765 .R43 2024 | DDC 347.73/05—dc23/eng/20231025
LC record available at https://lccn.loc.gov/2023050059

DOI: 10.1093/oso/9780197747414.001.0001

Printed by Integrated Books International, United States of America

Note to Readers

This publication is designed to provide accurate and authoritative information in regard to the subject matter covered. It is based upon sources believed to be accurate and reliable and is intended to be current as of the time it was written. It is sold with the understanding that the publisher is not engaged in rendering legal, accounting, or other professional services. If legal advice or other expert assistance is required, the services of a competent professional person should be sought. Also, to confirm that the information has not been affected or changed by recent developments, traditional legal research techniques should be used, including checking primary sources where appropriate.

(Based on the Declaration of Principles jointly adopted by a Committee of the American Bar Association and a Committee of Publishers and Associations.)

You may order this or any other Oxford University Press publication
by visiting the Oxford University Press website at www.oup.com.

" 'Professor Redish's tour de force deftly blends political theory, constitutional theory, and doctrine into a thoughtful, ambitious, and provocative reconstruction of the concept of due process. Scholars interested in constitutional law, interpretative theory, civil procedure, administrative law, legal ethics, remedies, free speech, the public-private distinction, or the American constitutional order as a whole—just to name a few topics covered in this bold and engaging work—will find themselves sometimes cheering, sometimes jeering, but always thinking. This is scholarship at its best.' "

Professor Gary Lawson, Philip S. Beck Professor of Law,
Boston University School of Law

" 'No scholar has written more cogently about the intersection of democratic theory with American constitutional due process. In this provocative new book Professor Martin Redish challenges conventional due process accounts based on originalism, utilitarianism, and dignity values. He suggests contemporary interpretations are flawed, constituting ' "an unhappy blending of unimaginative judicial thinking, mindless adherence to historical practice, or vague notions of political philosophy.' " The nub of Redish's argument is that due process accounts fail to ground it in underlying democratic theory or a proper appreciation of separation of powers doctrine. Redish revolutionizes due process thinking with a new theory based on concepts of liberal adversarial democracy and skeptical optimism. He illustrates his theory in settings such as complex multidistrict litigation, representative lawsuits, private contingent fee attorneys aligning with government attorneys, and administrative actions." '

Professor Linda S. Mullenix, Morris & Rita Atlas Chair in Advocacy,
University of Texas School of Law

" 'Procedural due process (PDP) is one of the most invoked and least understood concepts in American law. In this pathbreaking book, Professor Redish views PDP as an outgrowth of ' "liberal adversary democracy,' " rooted in mistrust of those who wield power. He uses this lens to illuminate problematic doctrine in civil procedure, administrative law, and constitutional law. Only a scholar of Redish's breadth and depth could write this sweeping and important book. It is a capstone achievement by one of America's preeminent constitutional theorists." '

Richard Freer, Charles Howard Candler Professor of Law,
Emory University

*To my wife, Caren, and my daughters,
Jessica and Elisa*

CONTENTS

ACKNOWLEDGMENTS xv
INTRODUCTION: DUE PROCESS AS AN OUTGROWTH OF AMERICAN DEMOCRACY xvii

1. LIBERAL ADVERSARY DEMOCRACY 1
2. DUE PROCESS AS LIBERAL ADVERSARY DEMOCRACY 7
3. MULTIDISTRICT LITIGATION, DUE PROCESS, AND THE DANGERS OF PROCEDURAL COLLECTIVISM 41
4. PROCEDURAL DUE PROCESS AND THE DAY-IN-COURT IDEAL: RESOLVING THE VIRTUAL REPRESENTATION DILEMMA 75
5. PRIVATE CONTINGENT FEE LAWYERS, PUBLIC POWER, AND PROCEDURAL DUE PROCESS 109
6. DUE PROCESS, FREE EXPRESSION, AND THE ADMINISTRATIVE STATE 135
7. CONSTITUTIONAL REMEDIES AS DUE PROCESS OF LAW 165

CONCLUSION 209
NOTES 215
INDEX 285

DETAILED CONTENTS

ACKNOWLEDGMENTS	xv
INTRODUCTION: DUE PROCESS AS AN OUTGROWTH OF AMERICAN DEMOCRACY	xvii
1. LIBERAL ADVERSARY DEMOCRACY	1
1.1 INTRODUCTION	1
1.2 (LIBERAL) ADVERSARY DEMOCRACY: A MARRIAGE OF OPPOSITES	1
2. DUE PROCESS AS LIBERAL ADVERSARY DEMOCRACY	7
2.1 INTRODUCTION	7
2.2 PROCEDURAL DUE PROCESS AND SKEPTICAL OPTIMISM	7
2.3 PROCEDURAL DUE PROCESS AND THE LEGITIMACY OF DEMOCRACY	10
2.4 APPLYING ADVERSARY DEMOCRATIC DUE PROCESS	11
2.5 PROPHYLACTIC NEUTRAL ADJUDICATION	13
2.6 MISGUIDED FAITH IN ADMINISTRATOR INTEGRITY	15
2.7 ELECTED STATE JUDGES	17
2.8 THE LAW OF JUDGMENTS AND THE "DAY-IN-COURT" IDEAL	18
2.9 CLASS ACTIONS	21
2.10 LEGISLATIVE DECEPTION	23
2.11 REBUTTING THE PRESUMPTION OF FAIR PROCEDURE	26
2.12 THE LIMITED OVERLAP BETWEEN *MATHEWS* AND ADVERSARY DEMOCRATIC DUE PROCESS	31
2.13 REJECTING ALTERNATIVE MODELS OF PROCEDURAL DUE PROCESS	32
2.14 CONCLUSION	38
3. MULTIDISTRICT LITIGATION, DUE PROCESS, AND THE DANGERS OF PROCEDURAL COLLECTIVISM	41
3.1 INTRODUCTION	41
3.2 HISTORY AND STRUCTURE OF MULTIDISTRICT LITIGATION	46
3.3 THE MECHANICS OF MULTIDISTRICT LITIGATION	47
3.4 MDL'S DUE PROCESS DIFFICULTIES	55
3.5 IS MDL CONSTITUTIONALLY SALVAGEABLE?	70
3.6 CONCLUSION	72

4. PROCEDURAL DUE PROCESS AND THE DAY-IN-COURT IDEAL: RESOLVING THE VIRTUAL REPRESENTATION DILEMMA — 75
   4.1 INTRODUCTION — 75
   4.2 VIRTUAL REPRESENTATION IN THE COURTS — 78
   4.3 THE DAY-IN-COURT IDEAL IN AMERICAN CONSTITUTIONAL AND POLITICAL THEORY — 83
   4.4 LITIGANT AUTONOMY, LIBERAL ADVERSARY DEMOCRATIC THEORY, AND THE DAY-IN-COURT IDEAL — 86
   4.5 LIMITATIONS ON THE DAY-IN-COURT IDEAL — 88
   4.6 INDIVISIBLE RELIEF, DUE PROCESS, AND VIRTUAL REPRESENTATION — 88
   4.7 THE DIFFICULTY OF INDIVISIBLE RELIEF — 92
   4.8 DEFINING ADEQUATE REPRESENTATION — 99
   4.9 RESOLVING THE VIRTUAL REPRESENTATION DILEMMA: A SUMMARY — 101
   4.10 SHAPING PROPHYLACTIC MEASURES TO AVOID THE VIRTUAL REPRESENTATION DILEMMA — 102
   4.11 INCENTIVIZING AVOIDANCE OF THE VIRTUAL REPRESENTATION DILEMMA — 103
   4.12 CONCLUSION — 106

5. PRIVATE CONTINGENT FEE LAWYERS, PUBLIC POWER, AND PROCEDURAL DUE PROCESS — 109
   5.1 INTRODUCTION — 109
   5.2 GOVERNMENTAL USE OF CONTINGENCY FEE ATTORNEYS: DEVELOPMENT OF THE PRACTICE — 113
   5.3 LIBERAL DEMOCRACY, STATE ACTION, AND THE PUBLIC-PRIVATE DICHOTOMY: IMPLICATIONS FOR PRIVATE CONTINGENCY FEE ARRANGEMENTS — 115
   5.4 THE PUBLIC-PRIVATE DICHOTOMY AND GOVERNMENT ATTORNEYS — 118
   5.5 CONSTITUTIONAL IMPLICATIONS OF THE STATE'S USE OF PRIVATE CONTINGENCY FEE ATTORNEYS — 127
   5.6 CONCLUSION — 132

6. DUE PROCESS, FREE EXPRESSION, AND THE ADMINISTRATIVE STATE — 135
   6.1 INTRODUCTION: ADVERSARY DEMOCRACY AND THE DUE PROCESS RIGHT TO A NEUTRAL ADJUDICATOR — 135
   6.2 A TAXONOMY OF UNCONSTITUTIONAL ADJUDICATORY BIASES — 142
   6.3 ADMINISTRATIVE ADJUDICATION AND DUE PROCESS — 146

6.4	AVOIDING THE MOST SERIOUS DUE PROCESS PATHOLOGIES OF THE ADMINISTRATIVE STATE	157
6.5	THE SPECIAL CASE OF FIRST AMENDMENT DUE PROCESS	159
6.6	CONCLUSION: PROCEDURE AS THE HANDMAID OF JUSTICE	164

7. CONSTITUTIONAL REMEDIES AS DUE PROCESS OF LAW — 165
    7.1 INTRODUCTION — 165
    7.2 THE CONSTITUTIONAL THEORY OF CONSTITUTIONAL REMEDIES — 169
    7.3 CHALLENGING THE INTERSECTION OF CONSTITUTIONAL DIRECTIVES AND CONSTITUTIONAL REMEDIES — 173
    7.4 CONSTITUTIONAL REMEDIES AND CONSTITUTIONAL TEXT — 174
    7.5 THE INADEQUACY OF EXISTING SCHOLARLY THEORY — 180
    7.6 ANTICIPATING AND RESPONDING TO COUNTERARGUMENTS — 185
    7.7 THE INCOHERENCE OF CONSTITUTIONAL COMMON LAW — 186
    7.8 CONSTITUTIONAL REMEDIES AND CONGRESSIONAL POWER TO CONTROL FEDERAL JURISDICTION — 191
    7.9 *LAUF*'S FUNDAMENTAL FLAW — 192
    7.10 STATUTORY ENFORCEMENT VS. CONSTITUTIONAL INTERPRETATION: SEPARATION OF POWERS AND LIMITS ON CONGRESS'S POWER TO CONTROL FEDERAL JURISDICTION — 194
    7.11 IMPLICATIONS OF CONSTITUTIONAL REMEDIES AS CONSTITUTIONAL LAW: CONSTRUING AND MISCONSTRUING *BIVENS* — 196
    7.12 IMPLIED STATUTORY REMEDIES — 198
    7.13 *BIVENS* AND IMPLIED CONSTITUTIONAL REMEDIES — 199
    7.14 IMPLIED STATUTORY REMEDIES VS. IMPLIED CONSTITUTIONAL REMEDIES — 204
    7.15 CONSTITUTIONAL REMEDIES AND ADVERSARY DEMOCRACY — 206
    7.16 CONCLUSION — 206

CONCLUSION — 209
NOTES — 215
INDEX — 285

ACKNOWLEDGMENTS

This book is the culmination of years thinking and writing about the theory and doctrine of procedural due process. As has often been the case, it wasn't until I had authored several articles on narrow aspects of the subject that I was able to glean from my earlier work a coherent and, I believe, innovative perspective on due process which links that constitutional protection to the underlying theory of American democracy.

Not surprisingly, then, many of the chapters derive from those earlier works, all of which are reproduced with the permission of the scholarly journals that published them. However, all of those prior articles have been modified to bring them into line with my underlying political theory of procedural due process.

Chapters 1 and 2 draw heavily on my article, coauthored with Victor Hiltner, *Adversary Democratic Due Process*, soon to be published in the Florida Law Review.

Chapter 3 derives from the article *One Size Doesn't Fit All: Multidistrict Litigation, Due Process, and the Dangers of Procedural Collectivism*, 95 B. U. L. Rev. 109 (2015) (coauthored with Julie Karaba).

Chapter 4 derives from the article *Taylor v. Sturgell, Procedural Due Process and the Day-in-Court Ideal: Resolving the Virtual Representation Dilemma*, 84 Notre Dame L. Rev. 1877 (2009) (coauthored with William Katt).

Chapter 5 derives from the article *Private Contingent Fee Lawyers and Public Power: Constitutional and Political Implications*, 18 Supreme Court Econ. Rev. 77 (2010).

Chapter 6 derives from the article *Due Process, Free Expression and the Administrative State*, 94 Notre Dame L. Rev. 297 (2018) (coauthored with Kristin McCall).

Chapter 7 derives from the article, *Constitutional Remedies as Constitutional Law*, 62 B.C. L. Rev. 1865 (2021).

My former students who coauthored several of the preceding articles—Victor Hiltner, Julie Karaba, Kristin McCall, and Bill Katt—deserve special thanks for the hard work and valuable ideas they contributed to each of their respective articles. To the extent I have added to the articles or rewritten or removed portions of them, all of the responsibility (and any mistakes) are mine alone.

There are, of course, additional thanks to be given. My thanks go to Jane Brock, who typed revision after revision with efficiency and good cheer. I also give thanks to the Northwestern University Pritzker School of Law for its moral, physical, and financial support in enabling me to complete this project.

Finally, I give the greatest thanks to my family—my wife, Caren, and my daughters, Jessica and Elisa. I have dedicated this book to all of them, for the very simple reason that I am blessed to have them in my life, and I am thankful every day for their love and support.

INTRODUCTION
DUE PROCESS AS AN OUTGROWTH OF AMERICAN DEMOCRACY

Procedural due process guarantees to individual members of the polity that government will treat each of them with fairness and respect when seeking to take their life, liberty, or property. It is not a guarantee that government will never seek to coerce them, imprison them, or deprive them of their property. It is, however, a guarantee that government will never do so absent the availability of fair procedure designed to determine whether the proposed governmental coercion is in fact grounded in law and legitimate as a matter of fact.

While both the Fifth and Fourteenth Amendments to the US Constitution guarantee such protection, neither constitutional text, history, nor doctrine provides a clear perspective as to what procedures do or do not constitute due process. To be sure, the phrase unambiguously dictates a generic requirement of fair procedure. But courts and scholars have battled amongst themselves for many years as to the specifics of such a requirement. Is "due process" to be defined as simply whatever procedures the political branches of government deem appropriate? Is it to be nothing more than the equivalent of whatever historical English or colonial practice dictated at the time the Constitution was adopted? Is it nothing more than the result of some sort of utilitarian calculus which balances the individual's interest in having available a particular procedure against the costs and burdens to which such a procedure gives rise? Or is it the outgrowth of some form of political theory of individualist self-realization? No one is sure, and the result has been an unhappy blending of unimaginative judicial thinking, mindless adherence to historical practice, and vague notions of political philosophy untied to the political system of which due process is a central part. In this book, I reject all of these alternatives as flawed for one reason or another. In their place, I fashion a theory of due process that is simultaneously intertwined with and an outgrowth of the proper understanding of American democratic theory.

The goals of this book are threefold. First, the book is designed to explain how the constitutional guarantee of procedural due process and the proper understanding of foundational American democratic theory are inextricably intertwined. In so doing, the book will explain why controlling American political theory is appropriately deemed to be a form of "liberal adversary democracy" and then describe why procedural due process, when properly viewed as an outgrowth of American political theory, should be shaped in a manner that recognizes the underlying assumptions and values of liberal adversary democratic theory. Second, the book explains why preexisting theoretical frameworks of procedural due process—primarily, the historical perspective, the utilitarian perspective, and the dignitary perspective—are either inconsistent with the broader structure of American constitutional theory or are theoretically flawed or incomplete. Finally, after developing and explaining the form of due process that grows out of liberal adversary democratic theory—what I refer to as "adversary democratic due process"—the book demonstrates how this form of due process applies to numerous areas of constitutional procedure.

While the chapters that follow explore both the theory and doctrine of due process in great detail, the book's thesis can be summarized in a straightforward manner. To this point, procedural due process theory and doctrine have suffered from a combination of judicial failure to attempt to ground that doctrine in underlying American democratic theory and the failure of either jurists or scholars to develop a legitimate, coherent theoretical framework for the shaping of due process doctrine. This theoretical void should be replaced by a version of due process that recognizes its vitally important intersection with American democratic theory.

The foundation of American political theory, as both a historical and normative matter, should be deemed to be adversary democracy—a democratic theory grounded, for the most part, in an overriding commitment to rule by those who are representative of and accountable to the electorate. Adversary democracy disdains a search for the "common good" in favor of a recognition of the inevitable existence of ideological and interest-based factions. Based on this empirical recognition, adversary democratic theory focuses on the need to manage the conflict among these groups in a manner which assures the continued vitality of representative democracy by preventing both winners' suppression of losers and individuals' right to protect their own interests in the process of governing.

This protection of individual interests, it should be emphasized, is by no means the equivalent of modern substantive libertarianism. Rather, its protections are confined to what can be called "meta-liberties"—that is, the liberty of participating in the democratic process. Individuals or entities may participate in the democratic process in two basic ways: first, by seeking to convince other private individuals or entities to support particular policies, or second, by attempting to influence governmental decisions in a manner consistent with their particular interests. This category includes attempts to influence decisions of *all* units of government—legislative, executive, or judicial—which may impact interests or values of the individual or entity in question. Adversary democracy reflects both the realities of modern society and the historical foundations of our democratic form of government, in which, as James Madison wrote so famously in *Federalist No. 51*, "ambition must be made to counteract ambition." Indeed, the nation's form of constitutional government was shaped in light of the recognition of the inevitability of competing factions, as Madison's even more famous *Federalist No. 10* so clearly shows. But recognition of the inevitability of ideological or interest-based factions as an inherent part of the operation of American government does not mean that our form of constitutional democracy was grounded in total pessimism or cynicism about the human character of the citizenry. To the contrary, much of the driving force behind the creation of the nation's Constitution was a belief in the possibilities of human growth, flourishing, and self-realization, all to be achieved by a foundational commitment to representative democracy. However, paradoxically conjoined with this optimism about human growth and development was a very real fear of the darker elements of the human personality, which push toward authoritarianism and the eventual demise of the democratic system. I refer to this theoretical paradox as "skeptical optimism."

Under the premises of adversary democratic theory, private individuals or entities may not be required to trust others to protect their interests except in the most rare and extreme circumstances. Individuals and entities may reasonably assume that no one else shares their particular viewpoints or interests. Rather, within the framework of adversary democracy, a presumption exists that others will pursue their own interests, rather than those of the particular individual or entity in question. This is true of all other private and governmental individuals or entities. To the extent feasible, then, it must be the irrefutable choice of individuals or entities to decide whether or not to rely on the protection of others in guaranteeing or enforcing their rights and interests in governmentally run proceedings. The threat to democracy which results from any approach that takes this choice away from the individual is unacceptably high.

These seemingly opposing visions of democratic theory actually work well together. When the two are conjoined in what can be called "liberal adversary democracy," the mistrustful presumptions of adversary democracy serve as the bodyguard of liberal democracy. In other words, only through resort to the protective reach of adversary democracy can we assure achievement of the positive goals sought to be achieved by liberal democracy.

Procedural due process is appropriately viewed as an element of this broader vision of the democratic process. When private individuals or entities defend themselves in judicial or administrative proceedings brought either by government or by other private individuals empowered by government to sue, they are participating in the democratic process in order to protect their interests. The same is true when private individuals or entities seek recourse through resort to judicial or administrative proceedings in order to protect or enforce their governmentally protected rights or interests against others. As is true of private individuals' or entities' efforts to influence other governmental branches, efforts to influence the decisions of judicial or administrative entities are appropriately seen as forms of adversary democracy—efforts to employ governmental processes as a means of furthering or protecting private interests. It is therefore both necessary and appropriate to determine which processes are required by the Due Process Clauses by viewing them through the lens of adversary democracy—that is, a framework in which all individuals and entities are allowed to assume that they are adverse to all other private and governmental individuals and entities, and they are therefore allowed to operate on a presumption of suspicion of the intentions of all governmental and private actors. To the extent others may be vested with authority to represent their interests without their authorization, it will be only in two situations: (1) where it is simply infeasible, under the circumstances of the surrounding situation, to vest in the individual or entity in question with that authority, and (2) where a truly compelling competing interest is demonstrated which justifies restriction of the party's ability to represent its own interests (or choose who will do so) before an adjudicator with strict, prophylactic protections of its neutrality and independence.

While liberal adversary democratic theory will prove relevant in some way to all issues which arise in the shaping of procedural due process, its primary implications for the functioning of adjudicatory procedure will involve preservation of the two key methods of implementing adversary democratic due process. The first is the centrality of the so-called "day-in-court" ideal—the fundamental right of individuals or private entities to defend their own interests when their property or liberty are at stake, or to choose who is to represent their interests. The second is the assurance of the prophylactically insulated independence and neutrality of the adjudicator. Both factors turn fundamentally on the application of the "skeptical optimism" premise: human flourishing can only be advanced if we are skeptical and mistrustful of the actions of governmental and other private actors in playing a role in the deprivation of an individual's liberty or property interests.

Alternative frameworks for shaping procedural due process—rigid adherence to historical practice, resort to a utilitarian calculus, or reliance on dignitary values—are invalid for a variety of reasons. Fundamentally, however, their flaws are their failure to recognize the role of procedural due process as one vitally important element of the broader democratic process in general, and, in particular, their failure to recognize the centrality of adversary democratic values within that democratic process.

Once the theoretical centrality of adversary democracy as the foundational element of procedural due process is recognized, it is possible to extrapolate this adversary democratic version of due process in specific subcategories of judicial and administrative process. These applications cross conceptual and doctrinal lines, sweeping within their reach issues of both civil procedure and constitutional law.

The chapters that follow may be viewed as a synthesis of liberal adversary democratic theory as applied in three seemingly distinct but ultimately related areas of law and legal theory. The first two chapters focus predominantly on political theory. Chapter 1 explores the structure and rationale of liberal adversary theory, as well as its grounding in the framework of the American Constitution. Chapter 2 demonstrates how the concept of procedural due process grows out of and is inherently related to this form of democracy.

Chapters 3 and 4 focus on the application of adversary democratic due process to the world of civil procedure—a world with which constitutional scholars are, for the most part, unfamiliar. Yet the Constitution is very relevant to the shaping of procedure in civil litigation. After all, property rights, which are explicitly guaranteed by both Due Process Clauses, are virtually always at stake in civil cases, and it is important to view controversial areas of civil procedure through the lens of adversary democratic due process. Chapter 3 does so for the controversial but widely used concept of multidistrict litigation. Through this process, cases deemed to be similar on some level are grouped together for pretrial procedure in one federal district. The chapter explains how the shockingly random, unguided, and nontransparent procedures employed in this practice are wholly inconsistent with the dictates of adversary democratic due process. It also suggests possible ways that multidistrict litigation practice could be altered to assure its constitutionality.

Chapter 4 applies adversary democratic due process to an area of civil procedure that in the past has seriously threatened the day-in-court ideal, a practice central to the tenets of adversary democratic due process. It is referred to as "virtual representation," a practice whereby an absent nonparty who had no say in the conduct of a litigation may be bound by the result of a case, solely because the losing party had overlapping interests with the absent nonparty. While the US Supreme Court has wisely held the practice to violate due process, in so doing the Court failed in a number of very important ways. Initially, the Court merely assumed the preeminent value of the day-in-court ideal. It did so, even though highly respected scholars have challenged the importance of that ideal. The chapter fills the theoretical void left by the Court by explaining the day-in-court ideal as adversary democratic due process. Equally important, however, was the Court's failure to recognize that in certain contexts, very significant interests may actually be undermined by adherence to the day-in-court ideal, on occasion even resulting in separate due process violations. Again, attempting to fill the void left by the Court, the chapter explores in detail the situations in which adherence to the day-in-court ideal must give way in favor of a competing compelling interest.

The remaining chapters shift focus from the area of civil procedure to an examination of the role of adversary democratic due process in the world of constitutional and administrative law. Chapter 5 focuses on the relevance of adversary democratic due process to a state's use of private contingent fee attorneys in civil damage actions brought against private individuals or entities. Contingent fee lawyers are naturally driven to a large extent by goals of personal financial gain. In the world of purely private litigation, of course, there is absolutely nothing wrong with this. When attorneys exercise the power of the state, however, their driving force must be pursuit of the public interest, not personal gain. If government prosecutors were to be paid by the conviction, it is difficult to imagine such a system being held to be consistent with due process. This is so, even though government prosecutors are of course advocates, not neutral adjudicators. But those exercising governmental power must be deemed controlled by the paradoxical concept of "adversarial neutrality." This should be equally true of private attorneys vested with the power of the state.

Chapter 6 applies adversary democratic due process to the field of administrative law, an area sorely in need of rethinking from the perspective of liberal adversary democracy. Adjudicators in the administrative context are invariably employees of the very governmental organization bringing the coercive action in the first place. On the basis of adversary democracy's foundational skepticism of the motivations of government actors in the exercise of their coercive power, this built-in relationship is inherently suspect. Yet puzzlingly, the Supreme Court has been far more trusting in the neutrality of administrative adjudicators than it has in that of judges. It has done so without the slightest explanation for this dramatic difference. The chapter sets out a taxonomy of disqualifying prejudicial influences which may plague adjudicators, and then demonstrates how most administrative adjudications suffer from one or more of these unconstitutional influences. The chapter then focuses on application of due process to administrative adjudication of the most important yet vulnerable of constitutional rights, the right of free expression. It sets out the argument that even assuming, solely for purposes of argument, that it is too late in the day to alter the foundations of the seriously flawed process of administrative adjudication, special procedures should be developed to insulate the free speech right from the scope of administrative adjudicatory authority.

Chapter 7 applies adversary democratic due process to the foundational precept of separation of powers. In doing so, the book returns to the core themes set out in the first two chapters on political theory—the extent to which due process guarantees parallel the entire framework of the Constitution, which evinces mistrust of all governmental organs by effectively having each one check the other. In light of this well-established adversary democratic constitutional framework, it is mystifying how scholars and courts have almost uniformly assumed that the shaping of remedies for constitutional violations by the political branches lies exclusively in the hands of those very political branches. As a result, the most interested and least neutral actors in the entire process—the political branches themselves—are able to effectively insulate their constitutional violations from judicial control. Nothing could be more inconsistent with the foundations of adversary democracy. The chapter explains how adversary democratic due process, as well as legitimate forms of textual interpretation, logically leads to the judiciary, rather than the political branches, possessing full power to shape remedies for constitutional violations by the political branches of either the state or federal government.

This brief summary of the thesis and scope of the book's analysis will hopefully lead the reader to several important insights. First, the theory and scope of procedural due process is far more complicated than either courts or scholars have, to this point, assumed it to be. Second, when properly understood, procedural due process is understood to be both an inherent element and outgrowth of the unique form of democratic theory to which the Framers committed us in shaping the Constitution: the paradoxical notion of liberal adversary democracy. This form of democratic theory grows out of the oxymoronic concept of skeptical optimism—optimism that humans are capable of self-realization and flourishing, and skepticism that the dark side of the human personality will always stand as a threat to that self-realization unless democracy begins with a healthy skepticism of the motivations of those other than the individual or those chosen as representatives by the individual. And this skepticism is especially true of those exercising the awesome power of the state. This is the lesson to be learned from the basic premises of American political theory, and it is the lesson to be learned from the application of those fundamental democratic principles to the essence of due process.

1
LIBERAL ADVERSARY DEMOCRACY

1.1 INTRODUCTION

The foundational thesis of this book turns on acceptance of its premise: that at its core, both normatively and descriptively, American democracy is properly seen as what is best described as liberal adversary democracy. To that end, it is the goal of this chapter to establish liberal adversary democracy as American democracy.

To be sure, neither liberal nor adversary democracy are the only conceivable forms that democracy can take. For example, communitarian democracy focuses on the individual as part of a broader community and gives primacy to pursuit of some understanding of the "common good." For reasons to be explained, however, this form of democracy has never characterized the American system, nor is it consistent with the foundational values embodied in the US Constitution. This chapter will argue that American democracy represents a synthesis of two seemingly conflicting forms of democratic theory: liberal democratic theory and adversary democratic theory.

1.2 (LIBERAL) ADVERSARY DEMOCRACY: A MARRIAGE OF OPPOSITES

Adversary democracy is designed to operate in the context of conflict and disagreement. In important ways, it is the antithesis of communitarian democracy. While communitarian democracy presumes the possibility that collective deliberation can give rise to an understanding of the common good, adversary democratic theory operates under no such illusion. Although the theory permits the emergence of consensus and alignment of interests, it in no way requires it. By Chapter 1, placing individual interest at the center of the governmental process, adversary democracy humbly avoids prescribing substantive or moral decisions *ex ante*. The theory rejects the notion either that morally correct answers can be determined externally to the democratic process or that substantive values must be shared by all. Rather, faced with the empirical reality of multiple diverging interests among the citizenry, adversary democracy ensures that individuals

Due Process as American Democracy. Martin H. Redish, Oxford University Press. © Martin H. Redish 2024.
DOI: 10.1093/oso/9780197747414.003.0001

have the freedom to influence—not *guarantee*—governmental decisions, and relies on some form of majority rule to aggregate interests and reach a collective decision.

To summarize, adversary democratic theory recognizes that (1) individuals or combinations of individuals possess both the moral right and the pragmatic need to take advantage of the political or judicial processes in order to protect or advance their personal or other selected interests; (2) on many important issues, these interests will not be identical (indeed, they will often be in diametrical opposition to each other); (3) there exists no empirically provable or intuitive basis on which to believe that those in power who do not share those interests will have as their goal the protection or advancement of that interest; and (4) even in situations of identical or overlapping interests, individuals or groups should not be required to trust or defer to the competence, resources, or enthusiasm of others in the protection or advancement of their chosen interest.[1]

The free competition among a wide range of diverse interests serves as a bulwark against the tyranny of any one faction coming to power and crushing the minority. This does not mean, however, that adversary democratic theory contemplates a type of total chaos. Rather, adversary democracy—much like an "adversary" boxing match—contemplates something similar to the Marquess of Queensberry rules that control boxing.[2] There are two foundational procedural guarantees which control the process of adversary democracy: (1) all competing factions must have full and equal opportunities to contribute to public debate, and (2) those in power must treat all members of society with fair and coherent procedures prior to coercing them. If either of these foundational process-based conditions is unsatisfied, the system is, as a definitional matter, no longer democratic in any reasonable sense of the term.

In a certain sense, adversary democratic theory is the antithesis of liberal democratic theory, much as it is the antithesis of communitarian democratic theory. But there are important differences between the two situations. Whereas adversary theory cannot be reconciled with the unwavering assumption of communitarian theory that a common good may be found, it is quite possible—indeed, necessary—to view the adversary and liberal forms of democratic theory as strange bedfellows. Superficially, they seem to proceed from opposite presumptions. Adversary theory presumes that humans operate from dark motives of self-interest, and therefore individuals are wise to mistrust the motivations and actions of others. Liberal democratic theory, in contrast, proceeds from the optimistic premise that democracy can help the individual grow both morally and intellectually. Yet in an important way, liberal theory needs adversary theory as a democratic catalyst. Adversary theory functions as a kind of bodyguard for liberal theory. In other words, by proceeding from the premise of mistrust of others—particularly those either in power or seeking power—adversary theory assures that the optimistic values of self-realization inherently linked to liberal theory will not be undermined by those seeking authoritarian power.

While there is some disagreement as to the proper characterization of history,[3] it is relatively clear that, in the words of one of adversary democratic theory's most prominent experts, "the framers of the American Constitution explicitly espoused a philosophy of adversary democracy built on self-interest."[4] The Framers' strategic preference for adversarial systems designed to protect against the risk of a dominant faction abusing its power is evident in, among other things, their definition of tyranny as the accumulation of power to a single group,[5] their preference for a republic rather than a pure democracy,[6] and their disdain for the notion of a compelled common interest.[7] Indeed, the form of government ratified in the Constitution is one of endless conflict embodied by horizontal division of power (separation of powers), vertical division of power (federalism), and even intrabranch division of power (bicameralism), all restrained by a set of countermajoritarian, individually held liberties (the Bill of Rights).

Unique to the Framers' conflict-ridden, self-interest-driven system, however, is its brilliant marriage of the two counterposed political theories described previously. The first theory is the pluralist[8]—or "possessive individualist"[9]—theory first associated with Thomas Hobbes, which is founded on self-interest, centered on property and capitalistic enterprise, and largely indifferent toward individual development.[10] Fearful of the natural "state of war of every person against every other,"[11] Hobbes himself could only ever appreciate the frightening, dark side of individualism to the point where he would have preferred an "absolutist government rather than democracy," finding democracy irredeemably "unstable."[12] But on the other side, there is the far more optimistic liberal theory associated with John Stuart Mill. Under this view, humans retain great potential for self-actualization which is to be achieved through intellectual development, and democracy is therefore desirable inasmuch as it "promot[es] the moral, intellectual, and active traits of its citizens."[13]

The Framers embraced the skepticism of Hobbesian pluralist adversary theory, but masterfully repurposed it as a protective tool to promote the second theory—optimistic values of human flourishing. The adversary democracy inherent in our constitutional system strives neither to eradicate conflict nor to promote it aimlessly. Rather, it is designed to *mediate* conflict under the liberal assumptions that (1) the individual possesses "decisive epistemic and hence moral authority . . . over his actions,"[14] (2) "[h]uman dignity would be threatened by absolute power,"[15] and (3) an individual acting to promote her self-interest "fosters [their] self-realization and self-determination" and is valid insofar as it does not "improperly interfer[e] with the legitimate claims of others."[16] As pluralist adversary theories do, this liberal infusion into adversary democracy accepts the inevitability of interpersonal conflict. But the Framers accepted this reality without accepting defeat, adhering to the belief that mediation of conflict and respect for the individual will promote widespread self-realization. In other words, adversary democracy effectively serves as the bodyguard for liberal democracy. The Framers wisely recognized the paradoxical form of "skeptical optimism" that necessarily characterizes any form of successful democracy.

The positive goals of a liberal democracy, it should be recalled, are to recognize the individual as an integral whole worthy of respect and capable of human growth and flourishing.

> This "developmental" versions of democratic theory proceeds on the premise that human dignity would be threatened by absolute power, for without an opportunity to participate in the regulation of affairs in which one has an interest, it is hard to discover one's own needs and wants, arrive at tried-and-tested judgements and develop mental excellence of an intellectual, practical and moral kind. Active involvement in determining the conditions of one's existence is the prime mechanism for the cultivation of human reason and world development.[17]

However, the goals can be achieved only by recognizing the dark side of the human personality, which causes many to seek power and oppress their opponents. This is where adversary democracy enters the picture. Adversary democracy warns all of us to watch our back, because someone is likely to want to insert knives into them. Thus, adversary democracy begins with a substantial mistrust of all of those enforcing governmental power as an essential means of preserving and protecting the foundational liberal value traditionally associated with optimistic forms of democracy. Our Constitution's form of adversary democracy, consequently, is best characterized as *liberal* adversary democracy.[18]

The theory of adversary democracy has been grossly underexplored by scholars. The most comprehensive description of adversary democracy to date is to be found in a few core chapters of a 1980 book by political scientist Jane Mansbridge,[19] but even Professor Mansbridge's persuasive account does not fully capture the elegant nuances of the Framers' uniquely *liberal* adversary democratic theory. Most legal scholars have done nothing more than attack the straw man of absolute pluralism without recognizing or acknowledging adversary democracy's central role in American political theory.[20] More often than not, a binary choice is presented between positivist, amoral pluralism on one hand and some variant of a communitarian, "common good"-driven theory on the other. To a certain extent, the opposition to an adversary liberal system that conceives of the "common good" as no more than a mechanical aggregation of self-interests may be understandable. But the false dichotomy presented by the scholarship overlooks the seductive dangers of communitarian theories and fails to appreciate the theoretical genius of the liberal version of adversary democracy.

As social beings, we might be partial toward a system that strives to achieve the collective satisfaction of consensus and harmony instead of a system of conflict and self-interest. Democracy in its classic Aristotelian form, it should be noted, reflects a belief in the capacity of a polity to achieve consensus for the sake of a common good, emphasizing unity, shared experience, and communal interests.[21] After all, collective pursuit of common interests can be a source of national security,[22] psychological satisfaction, and overall well-being.[23] In small, homogenous groups where consensus is achievable, unitary democracy may be the optimal approach. Yet the odds of achieving an idyllic state of unanimity rapidly decrease as the polity grows and diversifies,[24] rendering the allure of unitary theories of democracy a fatal attraction. In Professor Mansbridge's words, "the unitary vision appeals to humanity's most exalted sentiments—the deep joy of spontaneous communion, unselfishness, and commitment to a larger good," sentiments that are even more profound and inspiring when achieved at a larger scale.[25] At most, however, such a unitary vision of democracy could succeed only in a relatively small, homogeneous community, unified by agreed-upon aims. It could not possibly function successfully in a community as large and diverse as the United States, or even smaller levels of government within the United States. It is precisely at this larger scale where unitary theories begin to collapse. Given the virtual inevitability of conflict in large groups, it is all the more likely in these contexts that "rhetoric, propaganda, or fantasy that praises altruism or reason of state while disparaging self-regarding interests" will be used to benefit those launching these appeals to unity.[26] Championing this false assumption of common interest sends a clear message to the polity that conflict is not simply undesirable but illegitimate as well.

Demanding consensus and commonality in the face of unresolvable conflict inevitably leads either to a complete halt of societal progression or to a dystopian, authoritarian elimination of dissent. The liberal version of adversary democracy, however, avoids either outcome. Rather than fabricating a common good as communitarian theories of democracy inevitably do, the liberal form of adversary democracy provides the means to resolve conflict where there is little or no agreement about the meaning of the phrase "common good."[27] While the inability to eliminate faction or to guarantee favorable substantive outcomes may be frustrating, striving to eliminate rather than accommodate conflict is, in James Madison's words, to pursue a cure "that is worse than the disease."[28] This is the foundational premise of adversary democracy: recognition (in agreement with Madison in *Federalist No. 10*) of the inevitability of factions, and the goal of making these factions function within the framework of democratic government.

It should be emphasized that although adversary democracy is grounded in the pursuit of individual interest, it does not deny our social nature or reject the idea of "common interest" writ large.[29] It simply views these phenomena realistically. Individuals do not exist in a vacuum, nor do their interests. Even where there is conflict, group affiliation and membership remain influential parts of our daily existence and, indeed, who we are as people.[30] Common interests, norms, or shared beliefs will almost certainly form to varying degrees in an adversary democratic system.[31] Through coincidence, proximity, or the exchange of information, individuals may develop empathetic interests for the good of another, many others, or the polity as a whole.[32] But to a large extent it is irrelevant whether for purposes liberal adversary democratic theory, the interests are self-regarding (selfish), other/group-regarding (altruistic), or ideal-regarding (principle realization). In all cases, the very idea of democracy dictates that they still are the sole possession of the individual who holds them.[33]

In that same vein, even if the idea of aggregation of self-interest as the only true "common good" is not particularly morally satisfying, at least on a certain level there is a wealth of common good, universalism, and consensus implicit in adversary democracy. For starters, citizens must agree on the procedural ideals that sustain the adversary process itself (e.g., majority rule, nonviolent resolution of conflict, and equal protection of interests). Along the way, individuals may and often do make the interests of others their own and fight vigorously for them.[34] In fact, adversary procedures tend to "increase the frequency of a common good by handling technical decisions completely and by trying to resolve conflicts of interest on the basis of a rough principle of equal protection rather than denying the legitimacy of conflict."[35]

When founding a nation that, even in its nascency, was embroiled in conflict, the Framers made the prophylactic choice to instill our constitutional government with the skeptically optimistic principles of adversary democracy. And if there is any place in the Constitution where the reality of conflicting interests must be acknowledged, respected, and duly accommodated, one should look no further than the Bill of Rights, and the Due Process Clause in particular. Due process protections are only triggered if, at the hands of government, an individual may be "*deprived* of life, liberty, or property."[36] This language describes a quintessentially adversarial situation where two sets of interests are directly in tension—an individual's interest in life, liberty, or property on one hand, and the government's interest in law enforcement and administration on the other. The constitutional guarantee of due process ensures that the latter does not unfairly dominate the former and, in that sense, should be conceptualized as an essential liberty-protective tool born from adversary democratic values.

2
DUE PROCESS AS LIBERAL ADVERSARY DEMOCRACY

2.1 INTRODUCTION

Procedural due process is a countermajoritarian, confrontational, and individual-centered guarantee that is best understood as an outgrowth of adversary democracy. The existence of a constitutionally enshrined protection of this sort—untouchable by the typical political process—embodies the foundational mistrust of others inherent in adversary democratic theory. In the skeptically optimistic scheme of liberal adversary democracy, procedural due process is an essential defensive tool which safeguards individuals' paths toward self-realization by protecting against the threat of unjust governmental coercion which adversary democratic theory presumes to be always present. The foundational directive of liberal adversary democracy is that in furtherance of democracy's broader goal of human flourishing, due process must be imbued with the mistrustful, protective ethos that inheres in adversary theory.

Moreover, the distrustful check of procedural due process promotes the legitimacy of the democratic system itself. In guaranteeing procedures that scrutinize purportedly lawful coercive actions *before* they are taken against individuals, due process ensures that the law thoughtfully and democratically selected by the people is applied faithfully and accurately. At bottom, democracy cannot survive, let alone achieve its lofty goals, without due process of law guaranteed.

2.2 PROCEDURAL DUE PROCESS AND SKEPTICAL OPTIMISM

The notion that an individual constitutional guarantee is grounded in democratic theory is not novel. Key substantive protections of the Bill of Rights have been linked to democratic theory, free speech being one of the most notable.[1] Free speech promotes democracy's principal objective of self-realization and improves the quality of the democratic process. With respect to self-realization's inherent value, free speech facilitates the flow of information, thereby allowing individuals to make more informed decisions for themselves.

Due Process as American Democracy. Martin H. Redish, Oxford University Press. © Martin H. Redish 2024.
DOI: 10.1093/oso/9780197747414.003.0002

As for self-realization's instrumental value, protecting a wide range of expressive rights (individual, political, artistic, or otherwise) fosters the individual's intellectual development. The protection of free speech also shapes the relationship between individual and government, ensuring that individuals have a right to either seek assistance from government in protecting their interests or to advocate that others seek to influence government for those same purposes. But alongside the optimistic focus on human flourishing and self-realization, the common thread running through free speech theory is a darker, more skeptical one: individuals *cannot* and *should not* be required to trust anyone else to speak for them. Under the First Amendment, they never have to. Instead, individuals are rightly positioned as the foremost advocates of their own interests.

Due process, for its part, is distinct from other Bill of Rights protections in that in and of itself it does not make any substantive rights inviolable.[2] It is not a guarantee that government will never seek to coerce individuals, imprison them, deprive them of their property, or even deprive them of their lives. The clauses provide, instead, that an individual be afforded "due process of law" *before* the government strips that individual of her life, liberty, or property.[3] Due process is a personal guarantee which checks government power by providing a constitutional floor of procedural protections, which, like free speech, mediate the relationship between individual and government and empower individuals as the principal advocates of their own rights. When either the government or a private citizen is legally positioned to invoke the coercive power of law against an individual or entity, that individual is constitutionally—even if not legislatively[4]—guaranteed the benefit of fair procedures designed to determine whether the proposed coercion is both lawful and accurate.[5]

This constitutional guarantee of fair, lawful, and accurate government-authorized deprivation is best viewed as a manifestation of the skeptical optimism inherent in adversary democracy.[6] The choice to constitutionally empower individuals to protect themselves against improper deprivations at the hands of government reflects the view that, simply put, if individuals do not look out for themselves, no one else will. Recall that due process protections are only triggered if, at the hands of government, an individual may be deprived of life, liberty, or property. In this inherently adversarial context, the individual guarantee of procedural due process flows from the skepticism (or, one might say, sadly, the basic reality) that the agent acting to deprive an individual of life, liberty, or property is unlikely to keep that individual's best interests close to heart.[7] Procedural due process is a commitment to the notion that individuals do not have to idly accept—and in fact are empowered to actively challenge—the purported legal justification for the coercive action sought to be taken against them.[8]

In this way, procedural due process acts as a powerful, deeply skeptical bodyguard of the liberal value of human flourishing. While free speech affirmatively facilitates individual personal development through intellectual and creative expression, due process gives individuals the requisite security to realize the benefits of such freedoms by vigilantly defending against unjust coercion or loss of freedom. Where free speech provides individuals with the autonomy to advocate that government take action to their benefit, due process supplies them with the autonomy to implore government to abstain from acting to their detriment.

The constitutional stature of due process further evidences the skepticism that inheres in this guarantee. It is not a legislative protection subject to the ever-changing whims of the political majority.[9] Thanks to the constitutional guarantee of due process, an individual is not resigned to aimlessly hope and pray that elected officials or appointed bureaucrats will dutifully act in the individual's best interests. Individuals are empowered to see to it themselves that they are treated fairly, and the government is constitutionally bound to provide procedures accordingly.

Absent due process, an individual's interest in fair treatment and accurate application of the law would be nothing more than an externality for elected officials and bureaucrats, even though they are the ones required to make decisions affecting individual life, liberty, and property each and every day. One need not assume that corruption, laziness, or malice is pervasive (though all are well documented[10]) to justify the democratic need for procedural due process. The question is not if government will, at some point, unlawfully deprive individuals of, for example, their welfare benefits,[11] but when. Even if all government officials were to act only with the best of intentions, the risk of unlawful, unfair, or arbitrary deprivation will always be nonzero. Particularly in the modern era, with everything that government officials are responsible for, it would be foolish to expect anything else.[12]

This level of skepticism and self-centered rhetoric may strike some as too demanding. From a functionalist or collectivist perspective, one could imagine a system where, perhaps in the name of "efficiency" or "common good" or "sense of community," we overlook less-than-perfect execution of the law, set aside self-interested desires to control our own rights, and trust our wise political leaders to determine which procedures are worthwhile. But to the extent that there are any policy reasons to accept human error and trust in the good will of government, the Framers—through their enactment of the Due Process Clauses—chose a different system. Instead of leaving the lawfulness of government action in the hands of the relevant government agency itself, the Framers secured procedural guarantees to those who are most invested in avoiding mistreatment: the individuals facing purportedly lawful coercion.

Individuals cannot feel secure as participants in a democracy if the things they hold dear may be unfairly, unlawfully, or arbitrarily taken away from them without a meaningful opportunity to protect their legal rights. This foundational principle holds true whether individuals are defending themselves against government coercive action directly, or are seeking an adjudicatory forum to vindicate or protect their legal rights against another private individual. Leaving government unconstrained by any constitutional due process limitations—free to lawlessly coerce individuals directly or to turn a blind eye to individual claims of legal harms caused by others—constitutes a level of governmental unfairness and disregard for individual dignity that, as a definitional matter, cannot be called "democratic." Moreover, such unchecked discretion carves a loophole in our democratic system big enough to drive a truck through. Absent due process, the amount of unchecked power that government would retain at the moment of law enforcement and adjudication would be ripe for abuse, and our system would rapidly move toward tyranny.

2.3 PROCEDURAL DUE PROCESS AND THE LEGITIMACY OF DEMOCRACY

Though most of us would prefer otherwise, the reality is that we are governed by humans, not angels,[13] making the countermajoritarian check[14] of due process paramount not only to achieve the broader democratic value of self-realization but also to preserve the legitimacy of democracy itself.[15] At its core, a democracy must follow the self-governing decisions of the people, if only indirectly. But humans (even the ones occupying governmental offices) are fallible, and their malice, stupidity, bias, or simple error may sometimes lead them to apply the law in unfair, inaccurate, or even unlawful ways. This is where the need for constitutional safeguards is triggered. This is, ultimately, the lesson of adversary democracy. As an institutional, *ex ante* matter, government is not to be assumed trustworthy when it seeks to coerce private individuals or entities. There will, of course, be numerous individuals situations where the assumption of untrustworthiness will be unjustified. The problem, however, is that absent use of strong prophylactic protections designed to avoid governmental coercive improprieties, there is no way to know, *ex ante*, whether that will be true in the individual case. The essence of due process, then, is a preference for overprotection against improper governmental coercion, rather than underprotection.

Once again, a comparison to free speech is useful here, as both free speech and due process enhance the legitimacy of the democratic process in complementary ways. Whereas free speech improves the quality of the democratic process at the "front end," due process helps ensure that substantive rules actually mean what they say at the "back end" in critical moments where an individual is at risk of losing something. Free speech provides the front-end opportunity for the private individual (or collective) to advocate and attempt to influence government to enact the substantive rules the individual prefers. Due process, in contrast, provides the "back-end" opportunity for the individual to ensure that those substantive rules are applied fairly and accurately, both on their own terms and on the terms of the Constitution. The guarantee that individuals be provided with minimum procedures and a forum to either contest the government's coercive application of a law against them or to vindicate their own legal claims against others gives effect to the earlier guarantee that one may participate in the political, expressive, and advocative process that brought such laws into force.

This front-to-back form of constitutional protection fosters faith in the democratic system. As parties to the social contract of liberal democracy,[16] individual members of society will be more confident that they will get the benefit of their bargain if they know the agreed-upon terms (i.e., the rules the people have selected) will be respected by those in power. Procedural due process provides the adjudicatory guardrail for when they are not. After all, what legitimacy does democracy retain if individuals cannot be confident that the laws selected through the democratic process will be applied fairly and accurately when enforced against them (or when they seek to enforce them)? Individuals may debate, campaign, and advocate all they like in the political sphere to get a law on the books, but "[n]othing leaves a [government] agent as much room for venality, hatred, caprice, or carelessness as the power to ignore the applicable rules."[17] All of the rigorous and thoughtful front-end political advocacy will amount to very little if there is nothing to stop government from employing its power in arbitrary, invidious, or irrational ways. Procedural due process serves as a roadblock to prevent democracy's downfall, helping preserve our system as "[a] government of laws, and not of men."[18]

To that same end, the constitutional stature of due process and the minimum procedures it guarantees also reduce the risk of what can appropriately be called "legislative deception."[19] When government improperly enforces the law or sneakily undercuts its substantive guarantees through backdoor, sleight-of-hand procedural modifications unnoticed by the populace, citizens cannot reasonably maintain confidence in the democratic process by which they selected those laws. The democratic process becomes a farce, and separation of powers collapses. Providing individuals with procedural protections to ensure they receive the benefit of these laws as enacted fosters the faith in government necessary to preserve democracy's legitimacy. Thus, procedural due process converts individuals into the watchdogs of both their own personal liberty and of the democratic system as a whole.

2.4 APPLYING ADVERSARY DEMOCRATIC DUE PROCESS

A commitment to adversary democracy logically dictates a commitment to a presumptive mistrust of others. From adversary democratic principles flows liberal adversary theory's skeptically optimistic belief that defensively weaponizing mistrust as a shield against third-party or government intrusions on individual liberty will leave room for individuals (and thus society as a whole) to flourish. Due process, as an outgrowth of adversary democracy, is designed to implement this ethos of mistrust, fear, and skepticism and, as such, these values must pervade the procedural guarantees conferred by due process.

Once the infusion of adversary democratic precepts into due process is completed, it is necessary to prophylactically apply this defensive mistrust against three groups of "others" who are liable to threaten an individual's life, liberty, or property: those responsible for adjudication, third parties who seek or purport to represent the individual's interests, and the government charged with providing the substantive guarantees desired by the people writ large. Looking skeptically at the motives of each of the aforementioned groups yields three basic constitutional minimums or "bookends" of procedural due process. *First*, to ensure sufficient neutrality, adjudicators must be prophylactically insulated from all political and financial pressures with Article III–like protections of salary and tenure. Such strong prophylactic guarantees of neutral adjudication are foundational to any meaningful level of due process. *Second*, an individual's right to a day in court must be upheld in all but the most extreme circumstances. *Third*, legislative deception of prophylactic insulation imposed indirectly through denial of due process, must be categorically policed and rejected.

Between these foundational and nonnegotiable dictates of adversary democratic due process, reasonable minds may differ over what exact kind of process is due in particular cases,[20] but in all cases the adversary democratic ethos of due process must establish a strong level of skepticism against those who exercise the power of the law seeking to coerce individuals. It is important to note, however, that the presumption, while very strong, is not absolute, and adversary democratic due process does not subject the government to an "any means necessary" approach whereby it must overlook all danger, imminent harm, or verifiably serious risks of loss.[21] Government need not provide every conceivable procedural benefit in every case where individuals are (allegedly) acting unlawfully or seeking to exercise their legal claims against others.

That said, the foundational mistrust and skepticism of adversary democratic due process does compel an extremely protective approach to individual procedural rights. The indispensable nature of due process to our democratic system means that the process each individual is "due" cannot be circumvented as a matter of mere governmental convenience. As I said, the risk of the wrong guess favors overprotection rather than underprotection. Whereas the former risks delay and expenditure of fungible resources, the latter risks fundamental and irreparable violations of an individual's right to accurate, fair, and dignified treatment—all wholly incompatible with the premises of liberal democracy.[22]

2.5 PROPHYLACTIC NEUTRAL ADJUDICATION

The foundational mistrust toward others and the fear of abuse of power that inheres in procedural due process dictate intense vigilance toward the risk of outside pressures, incentives, or other influences that might reasonably compromise the independence of an adjudicator. The legal power of adjudicators over the parties before them is extraordinary, and the harm that would ensue if outside pressures were to corrupt that power makes the mere risk of such pressures constitutionally unacceptable. Though it has long been understood that "neutral" adjudication is part and parcel of due process, adversary democratic due process calls for a far stricter and more prophylactic definition of neutrality than that which current jurisprudence requires.

2.5.1 Structural Independence as a Constitutional Minimum

The quintessential fear of abuse of power that defines adversary democratic theory must bolster—or arguably transform—our conception of the neutral adjudicator requirement. Legal adjudicators wield a distinct and potentially dangerous power over the parties they adjudicate. With their word alone, they speak legally binding obligations, rights, and punishments into existence. At the swipe of an adjudicator's pen, individuals may be forced to forfeit their money, their property, their physical freedom, or their lives according to the adjudicator's orders. Once due process protections are triggered, the stakes are definitionally high,[23] and adjudicators must therefore be required to meet demanding standards of neutrality accordingly. With such great power in the hands of adjudicators, it is essential that judgments against individuals be the sole product of the issues, legal rules, and evidence presented.[24] When outside influences—including subtle ones, of which the judge herself may not even be aware—compromise an adjudicator's decision-making, all procedural protections and even controlling substantive law are effectively rendered meaningless.[25] For example, the right to effective counsel[26] is worth little if a judge's decision-making is affected by something other than counsel's presentation of the evidence and law. Precedent and even the strictest standards of review lose force when extralegal considerations enter the picture.[27]

It is for these reasons that the standard for neutrality under adversary democratic due process must err on the side of overprotection. Speaking only of *external* pressures, this overprotection does not require a zero-tolerance policy against ideological "bias," since it would be impossible to identify, let alone eliminate, every single idiosyncratic ideological preference or aversion that makes each person unique.[28] The reality, however, is that many of the pressures that compromise the neutrality of adjudicators are structural and external in nature, easily identifiable in practice, and therefore unjustifiable as a matter of procedural due process. Issues of coercive interference with the decision maker,[29] incentivized decision-making,[30] or associational prejudice[31] do not arise from unpredictable idiosyncrasies of human personality. They arise, instead, from predictable structurally imposed pathologies of poor organization and lack of adjudicatory insulation.

There is a straightforward, protective, and obvious means of prophylactically safeguarding litigants against these risks, and it is found in Article III: salary and tenure protections for adjudicators. Long before scientists researched the precise psychological impact of external social or financial pressures on decision-making,[32] the Framers recognized that prophylactically insured adjudicatory independence was necessary to minimize the risk of impermissible extralegal influence on the judiciary. Article III guarantees to all federal judges both life tenure during good behavior and protection against salary reduction. These tenure and salary protections reflect the Framers' decision to automatically insulate judges from incentives that could compromise their independence. If "a power over a man's subsistence amounts to a power over his will,"[33] as Alexander Hamilton wrote in the *Federalist*, then procedural due process leaves no room to tolerate the obvious and avoidable structural risk of adjudicators worrying about how the resolution of a dispute could impact their livelihood.[34] This intensely skeptical approach, consistent with the spirit of adversary democratic theory, rejects the idea that individuals should ever bear the burden of hoping that an adjudicator will remain neutral despite a structural risk of economic pressure, when that very risk can be eliminated *ex ante*.

To be sure, the tenure and salary protections of Article III are extraordinary ones, but the Framers "afforded these extraordinary powers and protections not for the comfort of judges, but so that an independent judiciary could better guard *the people* from the arbitrary use of governmental power."[35] Under the highly protective and skeptical ethos of adversary democratic due process, this insulation represents a necessary constitutional minimum. It is important that this is true, even where Article III itself is wholly inapplicable. This is so, because, at bottom, these employment protections for adjudicators must be seen as an essential requirement of due process, wholly distinct from their place in Article III. In short, the precepts of liberal adversary democracy dictate that adjudicatory neutrality require the prophylactic protections of salary and tenure associated with Article III. This is not because of Article III itself. It is, rather, because due process infused with the skepticism inherent in adversary democratic theory dictates a level of governmental fear and mistrust requiring, *ex ante*, prophylactic assurance of adjudicatory insulation from potentially important external pressures on decision-making.

The claim that Article III–like insulation is a constitutional minimum of due process may strike many as controversial, to say the least, but the critiques of such insulation do not and cannot rebut its importance to neutral adjudication. Many have argued for doing away with Article III protections even for Article III judges. Such arguments derive from scholarly hopes of achieving "political balance" in the judiciary,[36] "mak[ing] the system of [judicial] appointments fairer,"[37] and "renew[ing] . . . democratic consent and input into the process of judicial review."[38] But these critiques either unwisely discount or disregard the inevitable and dangerous erosion of neutrality that would flow from making adjudicators accountable to majoritarian political influences.[39] In such a system, it is the "undesirables" of the polity (for example, the indebted, the impoverished, or the imprisoned, to name just a few) who are likely to suffer the most when facing adjudicators who are beholden to the will of those in power. But the countermajoritarian constitutional guarantee of due process must apply in full force even to and, indeed, *especially* to those who are detested by the majority.

While the centrality of adjudicatory neutrality has been widely recognized in the abstract,[40] both scholars and the Court have failed to grasp the foundational and necessarily unyielding nature of the right, often allowing it to bend and break at the whim of political or economic concerns. Procedural due process, properly grounded in adversary democratic values, requires prophylactic adjudicatory independence in order to satisfy the neutral adjudication guarantee. This means there must be economic, associational, and political insulation of adjudicators when due process protections are triggered. In current due process jurisprudence, however, the Court has utterly failed to uphold this guarantee in three main areas: (1) the administrative state generally, (2) prison-system administration in particular, and (3) elected state courts.

2.6 MISGUIDED FAITH IN ADMINISTRATOR INTEGRITY

Even if we were to assume, solely for purposes of argument, that despite the lessons of liberal adversary democracy, due process is not to be construed to incorporate the equivalent of prophylactic Article III–like protection, serious problems in relevant Supreme Court doctrine would remain. The prominent risks of associational influences, coercive interference, and incentivized decision-making that inhere in the administrative state raise serious concerns about adjudicatory independence in a manner that is incompatible with the foundations of procedural due process. To make matters worse, tolerance of these structural pressures derives from a woefully misguided and unsupported assumption of administrative adjudicatory neutrality that disappears when real administrative adjudicators are involved.

To uphold adversary democratic values, procedural due process must look skeptically toward adjudicators selected to rule on individuals' rights. An individual should not have to rely on the unspoken assertions of personal integrity on the part of an adjudicator to negate obvious and easily remediated structural temptations, at least to a significant extent. The Court has affirmed this procedural due process value with regard to judges. In the landmark case of *Tumey v. Ohio*, the Court held that it violated due process for a judge to preside over liquor prohibition proceedings in which the judge would receive a cut of each fine issued.[41] The Court's holding was straightforward: the prospective financial incentive was a temptation that was constitutionally intolerable.[42] This was so, despite the lack of any evidence of impropriety on the judge's part in the specific case.

The *Tumey* Court further explained that due process in adjudication is not satisfied simply because of the categorical *ex ante* assumption that judges are people "of the highest honor and greatest self-sacrifice."[43] Rather, the *structural* pressures and the mere *possibility* of temptation tainted the system beyond repair as a matter of constitutionally dictated procedural due process.[44] The Court has followed this reasoning in subsequent cases, finding the potential for incentivized decision-making impermissible even with attenuated or associative incentives.[45] Given the choice between relying on the inherently honorable nature of judges and curing an obvious structural flaw that might compromise their independence, the Court held that due process requires the latter. All this was so, even though the Court did not expressly construe the Due Process Clauses to impose prophylactic protections parallel to those required of Article III judges.

In the administrative realm, however, the Court has inexplicably tainted procedural due process with the very naiveté that had been rejected in *Tumey* in the context of judges. When facing administrators-as-judges, the Court has advised litigants that any challenges to these regulators' neutrality "must overcome a presumption of honesty and integrity in those serving as adjudicators."[46] Without the slightest justification, this presumption flips the skepticism essential to adversary democratic due process on its head. Moreover, it is not only naïve, but dangerous, telling litigants that they need not worry about the obvious associational, financial, and career pressures pervading the administrative state.[47] Such reasoning is inconsistent with prior jurisprudence regarding the neutrality of administrators,[48] all jurisprudence on *judicial* neutrality,[49] and the wise insights of adversary democratic theory as a whole.[50]

Such optimism about and trust in the integrity of adjudicators is especially out of place when applied to the Goliath of the modern administrative state, where a single regulatory body often serves as the judge, jury, investigator, and prosecutor[51]—a bona fide one-stop shop for procedural due process violations. Since 1920, little to no case law has questioned the adjudicatory independence of administrators as a matter of procedural due process, leaving litigants to cross their fingers hoping that the same group of bureaucrats hired to punish them (and often under their own proprietary administrative rules, no less) will look out for the litigants' best interests when deciding whether such punishment is fair.[52]

Moreover, agency-deferential doctrines such as *Chevron*[53] and *Auer*[54] compound the problems posed by the structural temptations that compromise adjudicatory independence. These doctrines not only abandon all skepticism toward the political nature of administrative agencies but actually attempt to repackage a lack of independence as a virtue. Where agencies promulgate and enforce their own rules against individuals, litigants seeking relief from a reviewing court may well be told that the agency enforcer–interpreter–adjudicator ought be trusted *because* of its "political accountability."[55] Make no mistake, this so-called political accountability threatens the very foundation of neutral adjudication because, unlike independent judges, "executive officials are not, nor are they supposed to be, 'wholly impartial.' They have their own interests, their own constituencies, and their own policy goals," all of which may come to bear in their adjudications.[56] Such associative interests and structural temptations would be impermissible in the judicial sphere, and procedural due process should not afford them special treatment in the administrative sphere.

2.7 ELECTED STATE JUDGES

In the vast majority of state courts across the country, the prospective, forward-looking incentives of re-election and accountability to majoritarian considerations impermissibly tie our country's only courts of general jurisdiction to the "ill humours of society."[57] Although the Supreme Court has recognized time and again that prospective, forward-looking temptations impermissibly deprive litigants of a neutral adjudicator, it has somehow rejected the notion that subjecting judges to majoritarian elections raises any due process concerns.[58]

When asked to assess potential procedural due process issues relating to the neutrality of state judges, the Supreme Court has, of late, directed more attention toward retroactive gratitude[59] rather than to prospective influences. Granted, it is certainly reasonable to conclude that an adjudicator's gratitude toward the interest group, official, or corporation that put her in that position could impermissibly compromise her independence. But an overemphasis on gratitude and a disregard of prospective pressures simultaneously proves too much (after all, all Article III courts could be suspect for the "gratitude" of presidential appointment) and too little (ignoring importance of forward-looking temptations that interfere with neutrality).[60]

At a minimum, neutral adjudication requires prophylactic elimination of obvious prospective influences. But anything short of the equivalent of Article III insulation fails to take into account adversary democratic mistrust of government motivations and externalities. An electoral judicial system is wholly inconsistent with this constitutionally dictated requirement. Pressures of all kinds exist, but adjudicators regularly overestimate their ability to counteract or ignore them.[61] And unlike idiosyncratic personal preferences which are unpredictable, varied in effect, and difficult to control, majoritarian pressure is *categorically* both "inherently undesirable" and "easily avoidable."[62]

In order to uphold the values of adversary democratic due process, let alone the entire structure of our carefully constructed countermajoritarian Constitution, insulation from forward-looking, majoritarian influence is necessary in all adjudications in which the Due Process Clause is triggered.

2.8 THE LAW OF JUDGMENTS AND THE "DAY-IN-COURT" IDEAL

Ironically, while in many ways adversary and liberal theories are direct opposites, as explained in Chapter 1, in certain ways they share a key foundational premise, a commitment to the value and dignity of the individual. Adversary democracy is founded on the quintessential liberal principle that each individual "has privileged access to the contents of his own mind"[63] and is thus uniquely capable of accurately identifying, zealously promoting, and vigilantly defending his personal interests in a manner that no other person can. While adversary democracy accepts that individuals may take on altruistic, other-regarding interests and seek to defend them, this does not supplant the core concern that "as long as interests conflict, it is virtually impossible to ensure that one individual will protect another's as assiduously as his or her own."[64] Under an adversary democratic system, the individual must, wherever possible, have the opportunity to serve as the foremost representative of her own beliefs, interests, and fears.

This skepticism toward the capability of others—at least others not chosen by the individuals themselves—to diligently advocate for, let alone understand, an individual's unique interests is the reason why the exercise of individual will is the motor of adversary democracy.[65] Only the aggregation of many individuals either collectively or separately expressing their unique desires can legitimately bestow government with the power to act. For political activities such as voting, campaigning, or public debate, individuals are guaranteed the right to represent and speak to their own interests before their government. Anything departing from this model would not be democracy in the proper sense.

Under an adversary democratic model of due process, the same skeptical prioritization of individuals' right to speak for themselves (or choose those who do) is appropriately translated to the adjudicatory context. The judiciary is, at the end of the day, another branch of government with which individuals must interact. The strong presumption that favors individuals' right to represent their own interests both before and against government therefore corresponds to a strong presumption of individuals' access to the forum to engage in that very activity. In other words, where individual legal rights are or could be at stake in an adjudicatory dispute, due process guarantees individuals their day in court before they are deprived of their life, liberty, or property.

The skepticism and individualist supremacy of adversary democratic theory presumptively rejects the use of governmentally implemented paternalism for the sake of efficiency. "Paternalism" refers to a practice by which a supposedly wiser and more efficient government takes responsibility for (and away from) individuals in safeguarding their and legally guaranteed interests.[66] But while there may be room for paternalistic actions to supplant an individual's exercise of autonomy in situations where it is simply infeasible for the individual to do so herself,[67] reliance on paternalism in the absence of such circumstances constitutes an affront to the "decisive epistemic and hence moral authority [of] the individual" over his own beliefs and actions.[68] The default position in a system of adversary democracy, therefore, must favor the individual's strong presumptive right to participate in the governmental arenas where democracy operates—including the courts.

To be clear, limits on due process rights of participation on occasion do exist,[69] but there are core lines which, as a matter of adversary democratic theory, cannot be crossed. In a democratic system, we cannot impose political leaders upon a society that does not want them on the basis of the paternalistic justification that the people do not know what's good for them. We reject this system because "it is, according to basic tenets of liberal democratic thought, the individual who is to determine how to exercise his self-governing function when participating in the political process."[70] Adversary democratic thought demands no less when an individual enforces her rights via adjudication. Externally imposed paternalism is unacceptable in free expression and political choice; it is equally incompatible with procedural due process.

What's more, our constitutional democracy has long recognized the importance of an individual's legally protected interest in her own litigation. This interest, or "chose in action," is a historically established property right which, upon threat of deprivation, should trigger procedural due process protections. For this reason, res judicata and collateral estoppel (also known as "claim preclusion"[71] or "issue preclusion"[72]), which under certain circumstances extinguish an individual's litigation rights, must be seen through the protective lens of adversary democracy. Preclusion doctrine, consequently, must zealously prioritize individuals' right to appear in court to vindicate their legal interests rather than leave them to hope that someone else has done or will do it for them. In certain circumstances, modern due process jurisprudence, regrettably, fails to meet this standard.

Traditionally, with the exception of class actions—where all that is required is a finding of adequate representation[73]—res judicata and collateral estoppel could apply to nonparties only when the nonparties were "in privity" with a litigant in the prior case. In recent years, however, courts began to play fast and loose with the doctrine, expanding the category of nonparties to be bound by a case's resolution by relying on the same paternalistic "adequate representation" inquiry that controls class actions. Grounding procedural due process in this inquiry and this inquiry alone does not comport with adversary democratic values for two reasons. First, it fails to recognize the individual's unparalleled access to and understanding of her own interests relative to all others. Second, it implicitly suggests that the efficiency of avoiding "relitigation" of similar issues—without more—can override personal autonomy in the due process context, finding no inherent and overriding value in individuals' exercise of control over their own destiny through adjudicative advocacy.

Under adversary democratic due process, a finding that an absent litigant has been "adequately represented" is not, standing alone, a sufficient condition to deprive individual litigants of their day in court. Adversary democracy's emphasis on the unique ability of the individual to advocate for herself relative to all others, combined with its inherent skepticism of the competence and motivation of representatives not chosen by the litigants themselves, in most cases requires a clear showing that the litigant herself was not in a position to represent herself or choose her own representative. There are, of course, a limited number of situations where an individual's day-in-court guarantee may be overridden—for example, where it would impermissibly compromise the fundamental rights of another.[74] But such situations will be very few in number. In these circumstances, "adequate representation" is a necessary, but not sufficient, condition for rebutting the presumption in favor of an individual's day in court.

In the past, procedural due process jurisprudence has failed to live up to the day-in-court ideal principally in two main areas: (1) virtual representation doctrine, and (2) the modern class action generally. While the Court has modified the former situation, in doing so it failed to defend this "day-in-court" ideal against its critics. In the latter situation, however, there remains much work to do.

2.9 CLASS ACTIONS

The modern class action system gives rise to serious due process concerns relating to the day-in-court guarantee as well. Class actions, in theory, are a valuable tool to facilitate efficient multiparty litigation by grouping together commonly interested parties who may otherwise lack the resources or incentives to vindicate their rights as individuals. They can also safeguard defendants against the risk of duplicative litigation that might result in inconsistent or unduly burdensome legal orders. After a class is certified, both named and absent class members are bound to the final judgment and, with that judgment, res judicata attaches.

Recall that the day-in-court ideal is a constitutional protection which requires the utmost prioritization of an individual's right to appear in court and represent her own interests. The deep mistrust, inherent in the precepts of adversary democratic due process, of a third party's good faith of ability to adequately represent an individual's interest lies at the heart of this guarantee. Therefore, absent both a countervailing compelling interest that can only be met through deprivation of one's day in court *and* proof that the individual's rights will be adequately represented by a third party,[75] the individual is constitutionally entitled to a day in court.

As such, given the basic reality that absent class members retain far less control—if, indeed, any—over the administration of their legal rights in class litigation, there must be safeguards in place to ensure that their legal rights are not unfairly extinguished by res judicata. This is not to say that the action of binding absent class members to a final judgment is categorically problematic, only that, when taking such action, a court must be confident that either (1) absent class members have a meaningful opportunity to exercise their right of first refusal as to the transfer of their legal claim, or (2) that it is *necessary* to deprive them of that choice in order to avoid a far greater harm. The modern class action has not upheld either of these safeguards, contravening adversary democratic due process' prioritization of the day-in-court ideal.

The category of "mandatory" class actions, as a prima facie matter, exceeds permissible due process limits. Such class actions fall within Rule 23(b)(1)(A), (b)(1)(B), or (b)(2). If a class is certified under any of these categories, absent class members are prohibited from withdrawing from the litigation and their claims receive res judicata impact accordingly.[76] But by their very nature, mandatory classes take away from individual litigants control over the choice of who represents them. And with one possible exception, none of these mandatory categories comes even close to satisfying the compelling interest standard.

Rule 23(b)(1)(A) class actions are designed to prevent individual litigation from creating inconsistent or literally impossible obligations for defendants, otherwise known as instances of "indivisible relief."[77] That is, without a class action, individualized litigation could subject a defendant to (1) doubly punitive judgments requiring double payout of an indivisible "stake" (double liability);[78] (2) contradictory judgments that make it impossible for the defendant to satisfy the requirements of both orders (contradictory liability);[79] or (3) inconsistent judgments that require the defendant to give up a favorable ruling in one case (inconsistent liability).[80] The (b)(1)(B) mandatory class action is based on concerns that, absent a class action, the discrete, limited fund available to compensate claimants will run out or be distributed unevenly ("limited pie") or that a judgment in an earlier case will negatively impact a nonparty's later claim arising out of the same situation ("same-situation stare decisis").[81] Finally, there are the (b)(2) "institutional injunction class actions,"[82] where a defendant acts in a manner that affects a class generally and can be remedied via a single injunction.

Of these subcategories, the (b)(1)(A) "indivisible relief" class action is the only categorically justifiable mandatory class action as a matter of due process and the day-in-court ideal. Here, allowing all claimants to appear in court separately could yield judgments that, taken together, require a "stakeholder to pay a single debt twice or punish[] a litigant for failing to perform physically or legally impossible acts";[83] either result constitutes an erosion of law or deprivation of autonomy that itself violates due process. The same cannot be said of (b)(1)(B) or (b)(2) class actions, as concerns of equal distribution of funds, the impact of stare decisis, or the convenience of group injunctions can all be addressed through means *other* than stripping individuals of the choice of how (and whether) to exercise their legal claim.[84]

Additionally, there are the (b)(3) class actions which, unlike mandatory class actions, provide a means for individual class members to choose not to participate with an "opt-out" alternative. But whatever value these opt-out procedures provide to preserve litigant choice,[85] class incorporation by total passivity is an impermissibly unprotective mechanism that does not align with adversary democratic prioritization of individuals' right to represent or choose to abandon their legal claims as they see fit.

These opt-out procedures arguably undermine due process on multiple grounds. As a legal matter, the Court has long been wary of passive waiver of constitutional rights, particularly in the due process context.[86] As a psychological matter, the cognitive inertia against action and instinctive preference toward default choices means that opt-out procedures increase the likelihood of passive incorporation.[87] And, most importantly, as a matter of adversary democracy, skepticism toward others' desire to represent an individual's interests calls for more than mere inaction to facilitate the transfer of a protected interest to an unknown representative. The loss of procedural autonomy by pure omission is unparalleled in any other realm of American governance. In the political sphere, the phenomenon of representation through implied consent is outright nightmarish, yet our legal system has accepted this very phenomenon in class action litigation.[88]

These due process concerns are exacerbated by the fact that "adequate representation" alone has become the principal test for determining the propriety of class certification. Worse yet, this paternalistic inquiry is remarkably lazy in the class action context. Given the financial structure of the modern class action, class action attorneys are incentivized to certify the biggest class possible. This means they will often do all they can to *deprive* individuals of their control over their own legal claim—that is, the property that is their "chose in action"—to include them in the class, by having them categorized as a mandatory class. But this conflict of interests is universally left out of the "adequate representation" inquiry.[89] Such a half-hearted look into the incentives of a purported representative falls short of the skepticism and mistrust required by adversary democratic theory to protect individuals from unfair treatment.

2.10 LEGISLATIVE DECEPTION

Adversary democratic mistrust toward others also requires scrutinizing the actions of those in government who are responsible for enacting the substantive rights and obligations desired by the polity. When it comes time to enforce laws against individuals, adversary democratic safeguards of individual liberty call for rigorous review to determine whether the application of such laws is faithful to their own, democratically chosen terms.

Professor Edward Rubin refers to this tenet as the "rule-obedience principle," concluding that it is (at least as a matter of doctrine) a core element of procedural due process.[90] According to Professor Rubin, the government's failure to act according to law represents "the very antithesis of accurate decision making,"[91] and arguably violates the very definition of "rule" because the word necessarily carries "the obligation of obedience."[92] As a basic principle of justice, "[t]o deny one person the benefit of a right, whether substantive or procedural, that has been conferred upon the populace-at-large is the very essence of unfairness."[93] And as a matter of adversary democratic due process, heightened scrutiny to maintain rule-obedience increases the polity's confidence that they are receiving the benefit of their democratic bargain. In contrast, allowing obvious governmental departures from substantive law undermines the perceived and actual legitimacy of the democratic system.

When the actual substance of the law is undercut by subtle "back door" procedural modifications that either circumvent the political process or sneak by the polity, this too compromises the due process principle of rule obedience.

This phenomenon is called "legislative deception."[94] Where a law is enacted that, on its face, provides substantive right "A," legislative deception takes place when either the judiciary or legislature inconspicuously modifies the procedural mechanisms to vindicate that right such that the substantive "DNA" of the law is no longer "A," but instead "Y," "Z," or "∅." Legislative deception contravenes adversary democracy and does not survive the rigorous scrutiny of procedural due process. In this sense, adversary democratic due process reflects the same skepticism and mistrust of those who make the laws as employed for those who apply them.

When the legislature uses the smokescreen of procedure by promulgating unassuming procedural or evidentiary rules that inconspicuously mutate the substantive DNA of the laws they relate to, they unconstitutionally mislead the public. As a matter of both due process and separation of powers principles, the judiciary is constitutionally obligated to ensure the legislature has not deceived individuals as to how legislation actually impacts their lives.[95] Doctrinally, we can glean this principle from Supreme Court cases such as *United States v. Klein*, where the Court held that Congress had unconstitutionally altered evidentiary rules relating to the presidential pardon in an attempt to guarantee an outcome in a case without changing the substantive law at issue.[96] While the Court has recognized that Congress can only alter the outcome of cases to the extent it is "establishing new substantive standards,"[97] it has failed to connect this principle to procedural due process in any meaningful way.

From a political perspective, accountability of elected officials is integral for the democratic electoral process to function. When the legislature engages in "macro" legislative deception by altering substantive law with procedural or evidentiary rules, this impedes individuals' ability to hold their legislators accountable because it defrauds the polity into thinking that their representatives support or opposition to a law actually meant something.[98] The fraud is both subtle and effective because it may only ever be discovered by certain individuals. That is, people do not feel the impact of legislative deception until they attempt to vindicate a substantive right in court, only to find that the right they *thought* they had has been completely hollowed out by evidentiary or procedural caveats. This deceptive practice contravenes the principle of rule-obedience, damages the transparency, predictability, and fairness of the democratic process, and cannot comport with the adversary democratic spirit of due process.

Though scholars have not explored the idea that legislative deception violates procedural due process, the connection should be clear. Consider the case of *Michael H. v. Gerald D*, where the Court held that a putative natural father, whose blood tests indicated 98.07 percent probability of paternity, could be conclusively denied the right to establish his substantive paternity rights due to restrictive *procedural* state law.[99] California law provided all "parent[s]" with a substantive right of visitation.[100] Yet in a separate, procedural statute, the state established that even where biological testing, a parent–child relationship, or any other evidence proved paternity, if the mother of the child is cohabitating with her husband, the husband "is *conclusively presumed* to be a child of marriage."[101] Justice Scalia, writing for a plurality, held that this procedural provision was actually "implementation of a substantive rule of law"[102] and created no procedural due process violation.

The grant of a substantive right paired with a simultaneous denial of that right through elimination of any meaningful opportunity to vindicate it is a quintessential example of impermissible legislative deception. In *Michael H.*, the state legislature engaged in legislative deception by offering a substantive right with one hand and, via procedural modifications, categorically denied that right to an entire class of people with the other. Contrary to the assertions of the plurality, "the defect from which conclusive presumptions suffer is a *procedural* one: the State has declared a certain fact relevant, indeed controlling, yet has denied a particular class of litigants a hearing to establish that fact."[103]

Where, under law, a substantive interest in life, liberty, or property of some form is created, legislative deception strips that substantive interest away without due process.[104] Even when these procedural changes come from legislatures rather than courts, adversary democratic fear of abuse of power requires that significant modifications to substantive rights live up to democratic standards of accountability, transparency, and predictability. Otherwise, individuals will be misled by the same government that purports to represent them and will not even discover that they have been misled until it is too late. This is unacceptable as a matter of due process.

It is certainly true that procedural rules will virtually always impact or affect substantive rights in some manner, but the legislature cannot use unassuming changes to drastically alter the substantive DNA of the law. Regardless of how openly such evidentiary or procedural changes are debated, the grave risk is that individuals will not recognize the connections between procedural changes and the substantive law at issue until they attempt in vain to vindicate their (hollow) substantive rights in court.

At bottom, legislative deception fails to satisfy adversary democratic due process because it fails to provide individuals with the requisite governmental transparency and predictability needed for full and free exercise of individual autonomy. Allowing any branch of government—legislative, executive, or judicial—to modify substantive rights in a deceptive manner fosters unpredictability and destroys political accountability in violation of due process's basic rule-obedience principle.

2.11 REBUTTING THE PRESUMPTION OF FAIR PROCEDURE

Procedural due process is not absolute. While the presumption favoring individual protections must be strong—and considerably stronger than what current doctrine has provided—there is no private due process interest so powerful that it supersedes all other competing interests.

Once again, a comparison to the First Amendment is illustrative. That provision, too, has been construed to give rise to a strong, but not irrebuttable, presumption favoring individuals' free expression. Restraints on free speech are viewed with immense suspicion, leaving little room for government encroachment, and even less for economic complaints to justify such encroachment. Free speech doctrine has aggressively safeguarded the individual right to free expression, accepting intrusion only where there are compelling and demonstrable needs to limit that right with no other way to satisfy those needs.[105] Whether the particular limitation on free speech calls for "strict scrutiny" or one of various other "specialized tests," the doctrine has largely "maintain[ed] protection for speech equal to or greater than strict scrutiny."[106] As a matter of constitutional lathe inherent, democratic value of free speech is not left up for debate, judicial second-guessing, or case-by-case cost–benefit analyses. Proposed intrusions on free speech are often "*presumptively* inconsistent with the First Amendment."[107]

Procedural due process should be similarly construed to demand demonstration of a competing compelling interest before its requirements can be ignored. Yet due process doctrine has permitted a panoply of pragmatic interests which are hardly sufficiently relevant, let alone compelling, to override constitutionally guaranteed procedural protections of individuals' ability to preserve their life, liberty, or property with little to no judicial resistance. Adversary democratic protection of all individuals' right to retain their life, liberty, or property calls for skepticism tantamount to strict scrutiny when a third party attempts to shortcut the procedures an individual is presumptively owed. To justify infringing an individual's right to procedural safeguards, then, the party seeking to take coercive action against that individual—be it government or private citizen—must prove that circumvention of such procedures advances interests of the highest order and that the requested procedural shortcuts are narrowly tailored to achieve those interests. That is to say, if the counterparty can further those interests in a manner that does not deprive the individual of her procedural rights, "it must do so."[108] Though others may exist, two broad categories of compelling interests are worth discussing here, either one of which may rebut one's presumptive right to particular procedures: (1) severe urgency and risk of substantial loss or serious harm, and (2) risk of unacceptable intrusion on counter-litigants' fundamental rights. Both are examined in the following discussions.

2.11.1 Urgency and Lack of Alternatives

Timing of deprivation is a critical question in the due process context. A temporary deprivation is still a deprivation,[109] and it is well accepted that hearing-like procedures must be provided to individuals before they are deprived of life, liberty, or property. While, of course, a party seeking to deprive individuals of their property (whether that party is the government or another private person) would almost always prefer to do so swiftly and without undergoing the rigamarole of a hearing, procedural due process cannot tolerate a reckless system of "deprive first, ask questions later."

This starting presumption weighs strongly against shortcutting this process. As such, the skeptical question that must be asked when a party seeks swift deprivation is: "Why must this coercive action be taken *now*, prior to the holding of some sort of meaningful hearing?" In an adversarial system where all parties are motivated by self-interest, an adjudicator must scrutinize a party's desire to coerce another individual—especially where that party seeks to do so in a rapid or ex parte fashion. Only a demonstrably urgent and compelling *need* should be allowed to knock down the defensive wall of mistrust that stands between the threatened individual and her counterparty who seeks *immediate* coercive action.

There may be many contexts in which it is in some sense beneficial or convenient to take coercive action against an individual earlier rather than later, but constitutional due process is not defined by convenience alone. To safeguard individual liberty against improper coercion, the question of "why now?" must be unapologetically pressed by a neutral adjudicator. This inquiry into exigency requires placing the motives of the party seeking coercive action under a microscope and assessing whether there is a truly immediate need arising out of, for example, a risk of irrecoverable loss or irreparable harm.

The demand for a showing of exigency is anything but novel, but it has somehow failed to find a permanent home in procedural due process jurisprudence. To be sure, on occasion we have seen invocation of a standard at least approaching a true compelling interest test. Take, for example, the issuance of pre-hearing temporary restraining orders under Federal Rule 65. Under this rule, a court may only issue a temporary restraining order without notice to the adverse party if the party seeking the order (1) presents "specific facts [which] clearly show that *immediate* and *irreparable* injury, loss, or damage *will* result to the movant before the adverse party can be heard in opposition,"[110] and (2) the movant's attorney certifies efforts to give notice and reasons why notice should not be required.[111] Preliminary injunctions, which raise the less concerning but still important issue of prejudgment coercion, also require the movant to make a convincing showing of exigency.[112] Note also that in addition to a demand for a showing of exigency, these standards invoke the practice of scrutinizing the intentions of parties who seek to hastily deprive an individual, thereby capturing the skepticism associated with adversary democratic theory, which is mostly absent in the due process realm.

Rather than start from a presumption favoring procedural rights and apply strict scrutiny to the purported need for prompt coercive action, the Supreme Court has decided that the constitutional guarantee of due process should be subjected to a roughly equal balancing of pragmatic interests. This utilitarian balancing test, derived largely from *Mathews v. Eldridge*,[113] places four considerations on the scales: (1) the private interest of the individual affected by the deprivation, (2) the risk of an erroneous decision, (3) the burden on the government in providing the demanded procedure, and (4) (if an adversary private party is involved) the interest of the party seeking to deprive the individual.[114] With no built-in presumption favoring the individual seeking to assert her due process rights and no heightened scrutiny toward the interests of the party seeking to take coercive action, questions of urgency, exigency, or immediate and irreparable harm have become, at best, an afterthought.

Consider the case of *Kaley v. United States*, where the Supreme Court held that the government may freeze the assets of a criminal defendant without an adversary hearing, even when the defendant intends to use those assets to pay for counsel in that same criminal proceeding.[115] Prior to *Kaley*, the Court had held that freezing a defendant's property is constitutional as long as it is based on a finding of probable cause that the property will ultimately be proved forfeitable.[116] Combining this ruling with statutory forfeiture law, a defendant's property is forfeitable if there is probable cause to believe that (1) the defendant committed an offense permitting forfeiture, and (2) the property at issue has requisite connection to the crime.[117]

Although lower courts generally provide hearings on the issue of whether the property being seized is connected to the crime, the Court was only asked to resolve the question of whether a hearing was required to find probable cause supporting the prosecution, and answered in the negative.[118] Justice Kagan, writing for the majority, explained that our system already trusts ex parte grand jury proceedings to restrain a defendant's liberty, and property should be treated no differently.[119] Furthermore, as far as the *Mathews* balancing test was concerned, the Court asserted that the prosecution had a legitimate interest in not showing its hand, lest it reveal evidence to the defendant in an adversary hearing and perhaps be forced to choose between conviction or pretrial seizure.[120] The Court also asserted that the probable cause standard "is not a high bar" and thus found the risk of erroneous deprivation to be low even where defendants had a serious interest in retaining money to pay for counsel.[121]

In dissent, Chief Justice Roberts, joined by Justices Breyer and Sotomayor, argued that a system of such perverse prosecutorial supremacy "is fundamentally at odds with our constitutional tradition and basic notions of fair play."[122] Relying on *Mathews*, the dissent argued that the government's interest in preservation of trial strategy was unpersuasive and that the "emphasis ... on pretrial secrecy evokes an outdated conception of the criminal trial as 'a poker game in which players enjoy an absolute right always to conceal their cards until played.'"[123] Furthermore, even with the "low bar" of probable cause, the dissent countered that "[i]t takes little imagination to see that seizures based entirely on *ex parte* proceedings create heightened risk of error" because "[c]ommon sense tells us that secret decisions based on only one side of the story will prove inaccurate more often than those made after hearing from both sides."[124]

The fundamental flaw of the *Kaley* decision is not that the interests were improperly balanced under *Mathews* (though that point is certainly arguable) but that *Mathews* itself is a seriously flawed and constitutionally unacceptable as protector of the due process right. Even if there is room to question whether probable cause is the appropriate standard to justify prejudgment seizure, at no point did the Court ever require a showing of urgency, irreparable harm, or anything demonstrating *immediate* need to seize the defendant's property without providing an adversary hearing (i.e., "the fundamental instrument for judicial judgment").[125] What's more, while the dissent expressed laudable skepticism toward government coercion absent procedural protections,[126] its reasoning was trapped within the restrictive framework of *Mathews*—a test that undervalues individual liberty and overvalues pragmatic interests purporting to justify coercion.

This is not to say that procedural due process jurisprudence has left out exigency considerations entirely.[127] But *Kaley* is evidence that the exigency inquiry has all too often been kicked to the wayside or, at the very least, inconsistently applied. To uphold our constitutional commitment to adversary democracy, which is constitutionally implemented through the Due Process Clauses in the form of adversary democratic due process, procedural due process must require a categorical presumption against prehearing deprivations absent a clear showing of demonstrable, compelling, and unavoidable exigency.

2.11.2 Deprivation of Others' Constitutionally Protected Interests

Because the adversarial structure by its very nature pits self-interest against self-interest, preserving litigant autonomy for one party may inescapably infringe on the rights of an adverse private party. If the commitment to adversary democracy produces a presumptive commitment to autonomy for the individual litigant, a clear demonstration of threat to the counterparty's own procedural autonomy can in some instances constitute an overriding compelling interest. Thus, where demonstrated, it may be justifiable to restrict litigant autonomy to the extent necessary to respect the compelling procedural interests of the counterparty.

It is established that adversary democracy's mistrust of others and prioritization of the individual's ability to protect his interest implies a commitment to allowing and protecting the right of individual participation in the judicial sphere as much as in the political sphere. In both governmental arenas, individuals should not be forced to defer to others regarding the representation of their rights. And just like political participation rights such as freedom of expression, the adjudicatory participation rights that give rise to the day-in-court ideal are extremely important, but not absolute.

Various litigation tools reflect the inherent tension in our adversarial system—and adversary democracy more broadly—between the strong presumption favoring individual control of litigation and the very real possibility that such control becomes a weapon of unpredictability, abuse, or harassment which compromises another individual's right to meaningful autonomy.

An illustration of such compelling interests is a defendant's ability to invoke collateral estoppel where legally appropriate.[128] The presumption favoring the original nonparty's right to have her day in court is not a carte blanche to engage in as much legal abuse and harassment against others as desired. Rather, just as default judgments and statutes of limitations provide a check against the weaponization of the threat of litigation, so, too, does the availability to the defendant of the defense of collateral estoppel preclude a plaintiff from harassing a defendant with multiple suits on the identical set of facts. But invoking the day-in-court ideal that lies at the heart of adversary democratic due process, the well-established law of judgments precludes the use of collateral estoppel against a litigant who was neither a party nor in privity with a party in the prior litigation.[129]

As will be demonstrated in more detail in a subsequent chapter,[130] in a select set of extreme circumstances, the day-in-court guarantee itself may be overridden. Where there is a serious risk of one of two types of indivisible relief—(1) double liability, or (2) contradictory liability—abandonment of adversary democratic due process's requirement of litigant autonomy may be appropriate. For example, if an individual were required either to do the impossible by engaging in mutually exclusive behavior patterns or to suffer legally inconsistent double punishment because a second litigant was allowed to have her day in court and succeeded, this result would pose serious due process concerns. Individuals cannot reasonably be said to retain control over their destiny—a core liberal value of adversary democracy—where they are stripped of any meaningful choice to act lawfully or are punished beyond what the law permits. The threat of indivisible relief therefore constitutes a compelling interest that should be recognized to refine and limit the reach of adversary democratic due process's protection of the day-in-court ideal. It must be emphasized, however, that the adversary democratic skepticism toward the all-too-likely inadequacy of third-party representation would require, in all cases, proof of "adequate" representation of the interests of the absent party as a necessary condition for nonparty preclusion. If individuals are deprived of their opportunity to represent their own interests on the paternalistic basis that someone else already did so for them, the mandatory check of "adequate representation" cannot be circumvented.

2.12 THE LIMITED OVERLAP BETWEEN *MATHEWS* AND ADVERSARY DEMOCRATIC DUE PROCESS

By now, it should be clear that adversary democratic due process and the utilitarian calculus of *Mathews v. Eldridge* have very little in common. For example, when it comes to the requirement of a prophylactically insulated neutral adjudicator, adversary democratic due process permits no variation. *Mathews*, on the other hand, applies its vague and unprotective utilitarian calculus to *all* issues of procedural due process. Moreover, while adversary democratic due process demands clear demonstration of a truly compelling interest to override the almost sacrosanct right to a fair hearing, the *Mathews* test is all too ready and willing to abandon the individual's right to fair process.

The due process question, however, is not always a matter of all or nothing. On occasion—as in *Mathews* itself—the due process issue is not whether to provide a hearing or not, but rather whether a particular procedure is constitutionally required within that hearing. It is in this concept where some overlap exists between adversary democratic due process and the *Mathews* utilitarian calculus, albeit in a very limited manner.

Consider the following admittedly extreme hypothetical: a litigant asserts a due process right to recite the Gettysburg Address in the course of the hearing. Under the *Mathews* utilitarian calculus, this asserted procedural right would receive extremely low marks as a means of advancing the truth-finding process. To count on adversary democratic due process to protect a litigant's right to recite the Gettysburg Address, however, would render the entire due process concept nonsensical. Thus, as a trigger for invocation of adversary democratic due process, there would have to be an initial finding that the particular procedure in question can reasonably be viewed as a step forward in the truth-finding process.

In this limited sense, adversary democratic due process overlaps with the utilitarian calculus developed in *Mathews*: both consider the extent to which the procedure in question could advance the truth-finding process. But it is at that point that the overlap ends. No matter how strong and clear the sought-after procedure is in facilitating the truth-finding process, the utilitarian calculus of the *Mathews* test will balance it evenly against the other two or three factors in that test. In contrast, the adversary democratic standard fashioned here would require only an initial finding that the procedure in question has a reasonable probability of advancing or facilitating the truth-finding process. At that point, the compelling interest standard previously described would be triggered.

2.13 REJECTING ALTERNATIVE MODELS OF PROCEDURAL DUE PROCESS

The capacious and ambiguous nature of the phrase "due process of law" has led courts and scholars to create a wide range of theoretical approaches to define the purpose and outer limits of this constitutional protection. Measured against an adversary democratic theory of due process, however, each one comes up woefully short.

2.13.1 Dignitary Theory

The dignitary theory of due process, originally proposed by Professor Jerry Mashaw, derives from the liberal principle that "decisional processes [should] preserve and enhance human dignity and self-respect."[131] To determine what process is "due," a dignitary approach requires consulting a "taxonomy of dignitary values" to dictate processes that "make a worthwhile contribution to [a] process participant's sense of self-respect."[132] This taxonomy of dignitary values, according to Professor Mashaw, includes equality (each party's contribution receives equal respect),[133] "thin" rationality (an indication that the information presented was at least somewhat meaningful to the outcome),[134] participation (involvement in the decision-making process to avoid perceptions of unfairness),[135] and privacy ("the right to be let alone").[136]

Dignitary theory does not assign each value equal weight. Some dignitary values are deemed more "fundamental," and there is a "rough hierarchy" to guide how they should be implemented in the due process context.[137] In Mashaw's words, "equality (as embodied in majority rule), minimal or 'thin' rationality, and some set of privacy constraints have been seen to be more fundamental to the preservation of a political morality based on individual self-respect (*i.e.*, liberalism) than are other values."[138] These values consequently have a stronger claim to implementation.[139]

To illustrate, Mashaw considers the case of *Board of Regents v. Roth*, where a nontenured professor whose contract was not renewed asserted a due process right to a statement of reasons and an evidentiary hearing prior to termination.[140] Under dignitary theory, the professor would have no constitutional claim to a full hearing prior to deprivation. Reasoning that the professor has no claim to a denial of equality since all contracted professors are treated the same, only the rationality value is implicated; failing to provide the professor with an understandable explanation would be "an obvious affront to his self-respect."[141] Nevertheless, while "[a] reason must be provided as a constitutional minimum," the state could rebut the claim to a hearing with its practical concerns: "[T]he impact of such processes on the resources available for the principal mission of the school; the effects of contentious processes on the willingness of supervisory personnel to act on their convictions in replacing existing staff etc."[142] Thus, "[s]imple receipt of a reason" is sufficient.[143]

Dignitary theory shares some liberal tenets with adversary democratic theory, inasmuch as dignitary theory values an individual's right to participation and dignified treatment. But the dignitary theory suffers from a dangerous lack of protective skepticism and an overemphasis on a litigant's purely subjective feelings of fairness. Consider the *Roth* example, which, under dignitary theory, allows for a thinly rational explanation of deprivation to satisfy due process. Assuming for the sake of argument that due process applies at all in the *Roth* case (though the Supreme Court decisively held it did not[144]), the dignitary analysis of this case provides a meek procedural right that pales in comparison to the defensive shield required by adversary democratic due process.

For starters, the dignitary framework takes no moment to consider the importance of *who* is responsible for providing this "thinly rational" explanation for the deprivation in this context. It flatly accepts investigation, adjudication, and provision of reasoning by the same entity seeking to take coercive action against the individual without an iota of concern for the need for impartial adjudication. Simple receipt of a reason is insufficient when the reason comes from a non-neutral adjudicator.

Moreover, the assumption that the "rationality" value itself can be rebutted by weak, cookie-cutter appeals to pragmatic concerns is disturbingly deferential. In sharp contrast, under adversary democratic theory an individual's due process rights cannot be so easily circumvented by concerns regarding how procedures might "impact ... the resources available for the principal mission" of the agency or affect the willingness of bureaucrats to act "on their convictions" when taking coercive action against individuals.[145] To allow such deferential concerns to dominate the due process calculus is to accept the false premise that an agency's desire to act swiftly and cheaply, without more, should have any impact on an individual's constitutional rights.

Dignitary's theory most fatal flaw, however, is its emphasis on individuals' subjective perception, unmoored from instrumental concerns relating to the objective benefits of procedural protections. Adversary democratic skepticism toward unfair adjudication would not allow an individual's feelings alone to dictate what process is due, because a focus on subjectivity creates a serious risk of abuse. Under dignitary theory's disproportionately subjective approach, individuals are vulnerable to being misled as a result of, for example, a non-neutral adjudicator giving subjectively satisfying but objectively misrepresentative reasons for a decision. The prophylactic, objectively grounded skepticism of adversary democratic due process works to eliminate this opportunity for abuse *ex ante*.

2.13.2 Historical and Originalist Approaches

Though originalism (somewhat ironically) was never used as a method of judicial interpretation until the late 1900s, it has come to dominate constitutional analysis. As a result, at the very least it has to be considered a contender that warrants consideration when deciding which principles ought to shape our understanding of procedural due process. To the extent one believes that originalism is irredeemably flawed, as, for example, I do,[146] then the question of whether originalism should inform due process is easily answered in the negative. But assuming for the sake of argument that originalism is, in a broad sense, a valid theory of constitutional interpretation, its inadequacy remains especially apparent in the procedural due process context.

Doctrinally, the Court has almost never relied on originalist methods to set the boundaries of procedural due process,[147] and likely for good reason. One infamous, explicitly originalist Supreme Court opinion deciding an issue of procedural due process is *Burnham v. Superior Court*.[148] The opinion announcing the judgment of the Court, written by Justice Scalia, is wrought with flaws,[149] many of which epitomize the inconsistent and unreliable nature of originalism as applied to procedural due process. In *Burnham*, Justice Scalia wrote that so-called "tag jurisdiction"[150] satisfies procedural due process.[151] Justice Scalia reasoned that, while the Supreme Court's watershed 1940 opinion in *International Shoe Co. v. Washington* rejected the power-based principle that a state has no authority over persons beyond its territory, "that the courts of a State have jurisdiction over nonresidents who are physically present in the State" was "firmly established" and unaffected by *International Shoe*'s minimum contacts analysis.[152] To reach this conclusion, Scalia relied on common law practice allowing "transitory" actions against nonresidents temporarily present in England,[153] nineteenth- and twentieth-century opinions,[154] and the "continuing" nature of this practice in the majority of states.[155]

Justice Scalia's originalist and majoritarian-centered approach is seriously flawed for several reasons. To begin with, it ignores the fact that *International Shoe* had already been construed to impact the entirety of the antiquated power-based theory of personal jurisdiction, as the Court had previously explained in *Shaffer v. Heitner*.[156] The *Shaffer* Court stated that after *International Shoe*, "the relationship among the defendant, the forum, and the litigation, rather than the mutually exclusive sovereignty of the States on which the rules of *Pennoyer* rest, became the central concern of the inquiry into personal jurisdiction."[157] After all, the two state-power principles that guided personal jurisdiction's due process analysis prior to *International Shoe* can appropriately be seen as two sides of the same coin: states do not have jurisdiction over nonresidents beyond their borders but do have jurisdiction over those within them.

In conceding that one side of the state-power-theory coin was eliminated while affirming that the other side remained in effect, Justice Scalia's "due process originalism is a one-way ratchet; it permits innovation but shields from constitutional attack those procedures that were accepted at the framing."[158] Where due process would have been violated at the time of the framing, Justice Scalia's originalism allows due process to evolve if the protection "comes to be viewed as sufficiently inexpedient in light of contemporary economic standards,"[159] but procedures which satisfied due process at the time of the Framing somehow remain inviolable. And beyond this fractured approach to originalism, the *Burnham* decision strains to distinguish itself from *Shaffer* by asserting—in a manner directly contrary to the very essence of constitutional democracy—that majoritarian influence can alter the meaning of a constitutional right. Where the Court in *Shaffer* expressly warned that due process "can be as readily offended by the perpetuation of ancient forms that are no longer justified,"[160] *Burnham* responded that this rule only applies "when the 'perpetuation of ancient forms' is engaged in by only a very small minority of the States."[161]

The hallmark case of originalist procedural due process thus embodies: (1) a disregard for precedent; (2) an unfathomable and dangerous democratization of a constitutional, countermajoritarian-grounded right; and (3) a faint-hearted, one-way form of originalism itself. This is hardly an inspiring basis on which to ground originalist approaches in other procedural due process contexts. This may be why even the judiciary's most avowed originalists have otherwise eschewed the doctrine when confronted with the question of "what process is due."[162]

Originalist due process fares no better normatively. As a textual matter, there is only one constitutional provision that explicitly calls for an "originalist" analysis: the Seventh Amendment right to a jury trial in civil cases.[163] By its text, it "in effect adopted the rules of common law, in respect of [civil] trial by jury, as these rules existed in 1791."[164] If the Framers wanted "to freeze procedural law in amber, they would have used a formulation akin to that of the Seventh Amendment."[165] But they did not. Moreover, if we were bound to the minimum procedures guaranteed at the time of ratification of the Fifth or Fourteenth Amendments, we would be stuck with procedures that would not comport with "traditional notions of fair play and substantial justice"[166] given modern developments. The inevitability of societal change is the very reason why *Pennoyer*'s power-theory principles (or at least one of them) are dead and gone.

In any case, relying on the "original meaning" of language that well may have been "chosen precisely because of its indeterminacy"[167] runs head first into the evidentiary and archaeological problem that plagues all originalist inquiries. It is unclear what "due process" even meant at the time of the Framing. On one hand, it seems clear that the Due Process Clause that ended up in the Fifth Amendment, and then again in the Fourteenth, was inspired in part by the Magna Carta's "law of the land" provision.[168] Yet the Magna Carta's law-of-the-land provision was not directly transplanted into the Fifth and Fourteenth Amendments. Instead, the Due Process Clause of the US Constitution was taken from New York's bill of rights, a document so young that it could not have acquired any identifiable original meaning.[169]

Moreover, no one involved ever bothered to explain why this language was chosen over that of the Magna Carta.[170] There was no consensus among esteemed authorities such as Lord Coke, Blackstone, and Hamilton, as to how the "law of the land" provision functioned.[171] And despite Representative Bingham's unelaborated and unsupported assertion that case law between 1791 and 1868 clarified precisely what due process meant,[172] to this day scholars remain stupefied and divided on originalist interpretations of these clauses.[173] Insisting on an originalist approach to due process is, then, an unwise and fruitless endeavor.[174]

2.13.3 Utilitarianism

The final theory that warrants dissection is the one that has emerged as the basis for the procedural due process calculus: pure utilitarianism.[175] Not only is the basic functionality of utilitarianism questionable inasmuch as its "balancing" may well be objectively impossible or arbitrary in application, it also presents a serious risk of neglecting the rights, interests, and integrity of individual litigants.

Utilitarianism at its core constitutes the intersection of two principles. One focuses on the correct way to assess or assign value, and the other focuses on the theory of correct action. The two combine to form a "welfarist consequentialist" framework.[176] To assess value, we look to welfare, satisfaction, or people getting what they prefer, measured in units of "utility." To determine correct or ethical decisions, utilitarianism follows the "greatest happiness principle" of Bentham in one form or another: we strive for the greatest happiness for the greatest number.[177]

Reliance on utilitarianism as a basis for procedural due process is plagued with difficulties. Utilitarianism's logistical issues alone make it incompatible with due process. Regardless of how utility itself is defined,[178] even as a general matter we cannot "take[] for granted that utilities (however interpreted) are cardinally measurable and interpersonally comparable."[179] With subjective concerns of "happiness," "interests," or "self-realization" as the yardstick, it is not clear how to quantify, let alone properly compare these concepts. The *Mathews* Court held that due process's minimum procedures constitute the result of "balancing" and "weighing" individual and government interests, but while this "is a useful approach for dealing with bananas, [it] leaves something to be desired where factors such as *Mathews* are concerned."[180]

Utilitarianism also risks total subjugation of the individual's very real interests under a cost-balancing calculus. The aggregation mechanism of utilitarianism takes a "narrow view of a person" whereby "[p]ersons do not count as individuals in this any more than individual petrol tanks do in the analysis of the national consumption of petroleum."[181] The theory is wholly apathetic toward the value of personal autonomy or integrity. As such, it is no surprise that where the Court has applied utilitarian approaches to constitutional rights, such rights more easily fall by the wayside for being too "costly."[182]

The greatest pathology of *Mathews*, however, is that it overlooks the reality that any cost–benefit analysis pitting "individual interest" against "burden on the government" sets up an inherently unfair fight. "No man's liberty or property [is] safe when the court simply asks case by case what procedures seem worthwhile and not too costly."[183] Procedures always add costs which are easily calculable and immediately felt economically. The same cannot be said for the difficult-to-quantify, abstract values of "accuracy," "fairness," or "autonomy" on the other side of the scale. But the Constitution is not a business venture, and its protections are not designed to balance government budgets. Nothing in the Constitution or the democratic values it embodies suggests that procedural due process should succumb so easily to bureaucratic stinginess.

The tendency to bend and break at superficial complaints that individual procedural protections are "too costly" is readily apparent in modern due process case law. When, for example, a prison system points out that prison management is expensive,[184] or a metropolitan city complains that it is inconvenient to provide procedures *prior* to towing a car,[185] economic efficiency concerns dominate, forcing the individual to justify why she is worthy of the expenditure of government resources. Yet the real question the judiciary must ask when presented with these economic considerations is, "why do these concerns matter for due process?"

It is not that utilitarianism and cost-balancing have no place in procedural due process. Indeed, where the government can convincingly demonstrate exigency (e.g., a risk of irrecoverable loss or of imminent danger of harm[186]), exceptions to the default presumption favoring individual procedural rights may be proper. But utilitarian cost-balancing should be a method of last resort—that is, when used in a manner narrowly tailored to focus on specific immediate needs rather than general budgeting preferences.

2.14 CONCLUSION

The Fifth and Fourteenth Amendments' guarantee that no person be deprived of life, liberty, or property without "due process of law" has long been a source of confusion for legal minds. In the plethora of attempts to make sense of this capacious four-word guarantee, neither scholarly nor doctrinal developments have articulated a workable, meaningful approach to determine what process is due. Marred by a mix of poorly defined notions of fairness, dignity, or utilitarian cost-balancing, the legal landscape for procedural due process has left the doctrine detached from basic principles of American constitutionalism, and left litigants guessing as to what procedures are secured to them through these clauses.

There is no need for such guesswork. Just as we have done for similarly capacious phrases like "freedom of speech," we must recognize that procedural due process furthers a uniquely democratic purpose. Our particular constitutional democracy is unique, permeated by an adversary democratic spirit that is evident in our inherently divided system of government. By design, the multiple branches and hierarchical levels of our government find themselves in a state of virtually constant conflict. In a seemingly paradoxical manner, the Framers chose to promote conflict as the very means to keep it in check.

In reality, however, there is nothing paradoxical about the choice to mediate conflict rather than to hopelessly try to stomp it out. And given our ever-increasing and ever-diversifying polity, where conflict of interests is inevitable, the only epistemologically humble (and therefore defensible) position is one based on adversarial processes driven by individual interest. Of course, paternalism, at least at some minimal level, is inherent in the structure of our republic, since individuals are not guaranteed the right to directly participate in all governmental decisions. But when the stakes are high for particularly affected individuals, except in the most extreme instances the Constitution empowers those individuals to choose who is to advocate for their rights without having to depend on anyone else to do it for them. This is the lesson we learn from understanding the foundational precepts of the blend of the liberal and adversary forms of democratic theory on which our constitutional democracy was founded.

Procedural due process is appropriately viewed as both an integral component and outgrowth of this adversary democratic scheme, providing safeguards necessary to promote self-realization and legitimize the democratic system. The protective skepticism of adversary democracy pervades this constitutional guarantee, and its application and theoretical purpose must be defined accordingly. Recognizing the centrality of this adversary democratic framework to core notions of procedural due process would transform contemporary understanding and application of the right. Such change is long overdue. For the sake of individual liberty, the protection of vulnerable populations, and American democracy itself, it is time to do away with the hollow, confusing, and inadequate procedural due process jurisprudence of today. It is time to recognize the inherent symbiotic relationship between democracy and due process.

3
MULTIDISTRICT LITIGATION, DUE PROCESS, AND THE DANGERS OF PROCEDURAL COLLECTIVISM

3.1 INTRODUCTION

Given the manner in which complex litigation has evolved over the last forty years, it is surprising that no one has previously coined the phrase "procedural collectivism." That phrase, after all, effectively describes what has taken place during that time: what are, in their pristine substantive form, individually held rights which have no pre-litigation connection whatsoever are routinely grouped together for purposes of collective adjudication. This is often done, regardless of whether the individual claimants desire such a grouping or even whether such a grouping will hurt the interests of those claimants more than help them.

"Procedural collectivism" does not refer to all forms of aggregate litigation. For example, it does not include aggregate litigation in which all aggregated parties determine for themselves how to protect or pursue their own legal rights in the course of the litigation.[1] Rather, it refers solely to representative litigation in which the rights of purely passive claimants are adjudicated by selected parties, supposedly possessing parallel or at least similar interests, who litigate on behalf of those passive participants.

There are two forms of such litigation: class actions and multidistrict litigation (MDL). While class actions have generally been somewhat on the decline in recent years,[2] MDL practice has become so pervasive as to be almost routine.[3] Both courts and scholars have expressed concern about what they see as the pathologies of the modern class action, among which is the threat posed by the controversial procedure to the constitutionally protected interests of those passive claimants.[4] The Constitution protects such interests under the Due Process Clauses of the Fifth and Fourteenth Amendments, which guarantee that neither life, liberty, nor property may be deprived without due process of law.[5] The clause is triggered in the class action context because the absent class members' claims are deemed "choses in action," which are classified as protected property interests.[6]

There are legitimate reasons why the Due Process Clause is needed to police the class action process. All too often, neither representative parties nor their attorneys give sufficient attention to the interests of absent claimants.[7] But in important ways, the current practice of MDL actually makes the modern class action appear to be the pinnacle of procedural due process by comparison. At least in the class action context, the choice of representative party is controlled by explicit rule-based requirements. The representative parties' claims must share significant common issues with the claims of the absent parties.[8] Their claims must also be typical of those of the absent parties, and they must adequately represent those absent parties.[9] Moreover, these determinations are usually made in the context of a transparent process of adversary adjudication.[10] Finally, in at least the bulk of modern class actions—those brought pursuant to Rule 23(b)(3)—absent class members are given the right to opt out of the proceeding in order either to pursue their own claims individually or choose simply not to pursue them at all.[11]

In stark contrast, MDL involves something of a cross between the Wild West, twentieth-century political smoke-filled rooms, and the *Godfather* movies. The substantive rights of litigants are adjudicated collectively without any possibility of a transparent, adversary adjudication of whether the claims grouped together actually have a substantial number of issues in common, whether the interests of the individual claimants will be fully protected by those parties and attorneys representing their interests, or whether the individual claimants would have a better chance to protect their interests by being allowed to pursue their claims on their own.[12] Another important difference between class actions and MDL is that unlike class actions, *all* plaintiffs grouped together in MDL have what are called "positive value" claims, meaning claims that are sufficiently large to stand on their own.[13] This is so by definition, because MDL covers only those plaintiffs who have already filed their own individual actions.[14] In contrast, it is often the case that numerous absent class members have "negative value" claims, meaning their claims are insufficient to stand on their own,[15] and most of them have probably never even thought about bringing suit in the first place. Thus, often far more will be at stake for the passive member of an MDL than for the absent member of a class. Finally, whereas relatively few class actions are mandatory, *all* MDLs are mandatory.[16] The plaintiff whose claim is grouped together with countless others is given no choice in the matter.

One might respond that while the collective adjudicatory procedure in class actions will end in a final resolution which bars class members from future pursuit of their individual claims, the same is not true in the case of MDL. On the contrary, claims are grouped together solely for purposes of "pretrial" activities, including pleading motions, discovery, and summary judgment.[17] Actual trials, to the extent they ever take place, will usually be conducted either on a voluntary basis in the transferee court or on an individual basis in the district in which the individual plaintiff filed suit.[18] But even casual observation reveals that the notion that MDL is purely a preliminary procedural device is more theoretical than real. It is the rare multidistrict proceeding indeed that ever returns its members to their individual districts for adjudication on the merits.[19] But even if we were to take the process at face value as merely a collectivist form of pretrial practice, the interference with the individual litigant's control of the adjudication of her own claim remains substantial. There are usually many different pretrial strategies which litigants can choose, but for the overwhelming number of unwilling participants in an MDL, that choice is, as a practical matter, removed from them and their chosen attorney.[20]

Moreover, given the often extremely loose connection among the claims of the individual plaintiffs, it is certainly conceivable that some plaintiffs will have stronger claims and/or stronger fact situations than others, yet due to MDL they are all brought down to the lowest common denominator. And they are represented by attorneys whom they have not chosen or likely even met and who have never been formally adjudicated to adequately represent their interests. Also, individual plaintiffs have no meaningful opportunity to challenge either the legitimacy of their inclusion in the multidistrict process or the propriety of the representation chosen for them by judges in the judicial equivalent of a smoke-filled room.[21]

To be sure, scholars have long debated the merits of MDL.[22] But what seems to have been lost in the shuffle in all of that scholarly debate is any serious discussion of MDL's serious undermining of the individual plaintiffs' right to procedural due process. The Due Process Clause requires that before property rights may be taken away by governmental practice, the individual must be given some form of fair procedure by which she can protect her property interests.[23] At its core, that protection has been construed to require some form of "day in court," during which the litigant has the opportunity to plead his case openly before a neutral adjudicator.[24] As argued throughout this book, the strongest support for this day-in-court ideal is the Due Process Clause's grounding in core theoretical notions of American political theory: adversary democracy. Our entire democratic structure is grounded in the premise of skepticism and mistrust—the foundational commitment to the principle that in the absence of truly compelling circumstances, the choice of who should represent an individual litigant in court should be the individual's herself. Neither the motives, good faith, or competence of a representative chosen by others can be trusted to assure a full and fair defense of the litigant's interests. But not all versions of due process theory start from this same premise.

There appear to be two methodologies and rationales for this constitutional guarantee: what can be called the "paternalism" and "autonomy" models.[25] The paternalism version of due process demands that those who represent the legally protected interests of individual litigants adequately represent those interests in good faith.[26] The importance of this version of the constitutional guarantee has long been recognized in the shaping of the modern class action.[27] It may be seriously questioned whether such paternalism fully satisfies due process concerns when the litigant is available to legally protect his own interests and wishes instead to choose his own representative to litigate on his behalf.[28] Such an individualist-based choice flows from a conception of due process as protecting a form of "meta"utonomy—in other words, an individual's autonomy in choosing how to exercise his liberty to participate in the governmental process. This book consistently focuses on the dangers of paternalism by emphasizing the intersection between adversary democratic theory and due process. Adversary theory is grounded in the premise that for a variety of reasons, those in power cannot be trusted to protect the interests of others. Thus, we begin with a strong presumption that the individual has the right to control her own legal interests. In so doing, adversary democratic due process enables the individual to develop and flourish. This is the core of the autonomy model of due process. Use of the paternalistic model of due process undermines both the adversary and liberal values of American democratic theory.[29]

The debate between paternalism and autonomy as the ultimate rationale for due process has great relevance to the class action debate. However, the dispute between these alternatives turns out to be purely academic in the context of MDL, because that process miserably fails the dictates of the due process right to one's day in court from *either* perspective. From the perspective of the paternalism model of the day-in-court ideal, the failure of MDL procedure to provide any opportunity for a transparent, adversary-based adjudication of the adequacy and accountability of the chosen representative parties and attorneys as representatives of all of the nonparticipating litigants constitutes an unambiguous violation of the constitutionally dictated right to one's day in court.[30] The crude, almost random process by which claims are grouped together only compounds those due process problems.[31]

Nor does MDL fare any better from the perspective of the adversary-autonomy rationale. Individual litigants who possess positive-value claims—and have already demonstrated the desire to pursue those claims on an individual basis—are forced into a process in which their substantive rights will be significantly affected, if not effectively resolved, by means of a shockingly sloppy, informal, and often secretive process in which they have little or no right to participate, and in which they have very little say concerning the propriety of their inclusion in the process in the first place. It is difficult to comprehend how this process could even arguably be deemed to satisfy the Due Process Clause's protective reach, regardless of the assumed underlying rationale for that guarantee.

One might respond that the individual litigants do have the right to opt out of any settlement reached in the course of the MDL,[32] and therefore their due process rights have not been compromised. But it should be recalled that even if a litigant does withdraw from the collective settlement, his right to control adjudication of his own claim will have been substantially compromised by the collective, lowest common denominator control of the pretrial process, including all important discovery and pretrial motions.

More importantly, wholly apart from this serious due process concern, the option to remove oneself from a proposed settlement does not solve the significant constitutional problems to which MDL gives rise. First of all, the settlement has been determined on a one-size-fits-all collectivist basis, helping those plaintiffs with weaker individual cases while harming those plaintiffs whose individual claims are factually or legally stronger than the median.[33] Yet when making the decision of whether or not to accept the settlement, the individual litigant has no idea where his claim fits into this pecking order. While the individual plaintiff might reach out to his chosen attorney for advice as to whether or not to accept settlement, it must be recognized that the collective settlement may well have compromised the relationship between individual attorney and his client. The attorney knows at this point that if her client accepts the settlement, she will receive a fee while doing virtually nothing to have earned it. If, on the other hand, the client chooses to opt out of the settlement, any fee is now rendered uncertain and at best would come only after the attorney invests substantial effort to bring the individual litigation to a successful resolution. This potentially conflicting interest gives rise to the serious danger of a conflict in the attorney's fiduciary obligation to her client.[34] In this sense, multidistrict litigation actually manufactures threats to the relation between client and her chosen attorney that is supposed to serve as the ultimate guarantor of the goals sought to be achieved by adversary democratic theory.

It is true that, at least as a doctrinal matter, the due process calculus has in its modern form always included consideration of utilitarian concerns.[35] Thus, one might argue that this seemingly indefensible undermining of the individual's right to his day in court when his legally granted rights are at stake may be justified by the pragmatic need to limit the expenditure of governmental resources required by numerous individual litigations. But no court has even attempted to make that calculus, much less balance it against the significant interference with the individual litigant's right to his day in court. This is so, for the simple reason that no court appears to have even considered, much less ruled upon, a due process challenge to MDL. In any event, surely at *some* point there must be a floor on the individual's right to his day in court, lest the due process guarantee be rendered little more than a cynical sham. The sweeping deprivations of an individual's ability to protect his legal rights brought about by MDL cannot be justified by naked concerns of pragmatism if the concept of due process is to mean anything.

When the dust settles, then, there appears to be no way that the MDL process, at least as currently constituted, can satisfy the requirements of due process. In short, MDL is unconstitutional. This does not necessarily mean that the process is incapable of revision in order to satisfy due process by including measures demonstrating some respect for the rights of the individual litigants who are being herded into the process. But one cannot even reach that issue until one first decides that the process, as presently constituted, is unconstitutional. The Procrustean Bed that is MDL, whereby the claims of each individual are crudely and artificially reshaped into fitting some generic lowest common denominator, unambiguously violates the Fifth Amendment's Due Process Clause. The purpose of this chapter is to establish just that.

The first section of this chapter explores the history and structure of MDL. The second section explains the mechanics of the process, thereby revealing the serious dangers to individual rights to which this form of procedural collectivism gives rise. The third section discusses the nature of the due process problems from the perspective of constitutional doctrine and theory. The final section considers possible means of revising the multidistrict process in order to enable it to achieve the system's beneficial goals while showing greater respect for the integrity of individuals and their right to their day in court.

3.2 HISTORY AND STRUCTURE OF MULTIDISTRICT LITIGATION

Congress enacted the Multidistrict Litigation Statute[36] in response to the first modern mass litigation in the early 1960s, which stemmed from allegations of price-fixing in the electrical equipment industry.[37] Large-scale litigation was quite daunting in an era when fax and copy machines were just coming into widespread commercial use, and personal computers and the internet were decades in the distance. Chief Justice Earl Warren created the Coordinating Committee for Multiple Litigation of the US District Courts to coordinate discovery among the electrical equipment antitrust cases.[38] His project was successful and his idea legislatively codified; MDL was born.[39]

MDL refers to "coordinated or consolidated pretrial proceedings" in related cases taking place before a single federal district judge.[40] Since its inception in the late 1960s, MDL has become more and more common, to the point where today its use could almost be called routine.[41] Over the same period, the number of mass torts and antitrust cases has also grown, almost exponentially.[42] Also during that time, class actions became popular and then tapered off somewhat as a method of providing a national solution to mass litigation.[43] The majority of MDLs occur in products liability and antitrust cases, but the Judicial Panel on Multidistrict Litigation approves consolidation in a wide variety of substantive legal areas.[44] The Panel, made up of seven federal judges, decides whether an individual lawsuit is better suited to group treatment for pretrial purposes.[45] If several cases are found to share at least one common factual question and the Panel determines that consolidated proceedings will be relatively convenient for the parties and save judicial resources,[46] the Panel may transfer those cases to a specified federal district judge, who will preside over coordinated pretrial matters in one consolidated action.[47] The Panel may do so *sua sponte*, which means that seven federal judges can decide on their own to move thousands of cases into one forum.[48] Since 1968, they have decided to do so in over four hundred thousand cases involving millions of individual claims.[49]

The Panel can only transfer cases into an MDL for pretrial matters; the transferee court's jurisdiction extends only that far.[50] But as a practical matter, for almost all cases transferred into an MDL, there is no trial, let alone post-trial matters, left to conduct back in the transferor district.[51] Settlement is the endgame in almost all instances.[52] To get there, the transferee court appoints a small group of attorneys to strategize, conduct discovery, and try test cases on behalf of the group of plaintiffs.[53] This appointed group is frequently called a steering committee; it steers the strategy for discovery and guides the course for all other pretrial matters.[54] The steering committee effectively replaces the plaintiffs' chosen representatives and is expected to represent the interests of all plaintiffs in the MDL, no matter how varied they may be.[55] Every claimant enters MDL having made the decision to hire a particular lawyer and file suit against a particular defendant in a particular jurisdiction. But once her case is transferred to an MDL, the district judge decides who will really represent her interests in the MDL. Suddenly, all of the decisions the claimant made about exercising her rights through litigation—which lawyer to hire, when and where to file a lawsuit, and against whom—have been replaced by decisions made by federal judges and court-sanctioned attorneys.

3.3 THE MECHANICS OF MULTIDISTRICT LITIGATION

At the present time, more than one hundred thousand individual suits are part of an active MDL.[56] By at least one estimate, close to one-third of all pending federal civil cases are part of an MDL.[57] On the order of the Judicial Panel on Multidistrict Litigation, individual suits that share "one or more common questions of fact"—a "lenient"[58] standard—may be transferred to "any district" for all pretrial matters.[59] The chosen district may even be one that neither has personal jurisdiction over the parties nor constitutes a legally authorized venue for the individual suits.[60] That court then has complete jurisdiction over all pretrial matters, including discovery, motions for class certification, *Daubert* motions, dispositive motions such as summary judgment, and pretrial settlement.[61] Centralized management of numerous cases in an MDL aims to avoid duplicative discovery and increase efficiency in factually similar cases.[62] At the conclusion of pretrial procedures, cases transferred by the Panel into a single MDL proceeding are supposed to be remanded to the districts in which they were originally filed—the transferor districts.[63] In practice, however, consolidation into an MDL more often than not leads to settlement, not remand.[64] This is especially true in the realm of products liability suits.[65] This section describes the process by which cases become part of an MDL. It explains MDL case management and the scope of MDL courts' authority.

3.3.1 Initiating MDL

As of late 2013, 462,501 individual actions had been consolidated into 1,230 MDLs.[66] The Panel identifies pending civil actions that share one or more common questions of fact.[67] It uses its transfer powers to "avoid duplicative or possibly overlapping discovery . . . whenever there is a prospect of overlapping classes," and to "'eliminate the possibility of colliding pretrial rulings by courts of coordinate jurisdiction.'"[68] By statute, consolidation and transfer of multiple actions into a single MDL is appropriate when it "will be for the convenience of parties and witnesses and will promote the just and efficient conduct of such actions."[69] The Panel seems to focus primarily on the question of whether transfer will be more efficient than allowing the suits to proceed independently.[70] In making this determination, the Panel relies on the parties' attorneys to advise it about facts and circumstances relevant to "whether and where transfer should be effected in order to secure the just and expeditious resolution of all involved actions."[71] When it perceives that consolidation will save judicial resources, "transfer is almost inevitable."[72] Common questions of fact do not have to predominate over other questions, and arguments against transfer because of the existence of noncommon issues are unlikely to prevail.[73]

A party dissatisfied with the Panel's decision may move for reconsideration.[74] On appeal, transfer orders are reviewable only by an extraordinary writ to the court of appeals possessing jurisdiction over the district court handling the MDL.[75] However, an order denying transfer may not be the subject of an appeal.[76]

When the Panel decides to create an MDL, it designates a specific federal district court and a specific federal district judge to preside.[77] The Panel's choices are not guided by any particular set of factors; they are not cabined by statute or by the Multidistrict Rules of Procedure.[78] The selected judge (the "transferee judge") and court (the "transferee court") need not already have one of the consolidated cases on their docket,[79] though parties may lobby the Panel for a specific court or judge on that basis.[80] The Panel might choose a particular judge for his or her experience with similar cases or other MDLs.[81] The condition of a potential transferee court's docket appears relevant, as do the distribution of MDLs throughout the country,[82] the location of relevant evidence, and the "willingness and motivation" of the potential transferee judge.[83]

Prior to consolidation, most of the parties' disagreements have tended to focus on where the consolidation will take place; parties have often preferred particular venues and district judges.[84] When lobbying for transfer to a specific district, parties may not argue about applicable district and circuit law in potential courts (which may be more favorable to the plaintiffs or the defendants in a given set of facts); they are limited to administrative and convenience arguments.[85] Plaintiffs might strategically file cases in a particular district and then argue that the Panel should assign the MDL to that district because cases are already pending there. If those cases have advanced further in the discovery process such that a particular presiding judge appears to be leading the pack of cases to be transferred, this strategy might prove effective. On the other side, defendants might argue that creation of an MDL is premature or that, because only a few plaintiffs' lawyers are involved, the parties can informally coordinate the cases without formally consolidating them.

After the Panel creates an MDL, later-filed "tag-along" cases which share common questions of fact with the previously transferred cases may be added to the MDL.[86] A party to a tag-along case may seek a transfer order from the Panel,[87] which then reviews the complaint and docket sheet before issuing a conditional transfer order.[88] If the defendants agree not to object, tag-along cases can be filed directly in the transferee court, without regard to whether personal jurisdiction and venue would be proper in that court absent the MDL.[89]

3.3.2 MDL Management and Steering Committees

A single MDL can involve thousands of plaintiffs and thousands of lawyers.[90] Rather than deal directly with scores of attorneys, transferee courts appoint a limited number of lawyers to serve on "steering committees" to manage the litigation.[91] Because "'[t]he purpose of consolidation is to permit trial convenience and economy in administration,'"[92] they assert, a failure to designate lead counsel would be inefficient and counter to the very idea of MDLs. As a result, "the litigation is run in many ways by a relatively small number of counsel appointed to the case-management committees established by the court."[93]

Counsel appointed to management or leadership roles act on behalf of other counsel and parties, not just the clients who retained them.[94] MDL judges have total discretion to designate various leaders or committees among the involved attorneys. They are not required to use any particular titles or assign any particular duties. These designations fall into four general categories: liaison counsel, lead counsel, trial counsel, and committees of counsel.[95] "Liaison counsel" is essentially an administrator located near the transferee court who facilitates communications between the court and other counsel; this designee need not be an attorney.[96] "Lead counsel" is responsible for "formulating . . . and presenting positions on substantive and procedural issues."[97] This attorney (or attorneys) presents written and oral arguments to the MDL court, works with opposing counsel on discovery issues, conducts depositions, hires expert witnesses, manages support services for the MDL, and ensures that schedules are kept.[98] "Trial counsel" function as the principal attorneys at trial, and they coordinate the other members of the trial team.[99] "Committees of counsel," often called steering, coordinating, management, or executive committees, are appointed when there are sufficient dissimilarities among group members to warrant representation of those disparate interests on a larger litigation leadership team.[100]

The transferee judge has complete control over designating attorneys to play specific roles in the MDL.[101] In some cases, attorneys can apply to be on a steering committee or to take on another leadership role.[102] Though MDL judges entertain objections to applicants or nominees,[103] selection to the committee is not the result of a traditional adversary process refereed by the court.[104] In selecting counsel for leadership roles, the transferor judge may consider factors such as "physical (e.g., office facilities) and financial resources; commitment to a time-consuming, long-term project; ability to work cooperatively with others; and professional experience particular to this type of litigation."[105] Among attorneys, "[t]here is often intense competition for appointment by the court as designated counsel, an appointment that may implicitly promise large fees and a prominent role in the litigation."[106] Attorneys sometimes make side agreements about who will lobby to be appointed to a leadership role.[107] These preformed coalitions, which may be influential in establishing an MDL in the first place, often determine who ends up on the steering committee.[108] Of course, this backroom dealing is not transparent to individual claimants, and may not be open to first-time MDL attorneys, either.

Membership on the steering committee entails an enormous amount of work, but it can also come with a huge payoff—certainly larger than the contingency fee expected from representing one or even several individual plaintiffs—because attorneys who do work for the common benefit of the group typically receive a portion of every single plaintiff's payout. *In re Zyprexa Products Liability Litigation*[109] provides one example of how MDL courts commonly establish attorney compensation structures for the council appointed to steer the litigation. There, the MDL court capped attorneys' fees and created a common benefit fund, generated by a mandatory set-aside from all settlements and judgments in the MDL, to compensate members of the plaintiffs' steering committee.[110] The court also established fee restrictions and appointed special settlement masters with discretion to order reductions or increases of fees in negotiated settlement agreements.[111]

Appointment to the steering committee often reaps subsequent career benefits as well. After an attorney is selected for one steering committee, she may call herself an experienced MDL litigator the next time she participates in an MDL. That credential makes the next transferee judge more likely to appoint her to a subsequent steering committee.[112] The pattern repeats. Because the transferee judge has complete control over appointment to leadership roles, and there is fierce competition for those lucrative positions, experience in a prior MDL can tip the scales in favor of one attorney over another.[113] In this way, the group of powerful MDL plaintiffs' attorneys remains relatively small, and newcomers face formidable barriers to entry which they cannot overcome on their own accord.[114] Due to this positive feedback loop, if an individual plaintiff hires his local attorney for any reason other than the attorney's MDL experience, the odds of that local attorney being selected for a leadership role are quite low. Claimants are unaware of this when they retain counsel and decide to file a lawsuit, because unless they are tag-along plaintiffs, they are unaware that they will eventually be transferred into an MDL.

The existence of a steering committee lowers barriers to entry for tag-along plaintiffs, which may cause huge increases in the number of plaintiffs in a single MDL.[115] When attorneys appointed by the court will do the bulk of the work, the cost of participation to the individual claimant is lowered. The claimant might even file *pro se*, forgoing the cost of retaining a lawyer of his own, with the knowledge that a court-sanctioned attorney will litigate his case on his behalf, and that the case will likely never emerge from the MDL. Tag-along plaintiffs who file directly into an MDL do not have to make the same kind of investment as other plaintiffs, so it is possible that their claims are not strong enough to warrant filing individual lawsuits. If so, tag-along plaintiffs could dilute the overall strength of plaintiffs' claims, which could result in a weaker bargaining position for all the plaintiffs when settlement negotiations begin.

In the unlikely event that individual cases are remanded back to their jurisdictions of origin, the discovery conducted by the steering committee restricts what the individual claimant and her lawyer can do upon remand. Because one of the fundamental ideas behind consolidation into MDL is to avoid duplicative discovery, on remand transferor courts are hesitant to grant additional discovery requests.[116] As a more formal matter, transferee courts have authority to enter pretrial orders that "'govern the conduct of the trial'" back in a transferor court.[117] Furthermore, decisions made before trial can often be outcome-determinative; they dictate viable arguments and strategies. In these ways, even though the consolidated proceedings are restricted to pretrial matters, the steering committee exercises real and enormous influence over the direction of an individual's claim.

3.3.3 Bellwether Trials

As the Supreme Court made explicit in *Lexecon Inc. v. Milberg Weiss Bershad Hynes & Lerach*,[118] a transferee court's authority extends only to pretrial matters; it cannot try a transferred case without the parties' consent.[119] Within the limits of Section 1407 and *Lexecon*, though, MDL courts often work to obtain consent from some parties to conduct "bellwether" trials, which serve as a means of gathering information about the strengths and weaknesses of each side's arguments and often facilitate global settlement negotiations.[120] Bellwether trials are an expected element of the information-gathering process undertaken in transferee courts. These bellwether trials are, for the most part, information-gathering tools; while they of course bind the immediate parties, they are not binding on other parties in the MDL.[121] However, their holdings can be used offensively as collateral estoppel by plaintiffs in future cases, subject to the normal limits on that doctrine.[122] Cases selected as bellwether trials are usually tried by members of the appointed leadership team, not by the attorneys of record in the individual cases.[123] As such, bellwether trials give coordinating counsel an opportunity to "organize the products of pretrial common discovery, evaluate the strengths and weaknesses of their arguments and evidence, and understand the risks and costs associated with the litigation."[124]

Assuming the claims selected for bellwether treatment are "typical" of the group of claims, bellwether trials facilitate settlement by valuing cases in a way that can be extrapolated to other claims.[125] The utility of a bellwether verdict depends on whether the tried claim is a truly representative test.[126] But even if the transferee court conducts several bellwether trials in an attempt to account for claims of different strengths, they cannot account for all the unique features of all claims in the MDL. Relying on the results of bellwether trials to evaluate settlement offers can over- or undervalue individual claims, and there is no telling which is occurring more often.

If cases in an MDL are remanded to their jurisdictions of origin, bellwether trials may be useful for their creation of "trial packages," which local counsel can use in subsequent trials.[127] These packages typically include items such as discovery documents, background information, expert reports, deposition and trial testimony, information about potential witnesses, court rulings and transcripts, and coordinating counsel's work product.[128] But bellwether trials' primary function is to facilitate settlement in the transferee court.[129] Bellwether trials prioritize fact-finding and force appointed counsel to develop their theories of the case. These "contribution[s] to the maturation of disputes" "can naturally precipitate settlement discussions" because each side has "test driven" its theories before live juries.[130] Jury verdicts inform both sides about the relative strengths and weaknesses of their various strategies and arguments.[131] Knowing the persuasive value of bellwether trials when it comes time to negotiate a possible global settlement, "coordinating council often pull out all the stops," making bellwether trials "exponentially more expensive for the litigants and attorneys than a normal trial."[132] The more expensive the bellwether trial, the more likely the parties are to rely on its outcome in assessing the value of the remaining claims, because the parties have more riding on the bellwether trial being a useful tool. Similar to the preference for appointing experienced MDL litigators to leadership positions, reliance on bellwether trials is a self-reinforcing feature of MDLs.

Bellwether trials are not perfect predictors. Even if the transferee court conducts multiple bellwether trials that are representative of several subgroups of claims, the most useful bellwether cases for the greatest number of plaintiffs are not the extraordinary claims. So although the process of trying bellwether cases facilitates global settlement, by design it does not account for the unique characteristics of a particularly weak or strong claim.

3.3.4 Settlement

Settlement is the fate of almost all cases that are part of an MDL. Approximately 97 percent of MDL cases terminate in transferee districts; thus, relatively few are remanded back to the districts in which they were originally filed.[133] Parties to MDL cases and the transferee judges who preside over them face tremendous pressure to settle. Because a primary objective of consolidation into MDL is to avoid multiple federal judges having to deal with the same issues, some judges perceive failure to achieve a global settlement as a failure.[134] Transferee courts tend to take an active role in settlement negotiations. They appoint special settlement masters[135] and take a hands-on approach.[136] As Judge Fallon described, it is "not unusual" for a transferee court to "encourage a global resolution of the matter before recommending to the Panel that the case be remanded."[137] Individual litigants, whose personal litigation goals may or may not be monetary,[138] face pressure to accept defendants' monetary offers because their attorneys work for contingency fees.

Currently, the aggregate settlement rule governs global MDL settlements. It requires that each claimant give "informed consent" to a settlement, based on knowledge of the settlement terms, including other claimants' payouts.[139] However, that safety valve may be short-lived. A number of years ago the American Law Institute (ALI) published *Principles of the Law of Aggregate Litigation*.[140] The ALI proposal would allow clients, at the time they retained representation, to agree to be bound by an aggregate settlement approved by supermajority vote of all claimants.[141] Clients could empower their lawyers "in advance, to negotiate binding settlements on their behalf as part of a collective resolution of claims."[142] Although the ALI proposal is just that—a proposal—it demonstrates the pervasiveness of settlement in MDLs and the apparent consensus that facilitating global settlement is a certain function, if not the main purpose, of consolidation into an MDL.

3.3.5 Attorney Compensation

The huge responsibility placed on members of court-selected steering committees comes with potentially huge payoffs. Transferee courts structure compensation plans for lead counsel that reflect their responsibility to and efforts on behalf of the group. The courts justify that exercise of authority in the following way: " '[I]f lead counsel are to be an effective tool the court must have means at its disposal to order appropriate compensation for them. The court's power is illusory if it is dependent upon lead counsel's performing the duties desired of them for no additional compensation.' "[143] To compensate appointed counsel, courts set up common benefit funds from which they will later withdraw lead counsel's fees and costs.[144] They also enter orders requiring some portion of all claim payments, including settlements and judgments arising after cases are transferred back to their original jurisdictions, to be paid into the common benefit funds.[145] The "common benefit fee" comes from the fee that would be paid to the claimant's selected attorney—not from the claimant's portion.[146] In this way, MDL splits the attorney fee the plaintiff agreed to at the outset between retained counsel and appointed counsel. The contingent percentage of the plaintiff's recovery remains the same, but the retained counsel must share that percentage with the steering committee.

Transferee courts also establish how much lead counsel will be paid from the common funds. Many rely on a Fifth Circuit case, *Johnson v. Georgia Highway Express, Inc.*,[147] which established a twelve-factor guideline for determining a reasonable fee for each committee member.[148] In allocating fees, courts must "conform to 'traditional judicial standards of transparency, impartiality, procedural fairness, and ultimate judicial oversight.'"[149] They do so with input from lead attorneys, but ultimate discretion lies with the transferee court,[150] whose cost awards are subject to abuse of discretion review by the appellate court.[151] The transferee court cannot abdicate its responsibility of closely scrutinizing fee awards to appointed counsel.[152] Not surprisingly, given the large number of cases and attorneys involved, cost and fee allocation is a complicated and time-consuming part of MDL management. It can be difficult if not impossible for the transferee court to adequately predict what the nature of lead counsel's expenses will be as the MDL progresses, so all players must remain flexible and engaged in this part of MDL management. If they are not actively involved along the way, dissatisfied plaintiffs (or their retained attorneys) may forgo their opportunity to object to costs incurred and then requested by the steering committee.[153]

3.4 MDL'S DUE PROCESS DIFFICULTIES

As the foregoing description of MDL procedures illustrates, a case transferred into an MDL proceeding looks drastically different from a typical lawsuit, and presumably these procedures are not what the individual plaintiff expects when he files his claim. Despite this elaborate set of procedures and the enormous number of cases involved in MDL, the constitutional validity of this process has gone almost completely unexamined. In the name of efficiency, MDL— including its attendant procedures—has been embraced virtually without question.[154] This unqualified acceptance assumes that consolidation into MDL is totally benign and that individual claims retain their individualism even when they are temporarily adjudicated in a group with like cases. It also assumes—without any basis—that MDL procedures satisfy procedural due process.

The plain language of Section 1407 and the Supreme Court's decision in *Lexecon* have probably contributed to the unquestioning acceptance of the constitutionality of MDL, because both emphasize that transferee courts have jurisdiction solely over pretrial matters.[155] But consolidation into MDL, originally envisioned as a temporary transfer to facilitate convenience and avoid duplicative discovery, now all but guarantees that transferred cases will never return to their original jurisdictions for trial. The Panel's transfer orders are mandatory, one-way tickets to transferee districts—"black holes."[156] They are nontransferrable and nonnegotiable.[157] Instead of being temporarily and conveniently consolidated for discovery, individual claims become part of a massive group of cases plodding toward settlement. Although it is true that transferee courts have jurisdiction only over pretrial matters, individual claims are fundamentally transformed by virtue of their consolidation into MDL. And transfer back to the original jurisdiction—in the rare instances in which it actually takes place—cannot "save" the constitutionality of what happens in the transferee district.

Each claimant in an MDL has an individually held, constitutionally protected property right at stake. Those rights are guaranteed by the Fifth Amendment, which protects life, liberty, and property against deprivation absent due process of law.[158] The "property" right at stake in an MDL is the "chose in action." This historically established concept refers to the right to sue to enforce a legally protected claim, even the unlitigated right to sue.[159] Under the Fifth Amendment, then, MDL claimants cannot be deprived of their rights to a chose in action without due process of law.[160] MDL is a collection of individual lawsuits; it is not a vindication of some kind of substantively established group-held right. The constitutionality of MDL must therefore be assessed from the perspective of each litigant on an individual basis. As in other consolidated representative litigation (for example, class actions), MDL raises concerns about whether collectivization unconstitutionally modifies the claimants' individually held rights.

In MDL, individual litigants, for all practical purposes, lose a substantial degree of control over the procedural fate of their claims. For example, for the overwhelming number of claimants, the lawyers they hired are not selected for the court-appointed steering committee, which drives strategic and tactical decisions.[161] This impedes their ability to exercise control over the direction and course of their litigation. The lack of assurance that the selected attorneys can and will provide full and fair representation for each individual claimant is also unconstitutional because it does not comport with even the procedural protections afforded to absent class members in a class action, which are themselves constitutionally dubious to start.

This section of the chapter expands on these ideas and assesses whether the changes inherent in forced transfer into an MDL comport with the constitutional guarantees of procedural due process. It concludes that MDL fails to satisfy those guarantees. It begins with a discussion of the day-in-court ideal as the constitutional baseline for procedural due process. It argues that the day-in-court ideal is the *sine qua non* of constitutional due process—the basic structure upon which the adversarial system is built. Scholars disagree about the theoretical justifications for the day-in-court ideal, but no matter whether one subscribes to the autonomy model of the day-in-court ideal or is satisfied with a paternalistic notion of one's right to his day in court, MDL fails to provide a constitutionally adequate opportunity to litigate.

3.4.1 The Constitutional Baseline: Due Process and the Day-in-Court Ideal

Before delving into the constitutional merits of MDL, it is important first to identify the constitutional mandate against which MDL should be measured. In any given adjudication, the constitutional inquiry concerns exactly what process is "due." The Due Process Clause, on its face, does not provide a straightforward answer to that question, nor to the question of who gets to provide the answer. In attempting to answer the question of what procedures the Due Process Clause demands, the Supreme Court has repeatedly reaffirmed a "deep-rooted historic tradition,"[162] a principle that is "as old as the law" and "of universal justice": "[N]o one should be personally bound until he has had his day in court."[163]

The so-called day-in-court ideal is at the heart of constitutionally guaranteed procedural due process, according to the Court, and is central to the American conception of the adversarial model of litigation. Litigants, judges, and scholars frequently refer to the right to an individual day in court when they analyze whether due process requires, or forbids, a certain procedure. In some ways, "an individual day in court" has become a reflexive, shorthand description of what due process means. For a variety of reasons, MDL severely undermines the day-in-court ideal by depriving individual litigants of their opportunity to protect their interests through the litigation process. But before one can successfully indict MDL as a due process violation, one must first establish two things: (1) What does the day-in-court ideal specifically encompass? and (2) In what way does deprivation of one's day in court undermine the set of constitutionally dictated normative precepts encompassed by the concept of procedural due process? It is to answering these questions that the analysis now turns.

At the outset, it is important to define what an individual day in court entails. The right to one's own day in court means a right to meaningful control over litigation strategy and goals, including choice of legal representative.[164] It requires a "full and fair opportunity to litigate,"[165] which means, a "full opportunity to prepare [one's] own arguments and evidence."[166] At base, meaningful participation in the adjudicatory process—the day-in-court ideal—includes, in the words of a respected scholar, "the right to observe, to make arguments, to present evidence, and to be informed of the reasons for a decision."[167]

The Supreme Court has identified the "two central concerns of procedural due process" to be "the prevention of unjustified or mistaken deprivations and the promotion of participation and dialogue by affected individuals in the decisionmaking process."[168] The day-in-court ideal takes account of both of these concerns. First, an individual day in court helps achieve accurate outcomes (thus avoiding "unjustified or mistaken deprivations") because the stakeholders—those who will be most affected by the outcome and are the most motivated to protect their own rights—participate in the decision-making process.[169] In addition, individual participation is inherently valuable in a democratic system because it legitimizes the adjudicating entities in the minds of the litigants.[170] It fosters citizens' roles in democratic governance, which includes a legitimate, authoritative judiciary.[171]

3.4.2 The Foundations of Due Process Theory

Recognition of these and other benefits of an individual day in court does not, in itself, reveal the complex set of values underlying this procedural guarantee. Understanding the theoretical grounding for the day-in-court ideal helps one to grasp the importance of the tradition and determine the constitutional floor of procedural due process. Procedural due process can be thought to foster a variety of non-mutually exclusive values. But in reverse-engineering the day-in-court ideal as a manifestation of procedural due process, it is necessary to recognize a foundational conceptual dichotomy in due process theory. On the one hand, one may employ due process theory as a means of deciding which particular procedures are required to provide the individual whose constitutionally protected interests are at stake with a full and fair opportunity to defend those interests—in other words, exactly what procedures are essential to the exercise of the individual's right to her day in court. On the other hand, one may draw on due process theory in order to decide whether, in a particular situation, the individual has a constitutional right to her day in court in the first place. Those are not identical questions. Indeed, the theoretical analysis required to answer each of them is, in certain ways, fundamentally different.

When a court decides whether a particular procedure is required by due process in the course of an adjudicatory hearing, the traditional debate has been between the purely utilitarian approach adopted by the Supreme Court in its decisions in *Mathews v. Eldridge*[172] and *Connecticut v. Doehr*[173] on the one hand, and the so-called "dignitary" interest in permitting the individual to feel an appropriate level of respect from his government, on the other hand. Under the utilitarian test currently in vogue in the Supreme Court, a court is to balance competing utilitarian concerns: (1) the extent to which the procedure in question increases the likelihood of an accurate decision, (2) the nature of the individual's interest at stake, (3) the extent to which use of the procedure would burden government, and (4) the extent to which the use of the procedure would burden the other party or parties.[174] In contrast, the dignitary model, advocated by certain scholars and discussed as well as criticized in Chapter 2, places primary emphasis on an inquiry into the extent to which the procedure is necessary to allow the individual to believe that he has had a full and fair opportunity to plead his case, regardless of the impact of that procedural opportunity on the reaching of an accurate decision.[175]

One does not reach constitutional questions about the need for specific procedures, however, until one first concludes that the individual has a right to her day in court in the first place. It is generally assumed that before the individual's property interests may be undermined or taken away at least *some* form of governmental process is required.[176] Here, too, however, there exists a significant dichotomy as to the underlying rationale for that right. And, it is important to note, the choice between those theoretical alternatives is likely to have significant practical consequences for the shaping of a litigant's due process right to her day in court. That dichotomy is between the "paternalism" rationale for the day-in-court ideal and the "autonomy" rationale for the individual's right to her day in court.[177] Under the former rationale, the sole concern is that individual litigants' interests are, in fact, adequately protected by an advocate—whether or not of the individual's choosing—whose interests overlap with those of the absent parties and who possesses the resources and experience to advocate effectively on behalf those absent parties whose legal rights and interests are being adjudicated.[178]

Under the paternalism rationale for the day-in-court ideal, whether the absent party consents to the choice of advocate is irrelevant. In some situations, of course, it will be impractical, if not impossible, for the absent party to exercise choice even if she were permitted to do so. But under the exclusive focus on paternalism, the individual litigant's choice is irrelevant: the key is not whether the absent party has made a choice, but rather solely whether the absent party's legally protected interests have in fact been adequately represented. In effect, the paternalism model of the day-in-court ideal views the representative as a type of guardian, exercising protective authority over his wards who are categorically presumed to be unable to protect those interests themselves.

In stark contrast to the paternalism model of the day-in-court ideal is what can appropriately be described as the "autonomy" rationale for one's right to her day in court. The autonomy model views resort to the litigation process as simply one of several means by which the individual in a liberal adversary democratic society is permitted to participate in the governmental process—whether executive, legislative, or judicial—in an effort to protect her own interests.[179] In exercising the right to participate in the governing process, the individual is universally given the right to choose (within outer limits set by the law designed to preserve societal order and safety) how most effectively to influence decisions of a democratically shaped government. For example, government may not choose a representative to speak on behalf of the individual in the political process if she prefers either to choose her own representative or represent her interests herself. Nor can government tell the individual how to shape her appeal for governmental change in law or policy.[180] Such participatory choices are an essential part of the legitimizing function performed by preservation of the individual's right to seek to influence governmental decision-making. And this form of "meta"-autonomy (i.e., autonomy as to how to participate in the processes of democratic self-government—or, if you will, "democratic autonomy") logically applies to an individual's efforts to influence the judicial branch to protect his rights or interests as much as it does to the individual's attempts to influence the other branches of government. All three branches are, after all, part of a democratic government whose Constitution is committed to recognition of the individual as an integral whole, worthy of respect.

The foundational precept of adversary democracy underlies the autonomy model of due process. Under this version of what I have called adversary democratic due process, adversary democracy necessarily presumes an inherent mistrust of others—especially those in power—combined with the liberal democratic values of human flourishing and legitimation. In shaping the individual's due process right in the context of procedural collectivism, the Supreme Court has, all but exclusively, emphasized the paternalism model of the day-in-court ideal. There is no requirement that the individual litigant be given the opportunity to choose how best to represent his own rights and interests, as long as those chosen to represent those interests can be assumed to do so adequately.[181] Thus, in both *Hansberry v. Lee*[182] and *Amchem Products, Inc. v. Windsor*,[183] both class action cases, the Supreme Court found due process to be violated when a conflict in goals existed between the representative parties and the absent claimants.[184] But the Court has never extended similar recognition to the individual litigant's meta-autonomy right to choose how best to represent her own legally protected interests. For example, two out of the three categories of class actions authorized by the current version of Rule 23—a rule, after all, promulgated by the Supreme Court itself—are mandatory; members of the class are forcibly grouped together, even if they believe they are themselves better able to protect their own interests or even believe that they prefer not to pursue those interests legally.[185] It is true that in one decision, *Phillips Petroleum Co. v. Shutts*,[186] the Court upheld a state class action against a due process challenge only on the express condition that absent claimants be given the right to opt out of the class.[187] But while lower courts have on occasion read that decision broadly,[188] careful reading of the Court's opinion makes clear that the only reason for the requirement of a class member's option to withdraw from the class was the constitutional infirmity of lack of personal jurisdiction which would have resulted without the absent claimant's consent.[189]

One can, of course, make a strong case to support the need for paternalism as a means of assuring a full and fair day in court in the absence of an individual's ability to protect her own interests. It is in this manner that the Due Process

Clause may serve an appropriate guardian-like function. However, it would be dangerous to assume paternalism is a sufficient condition, as well as a necessary one. Where circumstances permit, due process is appropriately construed to provide the individual with autonomy to choose how—and indeed, if—to protect her own interests through resort to the adjudicatory process.

When one considers the implications of MDL for the Due Process Clause, it matters little, if at all, whether one chooses to view the paternalism model of due process as merely necessary or instead as both necessary and sufficient. From either perspective, MDL fails miserably. This is in stark contrast to the other well-known form of procedural collectivism, the modern class action. By both rule[190] and judicial decision,[191] class action procedure has taken care to assure that the paternalism model be satisfied. And while I have already severely criticized modern class action procedure because of its failure to satisfy the dictates of the autonomy model,[192] at least under the most common form of class action—that created by Rule 23(b)(3)—individual class members are given the right to opt out of the class proceeding,[193] thereby satisfying at least the minimum level of litigant choice and control demanded by the autonomy model.[194] But as the analysis will soon demonstrate, MDL satisfies the guarantees of neither the paternalism nor autonomy models of procedural due process. The inescapable conclusion, then, is that as presently structured, MDL is unambiguously unconstitutional.

3.4.3 Applying the Day-in-Court Ideal to MDL

On the surface, MDL practice seems largely innocuous; the Panel merely temporarily transfers cases to a different district court for pretrial matters. But for a variety of reasons, transfer effectively amounts to the end of the road for the overwhelming majority of cases. This is troublesome from a constitutional perspective, because not even the most minimal protection of the day-in-court ideal from the perspective of either the paternalism or autonomy models is satisfied.

Recall that unlike the class action, where most absent class members have not even considered individual suit and often possess claims not large enough to justify such suit,[195] MDL applies (with the exception of tag-along suits) only to claimants who have already chosen their own attorney and already filed suit.[196] Yet with no formal, open, and adversary participation by those claimants, the transferee court selects the attorneys who actually drive the litigation. This means that transfer into an MDL is by no means innocuous when it comes to the due process right to an individual's day in court. MDL plaintiffs in no sense meaningfully participate in, much less control, their day in court.[197] Nor are there any assurances that those in charge of the litigation are adequately representing the interests of the individual claimants.

One important way that litigants control their day in court is by selecting their attorneys. This is often the first expression of their autonomy: they seek the advice of counsel when they consider whether to even file a claim. Lawyers are contractually and ethically bound to vigorously represent their clients' interests—and no one else's—in court. Indeed, it would undoubtedly be unethical for an attorney to represent two parties in the same litigation when those parties' interests potentially differ. Permitting litigants to choose their representatives is central to providing a full and fair opportunity to litigate. The foundations of due process dictate that that choice belongs to the parties alone. But claimants forced into an MDL are deprived of that essential choice.[198] By virtue of his case's transfer into the MDL—a move that the plaintiff cannot prevent—his chosen lawyer will almost certainly not be the one actually representing his interests in the course of all the important MDL determinations. Rather, the lawyers on the court-appointed steering committee will take over, and they will do so without the protective assurances of their adequacy, good faith, or the extent to which the interests of the absent litigants truly overlap.[199] Thus, the method of choosing the attorneys who will represent the claimants in an MDL satisfies neither the autonomy nor the paternalism models of the day-in-court ideal.

When a transferee judge appoints a steering committee, she does so at her discretion, outside the strictures of any Federal Rule, statute, or adversary proceeding. Appointment to the steering committee comes after nothing more than a judge-designated period of nominations and written objections.[200] A more formalized, uniform adjudicatory approach could conceivably parallel the adequacy of representation protection of Rule 23(a)(4),[201] or the narrow "adequate representation" exception to the rule against nonparty preclusion.[202] Without such safeguards, however, the process fails to guarantee that the appointed representatives will zealously advocate on behalf of absent litigants in the same way that their hired representative presumably would have.

The dangers of MDL from the perspective of the paternalism model are exacerbated by the extremely loose connection required among the claims.[203] Wholly apart from the absence of a procedurally adequate method to determine the legitimacy of the attorneys in charge, there exist serious problems in having MDL satisfy the paternalism model of due process. Committee members' obligations to the mass of plaintiffs may undermine or dilute an individual plaintiff's unique interests, needs, or desires. If one plaintiff's best interests conflict with the majority's best interests (or even a small group's interests), how can the steering committee vigorously represent both? Indeed, one may question how these potentially conflicting responsibilities can be handled ethically.[204] The Model Rules of Professional Conduct define conflicts of interest between concurrent clients broadly, including even the "significant risk" of adverseness among clients.[205] MDL plaintiffs often seek the same thing—the largest cut possible of the defendant's limited funds. Their success can come at another plaintiff's expense. This is similar to what happens when one lawyer represents multiple parties seeking to form a joint venture. In that scenario, the lawyer is "likely to be materially limited in the lawyer's ability to recommend or advocate all possible positions that each might take because of the lawyer's duty of loyalty to the others."[206] Thus, even if the chosen attorneys are fully competent and acting in good faith, it is impossible to be assured that in the one-size-fits-all practice of MDL, they will be able to effectively protect the rights of individual claimants. In contrast, the modern class action demands close linkage among the claims, for the very purpose of assuring due process.[207] MDL claimants, on the other hand, are left in "a procedural no-man's-land,"[208] at the mercy of the transferee judge[209] and attorneys whose obligations are to the interests of many plaintiffs, which may not necessarily align with those of an individual plaintiff.

Moreover, the MDL judge's selection of lead counsel is not subject to effective appellate review, even though the choice may turn out to be outcome-determinative in many ways, including whether a plaintiff's claim will settle in the transferee court (and for how much), resolved on summary judgment, or be transferred back to the transferor jurisdiction. Repeat MDL plaintiffs' counsel can work behind closed doors to lobby for specific attorneys to be named to the steering committee. This makes it extremely difficult for a newcomer attorney to receive enough support to be selected for a leadership role.[210] The individual plaintiff's wishes are easily lost in this series of smoke-filled rooms, and only a narrow group of plaintiffs' attorneys are appointed to leadership roles.

Ignoring the claimant's choice of lawyer disrespects the claimant and undermines the procedural autonomy that adversary democratic due process is intended to protect. Such an approach contravenes core notions of both the adversary and liberal versions of democratic theory. Moreover, the established process of appointing lead counsel and ceding control to the court-appointed committees further undermines even the paternalism model of the day-in-court ideal by failing to build in safeguards that assure the choice of adequate representatives who are able to zealously advocate on behalf of *all* claimants.

In addition to the fact that appointed counsel are selected by the court, rather than by the individuals they represent, MDL claimants do not enjoy a traditional attorney-client relationship with the members of the court-appointed steering committee. The small group of attorneys chosen for leadership roles is charged with representing all of the possibly thousands of plaintiffs, whose cases have facts that are often only loosely linked. This arrangement treats plaintiffs as an indivisible group rather than as individuals who are integral wholes, worthy of respect. Individual claimants do not have a direct line to the steering committee in the way they would with their own lawyers. Steering committee members act as gatekeepers to discovery materials obtained from defendants.[211] Even if they were to freely grant access to those materials, committee members constitute a hurdle that is absent from the traditional attorney-client relationship. This severely attenuated attorney-client relationship between each claimant and the steering committee "inhibit[s] a client's ability to monitor her case as she would in an individual lawsuit."[212] This, too, violates both the autonomy and paternalism models of the day-in-court ideal.

If an individual plaintiff or her lawyer disagrees with a strategic choice made by lead counsel, they faces a steep uphill battle to reassert control over her representation.[213] That can hardly be characterized as a "full and fair opportunity to litigate" on her own terms. Because claimants forced into MDL effectively lose their chosen representatives, and the appointed representatives' loyalties are often likely to be divided, MDL falls far short of providing the "deep-rooted historic tradition" of an individual's day in court.[214] Due process demands much more.

Another nontraditional feature of the relationship between appointed lead counsel and individual claimants is the compensation structure common among MDLs. In consolidated proceedings, "the attorney's loyalty divides not only between clients, but also between clients and self-interest."[215] Compensation for attorneys who work on behalf of the group depends upon the value of every plaintiff's settlement or judgment.[216] As a result, lead counsel may push hard for settlement as opposed to remand, prefer a quick settlement in favor of a protracted discovery period, or advocate for settlement terms that may not be particularly favorable to some or many plaintiffs. The First Circuit has acknowledged existence of this "inherent conflict[] of interest" "between the PSC and individual plaintiffs in mass-tort MDLs."[217] But even after doing so, the court affirmed in substantial part an order awarding over $10 million to the appointed plaintiffs' steering committee, in large part because the plaintiffs did not object soon enough.[218] MDL plaintiffs, their chosen attorneys, and the appointed steering committee all want the largest common fund possible so that they can maximize their individual cuts. Still, how to allocate a common fund will usually be contentious,[219] and at that point, plaintiffs' and MDL counsel's interests become adverse. Complicating matters further is the fact that at the same time, the retained attorneys who were not selected for a leadership role want to guard their fees. That goal may impact the nature of their advice about settling or agreeing to specific settlement terms. All of this is to say that MDL muddles the traditional relationship between attorney and client, creating new adverse incentives. It introduces additional tension between attorneys' best interests and clients' best interests.

At the most basic level, MDL plaintiffs are not "given a meaningful opportunity to present their case[s]" as demanded by the Due Process Clause.[220] Individual claims lose their individual identities when they are clumped together in an MDL. Even if the transferee court were to employ a more exacting standard than Section 1407[221] to group like cases together for purposes of conducting discovery or bellwether trials, gone is the chance for unique discovery requests or personalized (let alone risky) litigation strategy. The primary idea behind MDL is to "coordinate" pretrial proceedings, and the court-selected steering committee or lead counsel is responsible for ensuring that such coordination occurs.[222] Rather than facilitating participation in democratic governance, however, the practice of judicial selection of certain attorneys to run an MDL hinders individuals' ability to participate in the legal system on their chosen terms.

One might argue that this concern about control over litigation strategy is exaggerated, because lawyers, rather than litigants, make most of the strategic choices anyway. While it may be true that an individual's chosen representative may make the strategic choices day to day, the very act of choosing one's representative is a clear expression of litigant autonomy protected by due process. Regardless of the relative merits of the steering committee compared to the litigant's retained attorney, selecting a representative to work toward an individual's litigation goals is the individual's prerogative and, indeed, is the foundation of the day-in-court ideal. MDL unconstitutionally undermines that choice.

It is true that theoretically, MDL only involves a temporary transfer for pretrial purposes; claimants' individual days in court await them back in the transferor courts. It is also true that no one is forcing these claimants to accept settlement offers in the transferee court; they can always hold out for remand to their preferred jurisdictions, where they will have the opportunity to have their personally chosen lawyers represent them and can attempt to implement their own strategies.[223] But this view demonstrates an incomplete understanding of the power of transferee courts. First, all players in an MDL, including the judge, face enormous pressures to achieve a global resolution in the transferee district. Not least of these pressures is the duration of the litigation to that point, which is usually several years, at a minimum.[224] Second, even if a claimant does elect to wait for remand, the steering committee has already dictated the direction of the suit. Transferor judges on remand are disinclined to grant discovery requests that seem at all duplicative of work the steering committee already did, or that seem like something the claimant should have asked the steering committee to address.[225] Transferee judges make decisions about expert testimony that carry over to remand, as well. In addition, transferee judges can and do rule on dispositive motions, so there is no guarantee that all parts of the litigant's claim will survive summary judgment in the transferee district.

If the day-in-court ideal stems from a democratic commitment to demonstrating respect for individual autonomy, then a set of procedures that undermines litigants' choices cannot satisfy the constitutional demand for an individual's day in court. In other words, a procedure cannot satisfy the right to a constitutionally dictated day in court if it does not protect the very values that gave rise to the constitutional right in the first place. MDL disrespects that individual autonomy. It does not provide claimants with the choices and control that are necessary to satisfy the individual's right to a day in court.

3.4.4 Utilitarianism, Due Process, and MDL

The analysis to this point has already demonstrated the seemingly insurmountable due process problems to which MDL gives rise. However, the question arises whether a utilitarian calculus of due process would justify MDL because of the litigation efficiency it is assumed to provide. Respect for individual autonomy dictates the right to an individual's day in court, but perhaps that right is not absolute. Like the right to free speech, the constitutional guarantee of a day in court may not be without limits; interests dictating such a right must be weighed against other interests when determining whether the government must provide a particular procedure or opportunity in a particular case.[226] The day-in-court ideal is admittedly not always the most efficient way to adjudicate rights. Indeed, there always exists inherent inefficiency in guaranteeing procedural due process in the first place. Reflecting that reality, the Supreme Court has fashioned a utilitarian test for determining whether specific procedures are required in specific circumstances.[227] But even a utilitarian view of due process cannot save the constitutionality of MDL.

Utilitarians argue that the paramount goal of all due process analyses must be accurate outcomes because they maximize social welfare.[228] According to this approach, the process that is "due" is the one most likely to prevent unjustified or mistaken deprivations, at the lowest cost.[229] To determine the value of a given procedure, these theorists rely on the procedure's effect on accuracy and its relative cost compared to other available procedures.[230] If a procedure is likely to produce more accurate outcomes, and the increased likelihood of accuracy is greater than the relative cost of the procedure, then the procedure is "due."[231]

3.4.4.1 The *Mathews-Doehr* Test
The Supreme Court endorsed a utilitarian view of the Due Process Clause in *Mathews v. Eldridge*. *Mathews* considered what process was due prior to deprivation of Social Security benefits. There, the Court emphasized, "[d]ue process, unlike some legal rules, is not a technical conception with a fixed content unrelated to time, place and circumstances."[232] Rather, "[d]ue process is flexible and calls for such procedural protections as the particular situation demands."[233] In laying out its oft-cited three-part test for identifying "the specific dictates of due process," the *Mathews* Court specifically identified "the probable value, if any, of

additional or substitute procedural safeguards" as a key component of the due process inquiry.[234] The Court proceeded to examine the "fairness and reliability" of the pre-deprivation procedures at issue.[235] It referred to "the risk of error inherent in the truth finding process."[236] The *Mathews* Court also assessed the public cost of a particular procedure, including "the administrative burden and other societal costs."[237] Finally, it left open the possibility that "[a]t some point the benefit of an additional safeguard to the individual affected by the administrative action and to society in terms of increased assurance that the action is just, may be outweighed by the cost."[238] Accuracy may be the paramount interest, but at some point it is outweighed by the cost of achieving it.

The Court extended this utilitarian view of the Due Process Clause to include suits between private citizens in *Connecticut v. Doehr*.[239] There it applied the *Mathews* test to a Connecticut statute that allowed prejudgment attachment of real estate without notice, a hearing, a showing of extraordinary circumstances, or a requirement that the party seeking attachment post a bond.[240] It concluded that the Connecticut statute did not satisfy due process, as measured by the *Mathews* three-prong analysis.[241] *Doehr* solidified the Court's commitment to using utilitarian balancing to determine whether due process demands a specific procedure.

As already noted, the *Mathews* test was designed primarily, if not exclusively, to determine whether *particular procedures* are required by the Due Process Clause, rather than whether there is a right to a day in court in the first place.[242] In *Mathews*, the Court faced only the question of "what process is due prior to the initial termination of benefits, pending review."[243] It outlined the elaborate procedures available to Social Security beneficiaries whose benefits are terminated, which included an evidentiary hearing after initial termination of benefits.[244] The *Mathews* test, then, was not fashioned in a case asking *whether* a day in court was required, but *when* it was required and what procedures it had to include. This is an important distinction. Though it clearly embraced a utilitarian approach to measuring procedural due process requirements, *Mathews* was not a case about an exception to the day-in-court ideal per se. The fact remains, however, that a utilitarian concern with burdens and efficiency always remains the elephant in the room in any due process analysis. It is therefore necessary to consider the extent to which efficiency concerns should be deemed to temper the stinging due process critiques of MDL.

The most immediate response to reliance on the utilitarian calculus is that it completely ignores any concerns with liberal adversary democracy, which are properly deemed to provide the theoretical DNA of the Due Process Clause. Yet while respect for individual autonomy and the need to invoke adversary theory to protect it justifies the day-in-court ideal in the first place, the *Mathews-Doehr* test ignores it entirely. The *Mathews-Doehr* balancing test explicitly considers the likelihood that a particular procedure will produce more accurate decisions, which outcome-based theorists consider the paramount goal of process. This is a limited view of the goals of due process protections; indeed, "[r]ights in a utilitarian system are strictly instrumental goods."[245] But the *Mathews-Doehr* doctrine and its utilitarian supporters ignore the other benefits of individual participation in litigation, such as those protected by adversary democratic due process. Ignoring these values is a mistake. For one thing, procedural rights have inherent value beyond maximizing social welfare. They also serve instrumental values because they facilitate social goods beyond accurate judicial decision-making, such as participatory democracy and governmental legitimacy. Were it to be applied to the day-in-court question, the *Mathews-Doehr* test might too easily dismiss an individual day in court simply because it would be more convenient, efficient, or easy for the government not to provide one. Conceptions of procedural due process which focus exclusively on outcomes and interest-balancing are underinclusive because they fail to account for the full breadth of values promised and protected by the Due Process Clause.[246]

An individual day in court demonstrates the government's respect for the individual by giving her a chance to speak for herself. It also fulfills the protective goals fostered by adversary democratic due process. Thus, in the words of one scholar, "[a]llowing individuals the freedom to act on and to govern their own legal affairs is a political and moral good."[247] These are the key premises of liberal democratic theory. Equally important, however, are the darker premises of adversary democratic theory, which imposes the categorical presumption that no one else may be trusted to make those choices on behalf of the individual against the individual's will. And nowhere is that procedural danger more serious than in the case of MDL. At least in class actions there exists a formal paternalistic process to determine adequacy of representation. No such comparable process exits in MDL. And as already explained, MDL certifiably further undermines the protections of adversary democratic due process by introducing a potential rift and high degree of mistrust between clients and their chosen lawyer. Thus, the choice of a form of forced wholesale justice, where the interests and needs of individual litigants are almost cavalierly ignored in favor of the myopic pursuit of efficiency, cannot possibly be deemed consistent with the dictates of due process, either as a normative or descriptive matter.

In any event, the day-in-court ideal *does* foster the utilitarian concern with accurate decision-making. The entire adversary system is premised on a notion of "litigation capitalism": the litigant's incentive to prevail gives that litigant the incentive to marshal the strongest possible case on her behalf. With both sides engaging in such a process, the passive adjudicator is informed in the most effective way possible. Where either the claimant or the defendant is denied an effective opportunity to present her case, the accuracy of the final decision is placed in serious doubt.

Viewed in this light, it is by no means clear that MDL actually fosters accuracy in decision-making. An individual claimant's attorney, who is presumably familiar with the specific facts of her client's case and is motivated solely to vindicate and protect those interests, is in the best position to assist the judge in reaching an accurate resolution of the litigation.[248] In contrast, where MDL attorneys know little or nothing of individual plaintiffs' cases when they control discovery or shape settlement, and the cases which have been herded together often are likely to have relatively little in common, accuracy in the resolution of individual suits is, at best, open to serious question.

MDL management is unbound by specific rules, so transferee judges do not conduct the coordinated proceedings uniformly. Each transferee judge selects lawyers to hold leadership positions on her own terms.[249] Appointment to the steering committee is not the result of an adversarial process, and it is not subject to any test for adequacy of representation. Similarly, bellwether trials occur without any guarantee that the tried cases are typical of the claims of the plaintiffs participating in the MDL. The results of those bellwether trials are then used to facilitate settlement and evaluate the strength of various arguments.[250] Even if cases are transferred back to the districts in which they were originally filed, the work of the steering committee and the pretrial orders entered by the MDL judge permanently impact the ultimate resolution of the claims. Transferee judges cannot and do not make individual rulings on all issues for all cases consolidated into the MDL. The fact that these procedures are unregulated makes it impossible to evaluate their accuracy for purposes of the *Mathews-Doehr* test, but the process smacks of a mass-produced form of rough justice. An individual lawsuit in federal district court, on the other hand, is the most accurate procedure available. The "probable value" of individual proceedings is high, because individual litigation would ensure that each claimant exercised control over how his rights were asserted.

Even assuming that MDL procedures are not as likely to be accurate as individual litigation would be, it might be argued that the government's interest in reducing litigation burdens justifies MDL. MDL seems attractive because it saves resources by forcing claimants to litigate as a group, instead of as hundreds or thousands of individuals in parallel actions. If MDL leads to outcomes that are at least as accurate as adjudication of individual claims does, then this cost saving is permitted under the utilitarian model of due process. Judge James F. Holderman put it this way: "Without the centralized control of an MDL transferee judge, the cost of duplicative discovery and e-discovery in each case consolidated as an MDL action for pretrial purposes would be a significant detriment to each case's litigants and justice in America as a whole."[251]

Judge Holderman's argument may be intuitively attractive, given the stated purpose of MDL and the sobering idea of thousands of cases stemming from one event. But assessments of the empirical benefits of MDL are not uniformly positive. Even members of the Panel recognize that "centralization does not benefit all parties equally and that, for some parties, it can be actually less efficient."[252] By several accounts, MDL takes much longer than individual litigation.[253] It is also at times inconvenient, for both plaintiffs and defendants.[254] All this is to say that it is not at all clear that MDL, as it now functions, is actually advancing the government's interests in efficiency and saving litigation resources.

Applying the *Mathews-Doehr* factors, then, MDL features an immeasurably high risk of inaccuracy or erroneous deprivations. At the same time, whether MDL actually advances the government's interest in efficiency is uncertain at best. The private interest in vindicating an alleged wrong through a fair, reasonably accurate process outweighs the potential efficiency gains of MDL. This means that MDL does not survive the *Mathews-Doehr* analysis even assuming its relevance. Even assuming MDL is more efficient than individual litigation, the uncertainty surrounding whether MDL leads to erroneous deprivations or inaccurate results is too great a risk to take when constitutionally protected interests are at stake.

3.5 IS MDL CONSTITUTIONALLY SALVAGEABLE?

For all of the reasons discussed in detail throughout this chapter, MDL, as currently structured, must be deemed unconstitutional, because it infringes on individual claimants' procedural due process rights. Measured in terms of *any* theory of due process—autonomy, adversary, paternalism, utilitarianism, or dignitary theories—procedural due process demands considerably more protection of the individual litigants' interests than MDL provides. But this conclusion does not necessarily mean that it is impossible to fashion a similar coordination procedure possessing many of MDL's benefits that nevertheless satisfies procedural due process. If so, however, Congress and the Panel would need to make significant changes to ensure that each MDL claimant is able to fully exercise his right to an individual day in court. The due process guarantee of a "full and fair opportunity to litigate" is not mutually exclusive with efficient, streamlined discovery and other pretrial procedures. But when they are in tension, due process calls for prioritization of litigant autonomy over efficiency. The tie goes to litigant autonomy because respecting individuals' choices reaps benefits that advance the American notion of the relationship between government and governed that lies at the heart of our constitutional structure.

The primary goal of this chapter is not to prescribe one particular solution or "fix" for the constitutional problems described here. The key to avoiding constitutional difficulties, however, is to recognize that if the benefits of MDL are to be achieved, they must be achieved through the free choice of the individual litigants to take part in the collectivist process. This would satisfy the autonomy and adversary concerns of due process. In other words, to ensure due process, transfer into an MDL must be made elective instead of mandatory. Claimants who choose transfer would benefit from the steering committee's large-scale discovery and other features of MDL. Especially if they were hoping only to settle their individual cases, they very well may choose this option. But if they preferred a faster resolution, or wanted more than money, or did not care to travel, or trusted their retained lawyer more than a stranger from across the country, they might opt out of consolidation. Opting in or staying out, however, must be their prerogative. Under this approach, participating in an MDL would become a strategic choice rather than a forced path.

Moreover, in order to satisfy the paternalism due process concerns, other adjustments need to be made. First, Congress should establish a uniform procedure for selecting attorneys to serve in leadership roles. As it stands, each transferee court appoints steering committees according to its own procedures and criteria. Instead, appointment should be the result of a process open to all affected parties and their retained representatives. The process should be designed to ensure that the leadership steering committees are made up of attorneys with different backgrounds and whose clients represent a wide array of the claims involved in the MDL, similar to the typicality requirement for class actions. Attorneys should not be permitted to trade favors of support behind closed doors, and the group of plaintiffs' attorneys who are appointed should not be a closed circle.

In order to reduce due process difficulties, transferee courts could also make changes to case management to ensure a more active, symbiotic relationship between steering committee members, other attorneys involved in the MDL, and the claimants. Communication between a plaintiff and the steering committee should be as fluid as it would be between the plaintiff and her retained counsel if her claim had not been transferred into an MDL. All retained plaintiffs' attorneys, not just those appointed to leadership roles, should—to the extent feasible—have some opportunity to take part in strategic decisions. If an individual plaintiff prefers a different strategy or wants to make a specific discovery request, ways to provide such opportunities should at least be explored.

An even more radical solution might be to coordinate and share discovery among cases that feature at least one common question of fact, but to do so remotely, without transferring the cases into a single district court. The advent of electronic discovery, video conferencing, and cloud-based data sharing are already transforming discovery practices.[255] Those technologies could facilitate the type of coordination and sharing that the MDL designers wanted in the first place. This type of cooperation could be more efficient, too.

Some of these suggested changes may seem burdensome, if not inefficient. They undoubtedly would require more time, effort, and creativity than the current procedures do, which may make MDL, as modified, less attractive. But constitutional rights cannot be sacrificed for mere convenience. These ideas are not meant to represent the perfect answer to MDL's insufficient due process safeguards. Rather, they are designed to provide only a starting point for a much-needed conversation about reconciling the day-in-court ideal with the overwhelming nature of mass torts and similar cases, which are often swept into MDL.

3.6 CONCLUSION

Although Anglo-American jurisprudence does have a venerable history of representative litigation, it is important to understand the fundamental differences between the historically acceptable form of representative litigation on the one hand and the procedural collectivism of the post-1966 era on the other. Historically, the only form of binding representative litigation involved claims that were legally intertwined in a substantive, pre-litigation context.[256] In those instances, the claims of the various plaintiffs are already linked at the point at which litigation begins—either by choice or by substantive law. In contrast, the modern forms of procedural collectivism—the class action and MDL—give rise to a far greater threat to the values embodied in the Due Process Clause. In these situations, substantive rights which are, in their pristine form, held solely by the individual, are lumped together—often quite crudely—in a manner which may significantly interfere with the individual claimants' due process right to their day in court.

One should not be so naïve as to believe that, in the modern day of complex litigation, it is feasible to avoid all forms of procedural collectivism. But there are ways to achieve at least some of the advantages of such collectivism without so blatantly undermining core procedural rights the way current MDL practice does. Indeed, with all of its serious drawbacks and problems, modern class action procedure provides a stark contrast to MDL practice. Whereas class action in every case requires a transparent judicial finding of adequate representation of the interests of absent claimants, MDL has no such requirement.[257] Whereas in most class actions absent class members have the right to opt out of the proceeding, MDL provides no means either for withdrawing from the proceeding or even meaningfully challenging the legality or propriety of inclusion within it.[258]

If our traditions and values of due process mean anything, the individual's right to a day in court must be preserved, even within the broader framework of procedural collectivism. MDL unconstitutionally infringes the procedural due process rights of claimants forced into all-important consolidated pretrial proceedings against their will.

Surprisingly, there have been no prior frontal assaults on the constitutionality of MDL. In advancing this attack, the chapter has sought to expose an extremely popular complex litigation procedure that today impacts a significant percentage of civil cases. MDL may seem to provide a cure-all to the difficulties of attempting to certify class actions on a massive scale, but it faces even greater constitutional roadblocks than does the modern class action. Despite its arguable efficiencies and perceived conveniences (which themselves are open to question),[259] MDL stealthily transforms fundamental characteristics of numerous claims so that they are unrecognizable as distinct actions filed by individual plaintiffs. Moreover, it may well do so even against the will of those plaintiffs, without providing them with meaningful recourse to challenge either their inclusion in the collectivist process or the adequacy of their representation in that process. Upon close examination, while MDL promises respect for the individual day in court, it delivers only a "Wild West" form of rough group justice, on the court-appointed steering committee's terms. Due process cannot tolerate such a system.

4

PROCEDURAL DUE PROCESS AND THE DAY-IN-COURT IDEAL

RESOLVING THE VIRTUAL REPRESENTATION DILEMMA

4.1 INTRODUCTION

The notion that the individual litigant possesses a foundational constitutional right to his day in court before his rights may be judicially altered has often been recognized as fundamental to our legal system. As this book has previously pointed out, recognition of the centrality of adversary democratic theory to a proper understanding of procedural due process underscores this importance and logically leads to a dramatic rethinking of the individual's right to a day in court.[1]

In the field of judgments, for the most part doctrinal adherence to this ideal has been sacrosanct. Virtually every first-year law student has learned that due process generally prevents a court from imposing either res judicata or collateral estoppel against litigants not represented by their chosen representative in the prior litigation.[2] To be sure, there exists a narrow group of well-accepted qualifications that allow a nonparty to be bound when he is in privity with a prior party.[3] Moreover, respected scholars have occasionally challenged the validity of the day-in-court ideal.[4] However, the day-in-court limitation on the imposition of res judicata and collateral estoppel has generally withstood the test of time—that is, until the modern development of the doctrine of so-called "virtual representation."

Virtual representation is a preclusion doctrine that permits a litigant to be bound by a judgment in a prior case in which she was not a party.[5] Unlike the other primary forms of nonparty preclusion, virtual representation (at least in some of its manifestations) does not require a preexisting legal relationship between the nonparty and a party in the case in order to bind the nonparty by the case's findings and judgment. Instead, the nonparty is bound if her interests are deemed to have been sufficiently aligned with a party in the prior case and certain other factors are satisfied,[6] even if there is no preexisting formalized relationship between them. As of the start of 2008, the definition of virtual representation

Due Process as American Democracy. Martin H. Redish, Oxford University Press. © Martin H. Redish 2024.
DOI: 10.1093/oso/9780197747414.003.0004

varied widely among the federal circuits, with at least one circuit disapproving its use almost entirely.[7] But as a general matter, the doctrine was widely recognized.

It is not difficult to recognize that virtual representation is in direct tension with the day-in-court ideal. By its very nature, the doctrine deprives litigants of their right to a day in court by binding them to judgments in cases in which they were not parties and in which they did not have the opportunity to defend their own interests. Because of this tension with the day-in-court rule, virtual representation was the subject of controversy in the lower courts right from its inception.

The Supreme Court provided important guidance on the viability of virtual representation in its 2008 opinion in *Taylor v. Sturgell*.[8] After recognizing the inherent clash between the day-in-court ideal and the doctrine of virtual representation, the Court pointed out the significant tension between the doctrine and the dictates of due process.[9] Specifically, it unanimously rejected the D.C. Circuit's multifactor balancing test for virtual representation.[10] In doing so, however, the Court quite clearly signaled the demise of all versions of virtual representation. For reasons subsequently explored,[11] the Court was correct to reject virtual representation as a general matter. In most cases, the doctrine unconstitutionally undermines the individual's due process right to his day in court—a doctrine whose value has generally been ignored by those courts and scholars who have advocated some form of virtual representation. However, the Court in *Taylor* failed in two important ways. On the one hand, it failed to articulate the true constitutional grounding for the day-in-court ideal, thereby leaving itself vulnerable to the charge of some that it has overvalued this right.

On the other hand, somewhat paradoxically, the Court simultaneously seemed to *overvalue* the day-in-court ideal, by at least implicitly rejecting virtual representation even in cases of indivisible relief, where the significant harm from failing to employ the doctrine potentially outbalances the harm from using it. The concept of indivisible relief refers to cases in which the relief sought by multiple parties from the same defendant demands that the defendant take singular action—in other words, that the defendant cannot, either legally or physically, provide wholly separate, disjointed, or inconsistent relief to the various plaintiffs. For example, when a municipality's ability to issue a bond is challenged in separate suits, it is impossible for the municipality to issue the bond in one suit, but not issue it in another suit; either the municipality issues the bond, or it does not.[12] Similarly, in the case of *Supreme Tribe of Ben-Hur v. Cauble*,[13] a fraternal benefit organization sought a financial reorganization, which was challenged in separate suits by different policyholders.[14] In this situation, either the organization financially reorganized, or it did not; it could not reorganize as to certain plaintiffs while simultaneously failing to reorganize as to others. In these situations, allowing separate suits could establish what Rule 23(b)(1)(A) of the Federal Rules of Civil Procedure, concerning class actions, describes as "incompatible standards of conduct."[15]

It is important to distinguish this situation from damage suits, where a defendant could, both practically and legally, be made to pay damages to some plaintiffs but not to others.[16] In situations of indivisible relief, it is quite conceivable that allowing separate suits to result in "incompatible standards" could cause severe hardships to a defendant. In these situations, not binding subsequent plaintiffs to the result in the first suit through virtual representation might threaten the defendant's due process rights, and at the very least threaten subconstitutional interests in reason and fairness.

As noted in earlier chapters, procedural due process has long been thought to involve a balancing of competing interests: the value of providing a given procedure is balanced against the cost, either to the state or to one of the parties, of providing it.[17] For the overwhelming majority of cases, the significant value of providing a litigant with her day in court outweighs the costs in providing it. Indeed, this calculus is so simple that in most cases a commitment to the provision of a day in court has become the presumptive rule. If one were to accept the alternative vision of adversary democratic due process advocated throughout this book, the answer becomes even more clear: except in the most extreme situations, adversary democracy places such decisions squarely in the hands of the individual herself. However, in multiple suit situations involving claims for indivisible relief, the issue becomes far more complex.

This chapter tackles the two glaring omissions in the *Taylor* Court's analysis of virtual representation: its failure to explain the theoretical grounding of the day-in-court ideal in American constitutional and political theory and its failure to explore the implications of indivisible relief for the viability of virtual representation. The first section of the chapter explores the facts and holding of *Taylor*. The chapter then fashions a theoretical explanation of the day-in-court rule. It concludes that the day-in-court rule springs from society's democratic commitment to the precept of process-based autonomy grounded in adversary democratic due process's inherent skepticism of one's rights being defended by those not chosen by individual litigants themselves. Just as the government cannot dictate to individuals how to participate politically in the democratic process, subject to generally applied rules of procedure and ethics, individuals should not be forced to defer to the judgment of others when pursuing their legal rights. But like political participation rights such as freedom of expression, the value of litigant autonomy is extremely high but not absolute.[18] The third section of this chapter explores the concept of indivisible relief and its implications for the constitutional viability of virtual representation. Indivisible relief can be subdivided into three categories: inconsistent liability, double liability, and contradictory liability. Each situation raises unique due process concerns that could be substantially avoided by use of virtual representation.

After conducting a detailed due process analysis, the chapter concludes that the constitutional value of avoiding the problems associated with double and contradictory liability is sufficiently significant to satisfy the compelling interest standard fashioned earlier in this book. The competing value of litigant autonomy grounded in precepts of adversary democratic theory is outbalanced and therefore virtual representation may be employed to avoid these problems.[19] It should be emphasized, however, that the threat of double or contradictory liability is necessary but not sufficient for virtual representation to pass due process strict scrutiny. As the analysis will show, virtual representation also requires a showing that the absent party has been adequately represented by a present party. Only if both conditions are satisfied should virtual representation ever be permitted.

The chapter's fourth part considers prophylactic measures that might be employed to avoid the entire dilemma caused by the problems associated with indivisible relief. Despite the conclusion that the limited recognition of virtual representation—confining its use to situations where failure to invoke it would produce intolerable results to opposing parties—satisfies due process, it nevertheless has the harmful effect of depriving litigants of their day in court and should therefore be avoided if at all possible.

4.2 VIRTUAL REPRESENTATION IN THE COURTS

Our legal system has long employed a presumption that each person has a right to her day in court. This ideal is most easily seen in the binding effect of judgments. The doctrines of res judicata and collateral estoppel preclude parties from relitigating claims or issues that have reached a final judgment. Because of the day-in-court ideal, however, these preclusion doctrines typically bind only the parties in the underlying suit; in most situations, imposition of a preclusive impact on a nonparty is deemed to violate due process.[20] In certain situations in which a formal prelitigation arrangement exists between a party and a nonparty, however, the nonparty may be bound. These prelitigation arrangements are often classified together under the heading of "privity."[21] Although a person in privity with a party is deprived of her personal day in court, the nature of the preexisting relationship is deemed to create an exception to the presumptive day-in-court ideal.

The doctrine of virtual representation departs from these traditionally accepted limitations. Unlike traditional exceptions to the day-in-court dictate, its preclusive bar is often not grounded in a formalized prelitigation arrangement between a party and nonparty. Instead, virtual representation, in some versions, binds a nonparty to a judgment any time that her interests are found to be sufficiently aligned with the interests of a party to that judgment.[22] Although the phrase's definition is a matter of some debate, having aligned interests essentially means that a nonparty to the first suit would, in the second suit, advance the same arguments and seek the same outcome as a party in the first suit.[23] Because of the broad range of situations in which a nonparty's interests may be aligned with a party's interests, since its inception, courts have labored to find ways to restrain virtual representation.[24]

The inception of the modern concept of virtual representation can be traced to a trio of Fifth Circuit cases in the 1970s.[25] The doctrine continued to evolve, with each circuit developing its own version, until the Supreme Court in 2008 called a halt to its use in *Taylor*.[26] The *Taylor* Court held that virtual representation deprives litigants of due process because it improperly denies them their right to a day in court before their rights are adjudicated.[27] The Court rightly rejected general application of virtual representation as a violation of due process. Nevertheless, as previously noted, the Court's analysis in *Taylor* failed to fully explain the basis for its commitment to the day-in-court ideal and failed to recognize the dangerous competing concerns arising in situations involving indivisible relief.

4.2.1 Modern Development of Virtual Representation

Virtual representation developed originally in the area of probate law. It provided that parties whose identity could not be determined (for example, the unborn) could be bound by an existing party whose interests were aligned with the undetermined party.[28] In the 1970s, however, the doctrine was transformed to apply not only to probate cases but also in the litigation context.[29] Initially, the litigation version of virtual representation authorized nonparty preclusion only when it was necessary to protect a prior judgment from being undermined by indivisible relief sought in a subsequent suit.[30] In this way, the modern concept of virtual representation paralleled its traditional role in probate as a doctrine of necessity. However, as time went on, courts lost sight of the doctrine's grounding in necessity.[31]

4.2.2 The Supreme Court Speaks: *Taylor v. Sturgell*

Greg Harrick filed a Freedom of Information Act (FOIA) request with the Federal Aviation Administration (FAA) for documents related to an antique F-45 aircraft he was restoring.[32] The FAA denied Harrick's request on the grounds that the documents included trade secrets of the aircraft's original manufacturer.[33] Harrick brought suit in federal court, seeking to require the FAA to produce the requested documents. The US District Court for the District of Wyoming granted summary judgment for the FAA, and the Tenth Circuit upheld the award, noting in its opinion two potential arguments that Harrick had failed to present.[34]

A month later, Brent Taylor, an acquaintance of Harrick, filed an identical FOIA request with the FAA. After the FAA failed to provide the documents, Taylor brought a suit in the US District Court for the District of Columbia to require production of the documents. His arguments were identical to Harrick's with the addition of the two arguments that had been suggested by the Tenth Circuit.[35] The district court concluded that Harrick's prior suit precluded Taylor's suit because given their identical interests, Harrick had effectively acted as Taylor's virtual representative.[36] In reaching this conclusion, the district court adopted the Eighth Circuit's seven-factor test for virtual representation.[37] This test required an identity of interests between the plaintiffs in both suits and in addition considered six factors that were found to weigh in favor of virtual representation in the present case: (1) a close relationship between the party and the precluded nonparty; (2) participation in the prior litigation by the precluded nonparty; (3) acquiescence to preclusion by the precluded nonparty; (4) deliberate tactical maneuvering to avoid the initial judgment; (5) adequate representation; and (6) a public law issue rather than a private law issue.[38]

The district court found that Taylor and Harrick had identical interests in obtaining the documents and that all of the relevant factors but one were satisfied. Accordingly, the district court held that Taylor's suit was precluded because of the disposition of Harrick's prior suit.[39] Taylor appealed to the D.C. Circuit, and that court affirmed.[40] In doing so, the appellate court adopted its own five-factor test for virtual representation, requiring both identity of interests and adequate representation.[41] In addition to these prerequisites, at least one of three additional factors had to be present: a close relationship between the party and the precluded nonparty, substantial participation in the prior litigation by the precluded nonparty, or tactical maneuvering by the prior party that indicated he was attempting to relitigate through a proxy.[42] The court found that Harrick had an identity of interests with and had adequately represented Taylor. The court also found that Harrick and Taylor had a close relationship. Having satisfied its test, the court held that Taylor's suit was precluded on grounds of virtual representation.[43] The Supreme Court granted certiorari and reversed.[44]

Justice Ginsburg began the Court's unanimous opinion by noting that an individual is generally not bound by a judgment in a suit to which he is not a party.[45] The standard rule, rather, is that each person has a right to her day in court.[46] However, the Court noted six recognized exceptions to this rule.[47]

First, if a person beforehand agrees to be bound, she may be bound despite not being a party to the suit. Second, a preexisting substantive legal relationship—for example, a successor in property interest—may dictate that a nonparty be bound. Third, in some situations a nonparty may be bound if she was adequately represented by a party to the prior suit. Fourth, a nonparty may be bound if she controlled the prior suit. Fifth, a second suit may be barred if the prior party is relitigating through a proxy. Sixth, a special statutory scheme within the bounds of due process may allow for nonparty preclusion. The Court concluded, however, that virtual representation unconstitutionally exceeds the limits of these recognized exceptions to the day-in-court requirement.[48]

The Court's analysis focused on the exception for when the plaintiff in the first case "adequately represented" the interests of the nonparty.[49] Its elaboration, however, made clear the narrowness of the exception, despite its seeming breadth. It developed the exception by reasoning from its prior decision in *Richards v. Jefferson County*.[50] In *Richards*, a class of taxpayers challenged an Alabama tax under both federal and state constitutions.[51] The State argued that taxpayers had been adequately represented in a prior suit, brought by individual taxpayers, where the tax had been upheld, and that the present suit should be found to be precluded by the prior judgment.[52] The Court in *Richards* rejected this argument, holding that the taxpayers had not been adequately represented.[53] The Court first noted that its decision requiring due process in class actions in *Hansberry v. Lee*[54] stood for the proposition that a prior proceeding must have been designed to protect the interests of the absent party in order to bind that party by the result of that proceeding.[55] Applying this logic to the prior tax challenge, the *Richards* Court stated:

> [T]here is no reason to suppose that the [prior] court took care to protect the interests of petitioners in the manner suggested in Hansberry. Nor is there any reason to suppose that the individual taxpayers in [the prior case] understood their suit to be on behalf of absent county taxpayers. Thus, to contend that the plaintiffs in [the prior case] somehow represented petitioners, let alone represented them in a constitutionally adequate manner, would be "to attribute to them a power that it cannot be said that they had assumed to exercise."[56]

From this negative language in *Richards*, the Court in *Taylor* inferred a positive dictate: if the interests of a litigant in a second case had in fact been adequately represented in the prior case, that litigant could constitutionally be bound by the result in the first case.[57] However, for a nonparty to be bound by a judgment based on adequate representation, the Court reasoned, one of two requirements must be met: either the prior court must have adopted "special procedures" to protect the absent person or the representative party in the prior suit must have understood itself to be representing the absent party.[58] Because the D.C.

Circuit's definition of virtual representation did not include these requirements, the Supreme Court concluded that it fell outside the recognized exception to the day-in-court rule on the basis of adequate representation.[59]

There is a strong argument that by limiting the "adequate representation" exception to cases involving "special procedures" or a preexisting understanding, the Court effectively stripped the exception of any meaning. The Court's only example of a sufficiently "special" procedure was a "properly conducted class action."[60] Class actions, of course, operate as an independent basis for nonparty preclusion, and it is not at all clear that any other procedures exist that would satisfy this limit on adequate representation-based preclusion. Furthermore, the preexisting understanding requirement is strikingly similar to the privity exception recognized by the Court for "a person who agrees to be bound."[61] The Court cited the Restatement (Second) of Judgments for the proposition that a person may expressly or impliedly agree to be bound.[62] It is unclear how a representative party could understand herself to represent the interests of an absent person without an express or implied agreement. Thus, the "adequate representation" exception—against which the Court tests virtual representation—appears to be void of any independent meaning.

Whatever one thinks of the Court's questionable logic concerning its "adequate representation" exception to the day-in-court ideal, the fact remains that the exception failed to include the D.C. Circuit's concept of virtual representation. The Court further rejected the argument that the existing exceptions should be replaced by virtual representation as fashioned by the lower court. First, the Court noted that prior decisions stressed the value of the day-in-court rule, and exceptions had been created only in discrete and narrowly limited circumstances.[63] In other words, existing precedent did not support virtual representation, and the Court was not about to expand that precedent. Second, the Court reasoned that adopting a virtual representation balancing test to govern nonparty preclusion could render the class certification process meaningless and effectively authorize the creation of "'de facto class actions at will.'"[64] Finally, the Court pointed out that while the preclusion doctrine is supposed to reduce the burden on the courts, the application of a complex balancing test and the discovery required to establish its elements could give rise to more judicial work than its use avoids.[65] The Court thus rejected the D.C. Circuit's balancing test for virtual representation and quite probably signaled the demise of the doctrine in its entirety.

4.2.3 What *Taylor* Did Not Consider

At the outset, I should emphasize my agreement with the *Taylor* Court's general skepticism about virtual representation. Because the day-in-court ideal reflects core democratic and constitutional values, the dictate should be ignored only in the most extreme circumstances, if at all. But while the Court has often noted its support for the day-in-court ideal as a dictate of due process,[66] surprisingly, at no point has it articulated any firm conceptual grounding or theoretical rationale for the precept. It is almost as if the Court simply intuits the normative basis for this important requirement of procedural due process. Yet as respected scholars have noted, even where relief is divisible, the day-in-court requirement is far from costless.[67] It has reasonably been contended that litigation is expensive, and relitigation of issues which have already been resolved is therefore wasteful.[68] Cost avoidance, of course, cannot be deemed the sole value involved in the procedural due process calculus. The problem, however, is that the Court's failure to articulate the counter-value leaves the day-in-court ideal vulnerable to attack on the basis of the competing considerations of cost and efficiency. The following discussion seeks to fashion an argument that the day-in-court ideal represents a core element of the participatory autonomy that is both pragmatically and conceptually central to American democracy. Although it is conceivable that in very rare cases counter-interests may be so compelling as to overcome it, absent the presence of such an extraordinary interest—one that must be far more compelling than the simple cost of litigation—the day-in-court dictate must be followed.

4.3 THE DAY-IN-COURT IDEAL IN AMERICAN CONSTITUTIONAL AND POLITICAL THEORY

The Court in *Taylor* noted the "'deep-rooted historic tradition that everyone should have his own day in court.'"[69] Indeed, the primary reason the Court rejected virtual representation was that applying virtual representation to bar Taylor's suit would have deprived him of his day in court. But why, exactly, is ensuring one's day in court so important? Although the Court in *Taylor* outlined the established exceptions to the day-in-court rule, it did so by merely recounting precedent. The Court failed to explain why a litigant's right to have her day in court should be protected as a moral, political, or constitutional matter or why exceptions to that rule are nevertheless permitted in certain situations. The following discussion provides a theoretical framework for understanding the importance of the day-in-court ideal.[70]

4.3.1 The Background of the Day-in-Court Ideal: Procedural Due Process Theory

In both its class action and res judicata jurisprudence, the Court has made clear that the day-in-court precept, much like the fifty-five-mile-per-hour speed limit of years past, is not just a good idea; it is the law. A litigant's right to a day in court is not merely a judicial policy choice. Rather, it is a constitutional directive that presumptively trumps any legislative or judicial choice to the contrary.[71] Therefore, to understand the precept's importance, it is first necessary to understand the scope and rationale of the procedural due process guarantee.

Procedural due process theories have traditionally been divided into two camps: outcome-based and process-based. Outcome-based theories measure the quality of procedure based solely on the procedure's effect on the accuracy of the outcome of cases. For example, utilitarianism, a common outcome-based due process theory, balances the ability of a given procedure to produce accurate outcomes against the costs of providing the procedure, either to the other parties or to the system itself.[72] If the marginal increase in the likelihood of attaining an accurate outcome produced by the procedure outweighs the costs of providing the procedure, the procedure is deemed to be required by due process. If, on the other hand, the costs of providing the procedure are found to outweigh the gain in accuracy, the procedure is prohibited. If two procedures produce the same level of accuracy but one is cheaper to provide, the more expensive procedure is not required by due process. This conclusion is unaffected by the fact that the more costly procedure might provide additional benefits that do not affect the accuracy of outcomes.

Process-based theories, in contrast, focus on nonutilitarian values associated with a given procedure.[73] Such process-based theories vary in their exact formulation, but one common characteristic is recognition of a value in permitting individuals to directly participate in the adjudication of their rights.[74] Participation may in some circumstances increase the accuracy of outcomes. For example, in the litigation context, a party has a strong incentive to vigorously pursue every possible argument because she bears both the risk and reward of the case's resolution. To the extent vigorous advocacy enhances the accuracy of outcomes in the adversary system, use of a procedure that enables participation may increase the accuracy of outcomes. A strictly outcome-based theory would reject the constitutional necessity of participation whenever another procedure could produce roughly the same accuracy at a lower cost or whenever the cost of enabling participation is deemed to outweigh the marginal increase in accuracy produced by participation. A process-based theory, on the other hand, values participation either for its legitimizing effect in the eyes of the litigants or its facilitation of the citizen's role in democratic governance, whether or not decision-making accuracy is improved as a result. Thus, there may be a value in permitting each litigant to personally participate—that is, have her day in court—that is entirely distinct from the value in securing an accurate outcome.

As explained in earlier chapters, exclusive focus on the utilitarian view of procedural due process is unduly truncated, because it ignores values inherent in liberal democracy that are appropriately deemed embodied in constitutional guarantees of liberty. Procedural due process is more appropriately viewed as a means of furthering and vindicating foundational democratic values. From this perspective, the litigant's ability to participate in the legal process as a means of vindicating his legally protected rights is seen as a core function in the democratic process. It is generally thought that participation in the judicial process, like the citizen's participation in the political process, is a means by which the individual asserts his dignity and worth, both necessary conditions to a viable liberal democracy. Therefore, the due process protection of litigant autonomy springs from a democratic commitment to process-based autonomy.

For the most part, all of this is true. However, as this book has argued throughout, the analysis to this point is dangerously incomplete. For it ignores the primary reason that American democratic theory has in virtually all cases prohibited anyone but the individuals themselves to choose who will represent their interests when constitutional rights are at stake: adversary democratic theory's inherent mistrust of the motives and/or competence of those not chosen by the individual litigants themselves.[75]

In fashioning the participatory right embodied in notions of procedural due process, it is important to distinguish between the concepts of autonomy and paternalism. "Autonomy" means that the individual has the right to choose how to fashion his own representation and to participate in the process as he sees fit, within the prescribed adjudicatory framework. In contrast, "paternalism" refers to the obligation of the government or other private individuals to assure representation of the citizen's rights in the course of an adjudicatory process in which the citizen plays no role. To be sure, due process may well require some form of paternalism when, even though his rights will be directly or indirectly affected by the outcome of the judicial process, it is either impossible or infeasible for the citizen to participate. However, when it is not beyond the bounds of practicality to allow an individual to protect her own interests by being afforded the opportunity to directly participate in the proceeding (or choose who will do so on her behalf), there is no need for paternalism to enter the procedural due process calculus. It is only when the individual's participation is not feasible, but her interests will inevitably be affected, that paternalism should be employed to provide a constitutional floor of protection.

Most of the Supreme Court's procedural due process doctrine affecting multiparties focuses on the need to satisfy the minimum requirements of paternalism, thereby failing to focus on the importance of liberal adversely democratic due process. The most authoritative statement on the paternalism version of procedural due process came in the landmark case of *Hansberry v. Lee*.[76] In *Hansberry*, in which the Court applied due process as a limitation on the class action procedure, the Court noted the "principle of general application in

Anglo-American jurisprudence that one is not bound in personam in a litigation in which he is not designated as a party or to which he has not been made a party by service of process."[77] Recognizing the class action as an exception to this rule, the Court emphasized the due process limits on this exception: "[T]his Court is justified in saying that there has been a failure of due process only in those cases where it cannot be said that the procedure adopted, fairly insures the protection of the interest of absent parties who are to be bound by it."[78] The Court in *Hansberry* failed to address the question of whether or not the class device permissibly infringes on litigant autonomy, even if the interest in paternalism is satisfied. Ignoring that question, the Court instead focused exclusively on what paternalistic protections are required to ensure a minimum amount of fairness even in the impacted individuals' absence. These required paternalistic protections, often grouped under the heading of adequate representation, are the primary legacy of *Hansberry* and form a cornerstone of the Court's procedural due process doctrine. The following discussion explains why paternalism fails to satisfy the demands of due process. Except in the most extreme circumstances, due process demands that litigant autonomy be respected.

4.4 LITIGANT AUTONOMY, LIBERAL ADVERSARY DEMOCRATIC THEORY, AND THE DAY-IN-COURT IDEAL

As already noted, the theoretical foundation of the nation's commitment to the day-in-court ideal is grounded in democratic theory.[79] At its core, of course, democracy is based on the notion of self-determination. Society as a whole expresses this self-determination through the election of governing representatives. However, individual self-determination drives this communal expression through the individual's participation at the voting booth. Whatever precise theory of democracy one ascribes to,[80] it must provide citizens autonomy in the way they choose to involve themselves in the political system. Participation in the activity of choosing leaders is a minimum requirement of any democratic theory.[81]

In order to effectively participate in democracy, individuals must also have the freedom to choose how to participate in the process of societal choice. The value of self-determination gives meaning to political participation, and a certain zone of individual autonomy is necessary to achieve self-determination.[82] Our constitutional commitment to this idea is found in both the Bill of Rights and the Fourteenth Amendment. For example, under the First Amendment, as a general matter government may neither suppress nor compel private expression.[83] This freedom of expression allows individuals to make decisions for themselves, free from external forces,[84] concerning what they say and how they say it.[85] The zone of individual autonomy created by the Bill of Rights and the Fourteenth Amendment allows individuals to interact effectively with the political branches of government in the exercise of democracy.

I should emphasize that—as emphasized throughout this book—the notion of autonomy represented by voting or speech rights is fundamentally different from the form of autonomy typically associated with general libertarian theory. Libertarian theory calls for expansive protection of what can be called substantive autonomy.[86] Substantive autonomy relates to the ability to conduct our lives in the way we choose—to own guns, to use marijuana, to cross the street. Substantive autonomy seeks to prevent government intrusion into our daily lives. In contrast, the ability to make choices about the way in which we interact with the political system, or what can be labeled process-based autonomy, seeks to assure that when the government intrudes on our lives, it is doing so in a manner that has been democratically authorized. In this way, process-based autonomy is agnostic as to a normative commitment to any particular substantive political policy; rather, process-based autonomy upholds the mechanisms without which we could not democratically express our personal policy preferences.[87]

Acceptance of process-based political autonomy leads logically to acceptance of the day-in-court ideal. The United States' commitment to participation in legal settings can be viewed as an outgrowth of the political commitment to process-based participation values.[88] Just as citizen participation in the electoral process legitimizes the decisions of democratic government, individual participation in the litigation process as a means of vindicating the individual's rights adds legitimacy to judicial outcomes. "Individuals are presumed to have no legitimate complaint if they were allowed to present their case in the way they chose to present it—or, to put it another way, had their 'day in court.'"[89] In this way, the day-in-court ideal does much more than increase the accuracy of outcomes; like the electoral process, it provides a foundation for citizens' trust in the decisions of an organ of the government. In one context that organ is the legislative or executive branch while in the other context it is the judicial branch, but this difference does not alter the fundamental democratic dynamic.

As in the other contexts examined throughout this book, the autonomy value of liberal democratic theory is inherently intertwined with the skepticism and mistrust that characterizes adversary democratic theory. Because government cannot be trusted to paternalistically look out for the litigant's interests, the system must assure the individual litigant her ability to control the procedural defense of her own interests. The adversary system and the day-in-court ideal each constitute an extension and further evidence of the nation's commitment to liberal adversary democratic theory.[90]

4.5 LIMITATIONS ON THE DAY-IN-COURT IDEAL

As mentioned earlier, although the Court in *Taylor* failed to explicate the theoretical underpinnings of the day-in-court ideal, it nevertheless relied on that ideal in rejecting virtual representation. The Court recognized that the value of a party's participation in litigation is a strong due process value that cannot be overcome simply because a litigant's interests are similar to those of a prior litigant.[91]

It would be unrealistic and unwise, however, to view the day-in-court ideal as an absolute. Procedural due process has always been thought to implicate some form of a balancing of interests.[92] As explained earlier in this book, this utilitarian balancing approach grossly undervalues the litigant's interest in procedural due process. The fact remains, however, that under currently established doctrine, the balancing test is universally employed. Therefore it is at least conceivable that, doctrinally at least, even highly valued autonomy interests may be outweighed by higher valued competing interests.[93] In many circumstances an individual's strategic litigation choices may be overridden by competing concerns. For example, rules of evidence restrict the way a case is presented. Compulsory counterclaims force a litigant to raise claims she might have preferred to bring later. Although neither example eliminates participation entirely, each restricts the litigant's procedural choices. But it should be recalled that under the adversary democratic due process model advocated throughout this book, the individual's constitutional right to choose her own representation can be overcome only by showing a competing and truly compelling interest—a far more demanding standard than that imposed by the traditional utilitarian balancing test. Although participation is a fundamental value of our litigation system arising from a commitment to liberal adversary democracy, in the face of a truly compelling competing concern, participation might be completely overridden within the bounds of due process. Because of participation's fundamental nature, however, a person should only be prevented from participating in the adjudication of her own legal rights for truly compelling reasons.

When the Court considered the legitimacy of virtual representation in *Taylor*, it was not presented with any compelling reason to prevent the initial litigant's participation; the gain in efficiency, standing alone, was deemed insufficient.[94] As the unanimous decision suggests, the Court apparently thought that *Taylor* was an easy case from a procedural due process standpoint. As the following discussion makes clear, however, the situation is not always that simple.

4.6 INDIVISIBLE RELIEF, DUE PROCESS, AND VIRTUAL REPRESENTATION

Indivisible relief refers to situations in which the relief granted in one suit and the relief sought in a second suit cannot be treated separately—in other words, the outcome in one is necessarily intertwined with the outcome in the other. Indivisible relief situations often involve cases in which injunctive relief is sought. For example, a judgment in one case might require that the defendant take a specific action, while a different plaintiff in a later suit against the same defendant might seek relief that would prohibit the defendant from taking the very same action. If the requested relief were to be ordered in the second suit, the defendant would be prohibited by law from performing the very act he had been required to perform in the first suit. In this scenario, the relief requested in the second suit is indivisible from the relief granted in the first suit because as both a legal and a practical matter the defendant can physically comply with only one of the conflicting orders.

In recognizing the dangers of indivisible relief to a defendant in multiple suits where inconsistent relief is sought, it is important to draw certain distinctions. The serious danger the defendant faces does not arise unless the relief is, in fact, truly indivisible. Thus, as long as it is physically possible for a defendant to treat different plaintiffs differently, the mere possibility of aesthetic inconsistency between the two suits should not be deemed prohibitive. To understand the distinction, consider two decisions from the Fifth Circuit: *Southwest Airlines Co. v. Texas International Airlines, Inc.*[95] and *Pollard v. Cockrell*.[96] In *Southwest Airlines Co.*, plaintiffs—first the City of Dallas[97] and later a group of airlines[98]—in two separate suits sought to apply a city ordinance to exclude Southwest from the Dallas airport known as Love Field.[99] In the first suit, the district court found in favor of Southwest and against the city, holding that the ordinance could not be properly applied to Southwest.[100] In the second suit, the airlines effectively sought the same relief against Southwest which had been denied to the city in the prior suit.[101] Because the airlines had not yet had their day in court, however, it seemed that there was a danger that the second suit could undermine, if not effectively revoke, Southwest's victory in the prior case. In the first suit Southwest had successfully prevented its exclusion from Love Field, yet a successful suit by the other airlines would obliterate that victory. Under the traditional day-in-court ideal, however, the second group of plaintiffs could not constitutionally be bound by the decision in the first suit. The airlines were clear that their goal in bringing the litigation was to undo the effect of Southwest's original judgment.[102] The district court in the first suit issued a preliminary injunction preventing the airlines from relitigating the question of whether the Dallas ordinance barred Southwest from operating at Love Field.[103] The Fifth Circuit affirmed the injunction on the grounds that the airlines were bound by the original judgment.[104]

It is puzzling that the Fifth Circuit emphasized that its decision to preclude the airlines' suit was not based on a theory of virtual representation. The court noted that the virtual representation "doctrine offers little analytical assistance . . . because of its wide and inconsistent application."[105] Southwest had argued that virtual representation applied to bind the second group of plaintiffs, in part because the City of Dallas, as a governmental body, had the power to represent private interests.[106] The court agreed with this position, but declined to "identify[] the doctrinal scope of virtual representation"[107] because it believed the case could be resolved without relying on that doctrine.[108]

The court found that res judicata—even without formal resort to virtual representation—barred the airlines' claims because their interests had been adequately represented in the first suit by governmental authorities.[109] The primary focus of the court's inquiry was the degree to which the airlines' interests aligned with the interests of the City of Dallas in the initial suit. According to the court: "Because [the] legal interests of the carriers do not differ from those of Dallas in . . . [the first suit, *City of Dallas v. Southwest Airlines Co.*[110]], we hold that they received adequate representation in the earlier litigation and should be bound by the judgment in that litigation."[111]

Although the court expressly declined to rely on a theory of virtual representation by name, its focus on alignment of interests and adequate representation is strikingly similar to that doctrine. Indeed, in a later case, the Fifth Circuit noted that its holding in *Southwest Airlines* was actually based on the theory of virtual representation.[112] Thus, *Southwest Airlines* is properly viewed as a virtual representation case in which the court found that the interests of the airlines and the City of Dallas were sufficiently aligned to bind the airlines to the result of the original suit.

In addition to its reliance on the parties' alignment of interests in the two suits, the court in *Southwest Airlines* recognized the fact that the relief sought in the second suit was indivisible from the relief granted in the first suit.[113] The court concluded its opinion with a discussion of due process, noting several factors that led to its finding of preclusion:

> [T]he due process balance must include the damage relitigation would visit upon the judicial system and Southwest. As discussed above, relitigation would constitute a blatant disregard for the decision of this Court and for the judgment of the federal district court in [City of Dallas v. Southwest Airlines Co.] It would threaten the rights granted Southwest by the [City of Dallas v. Southwest Airlines Co.] judgment. And finally, it would subject Southwest to the possibility of conflicting judgments.[114]

This calculation of the harm that could be visited upon Southwest if preclusion were not to be invoked is important in understanding the contours of virtual representation. The court was hesitant to permit nonparty preclusion because it would deprive the airlines of their day in court. However, the court faced a situation in which the relief sought in the second case would inevitably undermine the relief granted in the first case: Southwest could not simultaneously leave

Love Field and remain at Love Field. One can infer from the court's emphasis on alignment of interests that its desire to maintain the original judgment, on its own, could not establish virtual representation. However, when it was combined with the additional finding of adequate representation based on the alignment of interests of the plaintiffs in the two suits, virtual representation provided the court with a mechanism for preserving the prior judgment and maintaining a minimum amount of procedural fairness for the precluded nonparty.

In contrast to *Southwest Airlines*, the Fifth Circuit's decision in *Pollard* illustrates the *absence* of indivisible relief. In an effort to curb illicit sexual behavior, the City of San Antonio passed an ordinance strictly regulating massage parlors.[115] A group of massage parlor owners brought a suit challenging the constitutionality of the ordinance in state court.[116] The state trial court found that certain provisions of the statute were unconstitutional and therefore enjoined the enforcement of those provisions.[117] Both parties appealed, and the state intermediate appellate court reversed, holding that the statute was constitutional in its entirety.[118]

After the trial court's decision in the state suit, another group of massage parlor owners brought suit in federal court, challenging the statute's constitutionality.[119] The federal district court found that one additional provision violated the Constitution.[120] Before reaching the merits of the case on appeal, the Fifth Circuit faced the question of whether or not virtual representation precluded the federal suit based on the resolution of the state suit.[121] The court began its analysis with the definition of virtual representation it had previously adopted in *Aerojet-General Corp. v. Askew*.[122] Because the massage parlor owners in the state case and those in the federal case both sought to enjoin enforcement of the ordinance, they appeared to have aligned interests.[123] The *Pollard* court, however, held that the relationship between the two sets of plaintiffs was not close enough to justify a finding of virtual representation.[124] Instead of focusing on whether each set of owners had the same goal in the litigation—which had been the focus in *Aerojet* and *Southwest Airlines*—the court in *Pollard* shifted its focus to the lack of a substantive legal relationship among the owners. The court stated, "[v]irtual representation demands the existence of an express or implied legal relationship in which parties to the first suit are accountable to non-parties who file a subsequent suit raising identical issues."[125] Because no such express or implied relationship existed in the case, the court refused to find preclusion.

An important element of *Pollard* overlooked by the court was that, unlike in *Southwest Airlines*, the relief sought in the second case was divisible, both legally and practically, from the relief granted in the first.[126] In *Southwest Airlines*, the first suit determined that an ordinance did not apply to Southwest. The second suit sought a determination that the ordinance applied to Southwest—a result that would, of course, have been directly inconsistent with the conclusion of the court in the first case. As a practical matter, these forms of relief could not have been treated independently: the ordinance either applied to Southwest or it did not. In *Pollard*, in contrast, the first suit determined that the ordinance applied to one set of massage parlor owners, and the second suit sought a determination that it did not apply to a different set of owners. Although both suits were based on similar legal claims, the relief sought in each case could have been treated separately; the statute would simply have remained applicable to one group of owners but not to the other. Because there was no danger of indivisible relief, virtual representation should not have precluded the second suit. Thus, *Pollard* was correctly decided, albeit not primarily for the reasons it gave.

The threat of indivisible relief creates significant problems for strict adherence to the day-in-court ideal. In some situations, a second judgment may effectively undermine a party's prior victory. This was the situation the court faced in *Southwest Airlines*. A judgment in favor of the competitor airlines would have required Southwest to leave Love Field, despite Southwest's judgment from the first suit permitting it to stay. The second judgment could thus have forced Southwest to forgo a benefit that it is legally entitled to. It seems intuitively obvious that such a situation should be avoided if at all possible.

If the court in *Southwest Airlines* had considered the day-in-court ideal to be absolute, however, it could not have invoked virtual representation. Whether or not the City of Dallas could adequately represent the airlines' interests in a paternalistic sense, there is no doubt that their due process interests in autonomous control of their litigation had been denied. The Supreme Court's sweeping rejection of virtual representation in *Taylor* seemingly dictates a similar result. Because of the balancing nature of procedural due process, however, it is necessary to examine more closely the problems to which indivisible relief could conceivably give rise to determine whether or not the value in avoiding those problems is sufficiently compelling to outweigh the value of preserving a litigant's right to her day in court. The following subparts examine indivisible relief in detail, explore and apply the reigning procedural due process doctrine, and propose a coherent theory of virtual representation designed to reconcile the powerful competing interests.

4.7 THE DIFFICULTY OF INDIVISIBLE RELIEF

Although indivisible relief may arise in many legal situations, and occasionally has been legally recognized—most notably, in the circumstances recognized by Rule 23(b)(1)(A) of the Federal Rules of Civil Procedure,[127] concerning class actions—the problem has never been comprehensively analyzed, particularly in relation to res judicata and the day-in-court ideal. To fully understand this uncharted legal topic, the analysis here has organized indivisible relief into three distinct subcategories which we refer to as "double liability," "contradictory liability," and "inconsistent liability." This subcategorization is useful for two reasons. First, each subcategory represents a specific application of the problem of indivisible relief. Second, each subcategory gives rise to distinct due process problems. Because of their differing problems, the subcategories produce differing weights in the due process balance and therefore must be kept conceptually distinct. The following sections define each subcategory and describe the problems uniquely associated with each.

4.7.1 Double Liability

The core element of the concept of double liability, as defined here, is the existence of an indivisible "stake." A stake is "[s]omething (such as property) deposited by two or more parties with a third party pending the resolution of a dispute."[128] A stake may take the form of a specific sum of money, such as a capped insurance policy, or an identifiable piece of real or personal property. The person with whom the stake is deposited is called the stakeholder. A stake could conceivably be divisible, as where separate claims may legally be apportioned (for example, individual damage claims into an insurance fund). However, where mutually inconsistent claims may be made to the whole stake, the danger to the stakeholder of double liability arises. Assume that claimant A sues the stakeholder for the entire stake, and the stakeholder defends on the grounds that B is actually the proper recipient. Assume, however, that a jury finds that A is the proper recipient and awards the stake to A. Now assume that B files a subsequent suit against the stakeholder, asserting his legal right to the stake. Under traditionally accepted due process principles, the defendant stakeholder may not assert issue preclusion against B on the basis of the prior judgment in A's suit, because B has not yet had his day in court.[129] Thus, it is conceivable that a second jury could find for B, thereby legally requiring the stakeholder to pay twice, when in theory he could only be liable to pay either A or B, but not both.

Imposition of double liability on a defendant raises significant due process problems. Although the stakeholder was charged with holding a specific sum of money and she is obligated to pay out this sum to the proper claimant or claimants, the outer limits of the stake confine her legal obligations. As the Supreme Court has stated, "the holder of such property is deprived of due process of law if he is compelled to relinquish it without assurance that he will not be held liable again in another jurisdiction or in a suit brought by a claimant who is not bound by the first judgment."[130]

The constitutional danger of double liability could be avoided, of course, if we were to deem B in the later suit legally bound by the result in the first suit brought by A. Under traditional due process analysis, however, B could not be bound unless he had been found to be in privity with a party to the first suit. Otherwise, B would have been denied his day in court, constitutionally required by due process. But privity has traditionally been deemed narrowly confined to a small set of preexisting legally defined relationships,[131] and absent one of those situations, we are presented with a serious dilemma: either we deprive B of his day in court in contravention of due process, or we expose the stakeholder to the risk of unconstitutional double liability.

Use of virtual representation would avoid this legal dilemma by binding B to a party to the prior litigation who had adequately (if unsuccessfully) represented B's interests. In the hypothetical previously discussed, that would be the stakeholder who, we can presume, vigorously asserted the position that B was the proper claimant. The problem, however, is that if one adopts an adversary democratic rationale for procedural due process,[132] the fact that the stakeholder may have "adequately" represented B's interests in the first litigation is wholly irrelevant: B has not had his constitutionally dictated day in court, because he has not yet had an opportunity to assert and defend his own rights.

In this sense, the Supreme Court's decision in *Taylor v. Sturgell* correctly recognized the troubling implications of virtual representation for procedural due process. What it failed to recognize, however, was the necessary gradation in the stakes of refusing to invoke virtual representation. When the claims in the respective suits are legally divisible, as where the plaintiffs in the separate suits seek individual damages, the negative consequences of adhering to due process are relatively minimal: they are simply the costs to efficiency of relitigating. However, where the relief in the two suits is indivisible in a manner that imposes on a defendant the risk of double liability, we are presented with a serious constitutional dilemma. Before one seeks to resolve that dilemma, however, it is first necessary to explain the other categories of indivisible relief, so that the chapter may develop a holistic, comprehensive resolution of the problem.

4.7.2 Contradictory Liability

Contradictory liability occurs when a litigant faces an injunction awarded in case 1 commanding her to do X and an injunction in case 2 commanding her *not* to do X. Unlike double liability, contradictory liability does not involve an indivisible stake. Instead, the indivisible nature of contradictory liability centers around the inherent irreconcilability in the litigant's legally dictated actions: she cannot simultaneously do X and not-X.

As an example of contradictory liability, consider the facts in *Aerojet*. In the first case, Aerojet won a judgment for specific performance of the sale of a piece of land from both the Florida State Board of Trustees and the Florida Board of Education (collectively, State Boards).[133] In the second case, Dade County sought specific performance of the sale of the same piece of land from the State Boards.[134] Had the second suit succeeded, the State Boards would have been faced with contradictory judgments, requiring them to sell a single piece of land to two different parties. In that situation, there is no action the State Boards could have taken that would not have violated at least one of the judgments.

The due process problems imposed upon the defendant by contradictory liability are just as devastating as those that arise in the case of double liability. Contradictory liability places a litigant in a situation in which any action she takes will violate one or the other valid court judgment. If a litigant is simultaneously required to do X and not to do X, satisfying one requirement necessarily violates the other. Because in *Aerojet* each judgment could have been enforced by the state, failing to comply with one judgment is presumably punishable as contempt. It should not require complex analysis to recognize that it violates due process to punish someone for failing to do something she is legally or physically incapable of doing.[135] As Lon Fuller observed:

> A man who is habitually punished for doing what he was ordered to do can hardly be expected to respond appropriately to orders given to him in the future. If our treatment of him is part of an attempt to build up a system of rules for the governance of his conduct, then we shall fail in that attempt. On the other hand if our object is to cause him to have a nervous breakdown, we may succeed.[136]

Professor Henry Hart made a similar point: "People repeatedly subjected, like Pavlov's dogs, to two or more inconsistent sets of directions, without means of resolving the inconsistencies, could not fail in the end to react as the dogs did. The society, collectively, would suffer a nervous breakdown."[137] By punishing litigants for acting as they are required by legal judgments, contradictory liability inherently violates due process and therefore must be avoided.

Once again, use of virtual representation could conceivably avoid many of the constitutional problems to which contradictory liability gives rise. If the defendant in case 1 vigorously (albeit unsuccessfully) asserted the second plaintiff's legal position, the second court might conclude that that plaintiff's interests were adequately represented in the first case and therefore bind the second plaintiff, through issue preclusion, to the result in the first case, even though they were not a litigant in case 1. By summarily rejecting the doctrine of virtual representation,[138] the Court in *Taylor* left unrestrained the potential constitutional dangers of contradictory liability.

4.7.3 Inconsistent Liability

Inconsistent liability occurs when a litigant obtains an injunction authorizing (but not requiring) her to do X and later faces an injunction legally preventing her from doing X. Like contradictory liability, the indivisible nature of inconsistent liability centers around the litigant's out-of-court actions: she cannot both do X and not do X. The nature of the initial judgment is what distinguishes inconsistent from contradictory liability, however. In the case of contradictory liability, the first judgment requires the litigant to do X. In this situation, if a subsequent judgment requires her *not* to do X, any action the litigant takes will necessarily violate one judgment or the other. In the case of inconsistent liability, in contrast, the first judgment merely *permits* a litigant to do X. If a subsequent judgment requires her not to do X, it is of course legally and physically possible for her to simply forgo the benefit of her initial judgment.

It does not follow, however, that the system should necessarily be unconcerned by a second judgment's effective destruction of a right won by a party in the first suit. Again, the problem could be avoided by invocation of virtual representation to bind the second plaintiff to the result imposed on the plaintiff in the first case, as long as the first plaintiff is deemed to have adequately represented the second plaintiff's interests. However, the Court in *Taylor* exposed litigants involved in multiple litigation to the negative consequences of inconsistent liability by summarily rejecting virtual representation. But no safeguard can prevent virtual representation from depriving a litigant of her procedural autonomy. And it is this procedural autonomy that is required to protect against the dangers sought to be prevented by adversary democratic theory: a prophylactic, *ex ante* mistrust of any representative of a litigant's interests not chosen by the litigant himself. The only way to prevent the deprivation of litigation autonomy is to allow the litigant to participate in the adjudicatory process, which would render unacceptable a procedure such as virtual representation that is designed to prevent such participation. In order for a procedure that prevents participation to pass due process scrutiny, therefore, an interest must exist that is sufficiently compelling to outweigh litigant autonomy.

As an example of inconsistent liability, consider the facts in *Southwest Airlines*. In its first suit against the City of Dallas, Southwest obtained a declaratory judgment stating that the city ordinance did not apply to Southwest and, therefore, Southwest could stay at Love Field.[139] In a later suit, competitor airlines sought a declaratory judgment that the city ordinance did apply to Southwest and, therefore, Southwest had to leave Love Field.[140] Here, if the competitor airlines won the second suit, Southwest could leave Love Field, thereby complying with the second judgment and forgoing the benefits of the first judgment. In this way, it is possible for the judgments to coexist.

In order for the two inconsistent judgments to coexist, however, the holder of the first judgment must be forced to forgo the fruit of her prior victory.[141] A successful litigant possesses a property interest in a valid judgment that it has won through successful litigation. A chose in action has thereby been converted into a more definite form of property right—a judgment. When a risk of inconsistent liability exists, maintaining the second suit risks undermining the value of the first judgment, depriving the holder of that judgment of her property right without due process of law.

One should reasonably be sympathetic to the important constitutional values underlying the day-in-court ideal. Therefore, as a general matter, one should normally reject virtual representation because it contravenes core notions of procedural due process.[142] However, in cases of indivisible relief, the problem is not as simple as the Court in *Taylor* seemed to believe. As previously noted, even the demanding standards of adversary democratic due process may be forced to give way in the face of a truly compelling competing interest.[143] It is therefore at least arguable that the competing interests that counter the day-in-court ideal in cases of indivisible relief should be deemed to overcome the concededly important interest in allowing a litigant to defend his rights in court.

The upshot of this analysis is that the interest in avoiding the problems associated with double and contradictory liability is sufficiently compelling to overcome even the constitutionally significant value of litigant autonomy. Both double and contradictory liability themselves give rise to violations of due process, either by forcing the stakeholder to pay a single debt twice or by punishing a litigant for failing to perform physically or legally impossible acts. It is inconceivable that a system committed to fundamental fairness and the rule of law could tolerate such unfairness and legal incoherence except in the most dire of circumstances. Thus, as long as a court has assured itself that a litigant in the first case has adequately represented the interests of the litigant in the second case,[144] one must reluctantly conclude that in these situations, virtual representation should be invoked.[145] However, where the court concludes that the litigant in case 2 was not adequately represented in case 1, the day-in-court ideal should overcome even the incoherent and unfair consequences of both contradictory and double liability.

Whether or not the interest in avoiding the problems associated with inconsistent liability is sufficient to outweigh litigant autonomy is a much more difficult question than for the other two categories, because the problems arising from inconsistent liability do not include actual legal impossibilities. As discussed earlier, a protected property interest exists in an injunction permitting its owner to do X. Although a subsequent judgment preventing that person from doing X deprives her of the practical benefit of her original judgment and should be avoided where feasible, the fact remains that the two judgments are capable of reconciliation by forcing her to forgo the benefits of the first judgment.

While as a general matter it is of course preferable to avoid such situations, it is important in fashioning the controlling due process calculus to recall that the first judgment is, by its terms, binding only between the parties to the original case. In other words, the winning litigant's right to do X has been settled, but only between her and her former opponent, not between her and the world. To understand the distinction, one might well draw an analogy to the long-accepted distinction between judgments that are pure in rem (which bind the world) and those in the nature of rem (which bind only the particular persons named in the suit).[146] In the context of inconsistent liability, because the first judgment permitting its owner to do X presumably did not purport to bind the world, that litigant should, from the outset, be aware that later suits might arise which might have the effect of undermining her judgment in the prior suit. Although she may have no specific knowledge of the person who will later bring suit against her, she must nonetheless be aware of the possibility of subsequent suits by plaintiffs not involved in the first suit.

The conclusion that double and contradictory liability should be deemed sufficiently compelling to overcome a litigant's competing procedural participation interest, it should be emphasized, does not automatically mean that virtual representation will be permitted when these types of relief are sought. The possibility of the first two categories of indivisible relief is necessary but not sufficient for virtual representation to pass due process scrutiny. As already noted, there must also be assurance that the precluded party was adequately represented in the initial suit to which she will be bound. Adequate representation ensures that the precluded nonparty is not erroneously deprived of the substantive benefits of her legal rights. As argued throughout this book, a paternalistic governmental finding of adequate representation should never be allowed—except in the rare instances in which requiring litigant participation is overcome by an overwhelming competing compelling interest. The dangers of multiple or contradictory liability satisfy that very high standard. Even so, it should never be forgotten that even in those rare situations, the court must make an objective finding that the litigant in case 1 has, in fact, "adequately" represented the interests of the litigant in case 2. Thus, due process requires at least this floor of procedural protection, even in the face of competing interests that are sufficiently compelling to outweigh litigant autonomy. The following discussion examines the contours of the concept of adequate representation in the virtual representation context.

4.8 DEFINING ADEQUATE REPRESENTATION

The concept of adequate representation is not new. To the contrary, it has long been a central part of class action doctrine and forms the basis for much of the Court's procedural due process discussion in nonparty preclusion cases.[147] Particularly in the class action context, adequate representation is a fairly developed concept. As a prerequisite for class certification, Rule 23(a)(4) provides that "the representative parties will fairly and adequately protect the interest of the class."[148] This language has been interpreted to require that the representative party's interests be aligned with the represented party's interests,[149] the representative party possesses incentive to litigate vigorously,[150] and the representative party possesses sufficient resources to litigate vigorously.[151] These three prerequisites should also form the basis for the inquiry into adequate representation for purposes of virtual representation.

Any definition of adequate representation must demand total alignment between the representative party's and the represented party's interests. Because virtual representation does not require a formalized preexisting legal relationship between the parties, there is no reason to believe that the representative party is specifically advancing any interests other than her own; in other words, she is not necessarily looking out for the absent party. However, if the representative party's interests are inevitably and inescapably aligned with those of the represented party, a court will assume that the represented party's interests will be indirectly protected. This alignment of interests refers to a desire for the same outcome and the availability of the same legal theories in pursuit of that outcome.[152] If the absent party possesses legal rights that the representative party is incapable of raising, the representative party's interests cannot properly be deemed sufficiently aligned with those of the absent nonparty. Conversely, if the representative party desires the same outcome and has access to the same arguments as the absent party, their interests are aligned, even if they have different reasons for pursuing the same outcome. For example, in *Southwest Airlines*, the City of Dallas and the competitor airlines each sought to force Southwest to leave Love Field, and each presented the same legal arguments.[153] Their interests were aligned, despite the fact that the City of Dallas presumably wanted to force Southwest out in order to ensure the success of the new Dallas/Ft. Worth Airport while the competitor airlines wanted to prevent a competitor from using the more convenient Love Field, thereby gaining a competitive advantage.[154]

The second requirement of adequate representation is that the representative party possess sufficient incentive to vigorously litigate the first suit. To ensure the presence of this incentive, the representative party must possess a significant personal stake in the initial litigation. The motivation behind this requirement is similar to one of the motivations behind the injury-in-fact component of standing.[155] A party possessing a significant personal stake in the litigation is more likely to present her case in an effective manner. In the extreme situation, this requirement prevents a sham party from binding all others with aligned interests. At a more basic level, we simply do not trust someone to exhaust all plausible legal arguments unless she stands to suffer negative consequences as a result of an unsuccessful suit.

The final requirement of adequate representation is that the representative party possess sufficient resources to vigorously litigate the first suit. This element is purely practical. Even if the representative party's interests are perfectly aligned with the precluded nonparty's interests and the representative party has personal incentive to litigate vigorously, the representative party still may be incapable of providing adequate representation. Perhaps the party does not possess sufficient resources to present her case in an acceptably effective manner. Perhaps the party's lawyer is incompetent, despite her high fees. In either situation, it would not be fair to say that the absent party received adequate representation when the representative party clearly did not provide it. Of course, perfect lawyering is not required to satisfy this component. At the very heart of virtual representation is the fact that the absent party may disagree with certain strategic choices in the first suit but is nevertheless bound. Instead, this should serve as a practical inquiry that can be overcome only by insufficient party resources or incompetent lawyering.

To be sure, the lessons of adversary democratic due process—the outgrowth of the marriage between the liberal and adversary forms of democratic theory— clearly dictate that even when a court is satisfied that all of these criteria are satisfied, virtual representation is far from optimal. This is especially so, because the supposed "representative" litigant is not even aware of the litigant whose interests he is supposedly representing. The concern here is not so much the danger of improper motive, as it so often is. The concern, rather, is that the supposedly represented party may have chosen different attorneys and different litigation strategies. Also important is that a complete identity of interests between the two litigants may be rare. Even when the technical legal issue may be identical in both cases, the intensity of litigants' concern and the willingness to litigate may well differ. And a paternalistic determination of these issues by a court is to be avoided if at all possible.

Moreover, it is important to recognize that there exists an important difference between making a finding of adequate representation in the contexts of class actions on the one hand and virtual representation on the other. While the adequacy determination in the class action context must be made *ex ante*, that determination will be made *ex post* in the virtual representation situation. In class actions the court makes its adequacy finding before the actual litigation, rendering it merely a prediction of what is likely to happen in the future. In contrast, in the virtual representation context the court in case 2 has the luxury of being in a position to examine the conduct of case 1 to determine whether the absent party's interests had been adequately represented.

Having established a working definition of adequate representation, we can briefly return to the situations of double and contradictory liability[156] to understand how the adequate representation inquiry differs for each. Suppose two suits are framed as A v. B and C v. B. For a situation involving a danger of double liability, a stake must exist and B is the stakeholder. In the first suit, A claims a right to and receives a judgment for the entire stake. In the second suit, C also claims a right to the entire stake. For the reasons outlined previously, the compelling need to avoid this situation dictates resort to virtual representation. However, this is so if and only if C's interests had been adequately represented in the first suit. It is clear that A's interests and C's interests cannot be aligned: they have inconsistent and opposing claims to the same stake. It is possible, however, that B's interests are aligned with C's interests. But this would be the case only if B had defended the first suit on the grounds that A should not recover because C had a superior claim. In this situation, B is not wholly without incentive because she may be exposed to double liability down the road if A is awarded the stake in the first suit. If B's and C's interests were aligned and B possessed sufficient resources, there should be a presumption that B adequately represented C—a presumption that may be rebutted by a showing that B was not sufficiently interested or competent.

In the case of contradictory liability, the situation is different. Assume that in the first suit A wins an injunction requiring B to do X. Presumably, for whatever reason B would prefer not to do X; that is why she litigated the issue in the first place. In the second suit, C seeks an injunction *preventing* B from doing X—the same position that B favored in the first suit. As was the case with double liability, A's interests and C's interests cannot be aligned; they favor opposite outcomes. Instead, even though C is now suing B and the two are seemingly adverse, C's interests in the second suit are aligned with what were B's interests in the first suit. Assuming B had sufficient resources and incentives, the second court should find that B adequately represented C. Again, this is not an ideal solution for reasons already discussed. But under the circumstances, there is no viable alternative.

4.9 RESOLVING THE VIRTUAL REPRESENTATION DILEMMA: A SUMMARY

In the preceding pages, the chapter has presented the due process theory of virtual representation. The approach begins with a presumption in favor of the protection of litigants' right to their day in court but permits virtual representation in the extreme situations that involve the danger of double and contradictory liability. Virtual representation should be deemed permissible in these situations because the value in avoiding the problems that arise from these forms of indivisible relief is appropriately found to be greater than the value of maintaining a litigant's right to a day in court, even under the very demanding compelling interest standard imposed by adversary democratic due process. However, the approach does not allow virtual representation in cases of merely inconsistent liability, because the harm to the defendant in these situations is not intolerable as it is in cases of double and contradictory liability. The threat of the double liability and contradictory liability categories of indivisible relief, it should be emphasized, is necessary but not sufficient for virtual representation. There must also be a showing of adequate representation, evaluating whether or not the interests of the representative party and represented party are aligned and whether or not the representative party had sufficient incentive and resources to litigate vigorously.

4.10 SHAPING PROPHYLACTIC MEASURES TO AVOID THE VIRTUAL REPRESENTATION DILEMMA

4.10.1 Procedural Devices Available to Avoid the Virtual Representation Dilemma

This chapter has developed a concept of virtual representation that begins by recognizing the important due process value of litigant procedural autonomy as a baseline, but nevertheless allows for deprivation of that autonomy in the relatively rare situations involving the dangers of double and contradictory liability, assuming a judicial finding of adequate representation. However, virtual representation is little more than a barely acceptable *ex post* Band-Aid for the problem of indivisible relief. Because it necessarily deprives litigants of their day in court, virtual representation should still be considered a disfavored doctrine, albeit an occasionally necessary evil. The problem of virtual representation is a matter of timing. Indivisible relief, by its very nature, is sought in a second lawsuit and conflicts with an existing judgment. If the parties in the second suit had instead been parties in the first suit, there would of course be no problem. By the time the second suit arises, however, there is no way to go back in time and make them parties in the first suit.

Developing a principled and comprehensive account of virtual representation, however, allows us to anticipate when its use will be necessary. If procedures are capable of operating proactively (or prophylactically) in order to prevent the existence of separate actions seeking indivisible relief from occurring in the first place, need for the disfavored doctrine of virtual representation might be minimized or eliminated. The best way to prevent situations of indivisible relief from occurring is, of course, to bring all interested parties together in one suit so that the relief granted is binding on all. This might happen through creative application or modification of our existing joinder and intervention rules or by adopting new rules that directly address the problem of indivisible relief.

There already exist numerous procedural devices available to avoid the virtual representation dilemma. The currently available joinder devices that could conceivably be employed to avoid the harms of indivisible relief include (1) compulsory joinder under Rule 19, (2) intervention under Rule 24, (3) interpleader under either Rule 22 or 28 U.S.C. Section 1335, and (4) class actions under Rule 23(b)(1)(A).[157] Under each Rule, one actor in the process is provided the procedural opportunity in the first suit to include all those conceivably impacted, thereby avoiding the risk of the virtual representation dilemma in as second suit. In the contexts of compulsory joinder, interpleader, and the class action, the defendant in case 1 is capable of triggering the comprehensive adjudicatory process. The plaintiff in case 1 may do so in the class action context, and the potential second-suit party may do so through Rule 24 intervention into case 1. However, the devices do not always work as hoped, because the parties in the first suit either are unaware of the absent party's existence or lack the incentive to bring the outsider into the suit. The goal, then, must be to incentivize the operatives in case 1, in order to avoid the harmful dilemma created by case 2.

4.11 INCENTIVIZING AVOIDANCE OF THE VIRTUAL REPRESENTATION DILEMMA

As previously noted, numerous procedural devices already exist to comprehensively resolve a dispute in the first suit, thereby avoiding the dilemma of virtual representation.[158] The difficulty is in appropriately incentivizing either the litigants or absent parties in the first suit to trigger use of one of those devices. In the discussion that follows, we consider the possibility of developing such devices in the context of each of the permutations of indivisible relief.

4.11.1 Double Liability

Virtual representation can occur in situations of double liability only when the stakeholder in the second suit defends the judgment in the initial suit on the grounds that the absent party's claim is superior to the present claim.[159] It is only in this situation that a present party could even conceivably be said to have adequately represented the precluded nonparty by vigorously asserting the nonparty's arguments. A necessary condition for this to happen is that the stakeholder is aware of the absent party's claim during the initial suit; otherwise, he cannot reasonably be expected to present the absent party's arguments. In light of this knowledge, one might wonder why the stakeholder does not simply invoke interpleader or compulsory joinder to allow the second claimant to protect herself in suit 2. Indeed, this is the exact problem that interpleader was created to resolve, at least when there exists an identifiable stake that constitutes the requisite "res."[160] Similarly, in double liability situations, the absent claimant's joinder is required under Rule 19(a) because a second suit could expose the stakeholder to the risk of double liability.[161] The stakeholder's use of interpleader or compulsory joinder would prevent the possibility of double liability in the future, by including all those potentially affected in the initial suit.

One would hope that the very incentive of avoiding the risk of double liability would sufficiently induce the stakeholder to invoke either interpleader or compulsory joinder. However, in order to increase that incentive, it is advisable to impose the negative consequences for failure to invoke these devices in case 1 on the stakeholder in case 2. Thus, where a stakeholder adequately represents the absent claimant in the initial suit but fails to invoke either interpleader or compulsory joinder in that suit, the stakeholder should be precluded from binding the second claimant by virtual representation. The result would be that the stakeholder would be exposed to the risk of double liability in case 2. This assignment of risk, one could hope and expect, would force the hand of the stakeholder in case 1 to invoke the applicable multiparty devices.

Incentive-shifting mechanisms in civil procedure are by no means a new concept. The Supreme Court articulated a very similar scheme over a century ago in *Harris v. Balk*.[162] In that case, Harris owed Balk $180 and Balk owed Epstein $344.[163] Harris and Balk were residents of North Carolina, and Epstein was a resident of Maryland.[164] When Harris was in Maryland on business, Epstein was able to serve Harris with process and, by invoking quasi in rem jurisdiction, obtain an attachment of Harris's debt to Balk (deemed to be Balk's intangible property) requiring Harris to pay Epstein the $180 which Harris owed Balk as partial payment of the $344 Balk allegedly owed Epstein.[165] Due to a difference in state laws, once Harris returned to North Carolina, Balk was able to obtain a separate judgment against Harris for the same $180.[166] Harris appealed to the Supreme Court, arguing that he had already discharged his debt to Balk by paying it to Balk's creditor, Epstein, in the Maryland suit. The Court initially noted that "[i]t ought to be and it is the object of courts to prevent the payment of any debt twice over."[167] The Court went on to state, however, that Harris had a duty to inform Balk of the Maryland litigation at the time it was taking place, thereby enabling Balk to defend his rights against Epstein's claim against him in the Maryland suit.[168] The Court added that if Harris had failed to notify Balk of Epstein's Maryland suit, it would be proper to expose Harris to the possibility of double liability by forcing him to pay his debt a second time.[169] This was ultimately not required because Balk had been aware of the Maryland litigation and had chosen not to intervene.[170] Based on this knowledge on the part of Balk, the Court held that the Maryland suit barred Balk's suit to recover the original $180 debt from Harris.[171] As with the risk assignment system proposed here, the scheme in *Harris* apportioned risk based on who possessed information that could have prevented the problem.

Double liability may still arise in situations where the stakeholder is unaware of the absent claimant's existence. In such a situation there can of course be no case for virtual representation because no party in case 1—neither the stakeholder nor the first claimant—is in a position to present the absent claimant's arguments. However, incentive-shifting mechanisms still may be useful to combat indivisible relief. If the absent claimant is aware of the original suit and fails to seek Rule 24 intervention, his suit could be barred. Were such an incentivization system made clear at the outset, presumably the absent party would have been induced to seek intervention in case 1. When the stakeholder is unaware of the absent claimant and the absent claimant is unaware of the original suit, however, there exists no way to avoid double liability.

4.11.2 Contradictory Liability

Contradictory liability, it should be recalled, occurs when a person is judicially ordered, in different litigations, both to do X and not do X. Under these circumstances, there is no action the person can take without violating one court judgment or the other. As noted previously, this is the most severe and unfair form of indivisible relief.

Where no identifiable stake is involved, the remedy of interpleader is of course unavailable. However, if at the time of the first suit the party potentially subject to the risk of contradictory liability is aware of the existence of an absent party who might create that risk, it is appropriate to force that party to bring in the absent party as a necessary party through Rule 19 compulsory joinder.[172] However, where the party subject to the risk of contradictory liability is unaware of the absent party's existence but the absent individual or entity is aware of the initial suit's existence, it makes sense to shift the risk to that absent party. Instead of employing virtual representation in a subsequent suit, we could preclude subsequent suits based solely on the fact that the absent person had knowledge of the original suit, yet failed to intervene under Rule 24.

The constitutionality of this type of mandatory intervention scheme is somewhat controversial and therefore must be briefly examined. Mandatory intervention is a concept in which a party is required to intervene in order to protect her legal right—a sort of "use it or lose it" doctrine. The Court addressed the issue in *Martin v. Wilks*.[173] In that case, after a group of African American firefighters received a consent decree from the City of Birmingham granting them advanced seniority, a group of White firefighters brought a suit alleging that the decree indirectly discriminated against them by comparative demotion.[174] The Court addressed the argument that the White firefighters' suit should be barred based on their failure to intervene in the original action.[175] Rejecting the argument, the Court stated:

> The parties to a lawsuit presumably know better than anyone else the nature and scope of relief sought in the action, and at whose expense such relief might be granted. It makes sense, therefore, to place on them a burden of bringing in additional parties where such a step is indicated, rather than placing on potential additional parties a duty to intervene when they acquire knowledge of the lawsuit.[176]

This reasoning counsels in favor of placing the initial onus on the existing parties: they must join outsiders or risk a second suit challenging their victory or loss. The argument breaks down, however, when it is only the absent individuals who realize their own relevance to the suit. In *Wilks*, the Court's reasoning is based on the assumption that existing parties will have superior knowledge about who should be in the case. Whether or not the absent person is the sole actor to have actual knowledge of the first case's relevance to her, however, is simply a question of fact. While making this factual determination may be difficult, as noted by the Court in *Wilks*,[177] incurring this difficulty is a small price to pay for avoiding the danger of contradictory liability. Furthermore, although the reasoning of *Wilks* is generally instructive, Congress overruled its applicability to employment discrimination cases, essentially creating a legislatively dictated mandatory intervention scheme.[178] This statute has not been successfully challenged on constitutional grounds, suggesting that although mandatory intervention is not ideal, it is at least constitutional. In light of the particular danger of contradictory liability, under appropriate circumstances requiring mandatory intervention is permissible.[179]

4.12 CONCLUSION

Despite the Court's recent rejection of virtual representation in *Taylor*, the doctrine has never received a comprehensive constitutional analysis. This chapter has sought to provide that analysis. After deriving the day-in-court ideal from the foundational American political commitment to democracy, the chapter employs adversary democratic due process to create a workable, reasonable, and highly restricted theory of virtual representation. Although the day-in-court ideal should be adhered to in nearly all situations, when a litigant faces a risk of double or contradictory liability there are compelling reasons to preclude the subsequent suit. If we can be assured that the precluded nonparty has at least received paternalistic protection of her substantive rights through adequate representation, use of virtual representation is permissible in order to avoid the even more serious constitutional harms to which both double and contradictory liability give rise.

A far better solution, however, is to avoid the problematic situations of indivisible relief from occurring in the first place. This can be partially achieved by the use of existing joinder and intervention rules. In addition, the chapter proposes a system of risk allocation in cases of indivisible relief by imposing the risk on the party who failed to attempt to prevent it. It should be noted that this proposal is preliminary in nature and intended more to start rather than end the conversation. Despite the extreme problems that may result from indivisible relief, the topic has received little scholarly or judicial treatment. The concept is hinted at in nearly every multiparty tool, yet no one has presented a comprehensive analysis of the topic. Although this chapter has focused primarily on virtual representation as a means to combat indivisible relief, it can be hoped that the chapter's greatest contribution is its effort to bring indivisible relief into the due process conversation in a coherent manner.

5
PRIVATE CONTINGENT FEE LAWYERS, PUBLIC POWER, AND PROCEDURAL DUE PROCESS

5.1 INTRODUCTION

Imagine a system in which all police work is performed not by governmental employees but by private contractors, hired by the government, who are paid by the arrest: the more arrests, the more money they receive. Can anyone seriously imagine that such a system would be either constitutional or in any way consistent with the values of the American political system? It is certainly doubtful.

Now imagine a system in which prosecutors receive no set salary but instead are paid by the success of their prosecutions: the more convictions that are obtained, the more money they make. Once again, it is difficult to conceive that such a system would be held to satisfy the requirements of either legal ethics or due process. When the coercive power of the state is asserted against private individuals or entities, our legal, constitutional, and political traditions have been appropriately construed to demand that those exercising that power ground their decisions and conduct in a good faith assessment of the public interest, rather than in considerations of the narrow focus of personal self-interest.[1] Surely, the skepticism inherent in adversary democratic due process developed and invoked throughout this book would not tolerate the creation of such suspiciously perverse incentives on the state's assertion of its awesome coercive power against private citizens.

In contrast, when private individuals or entities act on their own behalf rather than on behalf of the state, the nation's tradition of liberal procedural autonomy, grounded in the protective precepts of adversary democracy, not only permits but also actually encourages them to establish and seek to realize their personal goals and to advance their personal welfare. To be sure, none but the most libertarian among us would suggest that individuals should be permitted to fashion or attempt to achieve these goals free from concern for or regulation in the public interest. None of us lives in a social vacuum. However, within the outer contours of the needs of the community (and the dividing line between the two is concededly a murky one which has been the subject of long and often bitter debate), basic values of liberal pluralism dictate recognition of the fact that individuals are integral wholes worthy of respect within our constitutional democracy.[2] As such, they are thought to operate within a sphere of litigation autonomy which permits them to choose their own legal strategies to vindicate their substantive rights. In so doing they will naturally often seek to satisfy their personal needs as well as protect and foster their own interests. As argued throughout this book, the foundational political theory of adversary democracy is fashioned to permit individuals to protect their own interests through resort to governmental organs, including the judiciary.

Because of an inherent skepticism of the motivations of all others, including government agents, adversary democracy vests exclusively in the individual herself the decision of who represents her in her interactions with the courts. It is only due to a truly compelling countervailing interest that this foundational democratic interest can be forced to give way. The theory is grounded in an inherent (and often fully justified) skepticism about government's willingness or ability to assure fair treatment to the private citizen absent the citizen's ability to protect his own interests. Both adversary democracy and procedural due process are grounded in skepticism about and fear of governmental behavior, but it is important not to ignore the subtle differences in the degree of that skepticism appropriate under specific circumstances. At the very least, government actors must be committed to some minimal level of neutral pursuit and protection of the public interest. The moment a governmental actor engaging in coercive legal action against a private individual is deemed not to be pursuing the public interest but instead pursuing primarily her own financial interest, the limits imposed by the adversary democratic version of due process are violated. For then the last line of the individual's protection—the governmental actor's good faith pursuit of the public interest—will have been breached.

To be sure, on occasion it will be difficult to separate public from private interests. After all, it would be unreasonable to expect governmental actors to completely ignore their own personal interests, any more than one could expect that of any individual. However, our democratic process demands more of public servants than it does of private actors. At the very least, then, where there exists an indisputable profit incentive that will be necessarily and contingently implicated by the public servant's success or failure, the Due Process Clause has been violated.

It is for these reasons that our constitutional tradition has long acknowledged the public-private dichotomy embodied in the so-called "state action" requirement of the Fourteenth Amendment.[3] Only the state is required to assure its citizens due process of the law and equal protection. Nothing in the Constitution itself requires private citizens to do so.[4] When the state acts coercively on behalf of the polity, however, all of the Constitution's array of protections and restrictions are triggered. As an ideal, at least,[5] when those who act on behalf of the state impose their coercive authority on private actors, they are deemed to be imbued with the fiduciary obligation to assess and pursue the public interest, rather than to foster primarily their own personal needs.[6]

As already noted, in a practical sense it will often be difficult, if not impossible, to police the motivations of those who wield state power. Any attorney who acts on behalf of the government may secretly hope that her effective enforcement of state interests will lead to fame, fortune, or at least a promotion. The same is at least conceivably true of a number of judges, who may believe that resolving a case in a certain manner may influence their chances of promotion to a higher court. Those facts, however, do not justify the failure to impose at least prophylactic structural limits on the pathological private incentives of those who exercise state power.[7] The difference is that one can be easily avoided, while the others cannot.

This fundamental precept of American political and constitutional theory is severely threatened by the relatively modern trend toward governmental use of private contingency fee-based attorneys to enforce state law and seek either civil damage awards or civil penalties against private actors. As any lawyer knows, under a contingency fee arrangement, an attorney effectively bets everything on attainment of victory in litigation. If she wins, she recovers a predetermined percentage of the award. If she loses, however, she receives absolutely nothing. In recent years, state governments have increasingly resorted to this practice in their efforts to pursue "big money" claims against alleged tortfeasors.[8]

In the private sphere, the contingency fee practice has much to recommend it. It enables victims of legal wrongs to vindicate their rights and recover legally authorized damages when they would otherwise be unable to do so because of the prohibitively expensive cost of lawyering. In this way, the contingency fee arrangement can be thought simultaneously to make victims whole and, as a byproduct, enforce societal proscriptions on governmental, individual, or corporate behavior. The situation is very different, however, when private contingency fee attorneys are vested with authority to vindicate the interests of the state through the litigation process. In this instance, we are presented with a dangerous mixture of public power and private motivation, effectively leaving us with the worst of all possible worlds.

To comprehend the problematic nature of the situation brought on by government's use of private contingent fee lawyers, one need only hypothesize a situation in which governmental prosecutors are given a financial arrangement in which they are to be paid when and only when they obtain a conviction. It is difficult to imagine an arrangement more rife with danger, cynicism, and potential abuse of power than this one. Such an arrangement is therefore wholly unacceptable in a constitutional democracy, where government is accountable to the electorate and where an implicit social contract restricting governmental power controls the relationship between government and the individual. And it is important to note that this is so, *even if, in a particular instance, all stipulate that the attorney did nothing improper.* Actual impropriety in a specific instance will generally be difficult to unearth, even when it exists. Indeed, it is quite conceivable that the government attorney herself would be unaware of the impact of the financial motivational twist on her behavior. It is for that reason that we generally establish *prophylactic* rules to ensure neutrality and adherence to the public interest by our governmental officers. Thus, were a government prosecutor to be paid if and only if her prosecutorial efforts are successful, such a practice would no doubt be deemed unethical,[9] as well as a violation of due process.[10]

There are, of course, two important distinctions between the hypothetical governmental prosecutor on the one hand and the private contingent fee attorneys suing on behalf of the government on the other. One is that the contingent fee lawyers are private individuals, not state officers. The other is that the contingent fee attorneys will function in civil cases, rather than criminal cases. Neither distinction, however, should make any difference in determining either the ethical acceptability or constitutionality of the practice. As to the former distinction, established Supreme Court doctrine makes clear that when government delegates to private agents authority traditionally exercised by government, those agents are to be treated as agents of the state for purposes of the Constitution's state action requirement.[11] As to the latter distinction, it is important to note that the Fourteenth Amendment's Due Process Clause[12] has been held to apply to civil litigation, as well as to criminal cases.[13] As a textual matter, the clause's protections are unambiguously triggered by the loss of property, as well as liberty. When government is enmeshed in a suit with private individuals or entities, the liberal democratic social contract, constitutionally embodied in the Due Process Clause, is at stake, even when the proceeding is entirely civil.[14] Therefore governmental attorneys even in civil cases have the obligation to respect and pursue the public interest in a manner that does not control the behavior of attorneys acting on behalf of private clients.[15] In any event, many civil suits brought by government are inherently coercive in nature, whether in the form of civil fines or punitive damages. In these situations, the role of the Due Process Clause becomes even more significant.

In sum, government's use of private contingent fee attorneys in civil litigation is (1) inconsistent with the nation's democratic tradition, (2) unethical, and (3) a violation of the Due Process Clause. The remainder of this chapter articulates and explains the political and constitutional arguments implicit in this thesis.

5.2 GOVERNMENTAL USE OF CONTINGENCY FEE ATTORNEYS: DEVELOPMENT OF THE PRACTICE

5.2.1 Growth and Rationale

While states have employed contingency fee contracts in litigation for many years, controversy has developed in recent years because of states' use of them in major tort litigation.[16] Most prominent of its uses was in the area of tobacco litigation, where most state attorneys general retained private attorneys on a contingency basis in their suits against the tobacco companies.[17] In addition to tobacco litigation, states have employed the device in such mass tort contexts as environmental harm and lead paint litigation.[18] In recent years, "trial lawyers representing public clients on contingency fee are suing businesses for billions over matters as diverse as prescription drug pricing, natural gas royalties and the calculation of back tax bills."[19]

While there may exist a variety of explanations for the development of the practice, the most obvious are the political and financial advantages to all involved—except, of course, for the defendants. In the words of one commentator:

> Trial lawyers love these deals. Even aside from the chance to rack up stupendous fees, they confer a mantle of legitimacy and state endorsement on lawsuit crusades whose merits might otherwise appear chancy. Public officials find it easy to say yes because the deals are sold as no-win, no-fee. They're not on the hook for any downside, so wouldn't it practically be negligent to let a chance to sue pass by?[20]

Another conceivable motivation for the use of private contingency fee attorneys is the attorney general's "need to bypass state legislatures."[21] According to Professor David Dana, "[b]oth critics and defenders of the AGs' use of contingency fee agreements concur that had the AGs sought legislative funding to hire a staff to prosecute the tobacco litigation or to pay outside lawyers on a pay-as-you-go, hourly basis, they would have been rebuffed."[22] The possibility of this strategy has led to separation-of-powers challenges against the contingency fee practice.[23] A number of states have passed legislation authorizing the practice.[24] Professor John Coffee, however, has questioned whether use of private contingency fee attorneys is truly designed to circumvent legislative authority. He has suggested that even if funding could have been secured through the legislative process, the attorneys general would have avoided it because the risks of losing the litigations would have been too great.[25] In response, Professor Dana asserts that Coffee's explanation "raises the same sort of democracy concerns as the pure legislative bypass explanation [because] by allowing AGs to cloud accountability for their actions, use of outside contingency fee counsel is [arguably] undemocratic inasmuch as transparency and accountability are regarded as core democratic attributes."[26]

5.2.2 Implications for Public Policy: Is It a Good Idea?

Professor Dana has pointed out that "[e]ven if we assume that AGs' use of contingency fee lawyers was not stupid, corrupt, or undemocratic, it does not mean the practice is a good idea overall."[27] If one were to consider the issue purely as a matter of concrete public policy, strong arguments can be fashioned on both sides. On the positive side, one could argue that the practice enables states to vindicate the public interest by policing illegal corporate behavior in ways they would be unable to do absent the practice. In this sense, states could be compared to the private plaintiffs who benefit from the use of contingency fee lawyers in situations when they would be unable to seek to vindicate their legal rights and interests otherwise because of prohibitive costs. Moreover, as already noted, even were we to assume that states, unlike financially strapped private plaintiffs, could come up with the necessary funds, the state's use of private contingency fee attorneys could avoid the risk to the state treasury—and therefore to the taxpayers—that would ensue from litigation failure. On the negative side of the ledger, it could be argued that "the public interest that the AGs purportedly seek to advance . . . will not always be best served by maximizing the states' monetary relief. Sometimes public interest considerations dictate dropping litigation altogether or focusing on nonmonetary relief more than monetary relief,"[28] something that contingency fee lawyers for obvious reasons are unlikely to pursue.

The concern focused on in this chapter, however, does not involve the interests of the state in particular or considerations of public policy in general. It concerns, rather, the constitutional interests of the defendants in such litigation: by creating potentially distorting private incentives for those who exercise the coercive power of the state, the contingency fee practice removes the protections assured to defendants politically by the social contract that inheres in liberal democracy and constitutionally by the Due Process Clause. Both dictate that those wielding public power be restrained by the constitutional and political constraints designed to assure good faith governmental pursuit of the public interest. The mistrust of government officers acting out of personal interest is the very essence of adversary democracy. While use of a contingency arrangement fits well within the nation's traditions of private action, when utilized by the state against private citizens, it is inconsistent with foundational precepts of constitutional democracy, and inconsistent with the constitutional dictate of procedural due process.

The constitutional and political elements of the attack on governmental use of contingency fee lawyers are inherently intertwined. Thus, before exploring the specific constitutional implications of the practice, it is first necessary to examine the public-private dichotomy that inheres in the traditions of American political theory. It is therefore to that analysis that the discussion now turns.

5.3 LIBERAL DEMOCRACY, STATE ACTION, AND THE PUBLIC-PRIVATE DICHOTOMY: IMPLICATIONS FOR PRIVATE CONTINGENCY FEE ARRANGEMENTS

5.3.1 The Political Theory of the Public-Private Distinction

Although democracy is by no means an unambiguous concept, at some level it necessarily assumes something about the individual citizens who make up society. Even the most communitarian form of democracy could not constitute a truly democratic society absent a commitment to the individual's ability to make certain choices on her own behalf. The more liberal versions of democratic theory, however, are explicitly grounded in precepts of individual pluralism and at least some level of autonomy: the individual necessarily retains some zone of autonomous behavior free from the state's control. This commitment may be explained by either of two non-mutually inconsistent rationales, what can be labeled the optimistic and pessimistic alternatives. The optimistic rationale (associated with liberal democratic theory) encourages a sphere of individual choice on both Kantian and utilitarian grounds. The former posits the value of individual choice as a foundational good, deriving from the assumption of the individual as an integral whole, worthy of respect. From the utilitarian perspective, recognition of a sphere of individual choice fosters personal and intellectual development, thereby assisting the individual in fulfilling her capabilities.[29] This describes the essence of liberal democratic theory. As this book has argued throughout, the pessimistic perspective on democratic theory dictates that individuals are invested with authority to pursue their own interests because otherwise those interests may never be respected by those in power.[30]

Whatever the underlying theoretical rationale, individual autonomy could not exist at any meaningful level in a constitutional democracy absent recognition of some form of dichotomy between the public and private spheres. Because of the mythical but nevertheless foundational social contract between government and individual inherent in liberal theory, some constitutional restrictions must be imposed on government to assure that individuals are treated fairly. To impose the very same restrictions on the individual would effectively gut the sphere of pluralistic choice essential to the individual's role in a liberal democratic society. We are, then, presented with the foundational premise of liberal democracy: individuals must possess the discretionary authority to treat others in ways that government may not employ. For example, the First Amendment freedom of association guarantees that individuals may shun others for no reason other than the political views of the shunned individual.[31] This discretion is denied to government, however, because of the First Amendment rights of the individual that government wishes to shun.[32] In the privacy of her home, the individual may shun others for no reason other than their race—power that the Fourteenth Amendment's Equal Protection Clause clearly denies to government. The Fourteenth Amendment's "state action" requirement is appropriately seen as the Constitution's means of recognizing and implementing this public-private dichotomy. While the state is prohibited from depriving individuals of their constitutional rights, with rare exception (for example, the Thirteenth Amendment's prohibition on slavery) no similar restrictions are constitutionally placed on private individuals or entities.[33]

Several respected commentators have posited that, at least as a descriptive matter, it is incoherent to believe in a sphere of private authority distinct from the public sphere.[34] According to this argument, today the state has so pervaded all aspects of existence that to the extent the state tolerates behavior, it is effectively condoning and facilitating that behavior. One may question the "sweeping assertion that individuals engaged in ordinary activities on their own behalf, far removed from the business of government, are wielding the power of the state—as though those individuals wore uniforms and badges—merely because their conduct is not prohibited by state law or protected by the Constitution."[35] The main problem with this perspective on state action is that it confuses what is designed to be a normatively structured framework with a purely descriptive one. The public-private dichotomy embodied in the state action requirement is not designed necessarily to empirically reflect social and political reality. Rather, it is designed to implement the divergent dictates of liberal democratic theory.[36] To function effectively as a liberal democracy, a society must simultaneously restrict government and empower private actors.[37] Except perhaps in the most unambiguous cases, then, the issue of state action turns not on a descriptive perspective but rather on a normative effort to insulate a sphere of private pluralism from the restrictive burdens of constitutional limitations—the very result we seek when the state, rather than a private individual or entity, is the actor.

5.3.2 Private Autonomy and Contingency Fee Arrangements for Private Clients

Private litigation represents the classic illustration of the normative, rather than descriptive nature of the public-private dichotomy. Were one to adopt a purely descriptive view, one could fashion a strong argument that the entire litigation system is inherently intertwined with the state and therefore an exercise of purely public power. In a certain sense, this conclusion is completely accurate.[38] In another sense, however, while attorneys operating within the litigation system are deemed officers of the court and subject to applicable legal and ethical restrictions, within those confines their allegiance is solely to their clients. In deciding both whether and how to pursue their clients' claims, private attorneys representing private clients make their choices solely on the basis on the interests of those clients. They are not required to inquire whether a particular strategic choice is in the public interest or beneficial for society as a whole. Instead, they base those decisions on their assessment of their clients' best interests, much as the individual may do for herself when her private concerns are implicated.[39]

As explained throughout this book, this is the underlying premise of adversary democracy. To be sure, in pursuing their clients' interests they may simultaneously—if incidentally or collaterally—be fostering the broader public interest by enforcing legislative policy to police a certain segment of corporate behavior. Indeed, such vindication of private rights is often contemplated by government as a means of implementing public policy and legislative proscriptions on illegal behavior.[40] But if so, it is largely as an incidental byproduct of their representation of their clients' interests.[41]

If one were to attempt to utilize a purely descriptive approach to the public-private divide, one might reasonably conclude that in representing a private client in the litigation system, an attorney is appropriately characterized as part of the state. In certain contexts, this is exactly the conclusion the Supreme Court has reached.[42] At the same time, the very nature of the adversary system precludes a finding that attorneys acting on behalf of private clients are state officers in *all* respects. Such a conclusion would be inconsistent with the liberal, pluralistic, and individualistic values underlying the public-private dichotomy in the first place. The litigation system is one means by which a private individual or entity resorts to governmental processes to vindicate her rights and interests. That the state makes such processes available to the individual is itself part of the liberal social contract.[43] To collapse the state and the private actors into the same category, while arguably a reasonable observation of modern realities, would undermine the very premises of liberal democratic society.

Once it is assumed that private attorneys acting on behalf of private clients are appropriately viewed predominantly not as state actors but rather as facilitators of private actors' ability to further their legally protected rights and pragmatic interests through resort to governmental processes, the constitutional legitimacy of the use of contingent fee arrangements can be seen as wholly appropriate. By enabling private actors to sue in situations where the cost of representation would otherwise be prohibitive, such an arrangement fosters private actors' ability to further state policies and interests by enforcing their private rights created by substantive law. Nor does such a structure in any way pervert the attorneys' proper incentives, since the all-or-nothing nature of contingency fees merely provides the attorney with an even stronger incentive to increase her client's recovery, thereby performing the attorney's proper function of serving her client's best interests.[44]

The purpose of this description of the role of the private attorney acting on behalf of private individuals or entities, its relationship to the public-private dichotomy, and its implications for the use of contingent fee arrangements has been to lay the groundwork for drawing a contrast to the moral, political, and constitutional obligations of full-time government attorneys. The analysis now turns to that issue.

5.4 THE PUBLIC-PRIVATE DICHOTOMY AND GOVERNMENT ATTORNEYS

5.4.1 Ethical and Political Limitations on Government Attorneys in Criminal Prosecutions

It has long been established that government prosecutors owe primary responsibility to the public interest, rather than to either their own personal concerns or a narrow, advocacy-based perception of their client's interest. In an often-cited passage, the Supreme Court in *Berger v. United States* wrote: "The United States Attorney is the representative not of an ordinary party to a controversy, but of a sovereignty whose obligation to govern impartially is as compelling as its obligation to govern at all; and whose interest, therefore, in a criminal prosecution is not that it shall win a case, but that justice shall be done."[45] Because attorneys for the government act on behalf of, not simply a self-interested private actor seeking to maximize personal gain and minimize personal loss, but rather the public entity who acts on behalf of all of us, their incentives must be different from those who do represent private actors. Occasions will arise where the public interest is not served by a conviction; there are cases in which a prosecutor, acting in the public interest, may determine that conviction of a particular defendant will not advance societal goals. This may be due to the prosecutor's serious doubt about the defendant's guilt, a relative choice that limited prosecutorial time should be devoted to more egregious criminals, or simply that the public interest would not be served by continued prosecution. These same considerations may influence the prosecutor's initial decision whether to proceed with a prosecution in the first place.

These are not considerations that either should or generally do influence the strategic litigation choices made by private attorneys acting on behalf of private clients. Creation of a distinctly personal incentive on the part of a prosecutor to pursue conviction would threaten prosecutorial pursuit of the public interest. Thus, the very idea that prosecutors could be subjected to an arrangement in which they make substantial money if they obtain a conviction but no money if they fail to do so would seriously undermine the public-regarding nature of a prosecutor's function.

The following implications can be reasonably drawn from the Supreme Court's conclusion in *Berger*: (1) at least in a prosecutorial setting, any sort of payment structure whereby prosecutors are paid solely for convictions is ethically and politically unacceptable; (2) the same political and ethical concerns about the need for government attorneys in criminal prosecutions to focus on considerations of public interest, rather than narrow interests of client success, apply with equal force when government attorneys participate in civil litigation; and (3) when government delegates the power to litigate claims on the government's behalf to private attorneys, those attorneys are subject to the exact same ethical and political limitations as are full-time government attorneys.[46] While there should be little that is controversial in any of these postulates, it is appropriate at this point to posit and then respond to conceivable criticisms of each of these assertions.

5.4.2 The Importance of Prophylactic Restrictions on Prosecutorial Motivation

It is difficult to imagine anyone seriously questioning either the wisdom or propriety of an unwavering ban on prosecutorial contingent payment arrangements in criminal cases. However, it is appropriate to consider the argument that any such prohibition would be futile since as a practical matter it is impossible to expunge all potential motivations of personal gain on the part of prosecutors. For example, even if we were to prohibit financial rewards for successful convictions, other personal motivations, particularly professional advancement, would remain in play. Public choice theory, it could be argued, posits that all governmental choices are, at some level, based on motivations of personal gain.[47] However, even if this sweeping assertion were assumed to be true (a fact that is by no means self-evident), it does not follow that reasonable efforts need not be made to reduce the dangers as much as possible. Indeed, while James Madison was all too aware of the dangers of factions and interest groups,[48] this recognition not only failed to deter him from seeking to control their invidious consequences, they actually spurred him to establish prophylactic structures of separation of powers within the governmental framework to reduce the harms to which they could give rise. That perhaps such prophylactic, formalized restrictions fail to avoid the problem completely in no way logically implies they are useless or should therefore be abandoned.

The same is true of prophylactic protections of judicial independence provided for in Article III of the Constitution. Section 1 of Article III provides federal judges with protections of their salary and tenure, in an obvious effort to insulate them from the political pressures that would inevitably result otherwise. Does this suggest that federal judges will be subject to no other improper personal motivations in deciding cases? Of course not. Judges may well still be motivated by their desire to have possible future political careers, to seek advancement within the judiciary, or to avoid retaliatory legislative restrictions on their jurisdiction. It surely does not follow, however, that there are no important benefits to judicial independence to be obtained by imposition of the formalized, prophylactic constitutional guarantees of judicial independence.

The same analysis applies with equal force to a formalized prohibition on contingent pay schemes for prosecutors. It is certainly true that such a prohibition will not avoid all extraneous or diverting personal incentives. But few could doubt that existence of such a prophylactic prohibition goes far in removing the most blatant and obvious influence distracting prosecutors from their obligation to the public interest.

5.4.3 The Elusive Nature of the Public Interest

While the prohibition on contingent payment arrangements for prosecutors may be deemed an appropriate means of focusing prosecutors on pursuit of the public interest, some have argued that there is no such thing as the public interest. What modern civic republicans refer to as evil-minded "pluralists" and others simply refer to as adherents of Adam Smith have argued that there is no such thing as the public interest, apart from the sum of all separate individual interests.[49] From this perspective, it could be argued that it is meaningless to attempt to force government attorneys to focus on pursuit of the public interest, because of the simple fact that there is no such thing.[50]

In the context of the present inquiry, it is neither necessary nor desirable to reconsider the long-standing debate over the tensions among public choice theory, individual pluralism, and civic republicanism. Other portions of this book have already done that. Whether or not one is somehow able to fashion a concept of the public interest that is distinct from an aggregation of individual interests, it is clear that a distinction exists between a government attorney's motivation to do justice as she perceives it on the one hand and an attorney's motivation to further her own personal economic interests on the other. In attempting to shape and focus prosecutorial motivations, then, the key is not what the public interest actually *is* but rather what it *is not*. Whatever the public interest is, it is most assuredly something different from the attorney's concern for his personal financial interests. Thus, a formalized prohibition on contingent payment arrangements for prosecutors has only the modest goal of removing one narrow but potentially invidious incentive from their strategic decision-making process.

5.4.4 The Civil-Criminal Connection

Even if one is forced to concede—as I believe one must—that criminal prosecutors may not properly be paid on the basis of some form of contingent payment arrangement that turns on the rate of conviction, the argument could nevertheless be fashioned that these considerations are inapplicable in governmental civil litigation. The argument might proceed in the following fashion: while prosecutors who have the power to bring to bear the government's resources to deprive private actors of their liberty should not be overtly influenced by considerations of personal financial gain, civil litigation involving the government is a strikingly different situation. In civil cases, the argument proceeds, the government stands in no different position from any private litigant. A private actor's liberty is not at stake. Rather than acting coercively as in criminal litigation, the state in civil cases is either defending itself or seeking to be made whole. As a general matter, however, this suggested distinction between state attorney obligations in criminal and civil cases has been rejected.[51]

At the very least, this argument would seem to be inapplicable in civil cases in which the state acts in a purely coercive manner. When the state acts as the plaintiff in civil litigation and seeks to impose purely punitive relief, rather than obtain compensatory relief, technical distinctions between criminal and civil litigation become far less significant. Criminal prosecutions, it should be noted, do not always threaten a private defendant's liberty. Criminal relief often includes the possibility of fines, either instead of or in addition to imprisonment. Indeed, in the case of corporate criminal defendants, the only possible punishment is financial. Even though only property rights are at stake in such situations, the inherently coercive nature of the action triggers the social contract inherent in liberal democracy: those imbued with public power are prohibited from acting out of motivations of private gain (to the extent it is reasonably possible to ascertain and prevent such a situation, of course). This is especially true of government attorneys. As Professor Steven Berenson has persuasively argued, "[i]t is an uncontroversial proposition in mainstream American legal thought that government lawyers have greater responsibilities to pursue the common good or the public interest that their counterparts in private practice, who represent nongovernmental persons and entities."[52] This is due to the fact that "the primacy of private values that exists within traditional conceptions of [an] attorney['s] professional role and responsibility when representing individual clients is based upon 'notions of individual dignity, privacy and autonomy.'"[53] However, "where the represented entity is the government, which is in at least one sense nothing more than the representative of all the people, the supplanting of public values with private ones seems particularly inappropriate."[54] Professor Bruce Green has added to this rationale. He argues that "[f]or government lawyers to hold themselves out to the public as 'seeking justice' when they are simply seeking to achieve partisan ends, regardless of where 'justice' may lie, is cynical and deceitful."[55] According to Green, "[w]hether one views the client as the government, a government agency or a government official, the client is distinctive in at least this respect: the client owes a fiduciary duty to the public."[56]

Professor Sanford Levinson has added an alternative explanation for the unique obligations of the state's lawyers. At some level, he argues, government lawyers are essentially "warranting" their legal arguments, due to their special status as representatives of the state.[57] Neither Green's nor Levinson's arguments, it should be noted, in any way turns on the criminal or civil nature of the proceeding in which the state lawyers are operating.

Judicial decisions have acknowledged that the special ethical obligations of government attorneys apply with equal force in civil cases. For example, Judge Abner Mikva, speaking for a panel of the District of Columbia Circuit, wrote that a government lawyer "is the representative not of an ordinary party to a controversy," as the Supreme Court said long ago in a statement chiseled on the walls of the Justice Department, "but of a sovereignty whose obligation . . . is not that it shall win a case, but that justice shall be done." The Supreme Court was speaking of government prosecutors—but no one, to our knowledge, has suggested that the principle does not apply with equal force to the government's civil lawyers.[58]

5.4.5 Applying the Public Interest Requirement to Private Attorneys Exercising Public Power: The State Action Question

Once it is established that under no circumstances may government attorneys receive payment on a contingency fee basis, it logically follows that private attorneys who have been delegated governmental power are equally restricted. The reasoning in support is simple: when the state, instead of performing traditional state functions itself, delegates to private actors the power to perform those functions, those private actors must be deemed part of the state in their interactions with other private actors. Any other conclusion would allow government to circumvent the political and constitutional limits on its authority simply by authorizing previously private actors to exercise public power. Under these circumstances, society would be left with the worst of both worlds: public power imposed on private citizens, without any of the obligations and limitations on public power normally associated with the dictates of constitutional democracy.

The point can be underscored by reference to an example no doubt recalled by many. Following *Brown v. Board of Education*,[59] certain southern states transferred the authority to operate what had previously been public schools to private actors. Surely, such devious circumvention of constitutional limitations could not be tolerated.[60] The Supreme Court has recognized that the state may not avoid constitutional responsibility merely by transferring its authority to private actors. For example, in *West v. Atkins*,[61] the Supreme Court held that a private physician contracted the Bureau of Prisons operated under of the color of state law when attending to prison inmates. The Bureau, the Court concluded, had a constitutional obligation to provide affirmative medical care to the inmates, which it transferred to the private physician.[62]

One may reasonably question how far this state delegation reasoning goes. Surely, it does not mean that every private actor who contracts with the state automatically is deemed to be acting on behalf of the state for purposes of the Constitution. The question seems to come down to whether the private contractor is performing the very same function it performs for numerous private actors—for example, waste removal. By this standard, perhaps it could be argued that private attorneys acting on behalf of the state, at least in the civil context, should not be deemed to bear all of the responsibilities of a state actor. Private contingency lawyers, after all, perform much the same function for private plaintiffs as well. However, the issue is not that simple. It is a legal and practical reality that the state is never fungible with a private litigant when the state seeks to exercise its awesome power in a coercive manner. For example, a defendant, where appropriate, may file a counterclaim against a private plaintiff. However, due to sovereign immunity it usually may not do so against the state as plaintiff, unless the state has consented to the suit. No private litigant has that option.

Once it is acknowledged that private actors suing on behalf of the state are to be deemed state actors, it logically follows that behavior deemed unacceptable for government attorneys must also be deemed unacceptable for private actors to whom state power has been delegated to perform the identical functions. As already shown, any contingent fee arrangement for government attorneys acting on behalf of the state would unquestionably be deemed an unethical violation of the social contract of liberal democracy, whether in the criminal or civil contexts, because it would confuse the attorney's obligations to pursue of the public interest with her own personal financial gain.[63] The state should not be permitted to circumvent its ethical and political obligations merely by delegating its litigating authority to private attorneys.

5.4.6 The *Qui Tam* Analogy

Professor Michael Dorf has defended the legitimacy of the state's use of private contingent fee lawyers to seek remedial relief through the litigation process by drawing an analogy to *qui tam* actions, which he describes as "a continuing tradition that pre-dates the American republic. . . ."[64] In *qui tam* actions, private plaintiffs are authorized, under defined circumstances, to sue to assert state remedial interests and recover a portion of whatever damages are recovered for harm to the state, even though the private plaintiffs have not suffered injury in fact. Today, as Dorf notes, the *qui tam* action is embodied primarily in the False Claims Act, which authorizes private citizens (described as "relators") to bring suit against defendants who have knowingly defrauded the US government. In order to induce private parties to take such action, the law allows them to recover a percentage of the proceeds from the suit.[65] In this way, "the *qui tam* provision works to provide an incentive for private litigants to expose the fraud and benefit from the recovery."[66] Professor Dorf also accurately notes that "at the time of the Founding . . . even private criminal prosecutions . . . were brought to enforce a wide variety of legal duties."[67]

Professor Dorf's reference to the historical use of *qui tam* actions for criminal purposes may well prove too much. Today, there can be little question that privately run criminal prosecutions would be deemed unacceptable and quite probably unconstitutional. Thus, the mere fact of historical pedigree does not automatically justify continuing constitutional validity. But he is surely correct that, at least in the civil-remedial context, what begin as government claims may under prescribed circumstances be pursued by non-injured private individuals who stand to gain financially from success in litigation. Whether relators under the False Claims Act are nevertheless wholly analogous to private contingency fee lawyers, however, is open to serious question.

The most obvious distinction is that the relator, unlike the private attorneys, is the named party to the suit. This distinction is not merely cosmetic. In holding that relators have standing under Article III, the Supreme Court found in *Vermont Agency of Natural Resources v. United States ex rel. Stevens*[68] that relators satisfy the Article III requirement of injury in fact because they are deemed assignees of the rights of the United States.[69] While the relator does not possess "representational standing" on behalf of the United States, he possesses Article III standing because he is deemed the partial assignee of the rights of the United States.[70] The Court noted that it routinely entertains suits brought by assignees, presumably because once the assignment is made the assignee stands in the legal position of the assignor. Viewed in this manner, relators in *qui tam* actions are suing to vindicate their own personal rights.[71] In this sense, they are far more analogous to private plaintiffs than they are to private contingent fee lawyers representing the state, who, of course, lack Article III standing in every sense.

It might be argued that in addition to recovering for themselves, relators recover also for the United States. Similarly, the relators take only a specified percentage of the damages awarded.[72] In this sense, the relator does appear analogous to private contingency lawyers suing on behalf of the state. For three reasons, however, the analogy ultimately fails. First, the fact that the relators in *qui tam* actions are suing at least in part on their own behalf conceptually distinguishes the two situations. Whether it is or is not appropriate to permit the relator, suing as an injured party to vindicate her rights, also to seek damages on behalf of the United States, the very fact of the relator's injury fundamentally alters the DNA of the contingent fee lawyer situation. In a relative sense, at least, private contingent fee lawyers representing the state in litigation are far more analogous to full time government lawyers representing the state in litigation, and, as previously shown, it is clear that such lawyers could not legitimately be paid on a contingency basis.

The full time government lawyer analogy is more apt also because it is far less likely to give rise to unacceptable governmental deception of the electorate. In the *qui tam* context, the very nature of the process makes formally clear to anyone concerned that a private actor motivated by financial concerns, in addition to the government, is a party to the suit against the private defendant. In the case of the contingency fee lawyers, in contrast, the sole named litigant is the state itself, necessarily conveying the message that it acts as the representative of the people and is therefore focused primarily on pursuit of the public interest, rather than the narrow financial concerns of private actors.

Finally, the *qui tam* analogy is inapplicable for an additional—and ultimately dispositive—reason: tradition. *Qui tam* actions are deemed legitimate today, despite the serious questions of separation-of-powers under both Articles III and II,[73] largely because they have existed for such a long period in English and American practice. In *Vermont Agency of Natural Resources*, the Court, in upholding *qui tam* actions, emphasized their concept's "long tradition . . . in England and the American colonies."[74] It pointed to their origins "around the end of the 13th century, when private individuals who had suffered injury began bringing actions in the royal courts on both their own and the Crown's behalf."[75] It further noted that such actions "appear to have been as prevalent in America as in England...."[76] One may seriously question, then, whether such actions would have been considered legal had they only recently been created.

One might reasonably question the legitimacy of blind reliance on tradition to determine modern constitutional validity. Our "tradition" includes such unfortunate practices as slavery and near genocide of the Native American population. The mere fact of tradition, then, amounts to something akin to proof by adverse possession—hardly a way in which modern constitutional analysis should be conducted.[77] Yet rightly or wrongly, tradition has played an important role in modern constitutional law.[78] If one were to reject such a significant role for tradition, one today might well dismiss *qui tam* actions as unconstitutional procedures in countless ways. However, if it is fundamentally tradition that is preserving the *qui tam* action in modern times, then of course it cannot be mindlessly bootstrapped into a rationale for use of an entirely new, equally suspect procedure. Yet that is exactly what Professor Dorf seeks to do. He gleans no valuable normative constitutional insight from *qui tam* actions by some form of constitutional reverse-engineering. Rather, he simply draws an analogy to an accepted practice: because *qui tam* actions are valid, and because use of private contingency fee lawyers by the state is analogous (in certain ways) to a *qui tam* action, it logically follows that modern private contingency fee suits on the part of the state are likewise valid.[79] But for reasons already explored,[80] modern contingency fee suits are not analogous to *qui tam* actions. Nevertheless, even if they were, they lack the tradition that quite clearly, in the Court's mind, insulated *qui tam* actions from serious and well-deserved constitutional attack.[81]

5.4.7 The Libertarian Paradox

The argument against the use of private contingent fee lawyers on behalf of the state at some point will likely come up against what can be called "the libertarian paradox." From the libertarian perspective, such an arrangement appears simultaneously to possess both very positive and extremely negative qualities. On the one hand, presumably a libertarian, already instinctively grudging in her concessions to the authority of the state, should be especially concerned that state power not be abused for purposes of personal gain. In the relatively rare instance in which the state should exercise power in the first place, a libertarian would presumably reason, it should do so solely in good faith and within the confines of that grant of power. For example, to the extent libertarians concede to the state the authority to raise and operate armed forces, presumably they would not want decisions about the conduct of the military to be grounded in the personal financial interests of those in charge, regardless of the impact on the welfare of the citizenry as a whole. On the other hand, because libertarians generally believe in the efficiency of the marketplace, where decisions are grounded in economic self-interest, they may well conclude that vesting decision-making authority in private contingent fee attorneys is more likely to produce efficient results than would vesting comparable decision-making power in officials charged with pursuing some mythical public interest. From this perspective, it might be thought that the private contingent fee lawyers are likely to make the wiser choices.

This libertarian perspective, of course, differs significantly from that of a liberal democrat, who recognizes legitimate roles for both the state and the individual. To the extent feasible, the liberal seeks to have governmental decision-making grounded in good faith efforts to ascertain the interest of the community, while vesting in the individual herself autonomy over a wide array of personal choices. Directly mixing considerations of personal financial gain and assessment of the public's interest thus unwisely swims halfway across a river. It would be absurd to assume, *ex ante*, that decisions that financially benefit the individual who exercises state power will automatically benefit society as a whole. Too many cases of cost overruns, contract kickbacks, and patronage deals have proven disastrous to justify such a prediction. Libertarians can reasonably debate the extent of the power to be vested in the state. However, it is unwise, if not reckless, to assume that once the decision has been made to cede the particular authority to the state, the same individual market dynamic thought to operate so effectively in the private sphere would produce the same efficient results in the public sphere.[82]

5.5 CONSTITUTIONAL IMPLICATIONS OF THE STATE'S USE OF PRIVATE CONTINGENCY FEE ATTORNEYS

5.5.1 Placing the Constitutional Argument in Perspective

The analysis has already demonstrated that the modern use by the state of private contingency fee attorneys is inconsistent with the political values and traditions of liberal democratic theory.[83] This section considers the extent to which the practice can actually be deemed unconstitutional. Before undertaking such an analysis, I should emphasize a number of important points. First, while I ultimately conclude that, purely as a matter of normative constitutional theory, the practice should be deemed a violation of the guarantee of procedural due process,[84] I fully acknowledge the controversial nature of my argument. Although I do believe that analogous legal precedent exists on which to support such a conclusion, certainly no prior decision is close to being on all fours, and the argument I make is admittedly on the frontiers of constitutional theory. I put forth my theory, then, more as something of a thought experiment in constitutional theory than anything else. Second, even if one were to reject my constitutional argument, that fact should not detract from my severe criticism of the practice from the perspective of American political and ethical theory.

5.5.2 Procedural Due Process and the Neutral Adjudicator

With those caveats in mind, my due process analysis begins with the doctrinally and conceptually uncontroversial assumption that whatever else procedural due process dictates, the guarantee requires that neither property nor liberty may be revoked absent the provision of a neutral adjudicator. A number of years ago, Professor Lawrence Marshall and I developed an elaborate constitutional defense of this proposition, and this book adds a wholly different perspective to that argument.[85] No other procedures really matter unless the adjudicator is completely free of predispositions in favor of or against one of the parties on grounds unrelated to the merits of the suit. Neither dignitary nor utilitarian concerns underlying procedural due process, therefore, can be deemed satisfied absent a neutral adjudicator. Indeed, the intersecting link between the theory of adversary democracy and the strict requirements of prophylactically neutral adjudicators has been emphasized throughout this book.

The neutral adjudicator requirement's origins are venerable, extending back to Lord Coke's famed opinion in *Dr. Bonham's Case*,[86] where he held that no man may be a judge in his own case. Since that decision, courts—including the US Supreme Court—have consistently held that "officers acting in a judicial or quasi-judicial capacity are disqualified by their interest in the controversy to be decided."[87] Most importantly, the absence of a prophylactically neutral adjudicator is inherently inconsistent with the dictates of adversary democratic due process developed throughout this book. Thus, the requirement of a neutral adjudicator must be applied in a prophylactic manner. For an adjudicator to be deemed to have violated the constitutional requirement of neutrality, actual perversion of the decision-making process in a particular case need not be shown. All that is necessary, rather, is that there exists a "possible temptation to the average [individual] as judge."[88]

5.5.3 Applying the "Adversarial Neutrality" Requirement to the Private Attorney Contingent Fee Arrangement

The neutral adjudicator requirement, of course, has no direct applicability to the constitutionality of the state's use of private contingent fee attorneys. Those who represent the state in litigation act as advocates, not adjudicators.

However, much the same reasoning that deems the absence of a neutral adjudicator a due process violation suggests that attorneys who represent the state must also be made as free as reasonably possible from distorting personally driven motivations.

One can reach this conclusion by drawing a series of probative (and troubling) analogies. First, imagine a situation in which public prosecutors are paid exclusively on a contingent fee basis: they are paid for convictions, but not for acquittals. While I am unaware of any case considering such a situation, there can be little doubt that such a scheme would be found to violate the due process rights of the defendant. The Due Process Clause stands as the constitutional enforcer of the political social contract which inheres in our nation's commitment to constitutional democracy. Moreover, when one adds the foundational "adversary" element to American democratic theory, as this book has argued throughout, the argument for imposing the purifying protections of procedural due process becomes even more important in the case of state prosecutors. The possible presence of inherently distorting motivations is obviously far greater in the case of prosecutors than in the case of a judge. Because such private abuse of coercive public power so fundamentally undermines core notions of governmental good faith in the treatment of its citizens and does so by resort to the judicial process, there should be little doubt that such a practice would constitute deprivation of liberty without due process of law.

Nor should such a distortion of prosecutorial good faith be deemed somehow purified by the presumed neutrality of the judge and jury. Presence of an improper personal motivation on the part of the judge is not purified by the presence of an honest jury, nor is improper jury behavior deemed purified by the presence of a wholly neutral judge. Thus, due process in the criminal context is rightly construed to demand good-faith pursuit of the public interest on the part of *all* levels of the criminal process. This properly includes the prosecutor, as well as the judge and jury.

It is of course true that, unlike the judge and jury, the prosecutor is an advocate on behalf of a client—the government. In an adversary proceeding, a lawyer for the government, similar to attorneys for private clients, needs vigorously to pursue her client's interests. Nevertheless, as shown in earlier discussion,[89] even as an advocate, a lawyer acting on behalf of the state is recognized to possess ethical and moral obligations far beyond those imposed on an attorney acting on behalf of a private client. State lawyers thus bear the obligation of what can appropriately be labeled—somewhat oxymoronically—"adversarial neutrality."[90] Under this dictate, while lawyers acting on behalf of the state will quite naturally assume the role of advocate and make strategic litigation choices on that basis, they simultaneously have an obligation under both due process and the democratic social contract to exercise their authority on behalf of the interests of the public, rather than on behalf of their own potentially competing personal interests.

On occasion, the public interest may be furthered not by continued litigation, not by gaining damage awards, but either by cessation of litigation or acceptance of a settlement which involves a form of nonmonetary relief. To be sure, the fact that state attorneys are to be paid solely out of damages awarded does not automatically imply that they will, in specific cases, base their litigation choices on something other than their good faith perception of the public interest. The same is true of judges who stand to gain from convictions. Nevertheless, the Supreme Court has readily found such schemes unconstitutional, without any requirement of a showing of specific judicial choices made because of that arrangement.[91] Such improper influence on the actual decision would likely be all but impossible to demonstrate in an individual case. Even more importantly, the *appearance* of judicial fairness would be destroyed by the mere existence of the arrangement. In addition, such arrangements are deemed violative of due process, even though it is effectively impossible to avoid other potentially distorting personal motivations, such as the hope for professional advancement. The fact that it is, as a practical matter, impossible to prevent all improper influences surely does not logically lead to the conclusion that the Due Process Clause should not be employed to prevent those which it can feasibly avoid.

The issue becomes admittedly more complex when the scenario is changed to apply to private advocates acting on behalf of the state, rather than those directly employed by the state. As earlier discussion demonstrated, the special status of—and the resulting additional controls on—lawyers acting on behalf of the state is well accepted in subconstitutional contexts, and it should therefore not be difficult to recognize their unique status for constitutional purposes, as well.

The very same logic applies to both criminal prosecutions and coercive civil actions—that is, an action to impose civil penalties—brought by the state against a private actor, where full-time state attorneys who are paid solely on a contingent fee basis represent the state. In the civil context, the constitutional implications may not be as readily obvious as they are in the context of a criminal prosecution, since a defendant's personal liberty is not at stake. Nevertheless, the two situations should be treated similarly, for a number of reasons. Civil coercive actions trigger virtually all of the same political and constitutional concerns implicated by criminal prosecutions. True, civil actions do not implicate the array of special constitutional protections traditionally associated with criminal prosecutions, such as the right to confront accusers or the requirement of proof beyond a reasonable doubt. The fact remains, however, that the potential loss of property, as much as the loss of liberty, triggers the protections of procedural due process.[92] When the state acts coercively against its citizens through the judicial process, its obligations to act in good faith in pursuit of the public interest, rather than out of potentially distorting personal motivations, the dictates of due process are equally applicable. It would, after all, be anomalous to provide a criminal defendant who faces nothing more than the possibility of a fine with greater due process protections than a civil defendant who faces the possibility of substantial civil penalties in an action brought by the state.

The final hypothetical permutation concerns a purely remedial civil action (as opposed to those seeking damages or a fine) brought by the state against a private actor. In this context, we have moved further and further away from the paradigm of the criminal prosecution. Nevertheless, the Court has made clear that procedural due process protections apply even in purely remedial civil actions between private litigants.[93] It would seem that *a fortiori*, procedural due process should apply in civil remedial actions when the state itself is the plaintiff. In purely remedial actions, no less than in coercive civil actions, the defendant's property rights are at stake, and when the judicial process threatens a private actor's property rights, procedural due process protections are triggered. Nevertheless, it is of course true that this fact does not necessarily tell us whether procedural due process requires that state lawyers pursue the public interest, rather than their personal financial concerns. That it does so require, however, flows logically from the following premises, previously established: (1) when either property or liberty is at stake, procedural due process protections apply, and (2) procedural due process requires that those acting on behalf of the state in the course of litigation pursue the public interest as they reasonably understand it, rather than their own personal or financial interests. Once these two premises are accepted, the conclusion is inescapable that the same due process dictate applies, even in civil remedial actions.

Once it is established that in criminal prosecutions, coercive civil actions, or remedial civil actions brought by the state against private actors, due process requires that attorneys acting on behalf of the state may not be paid on a contingent basis, the implications for private contingency fee lawyers acting on the state's behalf would seem to flow inexorably. As demonstrated by the prior analysis of the Fourteenth Amendment's state action requirement,[94] there can be little doubt that when private actors have been delegated the power of the state they simultaneously assume the constitutional, political and ethical obligations imposed on the state. Indeed, there could be no other answer: to allow the state to circumvent its constitutional and political responsibilities by the simple act of delegation of its responsibilities to private actors operating under the direction of the state would render those limitations on state power rather hollow. It would also invite cynical state maneuvering that could hardly be deemed consistent with the values of a constitutional democracy. All this leads to one conclusion: private contingency fee lawyers acting on behalf of the state, no less than full-time state attorneys, may not constitutionally benefit from a financial arrangement that tempts them to make litigation choices that further their personal financial interests, rather than the public interest.

5.5.4 The Fallacy of the "Continued Control" Alternative

Several courts have rejected constitutional challenges to governmental contingent fee schemes as long as government lawyers exercise sufficient and continuing control over the private contingent fee lawyers.[95] But such a restriction hardly serves even to dilute, much less expunge, the serious constitutional defects in the practice. This is so, on both the theoretical and practical levels.

Purely as a practical matter, it is impossible to see how a reviewing court could assure itself, in the individual case, that such control is in fact being exercised. In the words of one commentator, "[b]ecause reviewing courts are generally reluctant to outline particular mechanisms for achieving and maintaining such control, innovation and a desire to do better must come from within the state attorneys general offices themselves."[96] Use of an "honor system" by the very party whose behavior threatens to violate the Constitution can hardly be deemed an effective means of implementing judicial review. The whole idea of using private contingent fee lawyers is to relieve the burden on a state's justice department. For the state even to attempt to exercise sufficient control to avoid the threat to neutrality caused by use of private contingent fee lawyers, it would be forced to devote most or all of the very resources it had sought to avoid expending. Moreover, even if a reviewing court did intend to police the controls exercised by the state's justice department over the private contingent fee lawyers, it is difficult to imagine how the court could do so without seriously threatening to disrupt the state's conduct of the litigation.

In any event, purely as a theoretical matter the concept of "continuing control" is, in this context, incoherent. Presumably, the contingent fee lawyers are hired for the very reason that they will employ their expertise in shaping and conducting litigation. The greater the control the state is forced to exercise over the private attorneys, the less effective the strategy of using them in the first place becomes. Yet the less the state controls the day-to-day operation of the private attorneys, the greater the threat to constitutional values and dictates. Thus, it is far too facile to simply assume—as a number of courts have—that the state's exercise of such control is both possible as a theoretical matter and likely as a practical matter.

5.6 CONCLUSION

It seems to be such a simple, inviting alternative. By using private contingency fee lawyers to pursue its civil claims, the state appears to have the best of all possible worlds: from the state's point of view, it risks nothing, and potentially gains everything. As is often the case when government becomes involved, however, the issue is far from that simple. Private contingent fee attorneys representing private clients, within predetermined procedural rules and ethical boundaries, possess an obligation only to their clients. If their clients win, they win; it is as simple as that. When lawyers act on behalf of the state, however, we have long recognized their special moral and ethical obligations deriving from their association with public power in a constitutional democracy. When government acts within the framework of the legal system, it is not considered the typical adversary within the adversary system. At times, by the government choosing not to take legal action seeking financial relief, society wins, because government is obligated to pursue the best interests of society and at times that may mean bringing no litigation at all, or at least litigation that seeks relief other than the award of damages or financial penalties.

The irony in the state's use of private contingent fee lawyers is that were the state itself to employ such an arrangement for its own lawyers, there should be little doubt that the framework would be ethically improper and a due process violation as well. At the very least, this is true in the case of criminal prosecutions. Those exercising the full force of public power on behalf of the state should not be allowed to have their motivations shaped by stark personal financial considerations. Because procedural due process interests are triggered in purely civil cases as well, and because the unique ethical obligations of state lawyers apply in civil as well as criminal actions, it seems not a dramatic extension to find the state's payment of its lawyers on a contingency basis equally improper and unconstitutional in civil suits.

If there is anything clear about the often murky state action doctrine, it is that what would be unconstitutional for the state to do itself cannot be somehow constitutionally laundered by delegating the very same authority to private actors operating under ultimate state control. Thus, if one accepts each of the steps of the political and constitutional analysis to this point, there can be little doubt that an arrangement in which private lawyers are hired on a contingent fee basis to perform litigation functions traditionally performed by state attorneys is, at the very least, politically improper. It is highly likely that it is unconstitutional as well.

6
DUE PROCESS, FREE EXPRESSION, AND THE ADMINISTRATIVE STATE

The history of American freedom is, in no small measure, the history of procedure.

—*Justice Felix Frankfurter*[1]

6.1 INTRODUCTION: ADVERSARY DEMOCRACY AND THE DUE PROCESS RIGHT TO A NEUTRAL ADJUDICATOR

Procedural due process is, by its nature, a conditional protection. It does not guarantee that government will be unable to deprive an individual of her liberty, her property, or even her life. Instead, it does nothing more than impose the condition that government may deprive an individual of any or all of these valuable interests only if certain procedural requirements have first been satisfied. But for reasons discussed throughout this book, it would not be an overstatement to assert that this constitutional protection serves as a vital element of the foundation of a democratic system. As a matter of political theory, the implicit social contract between government and citizen in a liberal democratic state demands that the government treat its citizens with dignity and respect. If government seeks to take away a citizen's liberty or property for violation of law, the social contract therefore demands that government provide the citizen with a full and fair opportunity to challenge the allegations of legal wrongdoing; anything less would be inconsistent with its contractual obligations toward its citizens. In addition to this concern with due process's foundational grounding in liberal democratic theory, this constitutional protection grows out of the fundamental mistrust of government inherent in our nation's form of adversary democratic theory.

Of all the procedural requirements dictated by the demands of fair procedure, far and away the most important is the requirement of an independent, neutral adjudicator. Absent a truly neutral adjudicator, provision of any and all other procedural protections will be all but meaningless, since a biased or unduly influenced adjudicator is easily capable of ignoring all procedural protections in reaching a decision.

As important as procedural due process is in any case in which an individual's life, liberty, or property is at stake, special procedural considerations come into play when the liberty in danger of revocation is the individual's First Amendment right to speak. The First Amendment right of free expression is simultaneously foundational to the continued viability of American democracy and among the most fragile of all constitutional protections. Even when the right to communicate is vigorously protected, it takes courage to express one's views, and that courage is often easily lost at the first sign of even the slightest governmental intimidation or threat. It is therefore not surprising that both jurists and commentators have recognized a special category of procedural protection, known as "First Amendment 'due process.'"[2] This refers to the requirement that a would-be speaker be provided with procedures that satisfy the constitutional requirements of procedural due process before a claim of First Amendment protection for his expression may be rejected. The best way to view First Amendment due process is as a necessary but not sufficient condition. In other words, rejection of a claim of First Amendment protection absent the provision of the requisite procedures[3] will automatically be deemed unconstitutional. However, the mere fact that such procedural protections have been provided will not automatically be deemed to satisfy the requirements of First Amendment protection. In addition, the determination of whether the expression in question is constitutionally protected must satisfy the substantive requirements of First Amendment jurisprudence.

Due process in general and First Amendment due process in particular face perhaps their most serious threat in the context of the modern administrative state. When viewed through the lens of procedural due process, the fundamental structure of the adjudicatory process takes on a very different—and much more ominous—tenor in the administrative context than in the traditional judicial setting. In the traditional judicial setting, adjudication is presided over by what are for the most part independent judges who have no particular interest in who wins or loses the case. In sharp contrast, in the administrative setting adjudication is conducted and resolved by employees—often high-ranking employees—of the very agency whose existence is justified by the need for regulation and which has decided to institute the particular regulatory proceeding in the first place. Such potential sources of threat to adjudicatory neutrality and independence would never be tolerated in the judicial system. Indeed, given applicable precedent, it seems quite clear that such aberrations from adjudicatory neutrality would be deemed unconstitutional as violations of the Fifth or Fourteenth Amendment's guarantee of procedural due process. Yet to say these aberrations are commonplace in the administrative process would be an understatement.

Indeed, they represent the fundamental characteristics of the modern administrative process. On the basis of a poorly reasoned Supreme Court decision which feebly attempted to distinguish between the due process limits imposed on judicial and administrative adjudication, however, at least for the present time the highly dubious constitutionality of the modern administrative process—especially when free speech rights are implicated—is largely ignored.[4]

Some would no doubt argue that it is too late in the day to bring about so dramatic a constitutional upheaval within the administrative state, and as a practical and descriptive matter, at least, this is likely true. Some would also likely respond that whatever threats to due process values that occur regularly in the administrative state are more than justified by the regulatory benefits to society which flow from its existence. This view is both wrong and dangerous. There is no reason the administrative state cannot operate *both* effectively *and* fairly. Indeed, to the extent the goal of procedural due process is thought to be the utilitarian value of accurate decision making,[5] fair adjudication by a truly neutral adjudicator would seem essential to *both* effectiveness *and* fairness. Overregulation is no better for society than underregulation, and the danger of overregulation increases dramatically when the adjudicator begins the process with a built-in preference for the position taken by the very agency of which she is a part. We could avoid many of the due process dangers of self-interested adjudication simply by substantially increasing both the independence and decision-making power of administrative law judges.

One need not bring about so dramatic an upheaval in the administrative process in order to substantially rectify many of the serious due process problems that plague the modern administrative state. It is possible to view the due process pathologies of the administrative state on different levels of constitutional harm. Of course, if one were to accept the frontal due process attack on the fundamental operation of the administrative process, this multileveled analysis would be unnecessary; the process, as currently constituted, would be invalidated. But assuming for the moment that the foundational due process attack will be viewed as a bridge too far, it is important to recognize that there are especially harmful constitutional pathologies that are confined to much narrower forms of the administrative process.

Instead of invalidating *all* administrative adjudication on due process grounds, one could conceivably seek out legal contexts in which the threat to administrative adjudicatory neutrality is at its greatest. For example, when a *constitutional* challenge is presented to the agency's regulatory authority, either facially or as applied to the particular regulatory context, the constitutional stakes are raised significantly. From one perspective, the neutrality of an interested adjudicator is placed under even greater stress than when the issue for adjudication is simply whether a regulated party has or has not violated a regulation. When issues of constitutionality are raised, the challenge gives rise to a threat to the future scope of the agency's authority—one that would likely make any individual whose professional existence is intimately intertwined with the agency's power feel protective of that power, even if only subconsciously. From another perspective, the most foundational considerations involve constitutional challenges to agency action. It is therefore especially in such cases that the neutrality and independence of the adjudicator are most important.

Will an adjudicator tied to a specific agency be incapable of deciding neutrally in *all* cases? Likely not. But the foundation of adjudicatory independence is the assumption that we choose to *overprotect* independence by establishing *ex ante* categorical rules, rather than risk *underprotecting* it through use of a case-by-case inquiry into neutrality. If we learn nothing else from the lessons of adversary democratic theory, we learn at least that much. In many instances, the adjudicator herself will fail to recognize her implicit biases. It is for these reasons that due process is appropriately deemed to require use of categorical *ex ante* prohibitions on identification between the adjudicator and the enforcing entity. And, for reasons already explained, the need for such prophylactically insulated neutrality is at its most intense in the case of a constitutional challenge to agency action or authority.

As important as adjudicatory neutrality is in the case of any constitutional challenge to agency authority, for reasons already noted the need for such independence is arguably at its height when the constitutional challenge is grounded in the First Amendment right of free expression. It is for this very reason that the concept of "First Amendment due process" has been developed. *First Amendment* due process, then, must add an element above and beyond the level of constitutional protection afforded by procedural due process alone. What the content of that element actually is, however, is not immediately clear. This chapter seeks to answer this question by examining First Amendment due process in the specific context of the federal government's administrative state. In this sense, it involves a synthesis of First Amendment doctrine and theory with an analysis of procedural due process in the administrative context.

Claims of First Amendment protection may well clash with administrative regulatory schemes in a variety of contexts. At the state level, for example, such claims potentially clash with either state or local administrative zoning schemes or censorial boards created to limit or prohibit the distribution of obscene movies or publications. More important today, however, are the federal administrative regulatory schemes that may clash with claims of commercial speech protection. For example, when the Federal Trade Commission (FTC) attempts to regulate, punish, or halt allegedly false advertising, the advertiser may seek to challenge the allegation that its advertising is false, thereby triggering First Amendment protection for its advertisements. When the Food and Drug Administration attempts to prevent, stop, or punish so-called "off-label" advertising—that is, advertising of a prescription drug for uses for which the drug was not originally approved[6]—the pharmaceutical company may wish to challenge the constitutionality of such a regulatory scheme under the First Amendment.[7]

It is true that, historically, commercial speech has received considerably less First Amendment protection than more traditionally protected categories of free expression.[8] But both theoretically and doctrinally, this situation has changed dramatically in recent years.[9] The Supreme Court has wisely recognized that the constitutional stakes in the regulation or suppression of commercial speech are quite high, and that governmental restrictions on commercial expression can cause serious harm to traditionally recognized First Amendment interests.[10]

In both state and federal contexts, the first question that the doctrine of First Amendment due process poses is whether the administrative regulatory framework, in the first instance, satisfies the requirements of procedural due process for the adjudication of the regulated party's First Amendment claim. The concept of First Amendment due process raises the following questions about administrative adjudication of First Amendment challenges to the administrators' regulation or suppression of expression: (1) Can administrative adjudication (as opposed to judicially operated adjudication) *ever* satisfy the requirements of due process under such circumstances? (2) If not, does the provision of an opportunity for some form of judicial review of the administrative determination satisfy due process guarantees? The answer to both questions is no.

The conclusions reached in this chapter are multileveled. On the first—or what could be called the foundational—level, the chapter concludes that under no circumstances may regulatory administrative adjudication, as currently structured, be deemed to satisfy the requirements of procedural due process, much less the stronger requirements of First Amendment due process.[11] Procedural due process, at its foundation, demands a prophylactically protected neutral adjudicator. Absent such an adjudicator, other procedural protections are rendered all but meaningless, for a biased adjudicator is likely to ignore the evidence in any event.[12] This chapter's analysis will demonstrate that the modern administrative adjudicatory structure fails to satisfy this foundational constitutional requirement.

On a second level, should this foundational first-level conclusion be rejected on grounds of impracticality, at the very least, a prophylactically insulated adjudicator—of a type not seen in our current administrative structure—must be required to resolve a constitutional challenge to agency authority or actions. The inherent predisposition (if only on a subconscious level) of regulators to resist externally (i.e., constitutionally) imposed limits on the exercise of their own regulatory powers renders them constitutionally incapable of fairly judging the constitutionality of the exercise of their power to regulate.[13]

On a third level, when the constitutional challenge is grounded in the First Amendment right of free expression, the procedural assurances of adjudicatory neutrality need to be made even stronger. In non-free speech cases, the due process problem could arguably be solved simply by providing for de novo judicial review of agency action. When free speech rights are at stake, however, judicial review post-administrative adjudication, in anything but the most emergent situations, fails to satisfy the special requirements of First Amendment due process. In such situations, serious harm to constitutionally protected free speech interests may result from the interim restraints imposed until the judicial review mechanism will be in a position to remove the restraint on expression imposed at the administrative level. Moreover, requiring a subject of regulation to bear the costs and burdens of the administrative adjudicatory process before being able to have its First Amendment claim heard by a truly neutral adjudicator may well chill that subject's willingness to raise its constitutional challenge. In short, because of the simultaneous fragility and constitutional significance of free speech rights, a party challenging the constitutionality of administrative regulation under the First Amendment right of free expression must be permitted to circumvent the administrative process and immediately present the First Amendment challenge in court. The arguable inconsistency of this analysis with current doctrine must be acknowledged. But this chapter is written in the hope of stimulating a rethinking, if not an outright change in that doctrine.

The potential availability of judicially imposed preliminary restraint, issued following the administrative determination and prior to judicial review, on enforcement of an administrative directive regulating, suppressing, or punishing private expression seems theoretically to provide a conceivable safety valve. On closer examination, however, such a possibility is likely to prove to be less than effective, for several reasons. Initially, at the very start of an appellate proceeding, at a point at which the reviewing court is largely unfamiliar with the substance of the complex constitutional issues involved, the judicial instinct to defer to administrative expertise will be great. This is simply a practical reality. Moreover, once the regulatory body has found against the would-be speaker, the speaker's incentive to invest in pursuing the matter further may often be chilled at the point where review is to be sought.

Because of these serious constitutional difficulties, First Amendment due process must dictate (1) a categorical exclusion of the regulatory body from any consideration of a First Amendment challenge to its regulatory authority, and (2) an opportunity for a litigant to bring its constitutional challenge directly to the federal courts, once a regulator has decided to seek to suppress speech. While not certain, in some ways this is likely not the current procedure.[14] But to the extent this is in fact controlling law, the position taken here is that current procedure has been developed without sufficient regard to the constitutional imperative of First Amendment due process and needs to be rethought in that light.

The first section of this chapter reviews the theoretical foundations of procedural due process, focusing particularly on the essential due process requirement of a neutral adjudicator.[15] The analysis that follows that discussion consists of an analysis of the extent to which administrative adjudication of constitutional challenges to its regulatory authority or decisions satisfies the demands of procedural due process.[16] After concluding that administrative regulators categorically fail to satisfy the adjudicatory neutrality requirements of due process, at the very least in the context of constitutional challenges to their regulatory authority, the chapter will explain why the availability of post-administrative judicial review cannot cure the constitutional defect in administrative adjudication of First Amendment challenges to its regulatory authority.[17] Finally, the chapter will consider the extent to which modern administrative procedure authorizes the process here deemed constitutionally essential to enable the subject of administrative regulation to present its First Amendment challenge at a meaningful point in the process.[18]

There has never been a clear consensus as to the underlying theoretical framework of procedural due process. From the thirty-thousand-foot level, the conflict has been grounded in a debate between those who favor an "instrumental" rationale and those who prefer to employ a "noninstrumental" rationale. Those who adopt a noninstrumental rationale have framed their reasoning in terms of a "dignitary" theory, which focuses due process on the need to preserve and facilitate the individual's dignity within a liberal democratic society.[19] The Supreme Court, on the other hand, has employed a form of utilitarian—or instrumental—calculus, designed to balance the need for an accurate decision, the practical stakes for the litigants, and the burdens imposed on government.[20] Alternatively, the approach advocated throughout this book is grounded in the political theory of adversary democracy, which links the liberal democratic value of fulfilling the potential for human flourishing to the inherent skeptical mistrust of the competence or good faith of others—particularly those in government.[21] While all three theories logically lead to a commitment to a neutral adjudicator in some form, the mistrust inherent in adversary democratic theory places the greatest emphasis on the essential role played by adjudicatory neutrality.

As far back as the early 1600s, at the time of *Dr. Bonham's Case*,[22] the proposition that no man can be a judge in a case in which he has a personal interest was firmly established, and for good reason. Unless the adjudicator can be considered truly neutral between the parties, the provision of all other traditional due process guarantees is rendered meaningless. What difference would it make, for example, that a litigant has the right to call witnesses on her behalf or to cross-examine her antagonists, if the adjudicator's ultimate decision will not be based on the evidence presented but rather on the basis of extraneous prejudices or biases?

At least in the context of judicial adjudicators,[23] the Supreme Court has consistently adhered to the proposition that neutral adjudication represents the foundation of procedural due process. For example, as discussed in prior chapters, in *Tumey v. Ohio*,[24] the Court held unconstitutional an Ohio statute that designated half of any criminal fine imposed by a mayor's court to go to the township, municipality, or county that prosecuted the case. The local community in *Tumey* passed an ordinance that the judge would receive his costs from the village's share.[25] There was no evidence that the mayor/judge had actually taken his personal financial interest into account in deciding any of the cases. Seemingly recognizing that actual influence could only rarely be proven and further recognizing the importance of the appearance of fairness, the Supreme Court established a generalized, prophylactic standard of adjudicatory neutrality.[26] And as I wrote many years ago, "[t]he legal standard in *Tumey*—'possible temptation to the average man as a judge'—has not been seriously disputed."[27] The very words of this standard, which has been applied consistently by the Court,[28] suggest its highly demanding quality. There need be no showing of actual wrongdoing; rather, existence of merely a "possible temptation" to decide a case on the basis of factors other than a fair analysis of the evidence suffices to render the adjudicator insufficiently neutral for due process purposes. Thus, the Court has wisely adopted a prophylactically protective standard of neutrality. It is willing to overprotect adjudicatory independence, rather than risk underprotecting it. But this standard does not, by itself, inform us of what actually constitutes a "possible temptation." It is therefore appropriate to turn to an effort to categorize the different forms of constitutionally impermissible interferences with adjudicatory neutrality.

6.2 A TAXONOMY OF UNCONSTITUTIONAL ADJUDICATORY BIASES

This section proposes a taxonomy of biases that should be deemed to give rise to the same level of potential bias exhibited in all of the cases in which the Court has previously found the neutral adjudicator principle to have been violated.[29] This taxonomy of biases should be employed to determine whether the bias potential in a given case violates the due process-dictated neutral adjudicator requirement. This analysis conceptualizes three categories of the constitutionally impermissible prelitigation interests that encapsulate the biases recognized in the Court's prior cases and present problems for due process. These categories are (1) coercive interference, (2) incentivized decision-making, and

(3) associative or disassociative prejudices. If any one of these biases is present, then the threat to adjudicatory neutrality rises to an unconstitutional level and the judge's involvement in the adjudication must therefore be found to violate due process.

6.2.1 Coercive Interference

Coercive interference occurs when one of the parties or an outside individual or entity attempts to threaten or intimidate the adjudicator, thereby creating the potential for undue influence on the judge's decision-making. The potential for bias in this situation—that is, that the judge is likely to be influenced by the coercive party to decide the case in the way that party wishes—is high.

An extreme example of such coercive interference arguably occurred in Ecuador in *Republic of Ecuador v. Chevron Corp.*[30] In *Chevron*, the government of Ecuador allegedly actively supported the Lago Agrio plaintiffs in seeking redress against Chevron for alleged illegal polluting.[31] After President Correa was elected president of Ecuador, defendants claimed that he "openly campaigned for a decision against Chevron, at the same time that the Government made clear that any judge who issued opinions contrary to the Government's interests would be subject to dismissal and even possible criminal prosecution."[32] This is an extreme situation, but it nevertheless exemplifies the potential problem with coercive interference: a judge cannot be deemed neutral if he is being coerced to find a certain way.

6.2.2 Incentivized Decision-Making

Incentivized decision-making describes a situation in which an adjudicator is aware that she will gain a benefit from the outcome of the decision. In such a situation, the judge may have an incentive to decide the case in favor of a certain party, despite the fact that the evidence would dictate a contrary conclusion, so that she can gain a personal or associational benefit. If an adjudicator stands to gain a benefit from the outcome of the decision, the Due Process Clause has been violated. Indeed, *Tumey* stands as a perfect illustration of this category. In *Tumey*, the judge was paid for each conviction,[33] giving him an incentive to convict defendants whether they deserved it or not. In *Aetna Life Insurance Co. v. Lavoie*,[34] the judge stood a chance to gain a better outcome in his pending cases against other insurance companies based on the rule of decision applied in the case before him. Although the judge did not stand to get a direct financial gain, the potential beneficial effect on his pending cases may have created an incentive to him to rule one way. In both of these cases, the bias clearly rose to an unconstitutional level.

It should be emphasized that the adjudicator need not be consciously influenced by the incentive or disincentive. This underscores the prophylactic nature of the neutrality protection. Because the judge herself may not even be aware that her decision is being influenced by the incentive or disincentive, and because the legitimacy of the system turns as much on the appearance of fairness as the reality, the neutrality directive is properly construed to err on the side of overprotection.

The benefit to the adjudicator need not be personal. It could also be an associational benefit, as it was in *Ward v. Village of Monroeville*, where the mayor stood to gain a financial benefit for his city if the defendants were fined.[35] This was not a direct financial benefit to the mayor, but overall he stood to benefit indirectly from the outcome of each case because of his interest in maintaining the city's coffers. The associational benefit could also be reputational rather than financial. A hypothetical example would be if a judge works on the board of a group whose reputation could be helped or harmed by the outcome of the decision of a case. The judge would gain a benefit if she found in favor of the group because the group would gain a better reputation or avoid getting a worse one. Regardless of the nature of the benefit, in all of these scenarios the judge has an incentive outside the evidence to decide the case in a specific way, creating an unconstitutional level of bias potentiality.

6.2.3 Associative and Disassociative Prejudices

Finally, certain forms of association or disassociation with one of the parties in the case gives rise to a constitutionally unacceptable potential for bias. Associative and disassociative prejudices occur when some factor connects the judge to one side of the case, either favorably (associative) or unfavorably (disassociative). For example, associative prejudice would arise if a judge's family member is one of the parties, so the judge might be predisposed to rule in favor of that party. An example of a disassociative prejudice can be seen in *In re Murchison*.[36] There the Supreme Court held that due process is violated when the judge who issued the contempt citation for actions taking place in his courtroom adjudicates the trial for contempt.[37] In such a situation, the judge already has a negative attitude toward the defendant based on his earlier interactions with him in his courtroom.

Associative and disassociative prejudices carry a high risk of bias in the outcome of the case because the judge consciously or subconsciously risks being influenced by his connection with or feelings toward one of the parties in the case, wholly apart from the case's internal merits. As the Court reasoned in *In re Murchison*, a judge with such a connection to one of the parties "cannot be, in the very nature of things, wholly disinterested in the conviction or acquittal of those accused" because "[w]hile he would not likely have all the zeal of a prosecutor, it can certainly not be said that he would have none of that zeal."[38]

The potential for violations of impartiality in adjudications involving associative or disassociative prejudices is demonstrated by reference to the theory of motivated reasoning.[39] Motivated reasoning is the idea that "[p]eople are more likely to arrive at those conclusions that they want to arrive at."[40] The use of the word "want" is somewhat misleading, however. It suggests that a person consciously chooses the end result or conclusion and then does everything to achieve that result. This is not necessarily the case. Put another way, motivated reasoning "refers to the tendency of people to unconsciously process information—including empirical data, oral and written arguments, and even their own brute sensory perceptions—to promote goals or interests extrinsic to the decisionmaking task at hand."[41] Motivated reasoning therefore prevents individuals from making dispassionate, impartial, and fair judgments.[42]

Motivated reasoning operates through two mechanisms. The first is known as "biased search," in which individuals are more likely to search for information in a selective manner, focusing their inquiry on data that supports their group, belief, or position than information that challenges it.[43] The second mechanism is known as "biased assimilation," in which individuals are likely to credit or dismiss evidence or argument selectively based on how it conforms to their group, belief, or position.[44] Biased assimilation also includes the danger that individuals will credit individuals within their group with greater knowledge and therefore greater credibility than outsiders.[45]

It is important to note that motivated reasoning has its limitations. Generally, people will not believe anything they want simply because that belief furthers their ideology or interests. Assuming they are seeking to act in good faith, individuals will not make up evidence or irrational arguments to support their interests. The concern, rather, is that (if only subconsciously) they will selectively seek out evidence that supports their interest or weigh such evidence more heavily. As a result, motivated reasoning is extremely dangerous to the goal of fair adjudication because it prevents people from realizing that their reasoning is biased and instead allows them to believe that their beliefs are fair and objective.[46] In the case of a judge, the judge may well believe she was deciding a case fairly and impartially even though she was really viewing the evidence in a light more favorable to one of the parties. This means that a judge exhibiting motivated reasoning would exhibit a strong bias potentiality.

6.3 ADMINISTRATIVE ADJUDICATION AND DUE PROCESS

Although due process in general and the requirement of neutral adjudicator in particular has primarily been applied to the traditional judicial court system, it is well established that due process also applies in the context of administrative adjudication.[47] The traditionally applied test may play a lesser role in administrative adjudications due to the utilitarian nature of the Court's procedural due process balancing test.[48] However, because adjudicatory neutrality serves as the foundation of procedural due process, the requirement of a neutral adjudicator must still be satisfied in administrative proceedings.[49] In the judicial context, the Court has consistently held that an overlap in investigatory, prosecutorial, and adjudicatory powers creates a bias potentiality that violates due process.[50] However, in administrative adjudication the heads of an agency are generally empowered to function as adjudicators and make final agency decisions while also serving investigatory and prosecutorial roles.[51] This section will describe the federal administrative adjudicatory process. Then, the analysis will demonstrate that the power of agency commissioners to overturn Administrative Law Judge (ALJ) decisions and make the final agency decision violates the neutral adjudicator requirement that functions as the foundation of procedural due process.

6.3.1 The Federal Administrative Adjudicatory Process

The federal administrative adjudicatory process varies among agencies. Generally, the procedure that each federal agency follows is determined by a synthesis of the agency's organic act and the Administrative Procedure Act (APA). Although traditionally employed due process requirements for the most part still apply to agencies, the APA was enacted in part to offer additional protections beyond the minimum constitutional requirements of due process.[52] However, these statutory protections are triggered when the agency's organic act contains specific language requiring compliance with formal APA procedures.[53] In order to ensure impartial adjudications, the APA forbids "[a]n employee or agent engaged in the performance of investigative or prosecuting functions for an agency" to "participate or advise in the decision, recommended decision, or agency review."[54] Despite this protection from an overlap in conflicting powers, the APA creates an exception for "the agency or a member or members of the body comprising the agency" from this prohibition.[55] This means that the head of an agency or any of its commissioners may participate in the investigative or prosecutorial functions of the agency while also serving in an adjudicatory role.

Commissioners of each agency are often empowered to serve in investigatory and prosecutorial roles within their respective agencies. For example, the FTC can begin an investigation "by the Commission upon its own initiative."[56] Once the investigation is completed, the Commission votes on whether grounds exist to issue a complaint. If so, an adjudicatory proceeding is initiated.[57] FTC complaint counsel, made up of staff from the Bureau of Consumer Protection or a regional office of the FTC, conduct the prosecution on behalf of the Commission before an ALJ.[58] The prosecution is conducted on behalf of the Commission, assumedly with their oversight.

The Securities and Exchange Commission (SEC) provides another example of the synthesis of administrative, investigative, and prosecutorial powers. An administrative proceeding in the SEC begins when the SEC's Division of Enforcement staff conducts an investigation into a potential violation of federal securities laws.[59] If the Enforcement Division determines that a violation has occurred, it presents its findings to the Commission and recommends that the Commission bring a civil action before an ALJ.[60] If the Commission agrees that a violation has occurred, it files an order instituting proceedings, in which it directs an ALJ to conduct a public administrative proceeding and issue an Initial Decision.[61] The SEC may seek a variety of sanctions from the ALJ, including disgorgement of ill-gotten gains, civil penalties, censures, and cease and desist orders.[62] In these proceedings, the Commission is represented by attorneys from the Division of Enforcement.[63] As in the case of the FTC, these attorneys prosecute the cases on behalf of the Commission.[64] Thus, in the SEC, the Commission also decides whether to initiate formal proceedings, has the power to initiate proceedings, and oversees the prosecution.

The heads of each agency are also empowered to adjudicate hearings and make final agency decisions. The APA dictates that in formal proceedings the head of an agency or an ALJ adjudicates formal hearings and makes the initial decision.[65] In some agencies, this is the final decision, but in most agencies, the parties—including the agency, if it is a party—can appeal to a panel of judges in the agency or to the head of the agency.[66] This means that the agency itself can appeal an initial decision which is unfavorable to the agency and then overturn the initial decision in favor of the agency.

The FTC provides a good example of the nature of the adjudicatory authority exercised by the commissioners. In FTC adjudications an ALJ conducts the formal hearing.[67] Either party, including the FTC, may appeal the initial decision to the full Commission.[68] The Commission receives briefs, holds oral arguments, and issues its own final decision and order.[69] "The [C]ommission has the authority to 'adopt, modify, or set aside' the ALJ's initial decision" in making its final decision.[70]

This final decision is then appealable to a federal circuit court of appeals.[71] The court of appeals may review the final decision under the substantial evidence standard, as Section 5(c) of the FTC Act, which states, "the findings of the Commission as to the facts, if supported by the evidence, shall be conclusive," has been interpreted as analogous to the substantial evidence standard of the APA.[72]

The SEC adjudicatory process functions similarly to the FTC adjudicatory process. After the Commission files an order instituting proceedings, an ALJ conducts a public hearing and issues an initial decision.[73] Once the ALJ issues that decision, either party, including the SEC, may appeal to the Commission, which performs a de novo review and can affirm, reverse, modify, set aside, or remand for further proceedings.[74] The Commission's opinion constitutes the final agency decision of the SEC unless the initial decision is not appealed, in which case the initial decision is the final agency decision. That decision is reviewable by a federal court of appeals.[75]

Not all heads of agencies serve a role in the adjudicatory process. For example, in the Food and Drug Administration (FDA), an ALJ adjudicates the initial hearing,[76] and those appeals are heard by the Department Appeals Board of the Department of Health and Human Services (DHHS).[77] The Department Appeals Board consists of civil servants appointed by the DHHS Secretary who are meant to provide an impartial and independent review of the dispute.[78] Unlike the SEC appeals process, the standard of review for the Department Appeals Board is substantial evidence for issues of fact and clear error for issues of law.[79] The Commissioner of the FDA has no role in issuing initial or final agency decisions. However, the examples of the FTC and SEC demonstrate that the APA and many agency organic acts enable agency commissions to serve investigatory, prosecutorial, and adjudicatory roles in the same matter. As subsequent discussion will show, this overlap in roles creates a potential for bias that inescapably violates the neutral adjudicator principle.

6.3.2 The Neutral Adjudicator Principle Applied to Administrative Adjudication

As already noted, while due process has primarily been applied to the judicial system, it is well established that due process also applies to administrative adjudications.[80] After all, the Due Process Clause protects citizens against government's improper deprivation of property rights, and it cannot be disputed that administrative agencies exercise governmentally authorized coercive power to deprive private actors of their property. Regardless of the other procedures that due process requires in administrative hearings, an impartial adjudicator serves as a threshold requirement in administrative proceedings.[81] In its cases applying due process to the judicial system, the Supreme Court has consistently held that due process is violated if a judge also serves in a partisan role in the same case.[82] Applying this rule to the administrative adjudicatory process described in the previous discussion, it is clear that the power of agency commissioners to participate in investigations, prosecutions, and adjudications creates an impermissible bias in contravention of the dictates of due process.

One of the reasons the commissioners' roles in adjudications threaten due process is that it undermines the perception of fairness of administrative adjudications, which is one of the dignitary interests due process is meant to protect. More importantly, it directly contravenes the foundation of American due process's connection to adversary democracy, because those making the decisions are inherently compromised by the overriding danger of built-in associative prejudice. The commissioners are the heads of the agency. In fact, they are referred to as "The Commission" in the cases of the FTC and SEC, meaning that as a body they represent the agency. Regardless of whether the commissioners are actually biased, the other parties to the action may perceive bias. The commissioners are too closely tied to the agency itself and to the investigation and prosecution of each case for the people to perceive them as fair and unbiased judges of agency actions. The administrative adjudicatory process cannot function constitutionally if participants in the process cannot trust that it is fair and balanced.

The overlap in investigatory, prosecutorial, and adjudicatory roles performed by commissioners clearly violates the neutral adjudicator principle as shaped in *Tumey* and its progeny. First, the commissioners' position as heads of their agency automatically places them in a partisan role, necessarily inconsistent with the impartiality by which they are constitutionally bound. Like the mayor-judge in *Tumey*, the commissioners are the leaders of their respective agencies. In *Tumey*, the Supreme Court found that the mayor's dual role as mayor and judge violated due process because "[a] situation in which an official perforce occupies two practically and seriously inconsistent positions, one partisan and the other judicial, necessarily involves a lack of due process of law in the trial of defendants charged with crimes before him."[83] The commissioners also occupy both partisan and judicial positions: as heads of the agency and representatives of the agency in all matters, commissioners clearly occupy a partisan position in favor of the agency, and they are also empowered to adjudicate initial hearings and make final agency decisions. These two conflicting positions cannot be reconciled. When the agency is a party, agency officials prosecute the case on behalf of the commissioners, making the commissioners a party to the case. Thus, under *Tumey*, this overlap in roles unambiguously violates due process.

The commissioners' combined role in the investigatory and prosecutorial processes also gives rise to potential bias. In *In re Murchison*, the judge had effectively functioned as both victim and grand jury in the contempt hearing before serving as judge in the same case. In overturning the conviction, the Supreme Court stated that "[h]aving been a part of [the accusatory] process a judge cannot be, in the very nature of things, wholly disinterested in the conviction or acquittal of those accused" because "[w]hile he would not likely have all the zeal of a prosecutor, it can certainly not be said that he would have none of that zeal."[84] Commissioners are involved in the agency's accusatory process: they oversee the investigations conducted by their agencies, review the evidence collected, and decide whether to initiate formal proceedings. Throughout this whole process, they examine the case through the lens of a prosecutor. As heads of the agency, they are constantly attempting to determine if a party violated *their* rules and regulations. It is true that when they take on the role of judge, they may not have the same prosecutorial zeal that they may have had earlier in the process, but like the *Murchison* Court found, it cannot be said that the commissioners "would have none of that zeal." Thus, the potential for bias due to the overlap in accusatory and adjudicatory roles violates due process.

Even more important is the very associational connection between those working for the agency in question and the agency itself. The very point of a regulatory agency is to regulate, and those employed by the agency are surely aware of this fact. If only subconsciously, then, there exits an inherent danger that their judgments will be influenced by the pathology of motivated reasoning. When this pathology is combined with the very real potential for coercive distortion due to lack of employment security, direct involvement of agency employees in an adjudication brought by that agency contravenes the foundational dictates of adversary democratic due process developed throughout this book. By way of analogy, imagine a situation in which a judge in a legal case seeking civil or criminal fines holds an unprotected position in the governmental prosecutor's office which has brought the legal proceeding. Surely, no one could seriously believe that such a framework satisfies due process. When property rights are at stake in an administrative proceeding, there exists no legitimate basis on which to view the situation any differently.

Application of the taxonomy of biases to the administrative adjudicatory process, specifically those of the FTC and SEC, provides clear examples of these serious constitutional dangers. These examples demonstrate all too clearly that the overlap in investigatory, prosecutorial, and adjudicatory powers of commissioners creates an impermissible level of bias potentiality that violates the neutral adjudicator principle.[85] Because the commissioners are appointed by the executive and ultimately serve as part of the executive branch, a situation could arise in which they may be pressured by the executive to carry out more prosecutions or to be harder on white-collar crime. This could put pressure on commissioners to find against more defendants lest they lose their appointments in those agencies in which commissioners can be dismissed for cause.

More problematic, however, is the fact that administrative adjudications give rise to the serious danger of both associative and disassociative prejudices. The commissioners who make the final decisions in many of these agencies are members of the agency itself, meaning they have an associative connection to one of the parties (at least in those cases in which the agency is a party) and are thus likely predisposed to view the agency more favorably. Correspondingly, the commissioners' role in investigations and prosecutions creates a disassociative prejudice toward the party sought to be regulated. Commissioners often sign off on investigations and decisions to proceed, and oversee regulatory proceedings generally, meaning they may also look unfavorably upon the parties charged because of facts learned outside of the hearing. By deciding whether to initiate proceedings against a party, the commissioners have already made a determination that there is probable cause (or some similar weight of evidence) to initiate proceedings. Similar to the judge in *Murchison*, the commissioners may be predisposed to believe the parties charged are liable because they initially viewed the evidence through a prosecutorial or adversarial lens.

Motivated reasoning represents a very real danger in the context of the administrative adjudicatory process. Because they are a part of their respective agencies, commissioners begin with an attachment (or at least a perceived attachment) to their agency, which is often a party in a regulatory proceeding. This attachment potentially gives rise (at the very least) to subconscious motivated reasoning. Motivated reasoning may cause the commissioners to seek out information that supports the agency's case and to credit the agency's arguments and evidence more than those of the opposing side, both of which eliminate the possibility of an impartial, fair adjudication. These problems are amplified because the commissioners may have already played a role in deciding whether to initiate proceedings. This means that the commissioners have already examined the evidence through the agency's lens, weighed the evidence on behalf of the agency, and determined that the evidence merited further action.[86] While of course no one can know this for certain in the individual case, the danger is far from trivial or remote.

Moreover, because motivated reasoning is usually subconscious, the commissioners would never recognize that their association with the agency influences their decisions, and thus their motivational reasoning cannot be corrected. This is especially a problem when the challenge to regulatory authority is grounded in the First Amendment right of free expression. As I have previously written: "Nonjudicial administrative regulators of expression exist for the sole purpose of regulating; this is their raison d'être. [I]f only subconsciously, [they] will likely feel the obligation to justify their existence by finding some expression constitutionally subject to regulation."[87] Professor Thomas Emerson put the point more bluntly in discussing censorship agencies: "[T]he function of the censor is to censor."[88]

Will it always be the case that a regulator will possess an inherent instinct, conscious or subconscious, to favor regulation? Probably not. Indeed, conservative presidents generally opposed to regulation may well choose to appoint administrators who actually favor deregulation. The point, however, is that in the individual instance no one can know for sure. In the judicial context, the Supreme Court has wisely held that the due process-based demand for neutral adjudication cannot be satisfied by an individualized, case-by-case inquiry into an adjudicator's bias.[89] Rather, the Court finds factors that it deems *ex ante* to be disqualifying. Where we cannot be certain of possessing perfect knowledge in the individual case, due process requires that we risk erring on the side of overprotection, rather than underprotection. Thus, while there is no inherent reason to believe that the commissioners necessarily act with bias merely because of their role within the agency, adversary democratic due process and its prophylactically neutral adjudicator requirement are concerned not only with actual judicial wrongdoing but also with the possibility or appearance of bias.[90] As already explained, commissioners potentially exhibit all three categories of unconstitutional bias, and definitely exhibit associative prejudice due to their connection to the agency and their inherent role in the accusatory process. The danger of this bias inevitably violates the neutral adjudicator principle in which adversary democratic due process is grounded.

6.3.3 *Withrow v. Larkin*: The Supreme Court's Flawed Defense of Administrative Adjudication

As the analysis has shown, the association of investigatory, prosecutorial, and adjudicatory powers within agencies such as the FTC and SEC gives rise to the serious potential for unconstitutional bias that should, as a logical matter, be found to contravene due process's neutral adjudicator requirement established in cases involving judges such as *Tumey* and *Murchison*. However, when the Supreme Court has been asked to apply the neutral adjudicator requirement in the administrative context, it has categorically—and puzzlingly—rejected any due process challenge to the absence of complete adjudicatory independence. In its 1975 decision in *Withrow v. Larkin*, the Supreme Court addressed the question of whether a state administrative board's authority to investigate claims, present charges, rule on those charges, and impose punishment on parties violates due process.[91] The case involved a doctor who performed abortions in Milwaukee and was under investigation by the Wisconsin Medical Examining Board (the

Board) for alleged violations of state licensing requirements.[92] The Board held an investigative hearing to determine whether the doctor had engaged in certain prohibited acts.[93] This was followed by a final hearing to specifically determine whether the doctor had violated the state statute by practicing medicine under a different name than that under which he was originally licensed, by permitting an unlicensed physician to perform abortions at his clinic, and by splitting fees.[94] At this final hearing the Board found probable cause to revoke the doctor's medical license.[95] The Board was empowered by statute to conduct investigations, temporarily suspend medical licenses, and institute criminal actions or actions to revoke a doctor's license.[96]

The doctor challenged the constitutionality of the statute as a violation of procedural due process.[97] Applying the neutral adjudicator dictate from *Tumey* and *Murchison*, the district court found that the Board's involvement in the investigation and the final adjudication violated due process, stating, "for the board [to] temporarily ... suspend [the doctor's] license at its own contested hearing on charges evolving from its own investigation would constitute a denial to him of his rights to procedural due process."[98] The court reasoned that "[i]nsofar as [the statute] authorizes a procedure wherein a physician stands to lose his liberty or property, absent the intervention of an independent, neutral and detached decision maker, we concluded that it was unconstitutional and unenforceable."[99]

The Supreme Court rejected the district court's reasoning. The Court held that "the combination of investigative and adjudicative functions does not, without more, constitute a due process violation."[100] According to the Court, due process is violated when "the probability of actual bias on the part of the judge or decisionmaker is too high to be constitutionally tolerable."[101] The Court found that this combination of functions does not necessarily create an unconstitutional risk of bias.[102] The Court pointed to the variety of functions the members of administrative agencies are often called upon to perform, including "to receive the results of investigations, to approve the filing of charges or formal complaints instituting enforcement proceedings, and then to participate in the ensuing hearings."[103] The Court found that "[t]his mode of procedure does not violate the Administrative Procedure Act, and it does not violate due process of law."[104] The Court reasoned:

> The risk of bias or prejudgment in this sequence of functions has not been considered to be intolerably high or to raise a sufficiently great possibility that the adjudicators would be so psychologically wedded to their complaints that they would consciously or unconsciously avoid the appearance of having erred or changed position.[105]

In support of its conclusion, the Court noted that Congress had already dealt with the issue of combining investigative and adjudicatory powers through the

APA, seemingly implying that Congress had deemed this overlap of powers permissible.[106] The APA provides that no employee who investigates or prosecutes may participate or provide advice in the adjudicatory process though, as noted previously, the APA expressly exempts "the agency or a member or members of the body comprising the agency" from this prohibition.[107] The exemption allows the commissioners to engage in the investigation, prosecution, and adjudication of claims. The Court failed to address how the commissioners' direct role in all three processes might be impacted by due process, though the opinion implies that such behavior is constitutionally permissible.

Wholly apart from the fact that the APA has no applicability or relevance whatsoever to *state* administrative procedures, rendering the Court's reliance on the act both confusing and irrelevant, the Court's decision in *Withrow* flies in the face of its own due process decisions in the judicial context. In so doing, the Court established two separate due process standards—one for judges and one for administrators. Yet, in the Court's own words, the Due Process Clause "entitles a person to an impartial and disinterested tribunal in both civil and criminal cases."[108] As it had many years earlier in *Tumey*, the Court explained in *Marshall v. Jerrico, Inc.* that this constitutionally protected entitlement ensures "that no person will be deprived of his interests in the absence of a proceeding in which he may present his case with assurance that the arbiter is not predisposed to find against him."[109] This directly contradicts the Court's conclusion in *Withrow* some five years earlier. The commissioners in agencies such as the FTC and SEC authorize the initial investigation against a party, issue the complaint, control the prosecution, and then adjudicate any appeals filed by either party. As in the judicial context, the commissioners' role in the investigation and prosecution at the very least creates an appearance that the commissioners are predisposed to find against the party whom they investigated and prosecuted, especially since earlier in the proceeding they had a prosecutorial mindset and believed the defendants were liable. And yet the Court in *Withrow* found this practice to be consistent with due process.

One of the reasons the *Withrow* Court asserted in support of the constitutionality of this overlap of powers in the administrative context was that there is a "presumption of honesty and integrity in those serving as adjudicators." Therefore the Court must be convinced that "[u]nder a realistic appraisal of psychological tendencies and human weakness, conferring investigative and adjudicative powers on the same individuals poses such a risk of actual bias or prejudgment that the practice must be forbidden. . . ."[110] The Court's statement, however, directly contradicts the reasoning of the *Tumey* Court in the judicial context fifty years earlier. In *Tumey*, the Court did not care that some of the judges might not be affected by bias, or in the words of the *Withrow* Court, that many judges exhibit honesty and integrity. Instead, in *Tumey*, the Court invoked the very opposite presumption, holding that "[t]he requirement of due process of law in judicial procedure is not satisfied by the argument that men of the highest honor and greatest self-sacrifice could carry it on without danger of injustice."[111] And yet in *Withrow*, the Court, without any explanation, suggested that we now *presume* that administrative adjudicators have the "highest honor and greatest self-sacrifice." It is truly bizarre that the Court would assume that *administrators*, despite the countless reasons to question their inherent objectivity, will act without prejudice while at the same time assuming that *judges* may well not do so. At the very least, there is no justification for distinguishing between the two: On what possible basis could one assume that adjudicators are more likely to be free from prejudice than judges? But more importantly, for reasons previously noted, a strong case can be made that if a distinction is to be drawn at all, exactly the opposite is true, especially in cases involving challenges to the constitutionality of agency action or authority.

That the Court in *Withrow* drew a wholly unjustified distinction between the levels of neutrality required in judicial and administrative proceedings is demonstrated by how it attempted to distinguish its earlier decision in *Murchison*. The Court in *Withrow* attempted to distinguish the case before it from *Murchison* in two ways. First, the Court stated, "*Murchison* has not been understood to stand for the broad rule that the members of an administrative agency may not investigate the facts, institute proceedings, and then make the necessary adjudications."[112] The Court's meaning in this passage is clear: administrative law is different and normal due process requirements do not apply to it. Unfortunately, the Court had the situation completely reversed: it is the administrative context in which adjudicatory neutrality must be deemed far more suspect.[113]

Second, the *Withrow* Court noted that *Murchison* did not question the APA.[114] This is of course true; *Murchison* did not involve administrative law at all, and it did not involve a challenge to the APA. There was thus no reason for the Court in *Murchison* to question the validity of the APA or to even mention the APA, nor should it have. But the *Murchison* Court's failure to question the validity of the APA does not mean that the APA comports with the rule in *Murchison* or due process generally. In any event, as already noted, the APA is legally inapplicable to state administrative processes. Thus the Court's reliance on the APA remains mystifying.

In important ways, for due process purposes formal administrative hearings are functionally identical to traditional judicial adjudications. Both proceedings involve adversary parties standing before an adjudicator; both proceedings require notice to all parties involved; and both proceedings allow for presentation of evidence and cross-examination. Also, agencies are often empowered to impose sanctions that are as severe as those imposed by courts in civil cases.[115]

They can impose civil penalties, disgorgement of ill-gotten gains, censures, cease and desist orders, and license revocations.[116] Thus, when due process applies, the same constitutional standards should logically apply. This means that, above all, the traditional neutral adjudicator requirement should apply, because absent a neutral adjudicator, all other procedural protections are rendered irrelevant.

The *Withrow* Court implied that in the administrative context the requirements imposed by the APA are synonymous with those imposed by due process. This is shown by the fact that the Court states that it is normal for members of agencies to review investigation results, approve the initiation of charges, and then participate in the adjudication of the claim.[117] The Court goes on to say, "[t]his mode of procedure does not violate the Administrative Procedure Act, and it does not violate due process of law."[118] The Court appears to suggest that rather than conducting an independent due process analysis of agency action, the Court looks only to whether the APA is violated in order to determine the constitutionality of both state and federal administrative action. The clear implication is that satisfying the APA somehow automatically satisfies due process. But the APA, like any federal statute, is trumped by an inconsistent constitutional directive, and the Court failed to provide any basis for its implicit assumption that the limits imposed by the APA and the Due Process Clause are conterminous.

Like the mayor/judges in *Tumey* and *Ward*, agency commissioners occupy two different positions, one partisan and one judicial. Like the mayor in *Ward*, these commissioners may feel pressure to take a hard-line position against violators of their directives and maintain a high level of enforcement. By the standard set in *Tumey* and *Ward*, it seems clear that allowing commissioners to be directly involved in investigations, prosecutions, and adjudications of the same claim violates due process.

What brings the situations in the administrative context even closer to that in *Ward* is that these agencies often assess civil money penalties on defendants. Just like the mayor in *Ward*, who may be biased because fees from his court financed his executive needs, in the SEC's case, the commissioners could also be biased because civil money penalties indirectly affect their budget. As discussed previously,[119] in the SEC, most of the money collected through civil money penalties goes to the US Treasury General Fund, which in turn funds the SEC.[120] Over the last several years, the SEC has seen a significant increase in its budget.[121] It seems possible that this increase in the SEC budget could be related to the increase in civil money penalties the SEC contributed to the General Fund, suggesting that civil money penalties could affect the commissioners' budget. Under *Ward*, the commissioners' adjudication of appeals violates due process because there is a "possible temptation" for the commissioners to assess more civil money penalties in order to increase their budget.[122]

6.3.4 Fixing the Administrative State's Due Process Problem

A common reaction to this chapter's due process critique of the administrative state is likely to be that rectifying these constitutional difficulties, even if one acknowledges their existence, would effectively destroy the administrative state, and it is simply too late in the day even seriously to consider that possibility. It is certainly easy to understand the argument as a purely practical, if not theoretical matter. But one should be dubious of any such argument, for it necessarily tolerates the notion that government may violate core notions of constitutional democracy in the name of efficiency. Perhaps more importantly, one should not concede that the modern administrative state cannot coexist with rigorous adherence to the dictates of procedural due process in general and the requirement of a neutral adjudicator in particular. Transformation of the ALJ corps by making them employees of the US government generically, rather than of the particular agency, and significantly increasing their independence could go very far toward improving the adjudicatory neutrality of the administrative process.[123] If one were also to substantially increase judicial review of agency decisions—a move that would likely be viewed with alarm by supporters of the current system—the revised system could arguably satisfy due process. And it should always be kept in mind that none of these constitutional concerns impacts the rulemaking authority of administrative agencies.

The remainder of this chapter proceeds on the assumption that, for whatever reason, the broad constitutional challenge to the administrative process fashioned here has been categorically rejected. Even in the face of such wholesale rejection, one may reasonably confine the reach of this constitutional attack to enclaves consisting of situations where the dangers caused by the absence of adjudicatory neutrality are especially pathological. In so doing, we would be able to remove the most serious due process dangers while at the same time leaving the bulk of the administrative state unchanged.[124] It is therefore to an analysis of these narrower alternatives that the analysis now turns.

6.4 AVOIDING THE MOST SERIOUS DUE PROCESS PATHOLOGIES OF THE ADMINISTRATIVE STATE

To this point, this chapter has established that procedural due process and its requirement of a neutral adjudicator raise serious constitutional problems concerning the adjudicatory power currently exercised by administrative agencies. Even when prosecutorial and adjudicatory powers are not combined in the same administrators, the fact remains that those who make the ultimate decision are still part of the very same agency that has instituted the enforcement proceeding in the first place. Problems of motivated reasoning and cognitive dissonance plague the administrative decision-making process, threatening adjudicatory neutrality.[125] As serious as these concerns are, however, for reasons to be explained, they expand geometrically when the relevant issues of fact and law involve not merely the application of administrative regulation to the particular behavior of regulated private actors, but rather to the legitimacy of constitutional challenges to agency regulatory authority or action. And those constitutional concerns, in turn, become almost infinitely more problematic in one specific context: when the constitutional challenge is grounded in the First Amendment right of free expression.

6.4.1 Adjudicatory Neutrality and Constitutional Challenges to Agency Authority

The venerable doctrine of constitutional fact evinces fundamental mistrust of the ability of agencies to judge constitutional challenges to their authority, and with good reason.[126] This chapter has already explained why administrators, whose very purpose is to regulate, would likely have great difficulty maintaining objectivity in deciding between the claims of fellow agency members seeking to regulate and the private actor opposing regulation.[127] The problem of maintaining objectivity is far greater when an external constitutional challenge to the exercise of agency authority is presented. In such a situation, the scope of an agency's authority to act has been attacked on the basis of what are claimed to be restraints imposed by sources external to that agency. While courts are on occasion called upon to rule upon the constitutionality of their own authority,[128] their objectivity is generally not threatened in the same way as that of agency decision makers. Judges of state or federal courts are aware that as a practical matter, their general jurisdiction will remain in existence, regardless of whatever individualized tweaking takes place. The same cannot be said of agency decision makers, whose authority to act does not reach as broadly and is more fragile.

Moreover, to the extent a similar danger might be thought to arise in the judicial context, the doctrine of necessity, grounded in the need to preserve separation of powers, will usually justify vesting final say as to the constitutionality of restrictions on judicial authority in the hands of the courts themselves. Any other result would leave judicial jurisdiction dangerously vulnerable to a form of political guerrilla warfare, designed to emasculate the courts as protectors of countermajoritarian constitutional rights and values. The same rationale, however, in no way justifies deference to administrative determination of issues of fact or law on which the constitutionality of their exercise of authority turns.

For the most part, a categorical exclusion of judicial deference to agency fact-finding on constitutional challenges is already doctrinally precluded by the constitutional fact doctrine. To the extent doctrinal alteration is called for, it would be to demand a reinvigoration and clarification of the underlying rationale of such a doctrine.[129] But as problematic as is the general exercise of agency authority to make legal or factual determinations on which the constitutionality of agency authority turns, far more troublesome is an agency's exercise of such authority when that constitutional challenge is specifically grounded in the First Amendment right of free expression. It is therefore to an analysis of this unique context that the chapter now turns.

6.5 THE SPECIAL CASE OF FIRST AMENDMENT DUE PROCESS

That due process takes on a special quality when the First Amendment right of free expression is at stake is demonstrated by the recognition of the widely accepted doctrine known as "First Amendment due process."[130] To understand the unique aspects of First Amendment due process, it is first necessary to explore the concept's theoretical and doctrinal foundations and development. The following discussion will therefore explore both, and in so doing underscore both the unique aspects of the due process issues in the context of the First Amendment and how the current administrative adjudicatory structure must be altered in order to preserve both First Amendment and due process rights of those parties regulated by the administrative process.

6.5.1 The Concept and Origins of First Amendment Due Process

In the mid-1960s, the Supreme Court began to develop a special procedural due process doctrine for cases involving First Amendment rights. In *Freedman v. Maryland*,[131] the Court held unconstitutional a Maryland censorship statute, reasoning that "a noncriminal process which requires the prior submission of a film to a censor avoids constitutional infirmity only if it takes place under procedural safeguards designed to obviate the dangers of a censorship system."[132] The Court emphasized that "because only a judicial determination in an adversary proceeding ensures the necessary sensitivity to freedom of expression, only a procedure requiring a judicial determination suffices to impose a valid final restraint."[133] Professor Henry Monaghan, in his seminal article on the subject, explained the Court's conclusion, noting that the administrative censor does not play the role of "the impartial adjudicator but that of the expert—a role which necessarily gives an administrative agency a narrow and restricted viewpoint. Courts, on the other hand, do not suffer congenitally from this myopia; their general jurisdiction gives them a broad perspective which no agency can have."[134] The Maryland statute, the Court concluded, "provides no assurance of prompt judicial determination."[135]

Unfortunately, the *Freedman* Court left ambiguous exactly what should be considered "prompt judicial determination." Justice Brennan's opinion indicated that the censor must, "within a specified brief period, either issue a license or go to court to restrain showing the film."[136] But immediately after this sentence, he wrote the following: "Any restraint imposed in advance of a final judicial determination on the merits must similarly be limited to preservation of the *status quo* for the shortest fixed period compatible with sound judicial resolution."[137] He thus appeared to acknowledge the possibility of the imposition of a nonjudicial restraint on expression while the judicial determination of the constitutionality of the restraint proceeded.[138]

If this is in fact what Justice Brennan intended to say, the statement would represent a total departure from the reasoning underlying the rest of the opinion. The Court recognized the dangers of an interim restraint on speech. The simple fact is that an interim restraint is a restraint for however long it lasts, and therefore constitutes a *prima facie* violation of the First Amendment's free speech guarantee. The Court gave no reason why such interim restraints pending final judicial resolution cannot be issued by a court rather than the administrator. Indeed, the Court's opinion made clear that administrative restraint of speech *never* satisfies the dictates of First Amendment due process, so why—at least in the absence of some emergency where a court is somehow not immediately available—should not the interim restraints, much like the final restraints, be required to be imposed by a court through issuance of either preliminary injunctions or temporary restraining orders? It appears, then, that the Court in *Freedman* did not think through the inescapable logical implications of its own premises. Nevertheless, it is important not to undervalue the significance of *Freedman* in understanding the special status of the First Amendment in the context of procedural due process in general or adjudicatory neutrality in particular. As important as adjudicatory neutrality is to procedural due process in *any* context, *Freedma*n underscores its unique status when First Amendment rights are at stake.

There are three reasons for the special status of First Amendment due process. The first reason is, simply, the special status of free expression in our system of constitutional liberties. In contrast, in most administrative adjudications the stakes involve solely property rights—important and worthy of protection by procedural due process guarantees to be sure, but not presently considered to rise to the level of constitutional significance of the right of free expression. As a famous free speech scholar once wrote: "The principle of the freedom of speech springs from the necessities of the program of self-government. It is a deduction from the basic American agreement that public issues shall be decided by universal suffrage."[139] Absent free expression, self-government—whether on the collective or individual levels[140]—cannot function effectively. Therefore, greater procedural protection should be required before administrators are permitted to interfere with the right of free expression. The second reason is the consequential significance of the constitutionally pathological interim restraint resulting from administrative adjudication, even if sweeping judicial review is to follow. If, as the Court in *Freedman* correctly recognized, when rights of free expression are at stake, due process is judicial process, and any restraint imposed by an administrative body is inherently suspect—especially because a constitutional challenge to its authority challenges the very validity of its regulatory power. The third reason concerns the unique dangers of a chilling effect, which have been widely recognized in the First Amendment context.[141] Indeed, the Court in *Freedman* pointed to the concern about a chilling effect in recognizing the importance of prompt judicial action.[142]

6.5.2 Altering Federal Administrative Procedure in Light of First Amendment Due Process

Despite the venerable existence of the First Amendment due process doctrine, it appears to this point to have played no role at all in shaping federal administrative procedure. This should not be surprising, in light of the Court's bizarre, unfounded assumption, expressed in *Withrow*, that agency compliance with the APA somehow automatically signals compliance with the dictates of the Constitution.[143] At some point in law school, if not before, the Justices should have learned that the Constitution controls federal statutes, not the other way around, and to the extent a statute departs from constitutional dictates it is invalid.

There is much to be learned from a synthesis of this chapter's analyses of adjudicatory neutrality, procedural due process, and the special role played by the First Amendment in our constitutional system. First, administrators are constitutionally incapable of exercising final or even presumptive power to determine the constitutionality of their proposed regulation or authority in the presence of a First Amendment challenge.[144] This is so, even if an agency formally separates prosecutorial and adjudicatory functions. While perhaps such a formal separation could satisfy due process concerns in the case of subconstitutional adjudications (for example, in adjudications designed to determine whether a party's behavior has in fact violated an agency regulation or order), when a constitutional challenge to agency authority has been raised to agency action the inherent defensiveness of an administrator in favor of her agency and its powers gives rise to fatal constitutional problems of insufficient neutrality.

Second, in the context of First Amendment challenges, delaying judicial review until the close of the administrative process violates First Amendment rights because of the interim restraint that has been administratively imposed pending judicial review.

Third, even in the absence of an administratively imposed interim restraint, delaying judicial adjudication of First Amendment challenges to administrative action until completion of an administrative process should be deemed to violate First Amendment due process. The "deterrent" effect pointed to by the Court in *Freedman* should be recognized as raising a sufficiently serious concern that an individual or entity subjected to a complex administrative process before it can even raise its First Amendment challenge would deter the individual or entity from even seeking to engage in the expressive activity in the first place. The delay of judicial review of a First Amendment challenge until a subconstitutional administrative process has been completed surely cannot satisfy *Freedman*'s requirement of "prompt" judicial action.

It has been widely thought that the chilling effect concern should play no role in the context of commercial speech.[145] This conclusion is ironic, since the Court in *Freedman* found that the economic calculations of the film business might well deter the film industry from speaking.[146] The *Freedman* Court's insight is logically applicable as much in the context of commercial speech as it is to the film businesses in *Freedman*. Indeed, it is reasonable to assume that economic calculations are more likely to deter a would-be corporate speaker than they are to deter a speaker motivated by ideological belief rather than economic gain.

Acceptance of these conclusions would concededly require dramatic alteration in existing doctrine. That doctrine is best illustrated by the decision of the US District Court for the District of Columbia in *POM Wonderful LLC v. FTC*.[147] There the plaintiff, the largest processor and distributor of pomegranate products in the United States, sought a declaratory judgment that the FTC's new rule governing disease claims in food advertising exceeds the Agency's authority and violates the plaintiff's First and Fifth Amendment rights. The FTC moved to dismiss the complaint, and the court granted the motion. One of the primary factors leading to the dismissal was the fact that granting declaratory relief would require the resolution of an anticipatory defense.[148] The court quoted the Eighth Circuit's decision in *BASF Corp. v. Symington*: "[W]here a declaratory plaintiff raises chiefly an affirmative defense, and it appears that granting relief could effectively deny an allegedly injured party its otherwise legitimate choice of the forum and time for suit, no declaratory judgment should issue."[149] The court in

DUE PROCESS, FREE EXPRESSION, ADMINISTRATIVE STATE   163

POM concluded that "[c]ourts should not allow parties to use the Declaratory Judgment Act to engage in forum shopping,"[150] and that "[y]ielding here while the administrative action proceeds will not significantly prejudice POM."[151]

While the *POM* court's conclusion is consistent with the general rule on the subject of declaratory judgments seeking to raise an anticipatory defense,[152] to apply the same logic to First Amendment challenges to administrative action is grossly inconsistent with both the spirit and letter of the Supreme Court's First Amendment due process doctrine. Where First Amendment rights are at stake, as they were in *POM*, for the reasons developed throughout this chapter, it is simply wrong to conclude that the party asserting a First Amendment claim will not suffer significant prejudice by delaying its ability to raise its constitutional challenge until completion of the administrative process. Moreover, the logic traditionally relied upon to prohibit such anticipatory actions—that "[c]ourts should not allow parties to use the Declaratory Judgment Act to engage in forum shopping"[153]—is wholly irrelevant in the context of a First Amendment challenge to administrative action. We are not faced with a situation involving two private parties where the defendant is attempting to gain a strategic forum advantage over the plaintiff who chose the original forum. We are faced, rather, with the question of whether or not First Amendment due process will allow an agency to drain a private litigant of its resources, deterring it from continuing its constitutional challenge, by placing substantial procedural hurdles in its way that significantly delay its ability to have its First Amendment claim adjudicated in a judicial forum. To satisfy the requirements of First Amendment due process, then, the doctrine enunciated by the district court in *POM* must be rejected in the specific context of a First Amendment challenge to administrative agency action. A subject of regulation who possesses a plausible First Amendment claim[154] must, as a matter of First Amendment due process, be permitted to stay the administrative regulatory proceeding and seek declaratory relief on its First Amendment claim in federal court.

Pom should be contrasted with a seemingly inconsistent line of Supreme Court decisions, most recently illustrated by the decision in *Axon Enterprises, Inc. v. Federal Trade Commission*.[155] There the Court held that litigants challenging the constitutionality of administrative proceedings under certain circumstances may employ general federal question jurisdiction to make that challenge in federal district court. In so holding, the Court relied on the test it established in its 1994 decision, *Thunder Basin Coal Co. v. Reich*.[156] The D.C. Circuit in *Pom* failed even to cite *Thunder Basin*, however, presumably because it concluded that because Pom had engaged in misleading and deceptive advertising practices, there was no reason to allow a First Amendment challenge to proceed outside of the administrative proceedings. But if this was in fact the D.C. Circuit's reasoning, it appears to suffer from the serious logical flaw of question-begging. While it is true that established commercial speech doctrine categorically excludes false and misleading advertising from the First Amendment's scope, the first question in *Pom* would be whether Pom's advertising was in fact false or misleading. One of the key factors under the *Thunder Basin* test is whether the issue to be raised in the federal district court action falls within the agency's expertise, and finding whether advertising is false or misleading may well be deemed to fall within the FTC's expertise. But it should not be ignored that the presence of falsity constitutes a "constitutional fact"—a factual issue which, if decided one way, would render the government's regulatory action constitutional and if decided the other way would render that action unconstitutional. Such issues are, as a matter of due process, to be resolved not by an interested regulator but rather by a neutral adjudicator. In any case, at the very least, as a doctrinal matter *Pom* can be confined to situations of false or misleading advertising. In all other First Amendment challenges to administrative regulatory action, *Axon* should be held to apply, thereby allowing litigants to circumvent the administrative process to present a constitutional challenge in federal court.

6.6 CONCLUSION: PROCEDURE AS THE HANDMAID OF JUSTICE

As foundational to constitutional democracy as substantive constitutional rights clearly are, their protections would be meaningless absent the simultaneous existence of meaningful procedural devices by which those rights are effectively implemented and protected. As Judge Charles Clark—the father of the Federal Rules of Civil Procedure—once wrote, procedure is "the handmaid of justice."[157] This substantive-procedural intersection is nowhere more important than in the context of challenges to the exercise of governmental regulatory authority on the grounds of the First Amendment right of free expression. The primacy of that right is widely recognized, and for this reason the intersection of substance and procedure has been explicitly recognized by the Supreme Court in its doctrine of First Amendment due process.[158]

This chapter has argued that First Amendment due process is especially in peril in the context of the federal administrative state. For that reason, I have urged dramatic changes in administrative process. While significant changes in the doctrine of administrative due process are both necessary and important in all contexts, they are of special importance when First Amendment rights are at stake, due to those rights' widely recognized unique importance to the preservation of constitutional democracy and their inherent fragility. When First Amendment rights are at stake, the role of the administrative regulator must be significantly reduced, and the role of the reviewing court correspondingly increased. Absent such dramatic changes, the administrative process seriously endangers the all-important rights of free expression.

7
CONSTITUTIONAL REMEDIES AS DUE PROCESS OF LAW

7.1 INTRODUCTION

Consider the following scenario: a future federal government enacts a law directing federal agents to seek out and physically attack members of a particular ethnic minority group to which that government is hostile. In order to prevent the federal courts from ordering a halt to this obviously unconstitutional practice, Congress modifies the All Writs Act[1] to insulate the practices that this new statute authorizes from injunctive relief. The All Writs Act authorizes the federal judiciary to issue various forms of mandatory relief, including issuance of injunctions. Adopted in 1789, the Act has long been assumed to provide the federal judiciary with its power to issue equitable remedies, including injunctions that would halt such grievous violations of constitutional liberties.[2] Without authorization granted by the All Writs Act, presumably, the federal courts would be powerless to enjoin such practices.[3]

Although, theoretically, in such a case the state courts would be available, the long-standing prohibition on state court power to control federal officers through mandamus or injunction would, at the very least, create a cloud over state courts' abilities to enjoin the practices.[4] More importantly, if it is assumed—as it long has been—that, purely as a matter of substantive constitutional law, constitutional remedies lie totally within the power of the political branches of the federal government to control, presumably that power would allow those branches to limit state court ability to enforce the Constitution as well. For in such a situation, the issue is not one only of congressional power to control judicial *jurisdiction* but rather what the Constitution itself does and does not require. Thus, if, as a matter of substantive constitutional law, it is constitutional for Congress to exercise total control over constitutional remedies, state courts would be required to uphold the congressional modification of the All Writs Act, even if state courts were permitted to adjudicate such constitutional challenges on the constitutional merits. Thus, even if, in such a situation, a court—state or federal—were found to possess power to declare these actions unconstitutional, the constitutionally valid selective repeal of the All Writs Act would deny them the power to order the practices halted.

Due Process as American Democracy. Martin H. Redish, Oxford University Press. © Martin H. Redish 2024.
DOI: 10.1093/oso/9780197747414.003.0007

This situation would sound absurd, if it were not so frightening. Just try to imagine a court being unable to stop such an outrageous and unambiguous congressional violation of the Constitution, for no reason other than Congress does not want them to do so. Yet if one accepts the traditionally accepted view that constitutional remedies are subconstitutional and therefore ultimately lie in the hands of Congress, then this dystopic scenario becomes all too conceivable.[5] Nevertheless, the Supreme Court has consistently recognized the extremely deferential role that the judiciary must play in fashioning remedies for constitutional violations.[6] And the very existence of the All Writs Act inescapably implies that absent that statutory authorization, the courts would lack power to issue equitable writs, even to enforce and protect constitutional rights.

Surprisingly, the work of even the most respected scholars has been, at best, unhelpful and, at worst, downright harmful in understanding the relevant constitutional typography on the issue of constitutional remedies. Many have concluded that constitutional remedies present a subconstitutional issue and are therefore fully within the power of Congress to regulate as it sees fit.[7] Although several respected scholars have been far more sympathetic to the need for some sort of constitutional status for the remedies for constitutional violations, their analyses are only of slightly more value, because they advocate no more than a rebuttable *presumption* in favor of judicial control of constitutional remedies.[8] More importantly, these scholars fail to place the role of constitutional remedies within the broader framework of American political theory, or even to attempt to justify the constitutional status of remedies as a matter of constitutional interpretation.[9] What has long been needed, but to this point never supplied, is a detailed, coherent defense of the unbending constitutional status of constitutional remedies, grounded in core precepts of American constitutional democratic thought and justified as a matter of textual interpretation.

The argument fashioned here is that well-accepted, foundational principles of American constitutionalism, textually embodied in the Due Process Clauses of the Fifth and Fourteenth Amendments and grounded in belief in the foundationally countermajoritarian nature of the Constitution's directives as controls on the majoritarian branches of government, inescapably lead to the conclusion that constitutional remedies possess full status as constitutional law.[10] In other words, remedies for violations of the Constitution must be recognized as just as much a part of the Constitution as the substantive directives are, and therefore such remedies are fully in the control of the countermajoritarian judiciary, much as textual interpretation of the Constitution has been since the decision in *Marbury v. Madison*.[11] The connection to the Due Process Clauses should be obvious. Those clauses protect against the deprivation of "liberty" or "property" absent due process of law. As a matter of text, doctrine, and underlying political theory, these liberty and property protections—explicitly guaranteed by the Bill of Rights and incorporated by the Fourteenth Amendment—cannot be taken away from the individual without review by the neutral adjudication of the judicial process.

Such a conclusion most surely flows inexorably from the foundational insights of adversary democratic theory. Indeed, the very countermajoritarian nature of our constitutional system grows out of the mistrust and skepticism inherent in our form of democracy. And that mistrust is textually embodied in the Due Process Clauses of the Fifth and Fourteenth Amendments.

The US Constitution reflects a delicate balance between majoritarian rule and countermajoritarian limitations. Our system amounts to something of a paradox: a foundational commitment to the precept that the best way to assure democracy's continued existence is to limit and restrain it. The Framers sought to temper the worst impulses of democracy by making ours a democratic republic in which the people elect representatives rather than participate in democracy directly. The Founders recognized, however, that elected representatives could still threaten minority rights or even seek to impose tyranny. For the most part, the Framers sought to avoid tyranny by dividing political power, both horizontally (separation of powers) and vertically (federalism). The Founders generally sought to protect individual rights against majoritarian invasion through enactment of the Bill of Rights—with the first eight amendments guaranteeing various individual rights.[12] Later generations expanded countermajoritarian protection of individual rights to the states through enactment of the post–Civil War amendments. Although the post–Civil War amendments expressly provide for potential congressional enforcement, even those measures themselves require enforcement by the courts.[13]

In any event, even if Congress never enacted enforcing legislation, no one could reasonably doubt that the directives of those provisions are self-executing, to be enforced by the judiciary. But more importantly, none of the Bill of Rights' provisions mentions anything about enforcement mechanisms. On their face, none of these textually guaranteed protections provides for a judicial enforcement mechanism.[14] But absent such remedial measures, the mandatory countermajoritarian guarantees of individual rights are worth even less than the paper on which they are written. This is because their very existence will naturally lull the members of the electorate into a false sense of security that they in fact possess such rights. In reality, however, the rights are worth no more than their enforcement, and the existence of enforcement mechanisms belongs solely in the hands of the very majoritarian branches those rights are designed to restrain. The result amounts to the imposition of a fraud on the public. The simple fact, as a matter of both logic and practicality, is that the remedies required to vindicate these rights are just as essential as the substance of the rights themselves, and if control of remedies is ultimately vested in the very majoritarian branches that these rights presumably restrain, as a practical matter the rights do not exist. As a result, unknown to most, the entire structure of our constitutional system of minority rights possesses a potentially fatal Achilles heel that, in a time of stress, could bring the entire constitutional system down.

One might consider such dire warnings to be no more than hypothetical hyperbole. After all, our system has existed for well over two hundred years without this structural anomaly causing any serious problem. But constitutional law must be shaped with the most extreme circumstances in mind. Indeed, who would have thought that we would ever suffer the threats to American democracy that have ominously surfaced in recent years? When viewed from that perspective, our current system is woefully unprepared for the worst. This chapter seeks to remedy that glaring systemic weakness.

To protect minority rights from hostile majorities, the Framers of the Constitution intentionally established a judiciary insulated from majoritarian political pressures with salary and tenure guarantees in Article III.[15] The independence that these features ensured, as well as the power of judicial review vested in the federal courts, make it the only branch suited to review the constitutionality of the political branches' actions and, by extension, to create remedies to redress violations of individuals' constitutional rights. Recognizing the judiciary as the only institution capable of fashioning constitutional remedies acknowledges its proper role in our paradoxically countermajoritarian, yet democratic, system.

This chapter proceeds in five parts. The first section sets out a countermajoritarian constitutional theory and applies it to the issue of constitutional remedies. It explains how only a countermajoritarian institution (the judiciary) can both interpret and enforce the Constitution.[16] The second section shapes a theory of constitutional interpretation that justifies and rationalizes the courts' interpretive implication of constitutional remedies from constitutional text, including the Due Process Clauses.[17] The third section critiques existing scholarly theories concerning the legal status of constitutional remedies, showing the failure of even the most respected scholars to come to terms with the fundamental theoretical and practical flaws inherent in the vesting of control of constitutional remedies in the hands of the political branches.[18]

The fourth section addresses likely counterarguments to the theory of constitutional remedies as constitutional law, specifically Professor Henry Monaghan's characterization of constitutional remedies as constitutional common law and the view that constitutional remedies cannot be constitutional law because Congress maintains the power to control federal jurisdiction. Monaghan's constitutional common law posits that although the judiciary can use the same power to protect constitutional rights as it does to create rights and remedies that protect federal interests and implement federal legislative schemes, Congress has the authority to revise or reverse the courts' choice of constitutional remedies as constitutional common law. An additional counterargument suggests that just as the Constitution affords Congress the power to limit federal court jurisdiction, it assures that Congress can similarly control the judiciary's ability to fashion remedies for constitutional violations. Both arguments fail to recognize the judiciary's unique role as ultimate interpreter of the Constitution.[19] The chapter concludes with an examination of the implications for and lessons drawn from the *Bivens v. Six Unknown Named Agents of Federal Bureau of Narcotics* doctrine and implied constitutional damage remedies, highlighting the weakness of the *Bivens* doctrine itself and explaining why it constitutes a woefully inadequate means of vindicating and enforcing constitutional rights.[20]

7.2 THE CONSTITUTIONAL THEORY OF CONSTITUTIONAL REMEDIES

7.2.1 Countermajoritarian Constitutionalism

In sharp contrast to its British counterpart, which took an unwritten form and whose content was determined largely by a process of consensus understandings, the American Constitution took the form of written, mandatory positive law, subject to alteration only through a complex supermajoritarian process of amendment.[21] Much of the document imposed restrictions on the exercise of political power by the federal government as a whole as well as on the separate branches of that government. The subsequently enacted Bill of Rights—the first ten amendments—in varying ways placed further limits on the political branches, primarily on their ability to violate individual rights.[22] As the Supreme Court made clear in Chief Justice John Marshall's famed 1803 opinion in *Marbury v. Madison*,[23] it would make no sense to permit the political branches to ignore those written, binding limitations on their power.

If one starts with the premise that the majoritarian branches are not permitted to ignore the binding, written limits imposed by the Constitution, the inevitable next step is to conclude that they cannot serve as the final arbiter of those limitations. To vest such unreviewable power in the hands of the majoritarian branches would violate Lord Coke's famous dictate in *Dr. Bonham's Case* that no man can be a judge in his own case.[24] Indeed, what purpose would the Constitution serve if the very majoritarian branches it is designed to check are permitted to write, interpret, or eliminate those restrictions? The answer is obvious: the Constitution would be a dead letter. Without the countermajoritarian judiciary in control of remedies for constitutional violations, however, there is nothing, apart from Congress's and the president's magnanimity, stopping these admittedly radical scenarios from coming to pass. The Framers were not so naïve or trusting.[25] Obsessively fearful of and experienced with tyranny, they understood this democratic paradox—that the only way to preserve democracy and majoritarian rule that does not trample down minority rights was to make our system of government's undemocratic branch the ultimate guardian of democracy and the Constitution. This, in short, is the precept of judicial review, which grows directly out of the foundational premises of adversary democratic theory and which has become so fundamental to our constitutional system since *Marbury*.

Accordingly, "American judges came to be regarded as essential to the maintenance of the rule of law and the protection of individual rights."[26] The salary and tenure protections secured to the federal judiciary by the Constitution are a reflection of this regard and serve to ensure that federal judges remain independent of the political pressures to which the majoritarian branches must respond.[27] Because of these protections, the federal judiciary would be able, according to Alexander Hamilton, to "guard the Constitution and the rights of individuals."[28] He added that "the general liberty of the people can never be endangered from" the courts,[29] as long as they remain truly distinct from the majoritarian branches, and "that the courts were designed to be an intermediate body between the people and the legislature, in order ... to keep the latter within the limits assigned to their authority."[30] This then ensures that individuals subject to abusive government power or assaults on their individual constitutional rights "need not resort to revolution to vindicate th[ose] rights...."[31] Instead, they could rely on the countermajoritarian judiciary to keep the majoritarian branches in check.

The dictate of judicial review flows logically from the fears and concerns expressed throughout *The Federalist Papers* over the inevitable dangers of tyranny. Throughout those documents, Hamilton and James Madison express a fear—indeed, arguably an obsession—with the avoidance of this danger.[32] History taught them that tyranny was most likely to originate in the majoritarian branches. These concerns led the Framers of the Articles of Confederation to choose not to create an executive at all and to severely limit Congress's legislative power.[33]

One can rightly presume that the Framers adopted the Constitution under the premise that its terms and provisions were binding and had meaning, and that the people could rely on it for a relatively predictable form of government that would protect the rights and limits on the governmental power that it enumerates. Absent structural guarantees that the rights enshrined in the Constitution would be protected and enforced, the Constitution would be worse than meaningless. Indeed, it would create a framework of government under which the rights it is designed to protect are, as a practical matter, unprotectable. It would jeopardize the explicit constitutional rights of the most vulnerable. And it would cynically mislead the American populace into falsely believing that the people live in a constitutional democracy, even though the rights of minorities would last only as long as the majority acquiesced in them.

What has been said to this point should hardly be controversial. Indeed, it simply reflects the philosophy unambiguously expressed by Hamilton in *Federalist No. 78* and the reasoning of Chief Justice Marshall in *Marbury*.[34] It represents the core notion of American constitutionalism expressly guaranteed by the Due Process Clauses. But it inexorably leads to the conclusion that the judiciary must be fully in control of the scope and nature of our rights' enforcement mechanisms. It is logically and practically inconceivable that the Framers, who so carefully shaped a delicately structured system of separation of powers within the countermajoritarian, written, and binding Constitution, would have contemplated such a fatally large loophole that could so easily bring down the entire system that they spent so much time creating. It would all have been for naught if the effectiveness of the document's countermajoritarian limits would depend entirely on the good will, in instituting remedies for violations of constitutional rights, of the very branches it sought to control.

Were the political branches of government to possess ultimate control of the remedies for enforcing the Constitution's countermajoritarian directives, the entire concept of judicial review would be rendered all but meaningless, which in turn would render the very idea of a countermajoritarian, written, and binding Constitution all but meaningless. The courts would at best be rendered nothing more than advisory bodies, with no power other than to expound on the law in the abstract, subservient to the willingness of the political branches to enact means to make their decisions meaningful. At worst, the courts would be rendered completely irrelevant, as it has long been established that no Article III federal court possesses power to issue an advisory opinion.[35] Thus, absent legislative authorization to the courts to implement remedies as a means of enforcing constitutional directives, the courts could be virtually eliminated from the process of judicial review, while, paradoxically, leaving judicial review in existence (albeit in name only).

This approach to constitutional remedies—that they must be solely the province of the judiciary to maintain the power of judicial review and for the Constitution to retain its countermajoritarian directive—is entirely consistent with and an inherent part of the well-established framework of countermajoritarian constitutional theory.[36] And this dictate of this foundational skepticism of the majoritarian branches is textually embodied in the Fifth Amendment's Due Process Clause, which precludes governmental interference with liberty or property absent a fair, neutral adjudicator. To the extent the majoritarian branches can deprive the courts of all power to prevent such invasions of constitutionally guaranteed rights, due process is denied. In other words, as

I have written previously, it is "essential that the final say as to the [Constitution]'s meaning and the authority to enforce its provisions be vested in the [prophylactically] insulated judiciary."[37]

It is, then, both puzzling and ironic that both courts and scholars widely and simultaneously accept two totally inconsistent principles of constitutional law and theory, when the two cannot logically coexist—a point no one, until now, seems to have noticed. On the one hand, none but the most fringe constitutional scholars challenge the sanctity and security of the precept of judicial review. *Marbury* is the very first case to be read in virtually any course in constitutional law. And lest there be any doubt, the modern-day Supreme Court has reasserted the precept's continued existence whenever it perceives a threat to it. For example, the Court could not have been more clear in its 1958 decision, *Cooper v. Aaron*, when state government officials had the audacity to assert power to interpret the Constitution at least equal, if not superior, to that of the federal judiciary: "[*Marbury*] declared the basic principle that the federal judiciary is supreme in the exposition of the law of the Constitution, and that principle has ever since been respected by this Court and the [c]ountry as a permanent and indispensable feature of our constitutional system."[38]

Yet both the Court[39] and respected scholars[40] have for some reason failed to understand that to recognize judicial review while simultaneously rejecting ultimate judicial control over the fashioning of remedies for constitutional violations amounts to swimming halfway across a river, rendering the entire system an illogical failure. To the extent the system survives, it is only because it is effectively built on a house of cards. The political branches could bring it down any time they have a mind to, restrained only by the very same sort of vague consensus and tradition that the Framers conspicuously sought to avoid as the last line of protection against tyranny when they chose to reject the British system in favor of written, mandatory positive law as a means of controlling majoritarian government.

None of this should be taken to suggest that the insulated judiciary always acts as a perfect check on the majoritarian branches, or even an effective one. On more than one occasion, the Supreme Court has permitted or even endorsed majoritarian oppression of minorities.[41] But as Winston Churchill said of democracy, judicial control is the worst system—except for all the others.[42] Of the three branches, the insulated judiciary is far and away most likely to follow the Constitution's mandates because, unlike the executive, it possesses "neither FORCE nor WILL, but merely judgment,"[43] and possesses no military power to enforce those judgments. Furthermore, the judiciary differs from the legislature in that "it is not directly subject to the political pressures imposed by the ... prejudices of the electorate."[44]

For these reasons, remedies for constitutional violations must be deemed to have constitutional status, and the federal judiciary must have the final authority to craft the appropriate remedial scheme with no deference to Congress or the executive. To be sure, if Congress enacts remedies for violation of the Constitution pursuant to its authorized legislative power, the courts may choose to find those remedies sufficient, mooting the need for judicial fashioning of further relief. But if the courts do so, it is not because of some built-in deference, but simply because the courts, deciding independently, find the legislative remedy adequate to protect and implement constitutional rights. Judicial control of constitutional remedies is consistent with judicial review of the meaning of the Constitution's rights-bearing provisions. In fact, it is an essential feature of judicial review. Although it is true that the Constitution has little to say explicitly about remedies, the document also does not fully explain the meaning of the rights to be protected. Those rights, without judicial explication of their meaning and scope, would not be worth the paper on which they are written. But the interpretation cannot end there. Were the judiciary limited to expounding on the meaning of the rights-bearing provisions without the power to enforce those meanings through appropriate remedial schemes, those provisions would be as toothless as if their meaning and scope were never developed in the first place. Judicial review to interpret the meaning of the Constitution must therefore include the power to fashion the remedies for constitutional violations. One simply cannot logically accept the former without accepting the latter.

7.3 CHALLENGING THE INTERSECTION OF CONSTITUTIONAL DIRECTIVES AND CONSTITUTIONAL REMEDIES

One might respond to the compelling nature of the argument in favor of merging the power of constitutional interpretation and constitutional enforcement in two ways. First, one could argue that the fears of tyranny expressed here are grossly overstated. Our nation has survived as a constitutional democracy since its beginning with the understanding that the courts lack ultimate control of judicial remedies. Second, to the extent that the fears raised here are in fact legitimate, vesting ultimate control of constitutional remedies in the judiciary will be meaningless, because those involved in bringing about tyranny will no doubt refuse to enforce those decisions, much as President Andrew Jackson did in 1832 when he refused to obey Chief Justice John Marshall's order in *Worcester v. Georgia*[45] and as President Abraham Lincoln did in 1861 when he ignored Chief Justice Roger Taney's writ of habeas corpus in *Ex parte Merryman*.[46]

Although at some level there is truth in both of these assertions, they ultimately must be rejected as grounds for vesting ultimate control of constitutional remedies in the hands of the political branches. In the end, every measure that the Framers took to avoid the onset of tyranny can amount to no more than speed bumps. If the forces of tyranny are strong enough, nothing can stop them from ripping up the entire Constitution. But the fact that constitutional protections are merely speed bumps does not mean they are either useless or irrelevant. Although speed bumps cannot stop a car from going over and beyond them, they can force that car to slow down. Unless tyranny is imposed by outside enemies following a successful invasion, moves toward tyranny will demand some significant level of support within the populace. To the extent that those seeking to impose tyranny at the outset unambiguously violate controlling constitutional law, their legitimacy in the eyes of the populace is likely to be reduced. If majoritarian forces, as part of their move toward tyranny, are deemed to possess constitutionally valid authority to revoke all judicial remedies for violations of constitutional rights, it is likely to be that much easier for them to achieve their goal of gaining public support.

The fact that, at present, the fears expressed here may seem unrealistic does not mean that they are more theoretical than real, because once those issues do in fact become real, it is usually too late for constitutional theory to catch up.[47] It is, then, far better to debate these issues of constitutional theory at a time when they are in fact theoretical, rather than when they become all too real.

7.4 CONSTITUTIONAL REMEDIES AND CONSTITUTIONAL TEXT

There may be another reason why scholars and courts have largely assumed ultimate remedial authority to lie in the political branches. With very rare exception,[48] the text of the original document, as well as that of the Bill of Rights, makes no reference to remedial authority. And although the post–Civil War amendments expressly mention legislative power of enforcement, they similarly say nothing about judicial enforcement.[49] Thus, to deem constitutional remedies as having the status of constitutional law, one would have to infer the remedial power in the judiciary without any express textual basis.

Of course, the argument has already been made here that the explicit guarantee of due process effectively amounts to sufficient textual grounding to enable the courts to prevent majoritarian abrogation of all remedies to the deprivation of constitutional rights. In any event, even if this textual argument were to be rejected, it is quite possible to justify judicial control of constitutional remedies in a variety of other ways. For those who have no difficulty somehow gleaning from the written document a set of unwritten constitutional rights and directives,[50] inference from constitutional silence concerning judicial control of remedies should hardly seem shocking. I do not, however, include myself in that group. To the contrary, I believe in a form of constitutional textualism, which recognizes that although at some level constitutional text is often ambiguous, the total absence of linguistic grounding for constitutional dictates generally precludes judicial inference of constitutional authority.[51]

The easiest answer, as already argued, is to find textual support in the Due Process Clauses. As already explained, the terms "liberty" and "property" are properly construed to subsume the constitutional protections guaranteed by the Bill of Rights and the Fourteenth Amendment. Those "liberty" and "property" guarantees cannot be taken away absent "due process," properly defined to demand neutral judicial involvement.

Even if one were, hypothetically, to reject this texturally grounded due process argument, an alternative textual argument may be fashioned. Although I consider myself a textualist,[52] a commitment to textualism does not necessarily imply a commitment to textual literalism. Rather than focusing on the textual trees, the textual forest is far more important. In other words, the key for an interpreting court is to glean from the text some underlying purpose (which may or may not result from an originalist inquiry), and then to interpret the text in a manner that assists that provision in achieving that goal. This approach is properly described as "facilitative textualism." Thus, this interpretive approach justifies neither the Supreme Court's holding in *Lochner v. New York*[53] nor its decision in *Roe v. Wade*,[54] regardless of one's personal views on the social, political, or moral merits of either, because there is no plausible grounding for either decision in text, and because no one has fashioned a convincing argument providing real textual support in either instance.

In contrast to such naked, judge-made, nontextual additions to the Constitution which plague all forms of substantive due process, in certain instances facilitative textualism allows an expansion beyond the specific words in text in order to make the express textual directive meaningful. In the words of Justice Antonin Scalia and his coauthor, Professor Bryan Garner, "to say that one *begins* with the [text] is to suggest that one does not *end* there,"[55] for "[t]extualism, in its purest form, begins and ends with what the text says and fairly implies."[56] Thus, the form of textualism which they advocate does not prohibit taking into consideration the more general purposes, which the text is designed to serve.[57]

According to Justice Scalia and Professor Garner, this form of textualism is not a new development; indeed, it has its roots in early American jurisprudence and has been applied throughout the nation's history. For example, in the Supreme Court's 1819 holding in *McCulloch v. Maryland*, Chief Justice Marshall rejected a hyperliteral interpretation of Article I, Section 18's Necessary and Proper Clause.[58] Even earlier, in 1816, in the Court's decision in *Martin v. Hunter's Lessee*, Justice Joseph Story advocated for "reasonableness, not strictness, of interpretation"[59] and argued that "[t]he words [of the Constitution] are to be taken in their natural and obvious sense, and not in a sense unreasonably restricted or enlarged."[60] Much later, in the Court's 1946 holding in *Utah Junk Co. v. Porter*, Justice Frankfurter noted that "[l]iteralness may strangle meaning."[61] Rejecting a "narrow, crabbed reading of a text"[62] that is the essence of strict constructionism, textualists like Justice Scalia and Professor Garner acknowledge that the full text, given its fair, reasonable meaning, has implications that can alter the "hyperliteral meaning of each word in the text."[63]

Disposing of strict constructionism as "a doctrine [not] to be taken seriously,"[64] textualists such as Justice Scalia simultaneously reject the notion that departing from the literal approach to textualism gives judges free license to ignore the text entirely, while paying it lip service, and stray, unrestrained by anything other than their own moral compasses, into the realm of lawmaking. "[W]hile the good textualist is not a literalist, neither is he a nihilist. Words do have a limited range of meaning, and no interpretation that goes beyond that range is permissible."[65] The approach advocated here is entirely consistent with this idea, because finding the judiciary's power to fashion constitutional remedies in the Constitution does not require departure from the document's text. Such a power lies within that "limited range of meaning."[66] Not only is this interpretation entirely compatible with the principled textualist approach just outlined, it is also reinforced by "rules of interpretation called the canons of construction,"[67] tools often associated with and favored by textualists. Several, in particular, are relevant here.

The version of facilitative textualism advocated here is wholly consistent with the interpretive approach just described. Indeed, the Supreme Court has employed it on a variety of occasions.[68] One of the fundamental canons is the presumption against ineffectiveness, which states that "[a] textually permissible interpretation that furthers rather than obstructs the document's purpose should be favored."[69] The canon is based on "the facts that (1) interpretation always depends on context, (2) context always includes evident purpose, and (3) evident purpose always includes effectiveness."[70] It demonstrates that consideration of a legal text's purpose is not inconsistent with textualism.

The presumption against ineffectiveness applies not only to the rights-bearing provisions of the Constitution but also to the entire countermajoritarian document, for common-sense interpretive principles dictate that no provision of the Constitution can be construed to be meaningless. Application of this canon is quite straightforward. Two of the purposes of the Constitution are to restrain the majoritarian branches and to protect the individual rights enshrined in the document.[71] The countermajoritarian judiciary serves as the restraint on the majoritarian branches, Congress and the executive. It would be an understatement to say that without it, and without recognizing both this duty and power vested in the judiciary, a primary purpose of the Constitution would go unfulfilled. This purpose would be actively undermined and impossible to achieve, because the majoritarian branches would be left unchecked with little between them and possible tyranny, other than the parchment on which the Constitution is written. Similarly, without remedies, the Constitution's rights-bearing provisions would be wholly ineffective. Instead of serving their intended function of restraining the majoritarian branches, the provisions of the Constitution would function as nothing more than hortatory pleas. With no way to enforce or vindicate those rights, they would become worse than meaningless. Indeed, an interpretation that deprived the textual directive of mandatory countermajoritarian judicial enforcement would turn the Constitution into an instrument of deception, defrauding the populace into believing they possess rights that, as a practical matter, they do not have.[72]

In shaping a theory of implied enforcement powers, it is important to distinguish this "facilitative" form of nontextualism from the far less legitimate form of "supplemental" nontextualism. The former is merely a common-sense and principled means of analyzing the text of the Constitution in an effort to make sure the explicit text has meaningful impact. Absent these nontextual additions, the explicit textual directives are rendered all but meaningless as a matter of mandatory positive law. These ancillary directives are necessary as a matter of logic and practicality, in order to provide full force to the explicit provisions of the Constitution. The supplemental implied directives, in contrast, are not required in order to implement the Constitution's explicit mandates. Instead, the interpreter makes her own determination, often according to her personal ideology, that the unstated directive is essential. Their connection to the text is tenuous at best. Thus, recognition of the interpretive distinction between facilitative and supplemental nontextualism is necessary to rebut the charge that the former is illegitimate because the directives are not textually explicit and to mitigate the concerns that this approach would unleash judges to illegitimately stray from the text by fashioning supplemental implied constitutional directives wholly lacking foundation in the text.[73]

Supplemental nontextual directives, in contrast, "are not found to be essential to the successful implementation of an explicit provision, but instead represent nothing more than directives that the interpreter happens to conclude are foundational to a democratic society."[74] These are inherently problematic because allowing "unrepresentative, unaccountable judges" to "check the political branches when and only when the choices of those branches differ from the narrow political preferences of" the judicial interpreter completely undermines "our system of popular sovereignty."[75]

Consider, for example, the Court's discovery of an unenumerated right to privacy in *Griswold v. Connecticut* in 1965.[76] Justice Douglas, writing for the Court, reasoned that the "specific guarantees in the Bill of Rights," particularly in the First, Third, Fourth, and Fifth Amendments, "have penumbras, formed by emanations from those guarantees that help give them life and substance."[77] In doing so, Justice Douglas took principles or guarantees expressly provided in the Bill of Rights—such as the prohibition against the quartering of soldiers in individuals' homes during peacetime or the proscription against unreasonable searches and seizures—and fashioned something entirely new and distinct.[78] The right to privacy can be said to have been fashioned out of whole cloth because, although ostensibly starting with textual provisions, it becomes completely unmoored from the text and is not a necessary directive to effectuate or enforce the text. Justice Douglas's analysis, although purportedly, on some strained level, grounded in the text, is not textualism at all. Thus, my form of textual analysis categorically reject forms of supplemental nontextualism developed not to bring to life a specific provision but rather to simply advance the interpreter's own policy preferences. For reasons just explained, they are far different from the legitimate use of facilitative nontextualism advocated for here.

One should be equally wary, however, of the other extreme, which "leaves the political branches effectively unchecked, [so that] the essential values of counter[]majoritarian constitutionalism, so central to our political structure, [are] seriously undermined."[79] Although proponents of this view repudiate the contention that the judiciary should completely defer to the political branches when constitutional challenges to their actions arise, any model that vests any institution other than the judiciary with ultimate interpretive authority "effectively bring[s] about this result."[80]

Instead, a framework that remains fundamentally consistent with a faithful interpretation of the broad provisions of the Constitution's text can rest firmly in the middle ground between the two extremes of an unrestrained judicial power either to restrict or empower the political branches on the one hand and, on the other hand, leave those majoritarian branches so unchecked as to eviscerate the countermajoritarian nature of the Constitution. This approach gives rise to the possibility of ancillary constitutional directives, which never contradict the Constitution's explicit text but that are nevertheless indispensable to give meaning and effect to what the text does explicitly provide. "[C]onfined to the outer linguistic reaches of applicable constitutional text,"[81] the ancillary directives "are concepts that, while not explicit on the face of the text, are both logically and practically necessary to assure viability of the textually explicit directive."[82] One need not delve too deeply into the Supreme Court's interpretation of provisions of the Bill of Rights to find the Court's principled application of these directives.

Take, for example, the First Amendment right of free speech.[83] The Supreme Court has rightly inferred from the text of the First Amendment such facilitative freedoms as the freedom of thought and the freedom of association,[84] as well as a right to expressive anonymity,[85] despite the fact that there is no express provision of these rights in the text of the amendment. The Court has wisely reasoned that without inference of these additional facilitative mechanisms, the right expressly provided—the right of free expression—cannot be implemented effectively. In 1958, in *NAACP v. Alabama* ex rel. *Patterson*,[86] a case involving a state attorney general's demand for the disclosure of the NAACP's members, the Court found that "compelled disclosure of [the group's membership] [would] affect adversely the ability of [the NAACP] and its members to pursue their collective effort to foster beliefs which they admittedly have the right to advocate."[87] Because the freedom of association "will [frequently] function as a precursor to or facilitator of direct expression," it "can be seen as ancillary to and facilitative of the right of expression."[88] It is purely a matter of common sense that "the freedom of speech cannot survive, much less flourish, absent corresponding constitutional recognition of these supporting freedoms."[89]

What is true for these ancillary, facilitative First Amendment freedoms is equally applicable to implied enforcement powers. Indeed, the case for viewing implied enforcement powers as a legitimate form of facilitative textualism is far stronger than the case for recognizing ancillary facilitative First Amendment freedoms. Absent the ancillary First Amendment freedoms that the Court has recognized, the right of free expression would still possess independent force, albeit at a level significantly weaker than it possesses when those additional freedoms are added. In contrast, absent recognition of an implied power of countermajoritarian judicial enforcement, the foundational countermajoritarian nature of the entire document would be lost. As Chief Justice Marshall recognized in *Marbury v. Madison*, the only means by which courts may interpret the provisions of the Constitution is through a process of adjudication—a process that necessarily assumes a judicial exercise of mandatory remedial power. Absent such a remedial authority, courts cannot perform their function.[90] Thus, once one concludes—as our nation long has—that judicial review is itself an essential element of American constitutionalism, vesting in the courts a corresponding remedial power must similarly be recognized as an essential element of our constitutional framework.

One might respond that as long as the political branches remain willing to vest in the judiciary such remedial power, the system of American constitutionalism can continue to function properly. But as long as the judiciary's retention of its enforcement power remains entirely in the discretion of the political branches which the Constitution seeks to control, the system has a dangerously weak foundation.

Implied facilitative constitutionally guaranteed remedial authority, it should again be emphasized, is in no way logically confined to constitutional rights (though due process protections arguably are so limited). This facilitative enforcement power logically applies as well to other provisions of the Constitution relating to the powers of the federal government. The executive branch provides a good example. Article II vests the executive power in the president[91] and requires that he or she "take Care that the Laws be faithfully executed."[92] There is absolutely no reference in the text of Article II or any other part of the Constitution to executive privilege. It can only be justified as a means of protecting and facilitating the exercise of executive power. Although this power is neither absolute nor unqualified, the Supreme Court has recognized its constitutional foundations: "The privilege is fundamental to the operation of Government and inextricably rooted in the separation of powers under the Constitution."[93] Consequently, the combination of the Constitution's mandatory language and countermajoritarian nature, along with the understanding that ancillary directives are needed to effectuate the Constitution's rights-bearing provisions, demonstrates that a principled textualist approach to constitutional interpretation demands constitutional status for constitutional remedies.

7.5 THE INADEQUACY OF EXISTING SCHOLARLY THEORY

Issues surrounding the status of constitutional remedies have not escaped the attention of at least a few leading constitutional scholars, though it would not have been unreasonable to expect the subject to have received considerably more attention than it has. Some of the scholars who have examined the issue have moved in the direction of the firm stance taken here. All of them, however, have consistently failed to recognize the constitutional status of constitutional remedies, to recognize why only the judiciary by way of its final interpretative authority can appropriately fashion these remedies, or to integrate all of these elements into a comprehensive constitutional theory in line with the foundational principles of American constitutionalism.[94]

Professor Henry Hart briefly addressed the issue in his famous dialogue, recognizing broad congressional power to craft and select remedies. In his words, "[i]t must be plain that Congress necessarily has wide choice in the selection of remedies, and that [the status of these remedies] can rarely be of constitutional dimension."[95] He added, "that preventive relief is the exception rather than the rule . . . makes it hard to hold that anybody has a constitutional right to an injunction or declaratory judgment."[96] In so declaring, he made a serious mistake of overstatement. Hart fatally fails to distinguish between constitutional and statutory remedies.[97] Denial of remedies for constitutional violations are *always* and *necessarily* determinations of constitutional dimension. When constitutional rights have been violated, only a constitutional remedy can provide adequate redress, and basic notions of separation of powers and American constitutionalism inescapably dictate that those remedies are to be fashioned by the judiciary as an inherent element of the process of judicial review.[98] One cannot evaluate the proper respective roles for Congress and the judiciary without first recognizing this critical distinction. Moreover, this distinction allows for a clear dividing line: Congress controls statutory remedies because it legislates statutes, whereas the judiciary controls constitutional remedies because only the courts have final say as to the meaning of the Constitution.[99]

Professor John Harrison has also advocated strong congressional authority over constitutional remedies.[100] In his inquiry into the extent to which Congress can control constitutional remedies, Harrison argues that only Congress, under its substantive powers, can create affirmative judicial remedies.[101] Because remedies depend solely upon congressional authorization, Congress may withdraw what it also has the power to confer.[102] The implication of his argument is an exceedingly narrow view of judicial authority to protect constitutional rights—one lacking the power to provide affirmative remedies for constitutional violations. His theory also makes the same mistake as Hart's: the source of the right implicates the source of the remedy. The two must be one and the same. Otherwise, the entire process of judicial review would be rendered no more than the equivalent of the French Maginot Line immediately prior to World War II—on the surface appearing to provide strong protection yet in reality, easily circumvented by the very forces against whom protection is needed. Congress, as an inherent element of its legislative power, can create federal remedies for statutorily created rights.[103] In sharp contrast, as previously explained, the rights protected by the Constitution must be given final meaning by the courts empowered to interpret it. Thus, unless one rejects the foundational premise of judicial review—and none but fringe constitutional scholars has even seriously raised this possibility—protecting those rights is the role of the judiciary, and therefore, the means to protect constitutional rights are, as a logical matter, equally left to judicial determination. This is a fundamental reality of our entire democratic and countermajoritarian constitutional framework.[104]

Others have pushed back on Hart's and Harrison's arguments for congressional primacy, but unfortunately, they have failed to push back strongly enough. For example, Professor Daniel Meltzer[105] responded directly to Harrison's "radical" theory that "the Constitution is merely a shield and not a sword."[106] Meltzer questions Harrison's conclusion—that the scope of the judiciary's power to supply constitutional remedies is a narrow one—as "a doubtful leap" from Harrison's "originalist" premises.[107] "The nineteenth century practice on which

Harrison relies" for his conclusion, Meltzer argues, provides "weak support for [Harrison's] [argument] that that framework is the *exclusive* one called for by the Constitution."[108] Meltzer points out that Harrison fails to cite any legislative, judicial, or other contemporary authority in the early years of the United States for his proposition.[109] He then points to the "distinctive American ideas of a written higher law, enforceable by courts, and of individual rights protected by the Constitution" for a broad understanding of *Marbury v. Madison*'s notion that "it is a general and indisputable rule, that where there is a legal right, there is also a legal remedy by suit or action at law whenever that right is invaded."[110]

Meltzer's analysis up to this point is both fair and accurate. Not only does Harrison ignore the inherently constitutional nature of the rights and remedies, he also fails to ground his approach fully in the Constitution. Nevertheless, Meltzer missed an opportunity to strike even more forcefully at Harrison's framework. The Constitution cannot be reduced merely to a shield, meant solely to soften the blow of majoritarian attacks on individual constitutional liberties.[111] Rather, it must provide for the countermajoritarian judiciary to wield power in response so that the rights protected are actually vindicated and the people can exercise them. Any order a court issues to protect constitutional rights will necessarily require the political branches to do or refrain from doing something. The Constitution as a sword, in effect, allows individuals to take full advantage of the constitutional rights afforded to them rather than hide behind a shield while Congress or the executive searches for other ways to violate those rights.

Meltzer continued to develop this theory of constitutional remedies in an article coauthored with Professor Richard Fallon.[112] They recognize certain important remedial implications in the Constitution and argue that there should be "a strong though not unyielding presumption" in favor of "individually effective redress for violations of constitutional rights"[113] and that "constitutional remedies [must be] adequate to keep government generally within the bounds of law."[114] Meltzer and Fallon acknowledge the general lack of explicit reference to remedies in the Constitution but explain that "[t]o the [F]ramers, special provision for constitutional remedies probably appeared unnecessary, because the Constitution presupposed a going legal system, with ample remedial mechanisms, in which constitutional guarantees would be implemented."[115] They ground their theory in two basic principles served by constitutional remedies: "[t]he first is to redress individual violations" (i.e., for every right there is a remedy); and "[t]he second function is ... to reinforce structural values, including those underlying the separation of powers and the rule of law."[116] Both Meltzer and Fallon recognize that the Constitution was designed to serve as a necessary check on the political branches and that it is the judiciary's role "to represent the people's continuing interest in the protection of long-term values, of which popular majorities, no less than their elected representatives, might sometimes lose sight."[117] Nevertheless, they view this as merely "aspiration[al]" and "not an unqualified command" flowing directly and logically from the text of the Constitution.[118] This is their fatal mistake, for reasons explained throughout this chapter.

Meltzer and Fallon, along with Professor Walter Dellinger, acknowledge that Congress can and should play a legitimate role in crafting these remedies. For example, Dellinger argues that Congress can "substitut[e] an alternative remedial scheme [for the one created by the Court], provided it affords comparable vindication of the constitutional provision involved,"[119] and that in many cases the judiciary should actually defer[120] to Congress regarding constitutional remedies.[121] Even though scholars such as Dellinger claim that "[t]he source of the Court's power to create remedies will be found, if at all, in the spare language of [A]rticle III,"[122] they still assume "that Congress has the power initially to detail the remedial mechanisms available in the federal courts, [and that] Congress should be free to revise with an adequate alternative any remedy which is not determined by the Court to be indispensable but which is merely selected by the Court as one appropriate method of carrying into effect a substantive constitutional right."[123]

Despite acknowledging Congress's critical role in crafting remedial schemes, Dellinger seemingly leaves open the possibility that some remedies may lie solely within the province of the judiciary—in the "spare language of [A]rticle III."[124] But this notion remains grossly underdeveloped. Dellinger is correct in stating that remedies are part of the judicial power and manifested through judicial review. But left unsaid is that the judiciary's remedial power is fundamental to its countermajoritarian duty to enforce the Constitution and restrain majoritarian excesses. Also left unanswered is where exactly one is to find the line dividing those remedies that must be left solely to the judiciary and those that need not be. "If the Court is restricted in its development of constitutional remedies to only those remedies which are so indispensable that their absence would render the guarantee involved a 'mere form of words,' then the Court's implementation of the Constitution will be less than that reasonably implicit in the document."[125] Yet just a few pages later, he says, "where the judiciary independently infers remedies directly from constitutional provisions, Congress may legislate an alternative remedial scheme which it considers equally effective in enforcing the Constitution and which the Court, in the process of judicial review, deems an adequate substitute for the displaced remedy."[126] This also fails to account for Congress's inability to act as the final interpreter of the Constitution and the fact that the judiciary owes Congress no deference regarding what is or is not adequate. And the Constitution is the clear, principled dividing line. Rights that fall under the Constitution can be redressed, at the very least as a last resort, by the judiciary's remedial power.

Fallon has elaborated further on constitutional remedies in the context of congressional power to limit the jurisdiction of federal courts.[127] He emphasizes that "jurisdiction to decide constitutional cases would prove meaningless without judicial power to award remedies," adding that judicial "pronounce[ments] on constitutional issues" for which the courts "could not order [] remed[ies]," would run afoul of "Article III's prohibition against advisory opinions."[128] But he appears to backtrack on his premise of judicial power to shape constitutional remedies. He qualifies his analysis by asserting that although "the constitutional necessity of any particular remedy should be regarded as a function not only of the availability or unavailability of other remedies, but also of the particular constitutional provision under which a party seeks relief," the principle "that the Constitution requires some form of individually effective relief in all cases . . . is not absolute and will sometimes yield to interests in efficient government administration."[129] Nevertheless, Fallon states that "congressional attempts to preclude all possible remedies for the systematic or ongoing violation of constitutional rights . . . should be deemed intolerable."[130] But this sets the constitutional bar far too low; the mere fact that Congress has provided *some* remedy does not necessarily mean that the courts, exercising their independent final authority to interpret constitutional directives, must accept the congressional determination of what is adequate. In any event, Fallon does not go far enough, missing the inherent intersection between countermajoritarian substantive constitutional commands and constitutional remedies that are justified as a form of facilitative or ancillary textualism.[131]

Despite these serious flaws, there is much to approve of in the scholarship of Dellinger, Fallon, and Meltzer, to the extent that they argue that the judiciary possesses the power to fashion constitutional remedies and that this authority derives from the Constitution itself.[132] However, they either overlook or fail to recognize that this power can and must rest ultimately with the judiciary—*in all constitutional cases*.[133] It is a matter not only of textual and structural constitutional interpretation but also a logical outgrowth of the theory of the inherently paradoxical nature of American constitutionalism. And although these scholars have acknowledged the countermajoritarian role of the federal courts, they have not fully reconciled this role with giving final congressional authority to interpret the Constitution on its own—a political branch interpreting the restraints on its own action. In fact, these two ideas are irreconcilable, as majoritarian control of constitutional remedies and interpretation eviscerates the countermajoritarian nature of the Constitution. Moreover, such an approach completely ignores the lessons of adversary democracy, since it places ultimate trust in the political branches to police themselves. The inherent skepticism and mistrust which characterize adversary democracy surely does not permit such a result.

Professor Susan Bandes has sought to develop a more complete theory in her discussion of *Bivens*[134] remedies.[135] She recognizes "that the judicial branch can enforce the Constitution without congressional action," as "enforcement of the Constitution is not dependent on the assent of the political branches or of the states."[136] Bandes further claims that "[t]he insight at the heart of *Bivens* is that the judiciary has a duty to enforce the Constitution" and that "[i]f the remedy [for violations of the Constitution] is not forthcoming from the political branches, the Court must provide it."[137] Her argument relies on the "separation of powers principle demand[ing] judicial enforcement," declaratory and injunctive relief, as well as damages remedies.[138] Although Bandes is undoubtedly skeptical of a role for Congress in this area,[139] it appears as though she may allow for some congressional participation so long as the remedy it provides is adequate.[140] Mere skepticism is insufficient, however, and it is this point that ultimately distinguishes her theory from the one proposed in this chapter: the majoritarian branches cannot in any case be deemed to possess the ultimate say in "determin[ing] the proper means for effectuating constitutional guarantees."[141] The countermajoritarian nature of judicial review permits no deference to Congress in constitutional interpretation. It is the role of the judiciary alone to exercise the ultimate power to interpret the Constitution, and fashioning remedies for constitutional violations is an essential feature of that role. The judiciary must be able to create constitutional remedies because such remedies are necessary facilitative directives, required to effectuate the textually explicit directives.

The aforementioned theories of constitutional remedies either concede far too much power to Congress, fail to give remedies for constitutional violations the required constitutional status, or fail to place the theory of judicial control of remedies within a broader theory of American constitutionalism. I seek to fill these gaps by offering a theory fully consistent with and faithful to both the text of the Constitution and the paradox of American constitutionalism.

7.6 ANTICIPATING AND RESPONDING TO COUNTERARGUMENTS

To this point, this chapter has demonstrated that both constitutional theory and text, properly construed, point ineluctably toward a framework in which constitutional remedies are deemed to possess constitutional status. Furthermore, only the countermajoritarian judiciary, whose independence from political pressure is assured by Article III's prophylactic salary and tenure guarantees, may possess the ultimate power to fashion these remedies if our constitutional system is to function properly. This remedial power is appropriately viewed as an inherent element of the power of judicial review.

Nevertheless, courts, Congress, and scholars have largely rejected this constitutional theory throughout much of our nation's history.[142] This is not because the theory has been ignored, but rather because it has been rejected on other grounds. This discussion examines two of the most likely counterarguments. The first, set forth in an earlier discussion,[143] is Professor Henry Monaghan's theory of constitutional common law. This theory posits that the power to develop remedies stands somewhere between legislative and judicial power. The second is the well-settled power of Congress to control federal court jurisdiction which has often been assumed to subsume the power to control the remedies afforded by the federal courts. Careful analysis will demonstrate, however, that both are seriously flawed as a matter of constitutional theory.[144]

7.7 THE INCOHERENCE OF CONSTITUTIONAL COMMON LAW

In his review of the Supreme Court's 1974 term, Professor Monaghan articulated his theory of constitutional common law.[145] Monaghan contended:

> [A] surprising amount of what passes as authoritative constitutional "interpretation" is best understood as something of a quite different order—a substructure of substantive, procedural, and remedial rules drawing their inspiration and authority from, but not required by, various constitutional provisions; in short, a constitutional common law subject to amendment, modification, or even reversal by Congress.[146]

If the reader was not puzzled by this statement at the outset, a more careful reading should quickly demonstrate just how dubious Monaghan's theory actually is. In one breath, Monaghan points to "substantive, procedural, and remedial rules" inspired and authorized by the Constitution. These rules would necessarily be developed by the judiciary in the course of its interpretation of the Constitution. In the next breath, however, Monaghan claims that these judicial holdings can be amended, modified, or even overruled by Congress. This turns our system of separation of powers on its head. Congress has no authority to amend, modify, or reverse the Supreme Court's interpretation of the Constitution.[147] On the other hand, if a particular substantive, procedural, or remedial rule is truly part of the common law, how can it be properly characterized as constitutional interpretation? Constitutional law, by its very countermajoritarian nature, preempts congressional revision. In contrast, common law, again by its very nature, is inherently subject to congressional modification. Either the courts are construing the Constitution, or they are not. As a matter of the theory of American constitutionalism, then, Monaghan is swimming halfway across a river. In short, his entire theory is, as a matter of political theory, incoherent.

Uncovering more of the theory shines additional light on its foundational incoherence. The constitutional common law, Monaghan emphasized, was "rooted in the Constitution" and essentially a species of Judge Henry Friendly's "specialized" federal common law.[148] Monaghan set out his theory of the Supreme Court's constitutional common law power through an examination of Supreme Court developments in the field of criminal procedure, particularly the exclusionary rule—a doctrine recognized by the Court prohibiting the use of evidence obtained through violations of the Fourth, Fifth, and Sixth Amendments.[149] The Supreme Court's common-lawmaking power, however, extends beyond that, according to Monaghan.[150]

He points to the fact that the Supreme Court has used its power to create rights and remedies protecting federal interests and implementing federal legislative schemes. Accordingly, the Court should be free to employ the same kind of power to protect constitutional rights, as the Court's history of protecting individual rights make it a "singularly appropriate institution" to carry out this role.[151] Although Monaghan argues that this power is "rooted in the Constitution," he envisions "a coordinate role for Congress"—a form of Court-Congress "dialogue"—"in the continuing process of defining the content and consequences of individual [constitutional] liberties."[152] Congress's power to revise or reverse the Supreme Court's constitutional common law is, he argues, key to overcoming objections and concerns that constitutional common law violates separation of powers.[153]

Despite the critical role Monaghan sees Congress playing in protecting individual constitutional rights and liberties, particularly "where the Court's rule is perceived to have gone too far," he appears to acknowledge that there may be judicially crafted rules or remedies that may be beyond the reach of Congress to amend or reverse.[154] It is constitutional interpretation, and no longer common law, he reasons, when the Court views a particular remedy as an indispensable component of the underlying constitutional guarantee.[155] And, he continues, "[t]he Court undoubtedly has both the power and the duty to fashion 'interpretive' implementing rules to fill out the meaning of generally framed constitutional provisions."[156] Some of these rules may be "true constitutional interpretations within the meaning of *Marbury v. Madison*."[157] But his argument ignores the simple fact that constitutional interpretations, of course, can never be characterized as common law.[158] Only the judiciary has the final authority to interpret the Constitution and determine the remedies that are indispensable to its meaning, and Congress has no power to overturn the judiciary's interpretation of any constitutional provision.

In any event, Monaghan's theory leaves completely unanswered the question of where the dividing line is to be drawn. The deeper one goes, the murkier the water becomes. How does it fit within our constitutional structure for Congress to overrule judicial judgments when the Court is "interpreting the Constitution 'itself'"?[159] Monaghan's answer is unclear.[160] Ultimately, he appears content to settle on a "quasi-constitutional," twilight-zone-like law of remedies which the Court can fashion to vindicate constitutional liberties, subject—except apparently in the clearest instances of constitutional interpretation—to the power of Congress to revise or reverse the judiciary's remedial scheme with one of its own.[161] This resolution, however, is far from satisfactory. Indeed, the notion of "quasi-constitutional" law seems like nothing more than an attempt to have one's cake and eat it, too. Congress has no preemptive constitutional interpretive authority of the Constitution. Thus, in order for it to have any role at all, this area of the law must be something less than fully derived from the Constitution itself. That in itself is incoherent because the text from which these rules and laws are drawn is the Constitution—and only the judiciary can formulate those interpretations.

Leading scholars have weighed in on Monaghan's behalf.[162] Professor Daniel Meltzer has argued "that the Constitution 'authorizes' such lawmaking every bit as much as do federal statutes[,]" finding this authority to be unexceptional.[163] Moreover, he is not as troubled by the difficulty of drawing a "distinction between . . . common law and pure constitutional interpretation."[164] Meltzer, like the fiercest critics of Monaghan's theory (described later), acknowledges that there are instances in which congressional reversal or modification of a judicial decision of constitutional interpretation would violate the Constitution.[165] But this is far too generous. *Every* congressional attempt to reverse or modify the judiciary's interpretation of the Constitution is unconstitutional as a violation of separation of powers.

Monaghan's theory has been forcefully attacked by critics such as Professors Thomas Schrock and Robert Welsh.[166] They raise three primary objections to the theory of constitutional common law: "*Marbury*-style judicial review . . . separation of powers . . . [and] federalism."[167] *Marbury*, they argue, "legitimizes only constitutional review" and authorizes no "sub [-]constitutional powers over other branches."[168] They also contend that constitutional common law poses separation of powers problems with respect to both Congress and the executive branch.[169] The Court's regulation of subjects as diverse as "criminal law, welfare service, public employment systems, and the like" would improperly invade Congress's sphere of power.[170] That Monaghan's theory permits the judiciary to overrule the Congress in these fields does not solve the constitutional problem, for Congress's ability to defend "itself against judicial invasion of its sphere does not justify that invasion in the first place."[171] They also highlight Monaghan's tendency "to assimilate the constitutional common law to judicial review when he needs the benefit of the latter's established legitimacy" to reconcile his theory's separation of powers problem vis-à-vis the executive branch.[172] Finally, Schrock and Welsh object to constitutional common law on federalism grounds, which even Monaghan recognizes might "allow[] Supreme Court intrusion upon areas of state competence in a manner inconsistent with *Erie*'s fundamental presuppositions with respect to the limits of federal judicial power to displace state law."[173]

Schrock and Welsh also argue that Monaghan's concept of constitutional common law has no basis of authority in the Constitution, as "he can ultimately do no better than to infer authority from utility."[174] Neither general federal common law, nor analogies to some commerce cases, nor the Court's supervisory power suffice to overcome their objections and provide authority for the Court's constitutional common-lawmaking power that Monaghan claims.[175]

Schrock and Welsh are correct that, if one views the Court's actions in this realm as common-lawmaking, Monaghan's theory does concede a power to the judiciary that is not found in the Constitution.[176] But my disagreement with Monaghan's theory derives from a different perspective. In establishing remedial schemes necessary to give meaning and effect to various constitutional provisions protecting individual rights, the judiciary is not engaged in common-lawmaking. Rather, it is engaged in its appropriate and constitutionally granted roles of constitutional interpretation through creation of facilitative or ancillary constitutional directives or simple application of the theory of adversary democratic due process developed throughout this book. Indeed, when viewed from the perspective of adversary democratic due process, grounded in the inherent mistrust of adjudicatory self-interest, the very idea that Congress could exercise any meaningful control of the remedies to rectify its own violations of the Constitution is rendered nonsensical.

Proper analysis of Monaghan's theory of constitutional common law, the objections posed by Schrock and Welsh, and the theory developed in this chapter demand a sound understanding of the respective roles of both Congress and the federal judiciary, which, under this approach, keep each in its constitutionally dictated lane. Monaghan's constitutional common law theory assumes that both Congress and the judiciary can exercise powers found nowhere in the Constitution: Congress cannot legislate as to the meaning of the Constitution, and the judiciary may not interfere with Congress's constitutionally vested legislative authority. He asserts that the Constitution authorizes the judiciary to fashion a constitutional common law in the same way that certain federal statutes authorize it to fashion a federal common law.[177] The latter, however, arises directly from congressionally created authority and can therefore justifiably be reversed by Congress. In stark contrast, the Constitution itself, which is beyond Congress's power to alter, forms the basis of the judiciary's interpretive authority to fashion appropriate constitutional remedies. Here Monaghan gives Congress a power it simply lacks—the power to reverse judicial interpretations of the Constitution by arbitrarily labeling it constitutional common law.[178] If the judiciary invalidates legislation that conflicts with the Constitution, Congress has no authority to reverse that constitutional interpretation. Monaghan's constitutional common law theory is accordingly oxymoronic—"combin[ing] in one phrase authority that is simultaneously beyond yet within congressional power to overrule."[179]

The theory of constitutional remedies as constitutional law, on the other hand, preserves the proper balance between Congress and the judiciary in our system of separation of powers. It limits the judiciary to its role of serving as the ultimate countermajoritarian interpreter of the Constitution—"the bulwark[] of a limited Constitution against legislative encroachments"[180]—including the remedies inherent in and needed to give effect to constitutional provisions protecting individual rights. It also ensures that Congress does not become the constitutional judge of its own powers, which would "enable the representatives of the people to substitute their WILL to that of their constituents."[181] Providing statutory remedies is, indeed, within the proper province of Congress; constitutional remedies, however, are for the courts, which alone have the power to enforce the countermajoritarian Constitution against the majoritarian political branches.

There appears to be a general consensus, presumably beginning with the Supreme Court's decision in *Marbury*, that when the judiciary announces decisions and rules interpreting the Constitution, Congress is powerless to undo it. Nothing short of a constitutional amendment can accomplish that end. The critical distinction lies in where the judiciary's power to fashion remedies for constitutional violations is found. If it is part of the judiciary's supposed constitutional common-lawmaking power, then, by subjecting them to congressional reversal, they are not really constitutional remedies at all. Nevertheless, if they are deemed essential to the effective enforcement of enumerated constitutional rights—without which the rights-protecting provisions of the Constitution would be a "mere form of words"[182]—then they must possess constitutional status in that they are derived directly from the constitutional provisions themselves. But because only the judiciary is empowered to interpret and give controlling meaning to the Constitution, as a matter of pure logic only the judiciary has the ultimate power to fashion constitutional remedies.

Monaghan's theory of constitutional common law, then, is both unworkable as a practical matter and theoretically irreconcilable with the central precepts of American constitutionalism. Remedies are either constitutional or statutory. There is no murky middle ground where Congress and the judiciary engage in a "dialogue" to determine a form of "quasi-constitutional" remedies. As a practical matter, the process provides no platform or vehicle for the operation of any meaningful or realistic dialogic interchange. Moreover, Monaghan provides no clear, principled dividing line between too much and too little interference by one branch in the proper sphere of the other. By contrast, under the theory of constitutional remedies as constitutional law, the dividing line could not be made more clear. If the reviewing court deems the remedy an appropriate means to enforce the Constitution, the judiciary—and only the judiciary—can construe the document to give rise to implied remedies as a form of either due process or facilitative textualism.

Note the vitally important differences—often mysteriously forgotten or ignored—between implied *constitutional* remedies on the one hand and implied *statutory* remedies on the other hand. As a matter of democratic theory, the unrepresentative and unaccountable judiciary has no authority to construe a statute to include an important remedial provision that Congress chose not to include. It is reasonable to presume that Congress carefully chooses which remedies it wishes to include in a statute, and the courts' conclusion that additional remedies are called for is therefore irrelevant if not directly undermining of the congressional legislative scheme. In contrast, as previously explained, for the very reason that the federal courts are not representative, foundational principles of American constitutionalism dictate that determination of the most effective and appropriate means of enforcing the countermajoritarian Constitution and checking the majoritarian branches must lie solely in the hands of the politically insulated judiciary.

7.8 CONSTITUTIONAL REMEDIES AND CONGRESSIONAL POWER TO CONTROL FEDERAL JURISDICTION

One argument regarding Congress's constitutional power over the federal courts takes the form of "the greater includes the lesser"—that is, if Congress has broad power over the federal courts in some capacity, it must also possess any lesser power over those same federal courts.[183] For example, because Article III of the Constitution grants Congress discretion over the creation of lower federal courts,[184] Congress must also have the power to limit the federal courts' jurisdiction. Because the Constitution gives Congress the authority to control federal jurisdiction, the argument goes, it also confers on Congress authority to control the courts' remedial power. The Supreme Court said as much in its 1938 decision, *Lauf v. E.G. Shinner & Co.*, a New Deal–era case in which the Court explicitly linked congressional power to control federal courts' jurisdiction with a power to control remedies.[185] But this interpretation was mistaken. *Lauf* had nothing to do with jurisdiction, nor did it have anything to do with the Constitution. The Court's analysis in that case fundamentally misconstrued the issue, which was purely statutory rather than constitutional. Therefore, reliance on *Lauf* to justify denying the judiciary full control of constitutional remedies does not follow.[186]

Furthermore, Congress's control of federal jurisdiction is far from plenary. To the contrary, it is constrained by the separation of powers and due-process principles inherent in the text and structure of the Constitution. The Supreme Court has expounded on these limitations in several key cases described in the following, and these principles are critical to grounding the power over constitutional remedies in the judiciary alone.[187]

7.9 *LAUF*'S FUNDAMENTAL FLAW

In *Lauf*, the Supreme Court chose a peculiar case to hold that the judiciary's power over remedies can be limited by Congress's control of federal jurisdiction, as the case concerned merely the enforcement of a congressional statute.[188] Thus, in no way did the case implicate the judiciary's authority to interpret the Constitution. Accordingly, that federal courts must enforce constitutionally valid statutes enacted by Congress has no bearing on their power as the ultimate interpreters of the Constitution.

Prominent scholars such as Professor Henry Hart have suggested that there is a link between Congress's power to control federal jurisdiction on the one hand and its authority to create or deny remedies for constitutional violations on the other. In his famed "Dialogue," Hart poses this question: "The power of Congress to regulate jurisdiction gives it a pretty complete power over remedies, doesn't it? To deny a remedy all Congress needs to do is to deny jurisdiction to any court to give the remedy."[189] Although Hart's imaginary respondent refrained from answering this question completely in the affirmative, she did acknowledge that "[i]t must be plain that Congress necessarily has a wide choice in the selection of remedies, and that a complaint about action of this kind can rarely be of constitutional dimension."[190]

Lauf is the leading case espousing the view that Congress's power to control federal jurisdiction necessarily implies a power to control remedies.[191] In this labor dispute, Shinner, the owner of several meat markets in Wisconsin, sought a preliminary injunction to restrain Lauf and the labor union he led from picketing the business, forcing Shinner to fire employees who did not belong to this particular labor union, and running advertisements accusing Shinner of maintaining business practices that were unfair to labor.[192] The district court granted the preliminary injunction, and the US Court of Appeals for the Seventh Circuit affirmed.[193]

The case involved the meaning of "labor dispute" under both Wisconsin and federal law and specifically implicated the Norris-LaGuardia Act.[194] The relevant statutory provision provided that "no court of the United States shall have jurisdiction to issue a temporary or permanent injunction in any case involving or growing out of a labor dispute" unless the district court made certain findings set out in the statute.[195]

Because the district court issued the injunction without making the required findings, the Supreme Court held that the district court exceeded its jurisdiction.[196] It maintained that "the power of the court to grant the relief prayed depends upon the jurisdiction conferred upon it by the statutes of the United States."[197] As there was "no question of the power of Congress thus to define and limit the jurisdiction of the inferior courts of the United States," issuing the injunction without making the statutorily required findings went beyond the district court's jurisdiction as set out by Congress.[198] What follows, therefore, according to the Court in *Lauf*, is that the federal judiciary's remedial power is subsumed within Congress's power to control its jurisdiction.

The *Lauf* Court misconceived the fundamental nature of the issue in the case and consequently articulated a conclusion far beyond the proper grounds for upholding the statute. *Lauf* concerned purely a statutory matter—a directive embodied in the Norris-LaGuardia Act—not a constitutional one. The case involved purely an issue of substantive law—that is, whether or not the statute authorized an injunction under the circumstances of the case—not an issue of the courts' jurisdiction. Despite the use of the term "jurisdiction" in the relevant portion of the statute, then, the case demanded nothing more than that the courts enforce the statutory substantive law as set out by Congress. The statute authorized the courts to issue injunctive relief only in specific circumstances after making the statutorily required factual findings.[199] In a democratic system, the courts have no authority to supersede a constitutionally valid statutory directive, and it is well within Congress's power to instruct the judiciary in these matters.

"Jurisdiction," however, "is a word of many, too many, meanings,"[200] and the use of the term here harkens back to the days when the Court did not use the term as precisely as it endeavors to do today. For example, jurisdiction must not be confused with authority or power. To be sure, both may stem directly from the Constitution, but jurisdiction pertains to whether the case is properly before a court, whereas authority or power refer to the actions a court may permissibly take.[201] Therefore, the inquiry into a court's remedial power is distinct from that into its jurisdiction. Control over one does not necessarily imply control over the other. The fundamental mistake, then, is to view *Lauf* as a jurisdictional and constitutional case, rather than a statutory one.

7.10 STATUTORY ENFORCEMENT VS. CONSTITUTIONAL INTERPRETATION: SEPARATION OF POWERS AND LIMITS ON CONGRESS'S POWER TO CONTROL FEDERAL JURISDICTION

The distinction between statutory and constitutional issues cannot be understated. It does not follow that Congress's authority to set out rules of decision for the courts' enforcement of its statutes (with the caveat that it cannot force the courts to enforce unconstitutional statutes) necessarily entails a congressional power to instruct the Court on how to interpret and enforce the Constitution. The former lies at the heart of Congress's legislative power vested in it by the Constitution; the latter is fixed at the core of the Court's judicial power.[202]

Consider the 1871 Supreme Court case of *United States v. Klein*.[203] A congressional statute allowed for persons whose property had been seized during the Civil War to recover that property so long as they could prove that they gave no assistance to the Confederacy during hostilities, and the Supreme Court ruled that a presidential pardon could constitute the required proof.[204] While Klein's claim to recover the proceeds of his seized property was working its way through the federal courts and pending at the Supreme Court, Congress changed the law and instructed federal courts to treat a presidential pardon as proof of disloyalty—in direct contradiction of Supreme Court precedent—and dismiss Klein's case for lack of jurisdiction. This, the Supreme Court held to be unconstitutional.[205]

Although *Klein* arose from a congressional statute, its outcome necessarily turned on the Court's interpretation of the Constitution and the pardon power in particular. It is well established that federal courts must apply the law as it stands at the time of the final judicial decision, even if Congress changes the applicable law while a case is pending, and even if the government is a party.[206] Here, however, Congress's new directive to the courts "was unconstitutional because it denied to the presidential pardon—which the President was constitutionally authorized to issue—the effect the Court had ruled it had."[207] In short, the Supreme Court, not Congress, has the final authority to interpret the Constitution, and Congress cannot overturn the Supreme Court's interpretation of a constitutional provision by merely passing ordinary legislation.

When the issue involves the enforcement of constitutionally valid congressional statutes, the judiciary has no authority to substitute its will for that of Congress. Furthermore, Congress is free to prescribe rules of decision, even in pending cases, which the Court must follow. *Lauf* is much more akin to an 1855 case the Court distinguished in *Klein*, *Pennsylvania v. Wheeling & Belmont Bridge Co.*[208] That case concerned a bridge that the law at the time of the suit deemed a nuisance.[209] While the case was pending, Congress passed a statute legalizing the bridge as a post road, an act that the Court upheld as within the constitutional powers of Congress.[210] In both *Lauf* and *Wheeling Bridge*, the Court was called upon merely to enforce the law as it stood at the time of its decision. Neither case involved the Court's authority to interpret the Constitution nor its jurisdiction to decide particular cases. Consequently, one cannot rely on cases like *Lauf* to draw any conclusions about the judiciary's power over constitutional remedies. The more appropriate place to look is cases such as *Klein*, where performance of the Court's critical constitutional function was at stake.[211] The key constitutional dictate growing out of *Klein* is that "Congress may not control or direct the [Supreme] Court's interpretation of the Constitution."[212] Separation of powers and constitutional supremacy could not permit otherwise.[213]

There is no question that Congress can exercise significant power over both the Supreme Court's and lower federal courts' jurisdiction. Congress's power over federal jurisdiction, importantly, flows directly from the text of the Constitution itself.[214] But there are limits to this power. As *Klein* shows, Congress cannot employ its power over federal jurisdiction to dictate how the judiciary interprets the Constitution. These limits are dictated by the principle of separation of powers, but they extend beyond the prohibition against congressional directives to the judiciary on its authority to serve as the final interpreter of the Constitution.

Although the general assumption is that Congress cannot limit the Constitution's grant of cases to the Supreme Court's original jurisdiction, the Constitution clearly gives Congress authority over the Supreme Court's appellate jurisdiction. The textual support for this congressional power can be found in Article III's Exceptions Clause, which states: "In all the other Cases before mentioned, the supreme Court shall have appellate Jurisdiction, both as to Law and Fact, *with such Exceptions, and under such Regulations as the Congress shall make.*"[215]

It is beyond the scope of this analysis to re-examine the extent of Congress's power to limit the Supreme Court's appellate jurisdiction—other than to demonstrate its irrelevance to the power over constitutional remedies. Both the Court and scholars have opined extensively on that since at least the Reconstruction Era.[216] Some have interpreted the Exceptions Clause power broadly, while others view its scope as much more limited, referring only to the Supreme Court's review of questions of fact rather than questions of law.[217] For present purposes, however, the key point is that whether or not Congress has sought to make such an exception, it lacks constitutional authority to dictate to the Court how to interpret the Constitution.

Congress's discretionary authority to create lower federal courts is similarly widely assumed.[218] Again, the text of the Constitution is instructive, as Article III vests the judicial power "in one supreme Court, and *in such inferior Courts as the Congress may from time to time ordain and establish.*"[219] Because the Constitution does not require Congress to create lower federal courts, Congress can abolish them once they have been established. It could even stop short of abolishing them altogether by permitting the courts to exist while limiting their jurisdiction—"the 'greater' power to abolish the lower courts logically includes the 'lesser' power to limit the kinds or amount of cases they can hear."[220] This is a controversial power, since the Constitution does not explicitly grant Congress this authority, as it does regarding the Supreme Court's appellate jurisdiction, but it at least arguably makes logical, if only inferential, sense. Nevertheless, separation of powers, as we saw in *Klein*, demands that Congress cannot use this power to usurp the judiciary's authority to interpret the Constitution nor to co-opt it into rubber-stamping its unconstitutional actions.[221]

Klein and other cases[222] show that, despite the broad language in the Constitution conferring authority on Congress to control the jurisdiction of the Supreme Court (through the Exceptions Clause) and the lower federal courts (the "greater" power to establish these courts logically entails the "lesser" power to control the types and amount of cases they can adjudicate), this power is not unlimited. A common theme recurring throughout these examinations is that the Constitution's checks and balances are not designed to allow one branch of government to eviscerate the authority of another branch to carry out its constitutionally assigned functions and exercise its constitutionally vested powers. In this context, the problem is particularly severe when one of the majoritarian branches intrudes upon the independent, countermajoritarian judiciary and attempts to co-opt it into validating the majoritarian branch's potentially unconstitutional actions, or denies the judiciary the authority altogether to halt those unconstitutional actions. Congress cannot, in one breath, seek the "legitimacy provided by judicial validation of its actions" and, in the next, forbid it from exercising its independent judgment to determine the constitutionality of those actions.[223]

The inescapable conclusion that grows out of this analysis is that the power to control federal jurisdiction has nothing to do with constitutional remedies. Remedies for violations of constitutional provisions are not jurisdictional; they are a matter of constitutional interpretation. And there is only one ultimate interpreter of the Constitution: the judiciary. If, as this chapter argues, constitutional remedies are inherently linked to their associated constitutional provisions, the determination of the constitutional remedies required to vindicate constitutional rights is a matter of constitutional interpretation left solely to the courts. Congress's ability to control of federal jurisdiction is irrelevant.

7.11 IMPLICATIONS OF CONSTITUTIONAL REMEDIES AS CONSTITUTIONAL LAW: CONSTRUING AND MISCONSTRUING *BIVENS*

The theory of constitutional remedies as constitutional law developed here has profound practical implications for how the judiciary has dealt with remedies. It impacts the future of particular remedies the judiciary has already found within its authority to fashion and addresses the flawed argument that the judiciary's treatment of implied constitutional remedies should proceed parallel to its handling of implied statutory remedies. This dilemma has been front and center of the Supreme Court's development of *Bivens v. Six Unknown Named Agents of Federal Bureau of Narcotics* remedies. Judicial legitimacy and separation of powers, however, demand that constitutional remedies be analyzed discretely from statutory remedies because of the constitutionally prescribed limits on the powers of Congress and the courts. Put simply, implied statutory remedies are beyond the courts' power, but implied constitutional remedies fall squarely within the courts' constitutional authority.

The Constitution vests enumerated legislative powers in Congress.[224] The legislative power, quite naturally, includes drafting statutes which, upon presidential approval, become law. In drafting statutes, Congress decides on the behavior to be promoted or prohibited and whether any remedies will be available to those whose rights under the statute are violated. The judiciary plays no role in this process because it can claim no legislative power under the Constitution.

Interpreting the Constitution, on the other hand, is a different matter entirely. The Constitution vests the federal courts, at the top of which is the Supreme Court, with the judicial power.[225] The Supreme Court has the ultimate authority to interpret the Constitution and declare its meaning, and because constitutional remedies are part of the meaning of the relevant constitutional provisions, the whole power to fashion constitutional remedies lies with the judiciary, not Congress.[226]

The Supreme Court's foray into the subject of implied statutory remedies began in 1964 in its decision in *J.I. Case Co. v. Borak*.[227] The Court developed this doctrine further in key cases over the next fifteen years, setting out factors it would consider and limiting principles on this self-declared authority to infer remedies for statutory violations when none could be found in the text of the statute. A certain degree of deference to Congress, as well as the scheme set out in a given statute, would serve as two principal guideposts for determining whether courts could infer a statutory remedy.[228]

In the midst of this development, the Court also articulated its power to infer implied damages remedies for violations of the Constitution in the 1971 case of *Bivens*.[229] *Bivens* occurred in the context of the Fourth Amendment's prohibition on unreasonable searches and seizures,[230] and soon after, the Court extended these implied remedies for certain violations of the Fifth[231] and Eighth[232] Amendments. Nonetheless, apart from these examples, the Court declined to extend *Bivens* remedies, consistently narrowing its own authority to imply constitutional remedies.[233] *Bivens* and its progeny, in fact, suggested such a trajectory, because these cases emphasized deference to Congress. The Court has consistently built on this deference principle; since *Bivens* itself, the Court has held the doctrine of implied constitutional remedies in extreme disfavor, with each case seemingly putting another nail in the coffin of the *Bivens* doctrine.[234]

Many seem to have assumed that if the judiciary is required to defer to Congress in the realm of statutory remedies, it must also defer to Congress before creating constitutional remedies. After all, the Court in *Bivens* relied in part on *Borak* to declare this authority in the first place.[235] This argument, however, fails to recognize the difference between constitutional remedies and statutory remedies, as well as the very different functions and powers vested by the Constitution in Congress and the Supreme Court. In short, the judiciary's experiment with implied statutory remedies is as great an interference with Congress's vested authority and an affront to the principles of separation of powers as Congress's involvement in constitutional remedies and interpretation is to the judiciary's authority to interpret the Constitution. Any comparison between the two is inapposite: the foundations of the respective remedies are fundamentally different, and the respective roles of Congress and the courts in our democratic system are equally divergent.[236]

7.12 IMPLIED STATUTORY REMEDIES

As previously noted, the growth of implied statutory remedies began with the Supreme Court's 1964 decision: *Borak*.[237] The case involved a civil action filed by a shareholder of J.I. Case Co. for a deprivation of his and other stockholders' preemptive rights resulting from a merger allegedly affected through a false and misleading proxy statement.[238] After the US Court of Appeals for the Seventh Circuit reversed the trial court's ruling that the relevant statute empowered the trial court to issue only declaratory relief, the Supreme Court considered whether the statute "authorizes a federal cause of action for rescission or damages."[239]

Even though the statute contained no explicit reference to a private right of action, the Court inferred a statutory damage remedy based on the purpose of the statute.[240] The Court uncovered the statute's "broad remedial purposes" through its text and legislative history,[241] concluding that "[i]t is for the federal courts 'to adjust their remedies so as to grant the necessary relief' where federally secured rights are invaded ... [and] 'federal courts may use any available remedy to make good the wrong done.'"[242]

Not long after discovering this power to infer statutory damage remedies, the Court began to cut back and reinforce the notion implicit in *Borak* that Congress could limit this power. The Supreme Court declined to find an implied statutory damage remedy in the 1975 case of *Cort v. Ash*,[243] but notably, it set out the factors for doing so that it would consider in future cases. The principal issue in *Cort* was "whether a private cause of action for damages against corporate directors is to be implied in favor of a corporate stockholder under . . . a criminal statute prohibiting corporations from making 'contributions or expenditures'" in relation to particular federal elections.[244]

The Court listed four factors that it would consider in determining whether a private remedy can be inferred from a statute that explicitly fails to provide for one (all of which counseled against an implied statutory remedy in the case at hand): (1) whether the plaintiff is "one of the class for whose *especial* benefit the statute was enacted"; (2) whether there is "any indication of a legislative intent, explicit or implicit, either to create such a remedy or to deny one"; (3) whether an implied remedy is "consistent with the underlying purposes of the legislative scheme"; and (4) whether inferring a federal remedy would be inappropriate on the basis that such a cause of action is "one traditionally relegated to state law."[245]

Although the Supreme Court did not go so far as to curtail completely its power to infer statutory damage remedies (even with regard to criminal statutes), it did, through the explication of these factors, demonstrate a greater recognition that statutory remedies should be expressly supplied by Congress. Subsequently, the Court has adhered to these factors and has been reluctant to infer statutory remedies.[246] In 2008, in *Stoneridge Investment Partners, LLC v. Scientific-Atlanta, Inc.*, the Court refused to extend a private right, as "[c]oncerns with the judicial creation of a private cause of action caution against its expansion."[247] It further recognized that implied statutory causes of action and remedies such as those found in *Borak* are purely "judicial construct[s]," requiring a demonstration of clear congressional intent.[248]

7.13 *BIVENS* AND IMPLIED CONSTITUTIONAL REMEDIES

7.13.1 The Origins of the *Bivens* Doctrine

The Fourth Amendment to the US Constitution prohibits "unreasonable searches and seizures," but the text of the Amendment provides no remedy for violations of this prohibition.[249] In 1914, the Supreme Court ruled in *Weeks v. United States* that the Fourth Amendment bars from federal trials the use of evidence obtained by federal law enforcement officers in violation of this prohibition.[250] Without this exclusionary rule, the Court later explained, the Fourth Amendment would be nothing more than a mere "form of words."[251] Prior to 1971, however, the Supreme Court had not ruled definitively on the "question whether [the prohibition against unreasonable searches and seizures] by a federal agent acting under color of his authority gives rise to a cause of action for damages consequent upon his unconstitutional conduct."[252]

The Court answered this question affirmatively in 1971 with *Bivens*,[253] where the exclusionary rule was irrelevant because the plaintiff, mistakenly subjected to an unreasonable search, was never going to be prosecuted and no trial from which to exclude any illegally obtained evidence was ever going to occur.[254] Rejecting the notion that Mr. Bivens could only obtain money damages through a state tort law action,[255] Justice Brennan, writing for the Court, emphasized that "the Fourth Amendment operates as a limitation upon the exercise of federal power."[256] The Fourth Amendment must independently restrain federal power,[257] and "where federally protected rights have been invaded, it has been the rule from the beginning that courts will be alert to adjust their remedies so as to grant the necessary relief."[258] Furthermore, "federal courts may use any available remedy to make good the wrong done."[259]

The *Bivens* Court's logic necessarily leads to the conclusion that violations of constitutional rights require recognition of a federal cause of action and a remedy, notwithstanding congressional silence, lest explicit constitutional rights be rendered merely advisory. Nevertheless, Justice Brennan did not completely foreclose a role for Congress. He found it proper to infer a federal damage remedy in this case because it "involve[d] no special factors counselling hesitation in the absence of affirmative action by Congress."[260] In addition, he noted that there had been "no explicit congressional declaration that persons injured by a federal officer's violation of the Fourth Amendment may not recover money damages from the agents,"[261] but instead could only avail themselves of some other remedy "equally effective in the view of Congress."[262]

Justice Harlan's concurrence sought to distinguish between congressional and judicial roles in vindicating constitutional rather than statutory rights:

> [I]t must also be recognized that the Bill of Rights is particularly intended to vindicate the interests of the individual in the face of the popular will as expressed in legislative majorities; at the very least, it strikes me as no more appropriate to await express congressional authorization of traditional judicial relief with regard to these legal interests than with respect to interests protected by federal statutes.[263]

Justice Brennan added that "the judiciary has a particular responsibility to assure the vindication of constitutional interests such as those embraced by the Fourth Amendment."[264]

Despite this strong articulation of clearly distinct roles for Congress and the judiciary in protecting constitutional rights, Justice Harlan puzzlingly—and illogically—approved of judicial deference to Congress, saying that "it must be remembered that legislatures are [the] ultimate guardians of the liberties and welfare of the people in quite as great a degree as the courts."[265] The Court, through its "special factors counseling hesitation" language and other acknowledgments of Congress's role in contributing to constitutional remedies, failed to set out a complete framework for the fashioning of constitutional remedies. Moreover, by leaving open the possibility of some deference to Congress, it did not rest its decision on the countermajoritarian judiciary's final authority to interpret the Constitution and to restrain the majoritarian branches, thereby leaving unsettled the questions of how and under what circumstances this approach could extend to other constitutional provisions.

7.13.2 Extending *Bivens*

The subsequent story of *Bivens* remedies has been marked by the Supreme Court's imposition of limitation and restraint. In the more than fifty years since the Supreme Court articulated its authority to issue implied damage remedies for constitutional violations, it has rarely seen fit to extend the protection of the *Bivens* doctrine to other constitutional provisions. Those exceptions began in 1979 with the Court's holding in *Davis v. Passman*, which involved an allegation by a former congressional employee of wrongful termination on the basis of sex.[266] She brought suit under the equal protection component of the Fifth Amendment Due Process Clause, seeking damages in the form of back pay.[267] The Court considered whether, under *Bivens*, "a cause of action and a damages remedy can also be implied directly under the Constitution when the Due Process Clause of the Fifth Amendment is violated,"[268] despite the fact that Title VII's prohibition against sex-based employment discrimination specifically excluded from its protections congressional staff members.[269]

The Court extended a *Bivens* damage remedy to Davis's Fifth Amendment claim,[270] emphasizing that "the question of who may enforce a *statutory* right is fundamentally different from the question of who may enforce a right that is protected by the Constitution."[271] Congress, the Court made clear, creates statutory rights and these are enforced through means appropriately designed by Congress, whereas the judiciary is charged with interpreting and enforcing constitutional rights.[272]

The Court ostensibly made a strong claim for the judiciary's power, at the expense of Congress, to fashion remedies for constitutional violations. And even though the Court noted the presence of "special concerns counseling hesitation,"[273] it chose to extend a *Bivens* damage remedy—although not without highlighting that there was "no *explicit* congressional declaration that" litigants like Davis "may not recover money damages,"[274] leaving the door open to judicial deference to Congress if the legislature explicitly prohibited the issuance of money damages for constitutional violations. What, though, would the Court do if Congress were actually to take this step? Further, what if Congress denied any remedial relief altogether? Would this not render the Fifth Amendment a mere "form of words"?[275]

The Court again considered the issues surrounding the extension of *Bivens* remedies a year later in *Carlson v. Green*,[276] a suit brought by the mother of a deceased federal prisoner alleging that he died from personal injuries suffered during incarceration because the prison officials violated his Eighth Amendment right to be free from cruel and unusual punishment.[277] The majority directed attention to two situations in which an action for a *Bivens* damages remedy could be defeated: (1) when the defendants show "special factors counselling hesitation in the absence of affirmative action by Congress" and (2) "when defendants show that Congress has provided an alternative remedy which it explicitly declared to be a *substitute* for recovery directly under the Constitution and viewed as equally effective."[278]

Neither situation applied to Green's case. First, there were no special factors counseling hesitation because the prison officials did "not enjoy such independent status in our constitutional scheme as to suggest that judicially created remedies against them might be inappropriate."[279] Second, "nothing in the Federal Tort Claims Act (FTCA) or its legislative history ... show that Congress meant to preempt a *Bivens* remedy or to create an equally effective remedy for constitutional violations."[280] Once again, while extending *Bivens* remedies to another constitutional provision, the Court neither set out a comprehensive framework for constitutional remedies nor made clear that violations of constitutional rights require constitutional remedies to prevent those rights from becoming a mere "form of words." Unfortunately, the Court's deference to Congress had become part and parcel of its *Bivens* doctrine, leaving a gaping hole in the judiciary's final authority to interpret and enforce the Constitution.[281]

7.13.3 Limiting *Bivens*

The Supreme Court's willingness to extend *Bivens* damage remedies to other constitutional provisions was short-lived. Apart from the two exceptions just described, the Court has refused on each subsequent opportunity to infer damage remedies to enforce other constitutional protections.[282]

Although the seeds of *Bivens*'s demise can be found within the Court's *Bivens* decision itself, the true "turning point"[283] occurred in the 1983 case of *Bush v. Lucas*, which involved a request for "a new nonstatutory damages remedy for federal employees whose First Amendment rights are violated by their superiors."[284] Lucas, a NASA facility director, demoted Bush, a NASA aerospace engineer, allegedly as punishment for publicly criticizing the management of the space center where they both worked.[285] The Court first assumed that Bush's "First Amendment rights were violated by the adverse personnel action" and that the "civil service remedies were not as effective as an individual damages remedy and did not fully compensate him for the harm he suffered."[286] Despite explicitly stating that the remedy[287] that Congress provided was inadequate, the Court declined to extend *Bivens*, reasoning that Congress had established an "elaborate, comprehensive [remedial] scheme" to protect these rights.[288] Furthermore, it explained that Congress was "in a far better position than a court"[289] to make the "policy judgment"[290] of "balancing governmental efficiency and the rights of employees."[291]

The Court's deference to Congress was on full display throughout its analysis, which emphasized that "[w]hen Congress provides an alternative remedy, it may . . . indicate its intent, by statutory language, by clear legislative history, or perhaps even by the statutory remedy itself, that the courts' power should not be exercised."[292] It also combined the two factors set out in *Carlson v. Green*,[293] making "the existence of a statute . . . a factor counseling hesitation."[294] This move "obviated the need to find that the statute was equally effective—evidently its mere existence was reason for deference."[295]

The Supreme Court took yet another step toward near total deference to Congress in the context of *Bivens* action five years later in its 1988 decision, *Schweiker v. Chilicky*.[296] This case involved a Fifth Amendment Due Process Clause challenge to the denial of Social Security Disability Insurance (SSDI) benefits, allegedly through the use of impermissible quotas.[297] Congress had previously created an elaborate administrative remedial scheme for those who had been removed from the disability rolls, but the scheme only helped to restore SSDI benefits that were improperly withheld.[298]

Congress, in the context of *Bivens* actions, would now determine which remedies are adequate. Justice Sandra Day O'Connor's majority opinion contended that "[w]hen the design of a Government program suggests that Congress has provided *what it considers adequate remedial mechanisms* for constitutional violations that may occur in the course of its administration, [the Court] ha[s] not created additional *Bivens* remedies."[299] The Court again stressed that "Congress is in a better position to decide whether or not the public interest would be served by creating"[300] a new *Bivens* damages remedy. Following this case, the state of affairs seemed to be that Congress, not the judiciary, has the final say on whether the remedial mechanisms it provides adequately vindicate constitutional rights.

The doctrinal development of the *Bivens* doctrine continued with the Court's holding in the 2017 case of *Ziglar v. Abbasi*,[301] a suit involving the United States' post-9/11 detention policies brought against high-level Department of Justice officials for alleged Fourth and Fifth Amendment violations.[302] The Court first acknowledged that "[t]he decision to recognize an implied cause of action under a statute involves somewhat different considerations than when the question is whether to recognize an implied cause of action to enforce a provision of the Constitution itself."[303] Yet it drew the wrong conclusion from this difference. It referenced "separation-of-powers principles," noting that creating a judicial remedy for constitutional violations was "a significant step" under these principles.[304] Then, when considering the question of "'who [between Congress and the Court] should decide' whether to provide for a damages remedy," the Court answered, "most often [it] will be Congress."[305]

As these cases demonstrate,[306] the Supreme Court's *Bivens* doctrine, from its inception, has marched inexorably toward greater judicial deference to Congress in the field of remedies for constitutional violations, leaving the protection of individual rights increasingly subject to congressional determination of the adequacy of the remedies provided.[307] Left unanswered is the question of whether the Court would change course if Congress determined that *no* remedy was required to enforce certain constitutional provisions.

7.14 IMPLIED STATUTORY REMEDIES VS. IMPLIED CONSTITUTIONAL REMEDIES

The prior discussion has demonstrated that the Supreme Court's treatment of implied statutory remedies and implied constitutional remedies has largely settled into a state of rather generous judicial deference to Congress.[308] That was not always the case, however. Prior to the Court's decision in *Bush*, "[a] significant feature of the implied-remedies cases [was] the Court's disparate treatment of constitutional and statutory rights."[309] Leading up to this point, the Court seemingly recognized that Congress and the judiciary had fundamentally different roles to play with respect to constitutional remedies, which were ostensibly special and unique in the sense that Congress had no role in drafting or interpreting the document from which such remedies came—the US Constitution.[310]

The "turning point"[311] came when *Bush* "mark[ed] the beginning of a convergence in the Court's doctrine regarding constitutional and statutory remedies."[312] In that case, "[t]he Court declined to recognize a *Bivens* remedy where Congress had erected an 'elaborate, comprehensive scheme' of administrative remedies," a rationale strikingly similar to the Court's reliance "on the existence of 'elaborate' congressional legislation to infer the absence of congressional intent to create an implied damages remedy" in the context of statutory remedies.[313] It went even further in the cases of *Schweiker* and *Ziglar*, stating that Congress is far better positioned than the judiciary to determine whether and what kind of remedies are required to enforce constitutional rights.[314] In post-*Bush Bivens* cases, the

Court no longer stresses the distinction between constitutional remedies and statutory remedies or why its own role in creating the former might drastically differ from the latter.

There are at least two fundamental flaws with this approach, stemming from the principles of judicial legitimacy and separation of powers. When they assume the power of judicial review, the courts' legitimacy flows from the execution of their constitutionally mandated functions. The first function is "adjudicative . . . [resolving] the claims of [adverse] individuals and, in the constitutional context, . . . protect[ing] individual liberties."[315] The second is the "structural role: [the courts'] duty to ensure that the political branches do not exceed their constitutionally granted powers."[316] The judicial branch has the final say as to the meaning of the Constitution. Therefore, it is appropriate and entirely commensurate with judicial review to develop remedies that are essential to the meaning of the Constitution, necessary to protect constitutional rights, and effective in enforcing constitutional restraints. This role takes on even greater significance and further enhances the judiciary's legitimacy in cases where one of the majoritarian branches has encroached upon individual constitutional liberties. For statutory rights and remedies, on the other hand, the Constitution gives to the democratically elected Congress final decision-making authority. The judiciary's legitimate role here is limited to interpreting the statutes that Congress passes, leaving to that body the prerogative to decide how they are to be enforced.

The Court's approach to implied statutory and implied constitutional remedies also runs into multiple separation-of-powers problems. Judicially implied statutory remedies amount to an improper encroachment by the judiciary on the legislature's authority. Not only does Congress know how to provide a private cause of action and remedial scheme when it desires, but even if a judicially implied statutory remedy helps effectuate the purpose of the statute, that remedy "was not subjected to the formal requirements of the legislative process."[317] By inferring a remedy from a statute lacking one, the Court changes the statute and the law, violating Article I's bicameralism and presentment requirements.[318] Tempting though it may be, it is beyond the judiciary's authority to set out its own view of public policy or its theory of how a particular statute can best be implemented. That is left to Congress.

The Court permits Congress to violate separation of powers and improperly encroach on the judiciary's function when it allows the legislature to determine what, if any, remedies should be available for violations of the Constitution. Constitutional remedies are a matter of judicial interpretation—choosing and shaping them are an essential element of the judiciary's role, not Congress's. Furthermore, "exclusive enforcement authority [cannot] reside with the very political branches (and particularly the mistrusted legislative branch) whose power . . . the Bill of Rights . . . restrain[s]."[319] Viewing statutory remedies and constitutional remedies as one and the same strikes at the very foundation of the governmental structure established by the Constitution, transforms violations of separation of powers principles into judicial doctrine, creates an opportunity for both Congress and the judiciary to lose legitimacy, and leaves our constitutional rights unsecured.

7.15 CONSTITUTIONAL REMEDIES AND ADVERSARY DEMOCRACY

The intersection between the control of the constitutional remedies and adversary democratic due process should, by this point, be obvious. Recall that the premise of adversary democracy is an inherent skepticism and mistrust of those in power to ignore their own self-interest in favor of the interest of those whom they govern.

Such pervasive, foundational skepticism of those who govern logically dictates a categorical rejection of congressional power to control the scope of constitutional remedies. The very point of the countermajoritarian Constitution is to *limit* the otherwise all-powerful majoritarian branches. To trust those in power to have final say as to the limits on their own power contravenes the foundational premises of adversary democracy.

7.16 CONCLUSION

What difference does all this make? Does it ultimately amount to nothing more than a purely academic exercise? After all, all a court can do is issue a piece of paper. How, then, could the judiciary actually control constitutional remedies under the proposed framework? It has, as Alexander Hamilton said, "neither FORCE nor WILL...."[320] As a practical matter, this may be true, and the theory exposited here does nothing to alter that reality.

Under the current system, however, it is perfectly legitimate for Congress or the executive to treat issuance of that order as a mere piece of paper. By paying deference to the political branches in the creation, enforcement, or even existence of constitutional remedies—by ceding interpretive control over the very document and provisions adopted to restrain unchecked majoritarian power—the judiciary has itself effectively turned the Constitution into a mere piece of paper and the rights enshrined in our founding charter into a mere form of words. In so doing, the judiciary has ignored the adversary democratic foundations of our constitutional democracy, and the foundational precepts of adversary democratic due process.

It is undoubtedly true that, even if one accepts this theory of constitutional remedies in our countermajoritarian system, the Constitution is little more than a piece of parchment unless the institutions charged with enforcing it carry out their mandated functions. But under this theory, the stakes for flouting the Constitution or a court's judgment are much higher. Majoritarian-branch actions would be unlawful—and the people who, with the courts, can keep those branches in check will be better able to do so.

In any event, this criticism, grounded in judicial impotence, proves far too much. The very same criticism applies just as clearly to the very process of judicial review: courts have no independent means to enforce their decisions, yet virtually all concede that the loss of judicial review would be devastating to our constitutional democracy. At some level, the system collapses absent consensus adherence to it. But the popular force of an argument that failure to enforce the courts' exercise of judicial review will do much to deter abandonment of that consensus. I argue here that the very same is true of the need to permit the judiciary to exercise the ultimate power of fashioning constitutional remedies.

If one accepts the power of judicial review, if one acknowledges that enshrined in the countermajoritarian Constitution are individual rights that are meant to be protected, exercised, and enforced, and if one recognizes the principles of separation of powers and the countermajoritarian judiciary's checking role against its majoritarian counterparts, one must conclude that the political branches—given to majoritarian impulses and most threatening to constitutional rights—must not be permitted to judge the manner and extent to which they are restrained. And they certainly must not be allowed to do so with the judiciary's imprimatur.

This theory of constitutional remedies as constitutional law ineluctably grows out of the Constitution's text and the nature of our democratic system going back to the Founding Era and grounded in the Fifth Amendment's Due Process Clause. It recognizes the role and duty of the federal judiciary designed by the Framers, one in which they are "faithful guardians of the Constitution."[321] It is as relevant now as it was then—as are the rights protected by our Constitution.

CONCLUSION

If nothing else is clear at this point, it should be that the world of procedural due process is sorely in need of deep rethinking. The only even arguable advantage of the Supreme Court's vapid doctrinal focus on some vague form of utilitarian balancing is that it is not as misguided or manipulative as an impossible-to-apply (and therefore easy-to-manipulate) form of originalist inquiry. There exists no evidence that any of the Framers ever intended to tie the concept of due process to some narrow, photographic reproduction of the clause's interpretation at the moment of ratification. To the extent one does choose to look to historical evidence in the first place, it would make far more sense to view due process as an outgrowth of the complex form of democratic theory which the US Constitution so clearly embodies. And that is the first stage of this book's intended contribution to political and constitutional thought: due process and adversary democratic theory must be made to work together as inseparable elements of our system's inherent mistrust of those who possess power.

Adversary democratic theory is the pluralistic dark side of democracy—the effort to enable individual members or groups in society to protect themselves from those who act out of different motivations. It is only by recognition of the importance of adversary theory that the far more optimistic side of American political theory—liberal democratic theory—may be protected. Thus, American democratic theory is neither purely as pessimistic as adversary theory nor as optimistic as liberal democratic theory. But anyone who categorically dismisses the value or importance of adversary democracy is missing a foundational element of American political thought.

By recognizing the inherent intertwining of liberal adversary democracy with procedural due process, we can easily see how dramatically the foundations of due process doctrine and theory need to be rethought. The two "bookends" of adversary democratic due process are an overwhelming commitment to the so-called day-in-court ideal, which places preeminent value on the constitutional right of a litigant either to participate directly in the defense of her rights or to choose who will do so on her behalf. Except in the most extreme situations, government may not be allowed to paternalistically select who will represent a litigant's interests in court, any more than government may choose who will speak for an individual seeking to petition his government for redress of grievances. Recognition of adversary democracy's relevance would have a substantial impact on the constitutionality of modern class action procedure and provide a far more sophisticated theoretical basis for the presumptive rejection of the virtual representation doctrine.

Even more significant doctrinally would be adversary theory's impact on the constitutional requirement of a "neutral" adjudicator. Traditionally, the Supreme Court has construed due process to require a neutral adjudicator—a wise decision, because absent a truly neutral adjudicator, the provision of all other procedural protections makes no difference. The adjudicators' lack of neutrality renders all of them, as a constitutional matter, inherently inadequate.

Viewing the neutral adjudicator requirement through the lens of adversary democratic due process, however, dictates significant strengthening of current doctrine. The Court has defined neutrality to require a showing of some specific form of perverse decisional incentive or disincentive before it will dictate constitutional invalidation. The lesson of adversary democracy is that such thin protection is woefully inadequate. Adversary democracy, it should be recalled, is premised on a foundational mistrust of those other than the individual herself to protect that individual's interests. This is especially true of those exercising power over the individual. As a result, the due process guarantee of neutral adjudication must be strengthened.

The Constitution's Framers understood this concern. In Article III, they chose to prophylactically guarantee judicial salary and tenure, regardless of whether or not there is a showing of a specific perverse external influence on an adjudicator's decision. They did so, because they decided that in making a choice whether to risk overprotection or underprotection of judicial independence, they would choose overprotection. This is an example of what I have previously referred to as "the risk of the wrong guess." When one is forced to make a choice without certainty of the consequences of choosing the various options, the decider must ask herself, "Which way would I rather risk being wrong?" For example, in the criminal law, in choosing whether to risk convicting an innocent person or risk acquitting a guilty person, we have chosen to risk acquitting a guilty person. This is of course not the only decision that could have been made, but it was made presumably by careful consideration of the potential consequences of making the wrong choice, in both directions.

The Framers' decision to place the risk of the wrong guess in a manner which favors the risk of overprotection makes perfect sense, for a number of reasons. First, we begin with the foundational significance of judicial independence to the success of the constitutional democracy which they were establishing. Absent a truly independent and insulated judiciary charged with the final say as to the meaning of the countermajoritarian Constitution, the entire system would be in peril. Hence, placing the risk of the wrong guess in favor of underprotection could have calamitous results. Second, the likelihood of being able to ferret out improper coercive or incentivized influences in the individual case would often be near-impossible. Indeed, the undue influences on the judge may often be subconscious—yet very real nevertheless. While Article III does not apply to state courts, the insights of adversary democracy make clear that *ex ante* mistrust of those exercising power is fundamental to preservation of American democracy. However, as this book has demonstrated throughout, the Supreme Court has failed to recognize the foundational demand for prophylactic protections of adjudicatory neutrality.

Indeed, in the context of administrative adjudication the Court has mysteriously assumed an even smaller need to assure adjudicatory independence. At least when actual judges are involved, the Court has demanded that due process is denied in the event of a showing of some sort of improper temptation to the average judge. Yet where administrative adjudication is involved, the Court has actually expressed outrage at even the suggestion that the adjudicator's neutrality could be questioned. The irony here is that administrative adjudicators are far more likely to be subjected to improper influences than members of the judicial branch are. While for the most part, judges have no dog in the fight when they adjudicate individual cases, administrative adjudicators possess an inherent—even if unintended—bias in favor of the agency which has brought the action. The administrative adjudicators are themselves employees of that agency. They may well fear dismissal or discipline if their decisions are not satisfactory to those in charge of the agency. Even if this danger were assumed not to exist, regulators exist to regulate. The danger of their inherent favoritism to their own agency cannot be ignored—except by the Supreme Court, that is.

To crystallize the danger, imagine that judges, rather than being members of a wholly separate branch of government, were employees of the US Attorney's Office which brought proceedings before them. Can anyone imagine that this system would be deemed to satisfy due process (assuming, for the moment, that Article III protections did not exist)? Yet that is basically the state of our administrative system, with relatively limited judicial review available to cure the dangers. Yet that is exactly the system which the Supreme Court has constitutionally authorized. In shaping due process as an outgrowth of liberal adversary democratic theory and emphasizing the foundational importance of adjudicatory neutrality, this book is designed to serve as a wake-up call to both academia and the judiciary.

In this book, I have first explained the theory of liberal adversary democracy, and then expounded the inherent intersection between that vision of American democracy and procedural due process. I have then applied that vision to three areas of legal doctrine: (1) civil procedure, (2) administrative law, and (3) constitutional law.

I have focused first on the area of civil procedure, because the intersection between constitutional law in general and due process in particular are either unknown or even counterintuitive to many scholars. That situation should not be all that surprising, since only rarely do civil procedure scholars spend significant effort examining and understanding the nuances of constitutional theory, and even more rarely do constitutional scholars spend significant time grappling with the intricacies of civil procedure. But as I have shown in Chapters 3 and 4, constitutional values and protections often play an enormous role in the civil adjudication of private disputes. Property rights, as much as liberty, are protected by the due process clause. They therefore cannot be taken away from individual litigants without procedural protections which effectively implement the constitutional guarantees embodied in adversary democratic due process. Central to these guarantees is the right of a litigant to choose who will represent her interests in the litigation. This value has been embodied in the so-called "day-in-court" ideal. However, as Chapter 4 demonstrates all too clearly, both judicial doctrine and scholarly opinion have sought to undermine this value through creation of doctrines of res judicata which seriously threaten this value. Thankfully, the Supreme Court finally rejected this form of guerilla warfare. But in so doing, the Court failed to provide a coherent theoretical rationale of the ideal or an explanation of the circumstances under which the idea must give way. In Chapter 4, I do both. I conclude that although there exist extreme situations—those involving indivisible relief—where the day-in-court ideal must give way, viewing this ideal through the lens of adversary democratic due process both explains and strengthens the foundational role played by the day-in-court ideal in civil litigation.

Perhaps even more concerning to the day-in-court ideal is the truly bizarre system of multidistrict litigation (MDL), which has come to dominate complex litigation in the federal courts. Under this framework, litigants who have already chosen their legal representatives and filed lawsuits are forced into a single proceeding, usually in a jurisdiction with which they have no connection, legally or geographically, with countless other suits which may—or may not—be similar to their own. No adversary proceeding determines whether a suit should or should not be grouped together in this single proceeding; a judicial panel just does it. Are there individual differences among the suits, some of which may be significant? Well, it's close enough for government work, they seem to reason.

But what happens to the litigants' chosen attorneys? For the bulk of the process, at least, they are simply cast aside, replaced by attorneys selected by the judiciary without any formalized inquiry into the competence, interests, or representativeness of those attorneys. Yet the individual litigants effectively have no say as to their inclusion in the proceeding. The day-in-court ideal is nowhere to be found; nor has the issue of its assumed irrelevance ever been resolved in a constitutional challenge to this procedural monstrosity.

The supposed saving grace of this process is supposedly twofold. First, the process only applies to pretrial practice, including pleading motions, discovery, and summary judgment. If the litigation gets past this stage, the case is returned to the transferor district for adjudication on the merits. This protection, however, is of relatively little benefit to the individual litigants for two reasons. Initially, motions to dismiss and summary judgment motions can often resolve the suits prior to any transfer back to the transferor forum. Second, most MDL proceedings terminate in settlement before they ever have the chance to be referred back to the original forums.

It is at this point in the process, however, that the second justification for MDL processes comes into play. No case can be settled without the consent of the individual litigants. They have the ultimate option to remove themselves from the settlement and continue to litigate on an individual basis (controlled, of course, by all of the pretrial procedural rulings and discovery which were made in the MDL proceeding). But this asserted justification is of no more help than the first one was in justifying the constitutionality of the process. How is the individual litigant to make a competent decision on whether to accept or reject the settlement? The settlement, of course, takes into account the value of all of the suits—some of which will be larger (and possibly far larger) than others. Can the litigant know where her claim falls within that framework? Is her individual claim far smaller than most, so she would be getting a windfall by accepting settlement, or is her claim far larger, meaning that acceptance of the settlement would be unwise? This underscores the uncertain nature of the settlement process. Chapter 3 explores the MDL process's constitutional flaws in detail and recommends possible ways of modifying the process's framework to remove those flaws.

Chapter 5, concerning the process of the state employing contingent fee private attorneys to sue private individuals or entities, represents something of a bridge between the civil procedure and purely constitutional applications of adversary democratic due process. In some sense, this involves simply a matter of procedure in civil cases. However, because the practice triggers the important and complex issues of state power in relating to its citizens, in other ways the inquiry focuses heavily on pure constitutional law issues. From either perspective, however, the practice raises serious questions about the relevance of adversary democratic due process. Adversary democracy demands "adversarial neutrality" from lawyers seeking to assert state power. This means that while government attorneys are, of course, advocates within the adversary system, their ability to assert the awesome power of the state requires that they view lawsuits from something other than a narrow perspective of personal gain. Contingent fee attorneys, on the other hand, do nothing of the kind, and are not expected to do so in the conduct of purely private litigation. When the narrow self-interest of private attorneys operating from an all-or-nothing financial perspective is used to invoke state power, the constitutional calculus must change.

Chapters 6 and 7 focus more extensively on issues of pure constitutional law, moving away from the intricacies of judicial procedure in civil litigation. Yet Chapter 6 synthesizes a constitutional inquiry (a focus on First Amendment protection of free expression) with an examination of the highly problematic structure of administrative adjudication. It is at this point that the book fashions a frontal assault on the Supreme Court's poorly reasoned and very dangerous attitude toward adjudicatory neutrality in the administrative context.

Chapter 7 uses adversary democratic due process as a jumping-off point to engage in a detailed analysis of the role of constitutional remedies as a central element of our system of constitutional checks and balances. Understanding and acceptance of the foundational role of adversary democracy within our constitutional system and its manifestations in adversary democratic due process quickly demonstrate the serious fallacies in the widespread assumption that the creation and regulation of constitutional remedies lie ultimately in the hands of the political branches. If there is one insight that we must take from the premises of adversary democratic theory, it is that those being regulated cannot be given ultimate decision-making power as to how those regulations are to be implemented.

While a full understanding of some of the applications of adversary democratic due process may require some level of doctrinal sophistication, the most important message of this book does not. That message is this: since its inception, our constitutional democracy has been premised on a basic mistrust of all who exercise or seek to exercise power. To be sure, the optimistic vision of human flourishing which the Framers valued (at least for those protected by the Constitution at the time) was of great importance. But they also wisely recognized that unless closely watched and limited, self-interested factions could gain power and use it in ways that undermine the entire concept of self-rule. It is through the insights of adversary democratic theory that we recognize the necessity of mistrust. As one of the Constitution's most obvious and important implementations of adversary democracy, procedural due process must be reconfigured to implement the inherent skepticism of those who exercise or seek to exercise power.

NOTES

CHAPTER 1

1. Martin H. Redish, The Adversary First Amendment (2013), at 15–16.
2. Cf. *Marquess of Queensberry rules*, Encyclopedia Britannica (last visited June 10, 2022), https://www.britannica.com/sports/Marquess-of-preQueensberry-rules (explaining the nineteenth-century British boxing rules that heavily influenced modern boxing).
3. *See generally* Cass Sunstein, *Beyond the Republican Revival*, 97 Yale L.J. 1539 (1988).
4. Jane Mansbridge, Beyond Adversary Democracy (1980), at 16. *But see* Martin H. Redish, *The Adversary System, Democratic Theory, and the Constitutional Role of Self-Interest: The Tobacco Wars, 1953–1971*, 51 DePaul L. Rev. 359, 365 (2001) ("Under certain circumstances, adversary democracy as employed in liberal democratic society may apply, even where an individual is seeking to protect or advance an interest other than his own. Thus, liberal democratic adversary theory may operate within a framework of altruism or idealism.") [hereinafter Redish, *Tobacco Wars*].
5. Federalist No. 47 (James Madison).
6. Federalist No. 14 (James Madison).
7. Federalist No. 10 (James Madison) ("There are again two methods of removing the causes of faction: the one, by destroying the liberty which is essential to its existence; the other, by giving to every citizen the same opinions, the same passions, and the same interests. . . . The second expedient is as impracticable as the first would be unwise.").
8. The term "pluralism," as used here, refers only to interest-driven political theories of competition, not the pluralism that merely emphasizes the need to respect individuals' "divergent conceptions of the good life." For an illustration of this difference, compare David Truman, The Governmental Process 33 (1951) (describing how competing "norms[] or shared attitudes" emerge from group affiliation), with Harold J. Laski, Authority in the Modern State 26 (1919) (explaining that pluralism "urges that [society's] purpose has in fact been differently interpreted and is capable of realisation by more than a single method").
9. Joseph H. Carens, *Possessive Individualism and Democratic Theory: Macpherson's Legacy*, in Democracy and Possessive Individualism (Joseph H. Carens ed. 1993).
10. Mansbridge, *supra* note 4, at 15–17.
11. Gregory S. Kavka, *Hobbes's War of All against All*, 93 Ethics 291, 292 (1983).
12. Alan Apperley, *Hobbes on Democracy*, 19 Politics 165, 168, 171 (1999).
13. *See* David Brink, *Mill's Moral and Political Philosophy*, Stan. Encyc. of Phil. Para. 3.7 (Aug. 22, 2022).

14. Ian Shapiro, The Evolution of Rights in Liberal Theory 275 (1986).
15. David Held, Models of Democracy 89 (1987).
16. C. Edwin Baker, Human Liberty and Freedom of Speech 47 (1989).
17. David Held, Models of Democracy 89 (1987).
18. Both "pluralist adversary theory" and "liberal adversary democracy" have been referenced up to this point. Moving forward, if not specified, "adversary democracy" is shorthand for the latter.
19. *See generally* Mansbridge, *supra* note 4.
20. *See, e.g.*, Suzanna Sherry, *Civic Virtue and the Feminine Voice in Constitutional Adjudication*, 72 Va. L. Rev. 543, 545 (1986) ("The more common is adoption of an essentially pluralistic and non-teological view of human nature. This view holds that there is no unitary end towards which humans aspire, no transcendent concept of the good life."); Cynthia R. Farina, *Conceiving Due Process*, 3 Yale J.L. & Feminism 189, 241–49 (1991) (critiquing the "liberal-legalist" theory that the state exists to "safeguard[] the freedom of each individual to pursue his own interests as he perceives them" for creating an "incorrigible" due process jurisprudence); *see also* Daniel Markovits, *Adversary Advocacy and the Authority of Adjudication*, 75 Fordham L. Rev. 1367 (2006) (arguing the adversary litigation system is "necessary for the legitimacy of adjudication," stating that "the diversity of human experience and the complexity of human reason make pluralism the natural state of ethical life").
21. Mansbridge, *supra* note 4, at 8, 14 ("[Unitary democracy] makes formal and extends to the level of a polity the social relations of a friendship.").
22. Richard A. Epstein, *Modern Republicanism—Or the Flight from Substance*, 97 Yale L.J. 1633, 1635 (1988); *cf.* Redish, *Tobacco Wars*, *supra* note 4, at 359, 365 ("[N]othing builds national unity more than the presence of a common external enemy.").
23. Mansbridge, *supra* note 4, at 293; *see also* Ed Diener & Shigehiro Oishi, *The Nonobvious Social Psychology of Happiness*, 16 Psych. Inquiry 162, 163–64 (2005) (describing psychological scholarship finding that "social relationships" and "social connectedness" are "essential to well-being").
24. Mansbridge, *supra* note 3, at 293; *see also* Susan A. Wheelan, *Group Size, Group Development, and Group Productivity*, 40 Small Group Rsch. 247, 247–48 (2009) (describing psychological scholarship finding that increased group size is correlated with decreased cohesion and increased disagreement).
25. Mansbridge, *supra* note 4, at 293.
26. *Id.* at 295.
27. *Id.* at 30.
28. Federalist No. 10 (James Madison).
29. Nor is adversary democracy a theory of unhinged libertarianism, for that matter. Adversary democracy provides for meta-autonomy: the freedom to advocate and participate in the action of democracy as one pleases, but not the freedom to reject or disobey the substantive restrictions or obligations of law. While majority rule will almost always produce winners and losers, the losers must agree to respect these outcomes, avoid violence, and try again next time.
30. *See* David Truman, The Governmental Process 14–15 (1951).

31. *Id.* at 33.
32. *Cf.* Mitja D. Back, Stefan C. Schmukle, & Boris Egloff, *Becoming Friends by Chance*, 19 PSYCH. SCI. 439, 439 (2008) ("[M]ere proximity... as well as mere assignment to the same group... increases the likelihood of becoming friends."); Henry Solomon et al., *Anonymity and Helping*, 113 J. SOCIAL PSYCH. 37, 42 (1981) (finding that anonymity leads to "a reduction in helping behavior when helping is the [socially] appropriate response"); Andrew Silke, *Deindividuation, Anonymity, and Violence: Findings From Northern Ireland*, 143(4) J. SOCIAL PSYCH. 493, 497 (2010) (finding a correlation between anonymity and increased aggression and violence).
33. Mansbridge, *supra* note 4, at 26.
34. Redish, *Tobacco Wars*, *supra* note 4 (describing the self-interested and altruistic motives of the Black and white "Freedom Riders" of the 1960s as an example of adversary political advocacy).
35. Mansbridge, *supra* note 4, at 297.
36. U.S. CONST. amend. V, XIV (emphasis added).

CHAPTER 2

1. *See generally* Martin H. Redish & Abby Marie Mollen, *Understanding Post's and Meiklejohn's Mistakes: The Central Role of Adversary Democracy in the Theory of Free Expression*, 103 NW. U. L. REV. 1303 (2009); James Weinstein, *Participatory Democracy as the Central Value of American Free Speech Doctrine*, 97 VA. L. REV. 491 (2011); Robert Post, *Participatory Democracy and Free Speech*, 97 VA. L. REV. 477 (2011); Cass Sunstein, *Democracy and the Problem of Free Speech*, 11 PUB. RSCH. Q. 58 (1995).
2. Those who believe in "substantive due process" may disagree with this point. This chapter, however, focuses exclusively on the democratic value of *procedural* due process, the existence of which is noncontroversial.
3. U.S. CONST. amends. V, XIV.
4. Martin H. Redish & Lawrence C. Marshall, *Adjudicatory Independence and the Values of Procedural Due Process*, 95 YALE L.J. 455, 465 (1986) (explaining the superfluity of the Due Process Clause if legislative mandate controls the floor of procedural protections); *see also* Jerry L. Mashaw, *Due Process: The Quest for a Dignitary Theory*, 61 B.U. L. REV. 885, 891–96 (1981) (rejecting a positivist approach to due process).
5. *See* Edward L. Rubin, *Due Process and the Administrative State*, 72 CAL. L. REV. 1044, 1102 (1984) ("[A] consensus exists about the purpose of these procedures: to ensure accurate decision making.").
6. It is of course true that in a certain sense this approach can be deemed anachronistic, since due process finds its origins in preconstitutional English practice. However, as subsequent discussion will demonstrate, an originalist perspective toward due process seriously misapplies the concept. In any event, to the extent that some form of originalist analysis were assumed to be called for, it is important to recall that the Fifth Amendment's Due Process Clause was enacted by virtually the same Framers who implemented our system of liberal adversary democracy.

7. That the government is "unlikely" to do so may be debatable, but there is at least *some* risk that the government may not act in the individual's best interests. That risk alone is sufficient to justify guaranteeing procedural protections. It certainly was sufficient for the Framers.
8. It *especially* behooves the individual to make the most of the constitutional protections afforded to them by due process, as the clause is only ever triggered in a uniquely adversarial and frightening context. When individuals are directly threatened with deprivation, it would serve them well not to remain idle.
9. Arnett v. Kennedy, 416 U.S. 134, 167 (1974) (Powell, J., concurring in part) ("[T]he right to procedural due process . . . is conferred, not by legislative grace, but by constitutional guarantee.").
10. *See, e.g.*, Adriana S. Cordis & Jeffrey Milyo, *Measuring Public Corruption in the United States: Evidence From Administrative Records of Federal Prosecutions*, 18 PUB. INTEGRITY 127 (2016); Noel D. Johnson, Courtney L. LaFountain, & Steven Yamarik, *Corruption Is Bad for Growth (Even in the United States)*, 147 PUB. CHOICE 377 (2011); Noel D. Johnson et al., *Corruption, Regulation, and Growth: An Empirical Study of the United States*, 15 ECON. GOV. 51 (2014).
11. Landmark administrative procedural due process cases arose from government-benefits disputes. *E.g.*, Goldberg v. Kelly, 397 U.S. 254 (1970) (welfare); Mathews v. Eldridge, 424 U.S. 319 (1976) (disability).
12. *See generally* Christopher DeMuth, *Can the Administrative State Be Tamed?*, 8 J. LEGAL ANALYSIS 122 (2016) (describing growth of administrative state and legal mechanisms developed to oversee it).
13. *See* FEDERALIST NO. 51 (James Madison) ("If angels were to govern men, neither external nor internal controls on government would be necessary.").
14. *See* Lawrence Rosenthal, *Does Due Process Have an Original Meaning? On Originalism, Due Process, Procedural Innovation . . . and Parking Tickets*, 60 OKLA. L. REV. 1, 43 (2007) ("[L]egislative majorities do not have unfettered power to determine the manner in which persons c[an] be deprived of life, liberty, or property. . . . [Due process] ensure[s] that life, liberty, or property have some normative protection over and above that available by the grace of legislative majorities.").
15. *Cf.* Morton H. Halperin, *Guaranteeing Democracy*, 91 FOREIGN POL'Y 105, 118 (1993) (identifying "due process and equality before the law" as "necessary for a constitutional democracy").
16. *See* Martin H. Redish, *Good Behavior, Judicial Independence, and the Foundations of American Constitutionalism*, 116 YALE L.J. 139, 153 (2006) ("[T]o maintain their legitimacy all democratic governments must adhere to some form of social contract with their individual constituents.").
17. Rubin, *supra* note 5, at 1105.
18. John Adams, *Novanglus Papers, no. 7*, in THE WORKS OF JOHN ADAMS (Charles Francis ed. 1851).
19. Legislative deception here refers to situations where "the legislature leaves substantive law unchanged on its face, but alters it in a generally applicable manner by enacting procedural or evidentiary modifications that have the effect of transforming the

essence-or what can appropriately be described as the 'DNA' of that law." Martin H. Redish & Christopher Pudelski, *Legislative Deception, Separation of Powers, and the Democratic Process: Harnessing the Political Theory of* United States v. Klein, 100 Nw. U. L. REV. 437, 439 (2006).

20. For different approaches to the minimum procedures required by due process, *see generally* Henry J. Friendly, *Some Kind of Hearing*, 123 U. PA. L. REV. 1267 (1975); and Rubin, *supra* note 5.
21. *See* Martin H. Redish & Nathan D. Larsen, *Class Actions, Litigant Autonomy, and the Foundations of Procedural Due Process*, 95 CAL. L. REV. 1573, 1604–05 (2007).
22. This is referred to as "strict scrutiny" or "heightened scrutiny" in First Amendment jurisprudence. *See* Rodney A. Smolla, Smolla & Nimmer on Freedom of Speech § 4:13 (Oct. 2021).
23. For case law on what constitutes a cognizable "property" or "liberty" interest triggering due process, *see generally* Bd. of Regents of State Colls. v. Roth, 408 U.S. 564 (1972); Goldberg v. Kelly, 397 U.S. 254 (1970); Bishop v. Wood, 426 U.S. 341 (1976); Paul v. Davis, 424 U.S 693 (1976); Meachum v. Fano, 427 U.S. 215 (1976); Wolff v. McDonnell, 418 U.S. 539 (1974).
24. Mashaw, *supra* note 4, at 901 ("[T]here must also be some guarantee . . . that the issues, evidence, and processes were in fact meaningful to the outcome."); Melvin Aron Eisenberg, *Participation, Responsiveness, and the Consultative Process: An Essay for Lon Fuller*, 92 HARV. L. REV. 410, 413 (1978) ("What distinguishes adjudication from other forms of social ordering is . . . that the decision ought to proceed from and be congruent with th[e] proofs and argument [offered].").
25. *Cf.* Reed v. Town of Gilbert, Arizona, 135 S. Ct. 2218, 2226 (2015) ("Content-based laws—those that target speech based on its communicative content—are presumptively unconstitutional and may be justified only if the government proves that they are narrowly tailored to serve compelling interests.").
26. *Cf.* Gideon v. Wainwright, 372 U.S. 335 (1963).
27. *Cf.* Korematsu v. United States, 323 U.S. 214 (1944) (upholding internment of Japanese Americans under purported strict scrutiny analysis), *abrogated by* Trump v. Hawaii, 138 S. Ct. 2392 (2018); Bowers v. Hardwick, 478 U.S. 186 (1986) (upholding antisodomy law using disingenuous reframing of issue despite privacy right protected by *Griswold*), *overruled by* Lawrence v. Texas, 539 U.S. 558 (2003).
28. Even if this were possible, "there would probably be no one left to adjudicate anything" under such a standard. Redish & Marshall, *supra* note 4, at 492.
29. *See, e.g.*, Republic of Ecuador v. Chevron, 638 F.3d 384 (2d Cir. 2011) (Ecuadorian president accused of threatening judges with legal penalties for issuing opinions contrary to government interests).
30. *See, e.g.*, Tumey v. Ohio, 273 U.S. 510 (1927) (judge received financial reward for issuing fines).
31. *See, e.g.*, *In re* Muchison, 349 U.S. 133 (1955) (judge connected to one of the parties cannot be wholly disinterested in the proceedings).
32. *Cf.* Luis Garicano, Ignacio Palacios-Huerta, & Canice Prendergast, *Favoritism Under Social Pressure*, 87 REV. ECON & STAT. 208, 208 (2005) (analyzing how home-crowd pressure influences soccer referees).

33. FEDERALIST No. 79 (Alexander Hamilton).
34. Henry Paul Monaghan, *The Confirmation Process: Law or Politics?*, 101 HARV. L. REV. 1202, 1211 (1988) ("[W]hat relieves judges of the incentive to please is not the prospect of indefinite service, but the awareness that their continuation in office does not depend on securing the continuing approval of the political branches.").
35. Kisor v. Wilkie, 139 S. Ct. 2400, 2438 (2019) (Gorsuch, J., concurring in the judgment) (emphasis added).
36. Presidential Comm'n on the Sup. Ct. of the U.S., Final Report 114 (Dec. 7, 2021).
37. *Id.* at 116.
38. Rosalind Dixon, *Why the Supreme Court Needs (Short) Term Limits*, N.Y. TIMES (Dec. 31, 2021), https://www.nytimes.com/2021/12/31/opinion/supreme-court-term-limits.html (last accessed July 5, 2023).
39. *Cf.* Presidential Comm'n on the Sup. Ct. of the U.S., Statement by Former Federal Judges Thomas B. Griffith and David Levi (Dec. 7, 2021) ("[Term limits] are not related to any defect or deficiency in the Court or its procedures and they threaten judicial independence."); Presidential Comm'n on the Sup. Ct. of the U.S., Statement by Commissioner Adam White (Dec. 15, 2021) ("[A] term-limits framework would further corrode the appearance of judicial neutrality and independence, making the Court a spoil not just of politics, but of *presidential* politics exclusively.").
40. *See, e.g.*, Marshall v. Jerrico, Inc., 446 U.S. 238, 242 (1980) ("The requirement of neutrality has been jealously guarded by this Court.").
41. 273 U.S. 510 (1927).
42. *Tumey*, 273 U.S. at 523 ("[I]t certainly violates the Fourteenth Amendment and deprives a defendant in a criminal case of due process of law to subject his liberty or property to the judgment of a court, the judge of which has a direct, personal, substantial pecuniary interest in reaching a conclusion against him in his case.").
43. *Tumey*, 273 U.S. at 532.
44. *Tumey*, 273 U.S. at 532 ("Every procedure which would offer a possible temptation to the average man as a judge to forget the burden of proof . . . or which might lead him not to hold the balance nice, clear, and true between the state and the accused denies the latter due process of law.").
45. *See, e.g.*, Aetna Life Ins. Co. v. Lavoie, 475 U.S. 813 (1986) (due process violated where state supreme court justice presided over case which affected law relevant to justice's own pending lawsuit against one of the parties); Ward v. Village of Monroeville, 409 U.S. 57 (1972) (due process violated where mayor presided in court whose "fines, forfeitures, costs, and fees" substantially contributed to village revenue).
46. Withrow v. Larkin, 421 U.S. 35, 47 (1975).
47. The Court has recognized some limits to this presumption, finding it rebutted where there are obvious "prejudgment and pecuniary interests." Gibson v. Berryhill, 411 U.S. 564, 578 (1973).
48. Ohio Valley Water v. Ben Avon Borough, 253 U.S. 287, 289 (1920) ("[T]he state must provide a fair opportunity for submitting [the] issue to a judicial tribunal for determination upon its own independent judgment as to both law and facts; otherwise the order is void because in conflict with the due process clause of the Fourteenth Amendment.").

49. *See* section 2.5, *supra*.
50. *See* section 2.2, *supra*.
51. Martin H. Redish & Kristin McCall, *Due Process, Free Expression, and the Administrative State*, 94 NOTRE DAME L. REV. 297, 317 (2018) ("[T]he commissioners in agencies such as the FTC and SEC authorize the initial investigation against a party, issue the complaint, control the prosecution, and then adjudicate any appeals filed by either party.").
52. *See* Mathews v. Eldridge, 424 U.S. 319, 349 (1976) ("In assessing what process is due in this case, substantial weight must be given to the good-faith judgments of the individuals charged by Congress with the administration of [federal programs].").
53. Chevron v. NRDC, 467 U.S. 837 (1984) (reviewing court must defer to agencies' reasonable interpretations of ambiguous statute).
54. Auer v. Robbins, 519 U.S. 452 (1997) (reviewing court must defer to agencies' reasonable interpretations of ambiguous agency regulations).
55. Kisor v. Wilkie, 139 S. Ct. 2400, 2413 (2019) ("And agencies (again unlike courts) have political accountability, because they are subject to the supervision of the President, who in turn answers to the public.").
56. *Id.* at 2439 (Gorsuch, J., concurring in the judgment).
57. FEDERALIST NO. 78 (Alexander Hamilton). *See also* Martin H. Redish & Jennifer Aronoff, *The Real Constitutional Problem with State Judicial Selection: Due Process, Judicial Retention, and the Dangers of Popular Constitutionalism*, 56 WM. & MARY L. REV. 1, 9 (2014) ("[T]he very nature of what a judge does requires that she make decisions independent of popular sentiment.").
58. Republican Party of Minnesota v. White, 536 U.S. 765, 768 (2002).
59. *See generally* Caperton v. A.T. Massey Coal Co., 556 U.S. 868 (2009).
60. Redish & Aronoff, *supra* note 57, at 26–28.
61. *See, e.g.*, Emily Pronin, *Perception and Misperception of Bias in Human Judgment*, 11 TRENDS IN COGNITIVE SCI. 37, 37 (2006) ("People's tendency to deny their own bias, even while recognizing bias in others, reveals a profound shortcoming in self-awareness, with important consequences for interpersonal and intergroup conflict.").
62. Redish & Aronoff, *supra* note 57, at 30–31 (this system "exists out of tradition, not necessity").
63. IAN SHAPIRO, THE EVOLUTION OF RIGHTS IN LIBERAL THEORY 275 (1986); *see also* David Brink, *Mill's Moral and Political Philosophy*, Stan. Encyc. of Philosophy, para. 3.7 (Aug. 22, 2022) ("In the part which merely concerns himself, his independence is, of right, absolute. Over himself, over his own body and mind, the individual is sovereign.").
64. Martin H. Redish, *The Adversary System, Democratic Theory, and The Constitutional Role of Self-Interest: The Tobacco Wars, 1953-1971*, n 5/DePaul L. Rv.359,2001 ("Liberal adversary democratic theory recognizes the empirical reality that because individuals are integral units worthy of dignity and respect, it is quite conceivable that their interests will differ.").
65. *Cf.* SHAPIRO, *supra* note 63, at 275 ("[T]he individual will is the cause of all actions, individual and collective.").

66. *Paternalism*, BLACK's LAW DICTIONARY (11th ed. 2019).
67. Martin H. Redish & Nathan D. Larsen, *Class Actions, Litigant Autonomy, and the Foundations of Procedural Due Process*, 95 CAL. L. REV. 1573, 1579 (2007) (discussing *parens patriae* standing as an example of justifiable paternalism).
68. Shapiro, *supra* note 63.
69. *See* section 2.11, *infra*.
70. Redish & Larsen, *supra* note 67, at 1617.
71. *Res judicata*, BLACK's LAW DICTIONARY (11th ed. 2019) ("An affirmative defense barring the same parties from litigating a second lawsuit on the same claim, or any other claim arising from the same transaction or series of transactions that could have been—but was not—raised in the first suit. . . .—Also termed . . . *claim preclusion*.").
72. *Collateral estoppel*, BLACK's LAW DICTIONARY (11th ed. 2019) ("A doctrine barring a party from relitigating an issue determined against that party in an earlier action, even if the second action differs significantly from the first one.—Also termed *issue preclusion*.").
73. *See, e.g.*, Hansberry v. Lee, 311 U.S. 32, 42–43 (1940) ("It is a familiar doctrine of federal courts that members of a class not present as parties to the litigation may been bound by the judgment where they are in fact adequately represented by parties who are present."); Amchem Prods., Inc. v. Windsor, 521 U.S. 591 (1997) (reassertion of *Hansberry* rule as embodied in FRCP 23(a)(4) requirement that named parties "will fairly and adequately protect the interests of the class"). The adequate representation requirement was inserted into Rule 23 in 1966 "for the express purpose of assuring compliance with due process protections, as set out in *Hansberry*." Redish & Larsen, *supra* note 67 at 1598 (citing Proposed Amendments to Rules of Civil Procedure of the United States District Courts, 39 F.R.D. 73, 107 (Advisory Committee Note to Rule 23(c)(2))).
74. Brink, *supra* note 63 ("As soon as any part of a person's conduct affects prejudicially the interests of others, society has jurisdiction over it, and the question whether the general welfare will or will not be promoted by interfering with it, becomes open to discussion.").
75. *See* section 2.1, *supra*, for a detailed discussion on how the presumption favoring individual procedural protections can be rebutted by pragmatic concerns of the highest order.
76. Fed. R. Civ. P. 23(b)(1)–(2); (c).
77. Fed. R. Civ. P. 23(b)(1)(A) ("[P]rosecuting separate actions by or against individual class members would create a risk of inconsistent or varying adjudications with respect to individual class members that would establish incompatible standards of conduct for the party opposing the class.").
78. In generic terms:

> Litigant A sues Defendant D seeking payment of stake Z.
> Court orders D to give Z to A.
> Litigant B then sues D seeking payment of same stake.
> Court orders D to give Z to B.
> D is punished 100% more than legal bounds of stake would allow.

79. In generic terms:

> Litigant A sues Defendant D seeking specific performance to sell land Z to A.
> Court orders D to sell Z to A.
> Litigant B then sues D seeking same specific performance.
> Court orders D to sell Z to B.
> D cannot possibly act lawfully.
> See, e.g., Aerojet-General Corp. v. Askew, 511 F.2d 710 (5th Cir. 1975).

80. In generic terms:

> Litigant A sues Defendant D seeking injunction Y.
> Court denies injunction and holds D does not have to comply with Y.
> Litigant B then sues D seeking same injunction.
> Court grants injunction and holds D must comply with Y.
> D cannot make use of favorable judgment defeating injunction.
> See, e.g., Supreme Tribe of Ben Hur v. Cauble, 255 U.S. 356 (1921); City of Dallas v. Sw. Airlines Co., 371 F. Supp. 1015 (N.D. Tex. 1973), aff'd 494 F.2d 793 (5th Cir. 1974).

81. Fed. R. Civ. P. 23(b)(1)(B) ("[P]rosecuting separate actions by or against individual class members would create a risk of adjudications with respect to individual class members that, as a practical matter, would be dispositive of the interests of the other members not parties to the individual adjudications or would substantially impair or impede their ability to protect those interests.").

82. Fed. R. Civ. P. 23(b)(2) ("[T]he party opposing the class has acted or refused to act on grounds that apply generally to the class, so that final injunctive relief or corresponding declaratory relief is appropriate respecting the class as a whole.").

83. "Inconsistent liability" does not present the same issues, as it does not force an individual to do the impossible or receive punishment beyond legal limits.

84. For a discussion of alternative means to address the concerns of these mandatory class actions, see Redish & Larsen, supra note 67, at 1606–11.

85. See Richard A. Epstein, *Class Actions: Aggregation, Amplification, and Distortion*, 2003 U. CHI. LEGAL F. 475, 495–96.

86. Ohio Bell Tel. Co. v. Pub. Utils. Comm'n of Ohio, 301 U.S. 292, 307 (1937) ("We do not presume acquiescence in the loss of fundamental rights."); Coll. Sav. Bank v. Fla. Prepaid Postsecondary Educ. Expense Bd., 527 U.S. 666, 682 (1999) ("'[C]ourts indulge every reasonable presumption against waiver' of fundamental constitutional rights." (quoting Aetna Ins. Co. v. Kennedy, 301 U.S. 389, 393 (1937))).

87. See, e.g., William Samuelson & Richard Zeckhauser, *Status Quo Bias in Decision Making*, 1 J. RISK & UNCERTAINTY 7 (1988) ("In choosing among alternatives individuals display a bias toward sticking with the status quo."); see also Maurice Schweitzer, *Disentangling Status Quo and Omission Effects: An Experimental Analysis*, 58 ORG. BEH. & HUMAN DECISION PROCESSES 457 (1994).

88. It must be acknowledged that under Fed. R. Cir. P. 23(a)(4), before a class action may be certified, the District Court must certify that the representative plaintiffs are

"adequate" representatives on behalf of absent class members. But this requirement constitutes nothing more than the very form of governmental paternalism which adversary democratic due process categorically rejects.

89. For an argument that class action attorneys should be deemed the "real parties in interest" for the purpose of res judicata, see Martin H. Redish, *Rethinking the Theory of the Class Action: The Risks and Rewards of Capitalistic Socialism in the Litigation Process*, 64 EMORY L.J. 451, 474–75 (2014).
90. Rubin, *supra* note 5, at 1105.
91. *Id.*
92. *Id.* at 1106.
93. *Id.* at 1134.
94. Martin H. Redish & Christopher R. Pudelski, *Legislative Deception, Separation of Powers, and the Democratic Process: Harnessing the Political Theory of* United States v. Klein, 100 Nw. U. L. REV. 437, 452–53 (2006).
95. *Id.* at 437–38.
96. 80 U.S. 128, 148 (1872).
97. Bank Markazi v. Peterson, 578 U.S. 212, 231 (2016).
98. Redish & Pudelski, *supra* note 94, at 452–53.
99. Michael H. v. Gerald D., 491 U.S. 110, 121 (1989).
100. *Id.* at 115–16; Cal. Civ. Code Ann. § 4601.
101. *Michael H.*, 491 U.S. at 115–16; Cal. Evid. Code § 621 (emphasis added).
102. *Michael H.*, 491 U.S. at 119.
103. *Id.* at 153 (Brennan, J., dissenting).
104. The Securities Litigation Reform Act of 1995 may be another case of legislative deception. In imposing a significantly more burdensome pleading standard, the Act "worked to reduce more meritorious litigation, particularly aimed at smaller companies." Stephen J. Choi, *Do the Merits Matter Less After the Private Securities Litigation Reform Act?*, 23 J.L. ECON. & ORG. 598, 623 (2007).
105. Incitement to violence is a category of unprotected speech, but the category is limited to when there is a "clear and present danger" and lawless action is "intended and is imminent." Content-based restrictions are not categorically impermissible, but are subject to the rigors of strict scrutiny. For more examples, see Rodney A. Smolla, Smolla & Nimmer on Freedom of Speech § 2:12 (Oct. 2021).
106. *Id.* § 4:13.
107. Simon & Schuster, Inc. v. Members of N.Y. State Crime Victims Bd., 502 U.S. 105, 115 (1991) (emphasis added).
108. *Cf.* Fulton v. City of Philadelphia, 141 S. Ct. 1868, 1881 (2021) ("Put another way, so long as the government can achieve its interests in a manner that does not burden religion, it must do so.").
109. Fuentes v. Shevin, 407 U.S. 67, 84–85 (1972) ("[I]t is now well settled that a temporary, nonfinal deprivation of property is nonetheless a 'deprivation' in the terms of the Fourteenth Amendment.") (citing Sniadach v. Family Fin. Corp., 395 U.S. 337 (1969) and Bell v. Burson, 402 U.S. 535 (1971)).
110. Fed. R. Civ. P. 65(b)(1)(A) (emphasis added).

111. Fed. R. Civ. P. 65(b)(1)(B).
112. "A plaintiff seeking a preliminary injunction must establish that he is likely to succeed on the merits, that he is likely to suffer irreparable harm in the absence of preliminary relief, that the balance of equities tips in his favor, and that an injunction is in the public interest." Winter v. NRDC, 555 U.S. 7, 20 (2008).
113. Mathews v. Eldridge, 424 U.S. 319 (1976); *see also* Connecticut v. Doehr, 501 U.S. 1 (1991) (adopting modified *Mathews* approach for private civil litigation).
114. Mathews v. Eldridge, 424 U.S. 319 (1976); Connecticut v. Doehr, 501 U.S. 1 (1991).
115. Kaley v. United States, 571 U.S. 320 (2014).
116. *Id.* at 322 (quoting United States v. Monsanto, 491 U.S. 600, 615 (1989)).
117. 21 U.S.C. § 853(e).
118. *Kaley*, 571 U.S. at 324.
119. *Id.* at 329.
120. *Id.* at 335–36 ("[A]ny defense counsel worth his salt . . . would put the prosecutor to a choice: 'Protect your forfeiture by providing discovery' *or* 'protect your conviction by surrendering the assets.' It is a small wonder that the Government wants to avoid that lose–lose dilemma.").
121. *Id.* at 338.
122. *Id.* at 350 (Roberts, C.J., dissenting).
123. *Id.* at 352.
124. *Id.* at 355.
125. *Id.* at 355–56 (internal quotation marks omitted).
126. *Id.* at 350 ("[F]ew things could do more to 'undermine the criminal justice system's integrity' than to allow the Government to initiate a prosecution and then, at its option, disarm its presumptively innocent opponent by depriving him of his counsel of choice—without even an opportunity to be heard.").
127. *See, e.g.*, Fuentes v. Shevin, 407 U.S. 67, 93 (1972) ("There may be cases in which a creditor could make a showing of immediate danger that a debtor will destroy or conceal disputed goods. . . . [N]o such unusual situation is presented by the facts of these cases."); Calero-Toledo v. Pearson Yacht Leasing Co., 416 U.S. 663, 678–79 (1974) ("[P]reseizure notice and hearing might frustrate the interests served by the statutes, since the property seized—as here, a yacht—will often be of a sort that could be removed to another jurisdiction, destroyed, or concealed, if advance warning of confiscation were given."); United States v. James Daniel Good Real Property, 510 U.S. 43, 62 (1993) ("Unless exigent circumstances are present, the Due Process Clause requires the Government to afford notice and a meaningful opportunity to be heard before seizing real property subject to civil forfeiture.").
128. Parklane Hosiery Co. v. Shore, 439 U.S. 322 (1979).
129. For a discussion regarding impermissibly unfair use of offensive collateral estoppel, *see* Brainerd Currie, *Mutuality of Collateral Estoppel: Limits of the* Bernhard *Doctrine*, 9 STAN. L. REV. 281 (1957).
130. *See* generally Chapter 4.
131. Mashaw, *supra* note 4, at 886.
132. *Id.* at 899–901.

133. *Id.* at 899.
134. *Id.* at 901.
135. *Id.* at 903.
136. *Id.*
137. *Id.* at 924–25.
138. *Id.*
139. *Id.* at 925.
140. Bd. of Regents of State Colls. v. Roth, 408 U.S. 564 (1972).
141. Mashaw, *supra* note 4, at 928.
142. *Id.* at 929.
143. *Id.* at 929.
144. *Roth*, 408 U.S. at 578 ("[T]he respondent . . . did not have a property interest sufficient to require the University authorities to give him a hearing when they declined to renew his contract of employment.").
145. Mashaw, *supra* note 4, at 929.
146. *See, e.g.*, Martin H. Redish & Matthew B. Arnould, *Judicial Review, Constitutional Interpretation, and the Democratic Dilemma: Proposing a "Controlled Activism" Alternative*, 64 FLA. L. REV. 1485 (2012). *See also* Robert W. Bennett, *Objectivity in Constitutional Law*, 132 U. PA. L. REV. 445 (1984).
147. *See* Rosenthal, *supra* note 14, at 13.
148. Burnham v. Superior Court, 495 U.S. 604 (1990).
149. *See generally* Martin H. Redish, *Tradition, Fairness, and Personal Jurisdiction: Due Process and Constitutional Theory after Burnham v. Superior Court*, 22 RUTGERS L.J. 675 (1991).
150. "Tag jurisdiction" refers to the ability of a state court to assert personal jurisdiction over an individual served with process while present in the state, even if the person is only temporarily present and for reasons unrelated to the subject matter of the litigation. *See also* Tag, MERRIAM-WEBSTER, https://www.merriam-webster.com/dictionary/tag (last accessed July 5, 2023).
151. *Burnham*, 495 U.S. at 619.
152. *Burnham*, 495 U.S. at 610.
153. *Burnham*, 495 U.S. at 611.
154. *Burnham*, 495 U.S. at 612.
155. *Burnham*, 495 U.S. at 615.
156. 433 U.S. 186 (1977).
157. *Id.* at 204.
158. Rosenthal, *supra* note 14, at 25.
159. *Id.* at 26.
160. *Shaffer*, 433 U.S. at 212.
161. Burnham v. Superior Court, 495 U.S. 604, 622 (1990); *see also* Martin H. Redish, *Tradition, Fairness, and Personal Jurisdiction: Due Process and Constitutional Theory After* Burnham v. Superior Court, 22 Rutgers L.J. 675, 684 (1991) (relying on state practice as a basis to define due process "effectively begs the constitutional question").

162. *See, e.g.*, Jones v. Flowers, 547 U.S. 220, 225 (2006). The *Jones* Court held that due process requires additional notice before initiating a tax foreclosure residence sale if initial notice mailed to the owner's last known address is returned unclaimed. *Id.* Neither the majority opinion nor dissent by Justice Thomas made any reference to notice requirements at the time of the Fourteenth Amendment, even though history shows "service by mail was considered ineffective in 1868." Rosenthal, *supra* note 14, at 11.
163. "In suits at common law, where the value in controversy shall exceed twenty dollars, the right of trial by jury shall be preserved, and no fact tried by a jury, shall be otherwise reexamined in any Court of the United States, than according to the rules of the common law." U.S. CONST. amend. VII.
164. Dimick v. Schiedt, 293 U.S. 474, 487 (1935).
165. Rosenthal, *supra* note 14, at 24.
166. Int'l Shoe Co. v. State of Washington, 326 U.S. 310, 316 (1945).
167. Rosenthal, *supra* note 14.
168. *See* Randy E. Barnett & Evan D. Bernick, *No Arbitrary Power: An Originalist Theory of the Due Process of Law*, 60 WM. & MARY L. REV. 1599, 1606 (2019).
169. Rosenthal, *supra* note 14, at 34.
170. *Id.*
171. *Id.* at 30–34.
172. "[T]he courts have settled that long ago, and the gentlemen can go and read their decisions." Cong. Globe, 39th Cong., 1st Sess. 1089 (1866) (statement of Rep. Bingham).
173. *See* Rosenthal, *supra* note 14, at 33–34, 52 (describing how Rodney Mott "ultimately punted on the original meaning of the Fifth Amendment's Due Process Clause," how Learned Hand explained that "the Due Process Clauses are drawn 'in such sweeping terms that their history does not elucidate their contents,'" and that Arthur Sutherland asserted that "no one knows precisely what the words 'due process of law' meant to the draftsmen" of the Fifth and Fourteenth Amendments).
174. *Id.* at 52 ("[W]hen the evidence of original meaning of a particular constitutional text is unsatisfactory, the message of history is that the original meaning simply provides no reliable guide for decisionmaking.").
175. *See* Mathews v. Eldridge, 424 U.S. 319 (1976).
176. Amartya K. Sen & Bernard Williams, *Introduction* at 3–4, in UTILITARIANISM AND BEYOND (Amartya Sen & Bernard Williams eds. 1982).
177. James E. Crimmins, *Jeremy Bentham*, STANFORD ENCYC. PHIL. (Winter 2021), https://plato.stanford.edu/entries/bentham (last accessed July 5, 2023).
178. *See* Amartya Sen, *Utility: Ideas and Terminology*, 7 ECON. & PHIL. 277, 277 (1991) ("Any search for the 'true' and 'authentic' meaning of the term 'utility' must come to grips with the fact that the term is, in fact, used in a number of different senses.").
179. Jonathan Riley, *Utilitarian Ethics and Democratic Government*, 100 ETHICS 335, 338 (1990).
180. Rubin, *supra* note 5, at 1138.
181. Sen & Williams, *supra* note 176, at 4–5.

182. For example, when considering whether violations of the exclusionary rule of the Fourth Amendment could be claimed by habeas corpus petitioners, the Court in *Stone v. Powell* expressly stated: "The answer is to be found by weighing the utility of the exclusionary rule against the costs." 428 U.S. 465, 489 (1976). Infamously, the Court found "the substantial societal costs" of the rule too large. *Id.* at 495.
183. Cynthia R. Farina, *Conceiving Due Process*, 3 YALE J.L. & FEMINISM 189, 234 (1991).
184. Wilkinson v. Austin, 545 U.S. 209, 228 (2005) ("The problem of scarce resources is another component of the State's interests. . . . It follows that courts must give substantial deference to prison management decisions.").
185. City of Los Angeles v. David, 538 U.S. 715, 719 (2003) (holding that twenty-seven-day delay in holding a hearing after towing a car "reflects no more than a routine delay substantially required by administrative needs"); *see also* Van Harken v. City of Chicago, 103 F.3d 1346 (7th Cir. 1997) (Posner, J.) ("These calculations are inexact, to say they least; but they help to show, what is pretty obvious without them, that the benefits of requiring the police officer to appear at every hearing are unlikely to exceed the costs.").
186. For example, while the Court's prison-adjudication cases are problematic overall, it is not necessarily improper for a court to consider the dangers particular procedures might pose in that unique environment.

See, e.g., Wolff v. McDonnell, 418 U.S. 539, 466 (acknowledging witnesses may face "a risk of reprisal"); Wilkinson v. Austin, 545 U.S. 209, 228 (2005) (expressing concern that "nothing in the record indicates simple mechanisms exist to determine when witnesses may be called without fear of reprisal").

CHAPTER 3

1. *See, e.g.*, Fed. R. Civ. P. 20 (permissive joinder); *id.* Rule 22 (interpleader); *id.* Rule 24 (intervention).
2. *See* Robert H. Klonoff, *The Decline of Class Actions*, 90 WASH. U. L. REV. 729, 731 (2013) ("The class action device, once considered a 'revolutionary' vehicle for achieving mass justice, has fallen into disfavor." (citation omitted)).
3. *See infra* notes 56–57 and accompanying text.
4. *See, e.g.*, Martin H. Redish et al., *Cy Pres Relief and the Pathologies of the Modern Class Action*, 62 FLA. L. REV. 617, 641–51 (2010).
5. U.S. CONST. amend. V.
6. Logan v. Zimmerman Brush Co., 455 U.S. 422, 429 (1982) ("The . . . Due Process Clause[] protect[s] civil litigants who seek recourse in the courts, either as defendants hoping to protect their property or as plaintiffs attempting to redress grievances."); Standard Oil Co. v. New Jersey, 341 U.S. 428, 439 (1951) ("There is no fiction . . . in the fact that choses of action . . . held by the corporation, are property.").
7. *See, e.g.*, Lane v. Facebook, Inc., 696 F.3d 811, 828–29 (9th Cir. 2012) (Kleinfeld, J., dissenting) ("Facebook users [aside from the named plaintiffs] who had suffered

damages from past exposure of their purchasers got no money.... Class counsel, on the other had [sic], got millions."), *cert. denied sub nom.* Marek v. Lane, 134 S. Ct. 8 (2013).
8. Fed. R. Civ. P. 23(a)(2).
9. *Id.* 23(a)(3)–(4).
10. *See In re* Hydrogen Peroxide Antitrust Litig., 552 F.3d 305, 307 (3d Cir. 2008) ("In deciding whether to certify a class . . . the district court must make whatever factual and legal inquiries are necessary and must consider all relevant evidence and arguments presented by the parties.").
11. Fed. R. Civ. P. 23(c)(2).
12. *See infra* notes 203–06 and accompanying text.
13. *See* John C. Coffee, Jr., *The Regulation of Entrepreneurial Litigation: Balancing Fairness and Efficiency in the Large Class Action*, 54 U. CHI. L. REV. 877, 905 (1987) (recognizing that some class members have independently unmarketable claims).
14. *See* 28 U.S.C. § 1407(a) (2012) (allowing consolidation of pretrial proceedings "[w]hen civil actions . . . are *pending* in different districts" (emphasis added)).
15. *See* Coffee, *supra* note 13, at 905.
16. *See infra* notes 156–57 and accompanying text (describing the mandatory nature of MDL).
17. *See infra* notes 59–62 and accompanying text (describing the mechanics of MDL).
18. *See* 28 U.S.C. § 1407(a).
19. *See infra* note 133 and accompanying text.
20. *See infra* note 93 and accompanying text (describing court-appointed counsel's substantial control over the MDL).
21. *See* Joan Steinman, *The Effects of Case Consolidation on the Procedural Rights of Litigants*, 42 UCLA L. REV. 967, 976 (1995) (observing that, while some courts "have acknowledged the substantial disenfranchisement of nonlead counsel," they have nevertheless "upheld the lead counsel system"); *infra* notes 74–76 and accompanying text (describing a party's uphill battle when challenging transfer).
22. Others have analyzed MDL and even critiqued plaintiffs' lack of autonomy, but none has done so primarily from a due process perspective. *See, e.g.*, Elizabeth Chamblee Burch, *Litigating Together: Social, Moral, and Legal Obligations*, 91 B.U. L. REV. 87, 91 (2011) [hereinafter Burch, *Litigating Together*] ("My prescriptive objective is to enable plaintiffs to litigate together and self-govern through social norms and deliberative democracy ideals, such as arguing, bargaining, and voting."); Roger H. Trangsrud, *Mass Trials in Mass Tort Cases*, 1989 U. ILL. L. REV. 69, 69 (calling attention to plaintiffs' lack of autonomy in mass trials).
23. *See, e.g.*, Cleveland Bd. of Educ. v. Loudermill, 470 U.S. 532, 547 (1985) (holding that a public school board deprived an employee of due process by not providing him with a "pretermination opportunity to respond").
24. *See* section 3.4.1, *infra* (describing the day-in-court ideal).
25. *See* MARTIN H. REDISH, WHOLESALE JUSTICE 140–47 (2009) (discussing these models in the context of class actions).
26. *See id.* at 140.

27. *See infra* notes 181–84 and accompanying text.
28. *See infra* notes 203–06 and accompanying text (questioning whether a steering committee can protect the interests of a plaintiff whose interests conflict with those of the majority).
29. Redish, *supra* note 25, at 4 ("No one can doubt that the adjudication in the courts is as much a part of the governing process as are the actions of the legislative or executive branches.").
30. *See infra* notes 197–202 and accompanying text.
31. *See infra* notes 203–06 and accompanying text.
32. Lori J. Parker, *Cause of Action Involving Claim Transferred to Multidistrict Litigation*, 23 CAUSES OF ACTION 185 § 25 (2d ed. 2003) ("Opting out is the option available to plaintiffs who do not wish to accept a class settlement.").
33. *See* S. Todd Brown, *Plaintiff Control and Domination in Multidistrict Mass Torts*, 61 CLEV. ST. L. REV. 391, 412–13 (2013) (arguing that a collectivist, democratic settlement vote can reduce "fair compensation for those who believe they have suffered a loss").
34. *See* Edward D. Spurgeon & Mary Jane Ciccarello, *The Lawyer in Other Fiduciary Roles*, 62 FORDHAM L. REV. 1357, 1364 (1994).
35. *See* section 3.4.4, *infra* (discussing the background and implications of this utilitarian calculus in the MDL context).
36. Pub. L. No. 90-296, 82 Stat. 109 (1968) (codified as amended at 28 U.S.C. § 1407 (2012)).
37. *See* Richard L. Marcus, *Cure-All for an Era of Dispersed Litigation? Toward a Maximalist Use of the Multidistrict Litigation Panel's Transfer Power*, 82 TUL. L. REV. 2245, 2260–62 (2008).
38. Yvette Ostolaza & Michelle Hartmann, *Overview of Multidistrict Litigation Rules at the State and Federal Level*, 26 REV. LITIG. 47, 49 (2007).
39. *See id.* at 48–50.
40. 28 U.S.C. § 1407(a).
41. *See* John G. Heyburn II & Francis E. McGovern, *Evaluating and Improving the MDL Process*, LITIGATION, Spring 2012, at 26, 30.
42. *See generally* Judith Resnik, *From "Cases" to "Litigation,"* 54 L. & CONTEMP. PROBS. 6 (1991) (describing shifting attitudes toward mass tort litigation from the 1960s to the 1990s).
43. *See* Andrew D. Bradt, *The Shortest Distance: Direct Filing and Choice of Law in Multidistrict Litigation*, 88 NOTRE DAME L. REV. 759, 781–84 (2012) (summarizing developments that are making it harder to certify class actions); Klonoff, *supra* note 2, at 731.
44. *See* Calendar Year Statistics of the United States Judicial Panel On Multidistrict Litigation 10 (2013), http:// www.jpml.uscourts.gov/sites/jpml/files/JPML_Calendar_Year_Statistics-2013.pdf (last visited Oct. 26, 2014), *archived at* http://perma.cc/A3JE-VZP7 (depicting the areas of law in which MDLs are currently pending).
45. 28 U.S.C. § 1407(a), (d).
46. *See id.* § 1407(a).

47. *Id.* § 1407(b).
48. *Id.* § 1407(c)(1).
49. United States Judicial Panel on Multidistrict Litigation Statistical Analysis of Multidistrict Litigation Fiscal Year 2013 at 2, http:// www.jpml.uscourts.gov/sites/ jpml/files/ JPML_Statistical_Analysis_of_Multidistrict_Litigation-2013_1.pdf (last visited Oct. 26, 2014), *archived at* http:// perma.cc/9TQK-GYJ9 [hereinafter Statistical Analysis].
50. *See* 28 U.S.C. § 1407(a).
51. *See infra* note 133.
52. *See infra* notes 133–37 and accompanying text (describing the transferee judge's incentive to encourage a settlement).
53. *See* Eldon E. Fallon, *Common Benefit Fees in Multidistrict Litigation*, 74 LA. L. REV. 371, 373 (2014) ("The committees occupy leadership roles in the litigation— conducting documentary discovery, establishing document depositories, arguing motions, conducting bellwether trials, and in general, carrying out the duties and responsibilities set for in the court's pretrial orders").
54. *Id.*
55. *Id.*
56. United States Judicial Panel on Multidistrict Litigation, MDL Statistics Report— Distribution of Pending MDL Dockets, http:// www.jpml.uscourts.gov/sites/jpml/ files/ Pending_MDL_Dockets_By_District-February-19-2014.pdf (last visited Oct. 26, 2014), *archived at* http:// perma.cc/ DB8E-ZXTL.
57. Bradt, *supra* note 43, at 762. Others estimate the number to be smaller, closer to 15 percent of all civil litigation, which is still quite significant. *See* Fallon, *Common Benefit Fees*, *supra* note 53, at 373 (citing Heyburn & McGovern, *supra* note 41, at 26).
58. Bradt, *supra* note 43, at 786; *see also* Marcus, *supra* note 37, at 2269 ("[T]he Panel's willingness to combine cases, and its confidence that combination will be for the advantage of the litigants as well as serve judicial economy, is sometimes striking.").
59. 28 U.S.C. § 1407(a) (2012). "The common questions of fact must be complex, numerous, and incapable of resolution through other available procedures such as informal coordination." Manual for Complex Litigation (Fourth) § 22.33 (2004).
60. *See* Bradt, *supra* note 43, at 786 n.156; Fallon, *Common Benefit Fees*, *supra* note 53, at 371.
61. *See In re* Korean Air Lines Co., 642 F.3d 685, 699 (9th Cir. 2011) ("A district judge exercising authority over cases transferred for pretrial proceedings 'inherits the entire pretrial jurisdiction that the transferor district judge would have exercised if the transfer had not occurred.'" (quoting 15 CHARLES ALAN WRIGHT, ARTHUR R. MILLER & EDWARD H. COOPER, FEDERAL PRACTICE & PROCEDURE §3866 (3d ed. 2010)); *In re* Phenylpropanolamine Prods. Liab. Litig., 460 F.3d 1217, 1231 (9th Cir. 2006) (observing that a transferee judge's power "includes authority to decide all pretrial motions").
62. "Centralization under Section 1407 is thus necessary in order to eliminate duplicative discovery; prevent inconsistent pretrial rulings, including with regard to class certification; and conserve the resources of the parties, their counsel and the judiciary." *In re* Baycol Prods. Liab. Litig., 180 F. Supp. 2d 1378, 1380 (J.P.M.L. 2001).

63. 28 U.S.C. § 1407(a) ("Each action so transferred shall be remanded by the panel at or before the conclusion of such pretrial proceedings to the district from which it was transferred unless it shall have been previously terminated").
64. *See* United States Judicial Panel on Multidistrict Litigation, Multidistrict Litigation Terminated Through September 30, 2012, at 1, http:// www.jpml.uscourts.gov/sites/ jpml/files/ JPML_Terminated_Litigations-2012.pdf (last visited Oct. 26, 2014), *archived at* http://perma.cc/CMT8-W5LQ.
65. Ninety percent of pending cases that are part of an MDL are products liability claims. Bradt, *supra* note 43, at 784 (citation omitted).
66. Statistical Analysis, *supra* note 49.
67. John F. Nangle, *From the Horse's Mouth: The Workings of the Judicial Panel on Multidistrict Litigation*, 66 Def. Couns. J. 341, 341 (1999) ("[U]nder Section 1407, [the Panel] has the responsibility of . . . identifying civil actions pending in different federal courts involving one or more common questions of fact").
68. Marcus, *supra* note 37, at 2270 (quoting *In re* Westinghouse Elec. Corp. Uranium Contracts Litig., 405 F. Supp. 316, 319 (J.P.M.L. 1975)).
69. 28 U.S.C. § 1407(a) (2012). *See In re* "East of the Rockies" Concrete Pipe Antitrust Cases, 302 F. Supp. 244, 255–56 (J.P.M.L. 1969) (describing several factors relevant to the Panel's decision about whether to consolidate into an MDL); Note, *The Judicial Panel and the Conduct of Multidistrict Litigation*, 87 Harv. L. Rev. 1001, 1002 (1974) ("Section 1407 thus directs the Panel to balance gains in efficiency and economy for the judiciary and some parties against inconvenience, added expense, and loss of forum choice for others.").
70. *The Judicial Panel and the Conduct of Multidistrict Litigation*, *supra* note 69, at 1009 ("[T]he Panel has made the likelihood of significant judicial savings the operative factor in transfer decisions.").
71. Nangle, *supra* note 67, at 343.
72. *The Judicial Panel and the Conduct of Multidistrict Litigation*, *supra* note 69, at 1003.
73. *Id.* at 1006 ("The Panel's response has been to transfer all the cases and leave to the transferee judge any problems created by noncommon facts or conflicting interests among parties on the same side of a case."). This is in contrast to Rule 23(b)(3) class actions, in which common questions of law or fact must predominate. Fed. R. Civ. P. 23(b) (3); *see also* Wal-Mart Stores, Inc. v. Dukes, 131 S. Ct. 2541, 2565–67 (2011) (Ginsburg, J., concurring in part and dissenting in part) (suggesting that the majority opinion imported a predominance requirement into Rule 23(a)(2), which requires potential classes to share common questions of law or fact).
74. J.P.M.L. R. P. 11.1(c).
75. 28 U.S.C. § 1407(e) (2012).
76. *Id.* ("There shall be no appeal or review of an order of the panel denying a motion to transfer for consolidated or coordinated proceedings."); Ostolaza & Hartmann, *supra* note 38, at 62.
77. 28 U.S.C. § 1407(b).
78. Ostolaza & Hartmann, *supra* note 38, at 57–59.

79. *See, e.g., In re* Diet Drugs (Phentermine, Fenfluramine, Dexfenfluramine) Prods. Liab. Litig., 990 F. Supp. 834, 835–36 (J.P.M.L. 1998) (ordering consolidation of many actions into a district that contained none of them).
80. *See, e.g., id.* at 835 (listing districts to which the parties lobbied for transfer).
81. Ostolaza & Hartmann, *supra* note 38, at 60.
82. *Id.*
83. Bradt, *supra* note 43, at 787. *See* Manual for Complex Litigation (Fourth) § 22.33 (2004) ("[T]he Panel looks for an available and convenient transfer forum, usually one that (1) is not overtaxed with other MDL cases, (2) has a related action pending on its docket, (3) has a judge with some degree of expertise in handling the issues presented, and (4) is convenient to the parties.") (internal citations omitted).
84. Bradt, *supra* note 43, at 786–87.
85. *See* Nangle, *supra* note 67, at 343 ("[I]n selecting a transferee district, the panel does not consider the litigants' dissatisfaction with past or anticipated rulings of the transferee court. Nor does the panel consider the governing appellate law of the transferee district. And most empathically, the panel does not sit in review of decisions of the transferee court.").
86. *See* Manual for Complex Litigation (Fourth) § 20.132 (2004) (describing the transferee judge's management of tag-along actions).
87. The Panel may conditionally transfer the tag-along into the MDL for fifteen days, allowing the parties an opportunity to oppose the transfer. Ostolaza & Hartmann, *supra* note 38, at 63. When any transfer request is pending before the Panel, the potential transferor district court's authority is not affected—it can rule on pending pretrial motions, including motions to remand to state court. Until an effective transfer order is entered with the clerk of the transferor court, this remains true. Nangle, *supra* note 67, at 342–43; *see* J.P.M.L. R. P. 7.1.
88. Nangle, *supra* note 67, at 342.
89. Bradt, *supra* note 43, at 795–96.
90. Eldon E. Fallon, Jeremy T. Grabill, & Robert Pitard Wynne, *Bellwether Trials in Multidistrict Litigation*, 82 Tul. L. Rev. 2323, 2339 n.74 (2008) [hereinafter Fallon et al., *Bellwether Trials*]; *see, e.g., In re* Zyprexa Prods. Liab. Litig., 594 F.3d 113, 116 (2d Cir. 2010) (per curiam) (involving an MDL "brought by thousands of plaintiffs").
91. Though transferee courts appoint committees to represent both plaintiffs and defendants, "in practice, the [Defendants' Steering Committee] is generally selected by the defendant itself with the approval of the court." Fallon, *Common Benefit Fees*, *supra* note 53, at 373.
92. *In re* Air Crash Disaster at Detroit Metro. Airport on August 16, 1987, 737 F. Supp. 396, 398 (E.D. Mich. 1989) (quoting *In re* Air Crash Disaster at Florida Everglades on December 29, 1972, 549 F.2d 1006, 1014 (5th Cir. 1977)); *In re* Korean Air Lines Co., 642 F.3d 685, 700 (9th Cir. 2011) ("In discretionary matters going to the phasing, timing, and coordination of the cases, the power of the MDL court is at its peak.").
93. Bradt, *supra* note 43, at 791; *see* Elizabeth Chamblee Burch, *Group Consensus, Individual Consent*, 79 Geo. Wash. L. Rev. 506, 508–10 (2011) [hereinafter

Burch, *Group Consensus*] ("Presently, plaintiffs in nonclass aggregation have few opportunities for participation, voice, and control. Realistically, lawyers drive multidistrict litigation."); William W. Schwarzer, Alan Hirsch, & Edward Sussman, *Judicial Federalism: A Proposal to Amend the Multidistrict Litigation Statute to Permit Discovery Coordination of Large-Scale Litigation Pending in State and Federal Courts*, 73 Tex. L. Rev. 1529, 1547 & n.110 (1995) (asserting that "[a]ggregation tends to diminish plaintiffs' control over their claims" and citing an example in which nine lawyers or law firms represented over 10,000 claimants); Lawrence L. Jones II, *MDL Primer: Multi-District Litigation 101*, Jones Ward PLC (Aug. 5, 2011), http://www.the-recall-lawyers.com/2011/08/ mdl-primer-multi-district-liti.html, *archived at* http://perma.cc/LHS6-AW36 (last accessed July 5, 2023) ("After the [Plaintiffs' Steering Committee (PSC)] is appointed by the court, the lawyers on the PSC will control the litigation for all of the non-PSC members. All case strategy and much of the day-to-day work is completed by the PSC and the various 'subcommittees' created by the PSC.").
94. Manual for Complex Litigation (Fourth) § 10.221 (2004).
95. *Id.*
96. *See id.*
97. *Id.*
98. *Id.*
99. *Id.*
100. *Id.*
101. *See* Charles Silver & Geoffrey P. Miller, *The Quasi-Class Action Method of Managing Multi-District Litigations*, 63 Vand. L. Rev. 105, 118–19 (2010) (mentioning that judges are "free to pick the lawyers they want[] because the standards governing appointments of attorneys to managerial positions are extremely weak" and few if any attorneys appeal unfavorable appointment decisions, much less win a reversal).
102. *See, e.g., In re* San Juan Dupont Plaza Hotel Fire Litig., No. MDL 721, 1989 WL 168401, at *6 (D. P.R. Dec. 2, 1988) (describing nomination process for positions on Plaintiffs' Steering Committee).
103. *See In re* Bendectin Litig., 857 F.2d 290, 297 (6th Cir. 1988) (describing the process by which attorneys were appointed to the Lead Counsel Committee, the plaintiffs' failure to show cause why certain attorneys should not be appointed, and declaring, "[i]n complex cases, it is well established that the district judge may create a Plaintiffs' Lead Counsel Committee") (citing *In re* Air Crash Disaster at Florida Everglades on December 29, 1972, 549 F.2d 1006, 1014–15 (5th Cir. 1977); Vincent v. Hughes Air West, Inc., 557 F.2d 759, 773–74 (9th Cir. 1977); Farber v. Riker-Maxson Corp., 442 F.2d 457, 459 (2d Cir. 1971)); *San Juan Dupont Plaza Hotel*, 1989 WL 168401, at *5–11 (describing the purpose of the plaintiffs' steering committee; the main criteria for membership thereon; the primary responsibilities of the committee; and procedures for application and nomination to the committee, including written objections to potential members).
104. *But see* Manual for Complex Litigation (Fourth) § 10.224 (2004) ("[A]n evidentiary hearing may be needed to bring relevant facts to light or to allow counsel to

state their case for appointment and answer questions from the court about their qualifications.").
105. *San Juan Dupont Plaza Hotel*, 1989 WL 168401, at *6.
106. Manual for Complex Litigation (Fourth) § 10.224 (2004).
107. *Id.*
108. *See* Brown, *supra* note 33, at 398 ("In some cases, participants will agree to the entire composition of the steering committee and iron out any objections before presenting a list to the judge.").
109. 594 F.3d 113 (2d Cir. 2010) (per curiam).
110. *Id.* at 115.
111. *Id.* at 116.
112. *See* Stanwood R. Duval, Jr., *Considerations in Choosing Counsel for Multidistrict Litigation Cases and Mass Tort Cases*, 74 LA. L. REV. 391, 392 (2014) ("[P]revious experience in an MDL or other complex litigation is always considered.").
113. *See id.*
114. *See id.* at 392–93 (remarking on the danger of repeat MDL plaintiffs' attorneys becoming an "exclusive club").
115. For example, during the twelve-month period ending September 30, 2013, the Panel transferred 5,521 cases into MDLs, whereas 40,988 actions were filed directly in transferee courts during that time. Statistical Analysis, *supra* note 49.
116. *See, e.g.*, Pavlou v. Baxter Healthcare Corp., No. 98 Civ.4526, 2004 WL 912585, at *1 (S.D.N.Y. Apr. 29, 2004) (affirming, on remand from MDL, a magistrate judge's order limiting potential deponents and topics of deposition because "[p]laintiffs had sufficient opportunity to seek discovery during the MDL proceedings. To rule otherwise would undermine the MDL proceedings.").
117. Fallon et al., *Bellwether Trials*, *supra* note 90, at 2329 n.17 (quoting *In re* Factor VIII or IX Concentrate Blood Prods. Litig., 169 F.R.D. 632, 636 (N.D. Ill. 1996)); *see* Marcus, *supra* note 37, at 2264 (citing Stanley A. Weigel, *The Judicial Panel on Multidistrict Litigation, Transferor Courts and Transferee Courts*, 78 F.R.D. 575, 577 (1978)) (quoting Judge Weigel, an original member of the Panel, who "opined that the transferee judge's orders must be respected by the transferor judge").
118. 523 U.S. 26 (1998).
119. *Id.* at 28 (holding that a transferee court "has no ... authority" "to assign a transferred case to itself for trial"). This limitation does not extend to cases brought under Section 4C of the Clayton Act; the Panel can consolidate actions brought under that provision and transfer them for both pretrial and trial. 28 U.S.C. § 1407(h) (2012).
120. The method of selecting cases for bellwether treatment varies among MDLs. The process can involve grouping like cases and selecting from each group, allowing plaintiffs and defendants to propose cases featuring their strongest arguments, or some other process determined by the transferee court. *See* Fallon et al., *Bellwether Trials*, *supra* note 90, at 2343–51 (describing the selection process); *see also In re* Vioxx Prod. Liab. Litig., 869 F. Supp. 2d 719, 723 (E.D. La. 2012) ("Millions of documents were discovered and collated. Thousands of depositions were taken and at least 1,000 discovery motions were argued. After a reasonable period for

discovery, the Court assisted the parties in selecting and preparing certain test cases to proceed as bellwether trials."). There is no explicit requirement that cases selected for bellwether trials be typical of all claims.

121. Bradt, *supra* note 43, at 789–90; Fallon et al., *Bellwether Trials, supra* note 90, at 2337–38.
122. *Cf.* Parklane Hosiery Co. v. Shore, 439 U.S. 322 (1979) (holding that earlier SEC action could be used offensively as collateral estoppel in later shareholder derivative suit).
123. *See* Fallon et al., *Bellwether Trials, supra* note 90, at 2360 n.121 (noting that members of the steering committee tend to represent a significant number of plaintiffs, have extensive knowledge of the subject matter, and offer their cases to be tried as bellwether cases).
124. *Id.* at 2338.
125. Alexandra Lahav, *Bellwether Trials*, 76 GEO. WASH. L. REV. 576, 577–78 (2008) (explaining that bellwether trials "assist in valuing cases and to encourage settlement").
126. This is appropriate given the origin of the term "bellwether": The term bellwether is derived from the ancient practice of belling a wether (a male sheep) selected to lead his flock. The ultimate success of the wether selected to wear the bell was determined by whether the flock had confidence that the wether would not lead them astray, and so it is in the mass tort context. *In re* Chevron U.S.A., Inc., 109 F.3d 1016, 1019 (5th Cir. 1997). *See also* Fallon et al., *Bellwether Trials, supra* note 90, at 2324.
127. Fallon et al., *Bellwether Trials, supra* note 90, at 2325 ("At a minimum, the bellwether process should lead to the creation of 'trial packages' that can be utilized by local counsel upon the dissolution of MDLs."); *see id.* at 2340 ("Ultimately, the availability of a trial package ensures that the knowledge acquired by coordinating counsel is not lost if a global resolution cannot be achieved in the transferee court.").
128. *Id.* at 2339.
129. "The notion that the trial of some members of a large group of claimants may provide a basis for enhancing prospects of settlement or for resolving common issues or claims is a sound one that has achieved general acceptance by both bench and bar." *Chevron*, 109 F.3d at 1019.
130. Fallon et al., *Bellwether Trials, supra* note 90, at 2342.
131. *See id.* (explaining that bellwether trials let attorneys gain an understanding more grounded in reality due to the presence of a jury).
132. *Id.* at 2366.
133. As of September 30, 2013, 462,501 individual actions had been subjected to § 1407 proceedings. Statistical Analysis, *supra* note 49. The Panel remanded 13,432, or about 3 percent, of those. *Id.* 359,548 actions terminated in the transferee court. *Id.*; *see* Thomas E. Willging & Emery G. Lee III, *From Class Actions to Multidistrict Consolidations: Aggregate Mass-Tort Litigation After Ortiz*, 58 U. KAN. L. REV. 775, 801 (2010) (observing several MDL settlements that "suggest that the MDL process has supplemented and perhaps displaced the class action device as a procedural mechanism for large settlements").

134. *See* Marcus, *supra* note 37, at 2265 ("Almost inevitably, transferee judges are likely to feel that they have some responsibility to attempt to resolve the cases they have gotten—'The other judges are relying on me to finish this job.'").
135. *See, e.g., In re* Zyprexa Prod. Liab. Litig., 594 F.3d 113, 116 (2d Cir. 2010); *In re* Methyl Tertiary Butyl Ether (MTB) Prod. Liab. Litig., 578 F. Supp. 2d 519, 522 (S.D.N.Y. 2008); *In re* "Agent Orange" Prod. Liab. Litig., 597 F. Supp. 740, 760 (E.D.N.Y. 1984).
136. *See, e.g., In re* Patenaude, 210 F.3d 135, 139–40 (3d Cir. 2000) (describing transferee courts' resistance to remand unless "all avenues of settlement were exhausted"). Transferee courts even "may require individuals to attend settlement conferences." *In re* Korean Air Lines Co., Antitrust Litig., 642 F.3d 685, 699 (9th Cir. 2011) (citing *In re* Air Crash Disaster at Stapleton Int'l Airport, Denver, Colo., on Nov. 15, 1987, 720 F. Supp. 1433, 1436 (D. Colo. 1988)).
137. Fallon, *Common Benefit Fees, supra* note 53, at 373–74.
138. *See* Burch, *Group Consensus, supra* note 93, at 516–17 (citing the September 11th Victims Compensation Fund as an example of claimants whose goals transcended financial compensation); Howard M. Erichson & Benjamin C. Zipursky, *Consent Versus Closure*, 96 CORNELL L. REV. 265, 312–13 (2011) (arguing that tort law "is not simply a device for transferring wealth").
139. Erichson & Zipursky, *supra* note 138, at 296.
140. ALI, Principles of The Law of Aggregate Litigation (2010).
141. Erichson & Zipursky, *supra* note 138, at 293.
142. *Id.*
143. *In re* Guidant Corp. Implantable Defibrillators Prod. Liab. Litig., MDL No. 05-1708, 2008 WL 682174, at *5 (D. Minn. Mar. 7, 2008) (quoting *In re* Air Crash Disaster at Florida Everglades on December 29, 1972, 549 F.2d 1006, 1016 (5th Cir. 1977)) (alterations in original).
144. Fallon, *Common Benefit Fees, supra* note 53, at 374–75 (describing the practice of creating a common fund to spread the cost of the litigation across all beneficiaries).
145. *See, e.g., In re* Protegen Sling and Vesica System Prod. Liab. Litig., Nos. 1:01-01387, 1387, 2002 WL 31834446, at *1 (D. Md., Apr. 12, 2002) ("The obligation shall follow the case to its final disposition in any United States court including a court having jurisdiction in bankruptcy."). The process described is most typical for plaintiffs' steering committees; clients typically compensate the defendants' steering committees on a periodic basis. Fallon, *Common Benefit Fees, supra* note 53, at 374.
146. Fallon, *Common Benefit Fees, supra* note 53, at 376 (justifying the common benefit fee's extraction from the primary attorney because the primary attorney is the beneficiary of the common benefit work).
147. 488 F.2d 714 (5th Cir. 1974).
148. *See, e.g., Guidant Corp. Implantable Defibrillators*, 2008 WL 682174, at *7 (explaining that courts have wide discretion in applying the elements of the *Johnson* twelve-factor test). The *Johnson* factors are: (1) the time and labor required; (2) the novelty and difficulty of the questions; (3) the skill requisite to perform the legal service properly; (4) the preclusion of other employment by the attorney due to acceptance of the case; (5) the customary fee for similar work in the community; (6) whether

the fee is fixed or contingent; (7) time limitations imposed by the client or the circumstances; (8) the amount involved and the results obtained; (9) the experience, reputation, and ability of the attorneys; (10) the undesirability of the case; (11) the nature and length of the professional relationship with the client; and (12) awards in similar cases. *Id.* (citing *Johnson*, 488 F.2d at 719–20).

149. *In re* Vioxx Prod. Liab. Litig., 802 F. Supp. 2d 740, 772 (E.D. La. 2011) (quoting *In re* High Sulfur Content Gasoline Prod. Liab. Litig., 517 F.3d 227, 234 (5th Cir. 2008)).

150. Fallon, *Common Benefit Fees*, *supra* note 53, at 387. District courts derive authority to establish these structures from their equitable powers. *Id.* at 379–80 (explaining how courts derive this equitable authority from Rule 23 of the Federal Rules of Civil Procedure). Settlement agreements also sometimes give express consent to the transferee judge setting common benefit fees. *See id.* at 378–80 ("[S]ettlements usually contain[] a specific agreement addressing the court's authority regarding attorneys' fees.").

151. *In re* San Juan Dupont Hotel Fire Litig., 111 F.3d 220, 228 (1st Cir. 1997). *See High Sulfur Content Gasoline*, 517 F.3d at 227 ("We must determine whether the record clearly indicates that the district court has utilized the *Johnson* framework as the basis of its analysis, has not proceeded in a summary fashion, and has arrived at an amount that can be said to be just compensation." (internal quotation marks and citation omitted)).

152. *See High Sulfur Content Gasoline Prod. Liab. Litig.*, 517 F.3d at 227 (admonishing the district court for "abdicat[ing] its responsibility to ensure that the individual awards recommended by the Fee Committee were fair and reasonable").

153. *See, e.g., San Juan Dupont Hotel Fire Litig.*, 111 F.3d at 228 ("[A]ll litigants must share in their mutual obligation to collaborate with the district court *ab initio* in fashioning adequate case management and trial procedures, or bear the reasonably foreseeable consequences for their failure to do so.").

154. *See* Marcus, *supra* note 37, at 2248 ("The Panel's activities have generally not caused the sort of controversy the class action produced.").

155. Lexecon Inc. v. Milberg Weiss Bershad Hynes & Lerach, 523 U.S. 26, 28 (1998).

156. *See* Fallon et al., *Bellwether Trials*, *supra* note 90, at 2330 ("Indeed, the strongest criticism of the traditional MDL process is the centralized forum can resemble a 'black hole,' into which cases are transferred never to be heard from again.").

157. "Imagine you are minding your own business and litigating a case in federal court. Opening your mail one day, you find an order—from a court you have never heard of—declaring your case a 'tag-along' action and transferring it to another federal court clear across the country for pretrial proceedings. Welcome to the world of multidistrict litigation." Gregory Hansel, *Extreme Litigation: An Interview with Judge Wm. Terrell Hodges, Chairman of the Judicial Panel on Multidistrict Litigation*, 19 Me. B.J. 16, 16 (2004).

158. U.S. Const. amend. V.

159. Sheldon v. Sill, 49 U.S. 441, 444 (1850) (defining a "chose in action" as a right "which can be realized only by suit").

160. Phillips Petroleum Co. v. Shutts, 472 U.S. 797, 807 (1985) ("[A] chose in action is a constitutionally recognized property interest").

161. *See* section 3.3.2, *supra* (explaining the selection process and power of steering committees).
162. Ortiz v. Fibreboard Corp., 527 U.S. 815, 846 (1999) (internal quotation marks omitted).
163. Mason v. Eldred, 73 U.S. 231, 239 (1867). *See* Taylor v. Sturgell, 553 U.S. 880, 892–93 (2008) (pronouncing the general rule that persons are not bound by cases in which they are not parties); Hansberry v. Lee, 311 U.S. 32, 40 (1940) ("It is a principle of general application in Anglo-American jurisprudence that one is not bound by a judgment *in personam* in a litigation in which he is not designated as a party or to which he has not been made a party by service of process.").
164. Martin H. Redish & William J. Katt, Taylor v. Sturgell, *Procedural Due Process, and the Day-in-Court Ideal: Resolving the Virtual Representation Dilemma*, 84 Notre Dame L. Rev. 1877, 1890 (2009) ("'Autonomy' means that the individual has the right to choose how to fashion his own representation and to participate in the process as he sees fit."); *see* Mathews v. Eldridge, 424 U.S. 319, 333 (1976) ("The fundamental requirement of due process is the opportunity to be heard at a meaningful time and in a meaningful manner.") (internal quotations omitted).
165. *Taylor*, 553 U.S. at 892.
166. Martin H. Redish, *The Adversary System, Democratic Theory, and the Constitutional Role of Self-Interest: The Tobacco Wars, 1953–1971*, 51 DePaul L. Rev. 359, 391 (2001) [hereinafter Redish, *Tobacco Wars*].
167. Lawrence B. Solum, *Procedural Justice*, 78 S. Cal. L. Rev. 181, 280 (2004).
168. Marshall v. Jerrico, Inc., 446 U.S. 238, 242 (1980).
169. *See* Solum, *supra* note 167, at 259 ("[P]rocedural fairness requires that those affected by a decision have the option to participate in the process by which the decision is made.").
170. *See* Alexandra D. Lahav, *Due Process and the Future of Class Actions*, 44 Loy. U. Chi. L.J. 545, 554 (2012) ("Dignitary theory dovetails with social-psychological studies of procedural justice finding that people perceive outcomes as more legitimate when the participants are given the opportunity to be heard."); Redish & Katt, *supra* note 164, at 1893–94 ("[I]ndividual participation in the litigation process as a means of vindicating his rights adds legitimacy to judicial outcomes."); Solum, *supra* note 167, at 274 ("Procedures that purport to bind without affording meaningful rights of participation are fundamentally illegitimate.").
171. Redish & Katt, *supra* note 164, at 1889–90 (describing "process-based theory['s]" "facilitation of the citizen's role in democratic governance"). *See* Martin H. Redish & Nathan D. Larsen, *Class Actions, Litigant Autonomy, and the Foundations of Procedural Due Process*, 95 Cal. L. Rev. 1573, 1582 (2007) ("The procedural due process guarantee is appropriately viewed as a constitutional outgrowth of democracy's normative commitment to . . . process-based political autonomy."); Susan P. Sturm, *The Promise of Participation*, 78 Iowa L. Rev. 981, 996–97 (1993) (describing the benefits of direct participation to public law remedies).
172. 424 U.S. 319 (1976).
173. 501 U.S. 1 (1991).

174. *Id.* at 10–11.
175. *See* Jerry Mashaw, *The Supreme Court's Due Process Calculus for Administrative Adjudication in* Mathews v. Eldridge: *Three Factors in Search of a Theory of Value*, 44 U. Chi. L. Rev. 28, 49–52 (1976).
176. *See Mathews*, 424 U.S. at 333 ("This Court consistently has held that some form of hearing is required before an individual is finally deprived of a property interest.").
177. *See supra* note 25 and accompanying text.
178. *See* Redish, *supra* note 25, at 140.
179. *See supra* note 29 and accompanying text.
180. *See, e.g.*, Cohen v. California, 403 U.S. 15, 26 (1971) (individual has First Amendment right to display in public a jacket saying "Fuck the Draft" on the back).
181. The paternalistic version of the day-in-court ideal is explored in Redish, *supra* note 25, at 140–47.
182. 311 U.S. 32 (1940).
183. 521 U.S. 591 (1997).
184. *Hansberry*, 311 U.S. at 45; *Amchem Prods.*, 521 U.S. at 626; *see also* Stephenson v. Dow Chemical Co., 273 F.3d 249, 260–61 (2d Cir. 2001), *aff'd by an equally divided court*, 539 U.S. 111 (2003).
185. *See* Rima M. Daniels, *Monetary Damages in Mandatory Classes: When Should Opt-Out Rights be Allowed?*, 57 Ala. L. Rev. 499, 499 n.1 (2005) ("Classes certified under 23(b)(1) or (b)(2) are known as 'mandatory' classes because absent class members have no inherent right to remove themselves.").
186. 472 U.S. 797 (1985).
187. *Id.* at 811–12.
188. *See, e.g.*, Brown v. Ticor Title Ins. Co., 982 F.2d 386, 392 (9th Cir. 1992), *cert. granted in part*, 510 U.S. 810 (1993), *cert. dismissed as improvidently granted*, 511 U.S. 117 (1994) (holding minimal due process protection requires opportunity for plaintiff to remove himself from the class where forum court had personal jurisdiction over plaintiff).
189. *Shutts*, 472 U.S. at 811–12.
190. *See* Fed. R. Civ. P. 23(a)–(b) (requiring parties be "fairly and adequately protect[ed]" and allowing a class action if "prosecuting separate actions" "would substantially impair or impede [individual class members'] ability to protect their interests"); *supra* note 185 and accompanying text.
191. *See supra* note 184 and accompanying text.
192. *See* Redish, *supra* note 25, at 135–75.
193. Fed. R. Civ. P. 23(c)(2)(B)(v) ("[T]he court will exclude from the class any member who requests exclusion").
194. *See supra* note 164 and accompanying text. It could be argued that an opt-out procedure is insufficient to satisfy the autonomy model because it preys on the inertia of class members, and that instead autonomy demands use of an opt-in procedure. That issue, however, is irrelevant to MDL, which provides for neither procedure.
195. *See supra* note 15 and accompanying text.
196. *Supra* note 14 and accompanying text.

197. Sturm, *supra* note 171, at 1001 ("Lawyers' control over the process detracts from the client's sense of autonomy and responsibility.").
198. "In fact, a party loses some control over litigation as soon as she is forced to share the litigating stage with even one other litigant." Robert G. Bone, *Rethinking the "Day in Court" Ideal and Nonparty Preclusion*, 67 N.Y.U. L. Rev. 193, 198 n.16 (1992). "Indeed, the judicial willingness to sacrifice party control in the aggregation context seems inconsistent with the firm commitment to individual litigant control in the preclusion area." *Id.*
199. *See supra* notes 90–93 and accompanying text.
200. *See supra* notes 101–04 and accompanying text.
201. Fed. R. Civ. P. 23(a)(4) ("[T]he representative parties will fairly and adequately protect the interests of the class.").
202. *See* Taylor v. Sturgell, 553 U.S. 880, 894 (2008) ("[W]e have confirmed that, 'in certain limited circumstances,' a nonparty may be bound by a judgment because she was 'adequately represented by someone with the same interests who [wa]s a party' to the suit." (quoting Richards v. Jefferson Cnty., 517 U.S. 793, 798 (1996))).
203. *See supra* note 58 and accompanying text (describing the lenient standard by which claims are aggregated).
204. *See* Burch, *Litigating Together*, *supra* note 22, at 97 (examining "how to effectively and ethically represent multiple clients when one client's best interest conflicts with the majority's best interests").
205. A concurrent conflict of interest exists if: (1) the representation of one client will be directly adverse to another client; or (2) there is a significant risk that the representation of one or more clients will be materially limited by the lawyer's responsibilities to another client, a former client, or a third person or by a personal interest of the lawyer. Model Rules of Prof'l Conduct R. 1.7(a) (1983).
206. *Id.* R. 1.7 cmt.
207. *See supra* notes 8–9 and accompanying text.
208. Burch, *Litigating Together*, *supra* note 22, at 95.
209. For an example of the criteria used to select members of a plaintiffs' steering committee, see *In re* San Juan Dupont Plaza Hotel Fire Litig., No. MDL 721, 1989 WL 168401, at *6 (D. P.R. Dec. 2, 1988). There, the transferee court listed "physical (e.g., office facilities) and financial resources; commitment to a time-consuming, long-term project; ability to work cooperatively with others; and professional experience particular to this type of litigation" as the main criteria for membership on the plaintiffs' steering committee. *Id.*
210. A survey of about ninety attorneys who practice in MDL cases indicates that snubbed attorneys resent this reality. As the surveyor wrote, "A substantial group of local plaintiffs' counsel resent the panel's role in facilitating national plaintiffs' counsels' 'takeover' of their cases. They criticize a repeat-player syndrome in the selection of plaintiffs' MDL counsel." Judge John G. Heyburn II, chair of the Judicial Panel on Multidistrict Litigation, responds: "We know that our orders can effectively disenfranchise some local plaintiffs' counsel. In every case, we ask ourselves whether centralization sufficiently promotes justice and efficiency, so much so that we should

inconvenience some for the benefit of the whole." Heyburn & McGovern, *supra* note 41, at 30.
211. *See* Fallon, *Common Benefit Fees*, *supra* note 53, at 373 (observing committee's role in conducting and overseeing discovery).
212. Burch, *Litigating Together*, *supra* note 22, at 95 (advocating a plaintiff-consensus approach to managing nonclass aggregate litigation).
213. *See, e.g.*, San Juan Dupont Plaza Hotel, 1989 WL 168401, at *10 (outlining the procedure to be followed when an individual plaintiff's counsel disagrees with the PSC, stressing "that counsel must not repeat any question, argument, motion, or other paper propounded or filed, or actions taken by the PSC" and warning that "[f]ailure to abide by these terms shall result in sanctions against counsel personally"). In *In re Bendectin Litigation*, a group of plaintiffs complained that the transferee judge's appointment of lead counsel denied them the right to freely choose counsel. None responded to the judge's order to show cause why the selected attorneys should not be appointed. The Sixth Circuit found no error in the appointment, noting that the practice of appointing such committees is "well established" and the plaintiffs' "failure below to object to such a procedure." *In re* Bendectin Litig., 857 F.2d 290, 297 (6th Cir. 1988).
214. *See supra* note 162 and accompanying text.
215. Burch, *Litigating Together*, *supra* note 22, at 98.
216. *See supra* notes 143–46 and accompanying text (discussing common benefit fund attorney compensation); *see also* Trangsrud, *supra* note 22, at 83 ("The inherent tensions of contingency fee representation have been intensified to such an extent by the mass trial that the adversary system may break down.").
217. *In re* San Juan Dupont Plaza Hotel Fire Litig., 111 F.3d 220, 238 (1st Cir. 1997).
218. *Id.* ("[D]espite reasonable notice of the obvious peril to their own financial interests, and their clear obligation to forfend against it from the outset, appellants did not turn serious attention to the PSC cost reimbursement regime deficiencies until the Gordian knot could no longer be undone. [T]he requested relief has been rendered impracticable, through appellants' inaction.").
219. *Id.* at 227 ("[I]nternecine differences as to subsidiary matters—particularly the appropriate allocations from the common fund for their respective attorney fees and costs—are commonplace.").
220. Mathews v. Eldridge, 424 U.S. 319, 349 (1976).
221. Section 1407 requires that there be "one or more common questions of fact" among cases that are to be consolidated into an MDL. 28 U.S.C. § 1407(a) (2012).
222. *See* Manual for Complex Litigation (Fourth) § 40.22 (2004) (listing plaintiffs' lead counsel's responsibilities for coordinating pretrial proceedings).
223. *See supra* notes 118–19 and accompanying text (emphasizing that a transferor court's authority extends only to pretrial matters; it cannot assign itself a case for trial).
224. *See* Cory Tischbein, *Animating the Seventh Amendment in Contemporary Plaintiffs' Litigation*, 16 U. PA. J. CONST. L. 233, 258 (2013) ("MDL courts consistently take several years to conduct discovery alone."); *see also infra* note 253.

225. *See supra* note 116 and accompanying text.
226. *Cf.* Ward v. Rock Against Racism, 491 U.S. 781, 791 (1989) ("[E]ven in a public forum the government may impose reasonable restrictions on the time, place, or manner of protected speech").
227. *See supra* note 174 and accompanying text (outlining this test).
228. Mashaw, *supra* note 175, at 47.
229. *See* Bone, *supra* note 198, at 239 ("[A]n efficiency-based, outcome-oriented theory aspires to that level of accuracy that minimizes social costs, including the error costs of incorrect decisions and administrative or direct costs of adjudication itself, and it dictates that one should forego even substantial accuracy gains if one must invest even greater amounts to achieve those gains."); Richard A. Posner, *Utilitarianism, Economics, and Legal Theory*, 8 J. LEGAL STUD. 103, 111 (1979) ("An act or practice is right or good or just in the utilitarian view insofar as it tends to maximize happiness, usually defined as the surplus of pleasure over pain.").
230. *See, e.g.*, Bone, *supra* note 198, at 239.
231. *See* Robert G. Bone, *Procedure, Participation, Rights*, 90 B.U. L. REV. 1011, 1017 (2010) ("[F]ew people, if any, would think that reducing the risk of error is always important enough to justify substantial social investments that could otherwise be used to improve roads, schools, public health, and the like."); Mashaw, *supra* note 175, at 48 ("[U]tility theory can be said to yield the following plausible decision-rule: 'Void procedures for lack of due process only when alternative procedures would so substantially increase social welfare that their rejection seems irrational.'"); Solum, *supra* note 167, at 244–47 (describing and critiquing the "accuracy model").
232. *Mathews v. Eldridge*, 424 U.S. 319, 334 (1976).
233. *Id.*
234. *Id.* at 335.
235. *Id.* at 343.
236. *Id.* at 344.
237. *Id.* at 347.
238. *Id.* at 348.
239. The Court altered the third *Mathews* factor slightly, describing it as "principal attention to the interest of the party seeking the prejudgment remedy, with, nonetheless, due regard for any ancillary interest the government may have in providing the procedure or forgoing the added burden of providing greater protections." Connecticut v. Doehr, 501 U.S. 1, 11 (1990).
240. *Id.* at 4.
241. *Id.* at 24.
242. *See supra* notes 172–75 and accompanying text (contrasting *Mathews* and *Doehr*'s emphasis on procedures with the dignitary model's emphasis on an opportunity to plead a case).
243. *Mathews*, 424 U.S. at 333.
244. *Id.* at 339.
245. Posner, *supra* note 229, at 116.
246. *See* Mashaw, *supra* note 175, at 48 ("As applied by the *Eldridge* Court the utilitarian calculus tends, as cost-benefit analyses typically do, to 'dwarf soft variables' and to ignore complexities and ambiguities.").

247. Jay Tidmarsh, *Rethinking Adequacy of Representation*, 87 Tex. L. Rev. 1137, 1142 (2008).
248. Sturm, *supra* note 171, at 985 ("Adversarial presentation by parties' lawyers enhances the likelihood of reaching a correct decision.").
249. *See supra* note 103 and accompanying text.
250. *See supra* notes 129–32 and accompanying text.
251. James F. Holderman, *Sua Sponte: A Judge Comments*, Litigation, Spring 2012, at 27, 27.
252. Heyburn & McGovern, *supra* note 41, at 32.
253. *See* Delaventura v. Columbia Acorn Trust, 417 F. Supp. 2d 147, 150 (D. Mass. 2006) ("[A]s compared to the processing time of an average case, MDL practice is slow, very slow"); Fallon et al., *Bellwether Trials*, *supra* note 90, at 2325, 2330 (observing the "traditional delay associated with MDL practice" and that "[t]he relevant comparison is not between a massive MDL and an 'average case,' but rather between a massive MDL and the alternative of thousands of similar cases clogging the courts with duplicative discovery and the potential for unnecessary conflict").
254. *See In re* "East of the Rockies" Concrete Pipe Antitrust Cases, 302 F. Supp. 244, 254 (J.P.M.L. 1969) (Weigel, J., concurring) ("[C]oordination and consolidation may impair, not further, convenience, justice and efficiency There are a number of inherent inconveniences in transfers for coordinated or consolidated pretrial. Some plaintiffs are temporarily deprived of their choices of forum and some defendants may be forced to litigate in districts where they could not have been sued. Considerable time and trouble are involved in the sheer mechanics of transferring and remanding.").
255. *See, e.g.*, Virginia Llewellyn, *Electronic Discovery Best Practices*, 10 Rich. J.L. & Tech. 51 (2004), *available at* http://jolt.richmond.edu/v10i5/article51.pdf, *archived at* http://perma.cc/U6L5-3XPX (last accessed July 5, 2023) ("With preparation and the proper technology the document review and production process can be easier and more efficient than procedures used in the 'paper world.'").
256. *See* Redish, *supra* note 25, at 1–12.
257. *See supra* notes 9–10 and accompanying text.
258. *See supra* note 21 and accompanying text.
259. *See supra* notes 252–54 and accompanying text.

CHAPTER 4

1. *See, e.g.*, Ortiz v. Fibreboard Corp., 527 U.S. 815, 845–46 (1999) (discussing the "day-in-court ideal" as it relates to class action suits). *See generally* Chapters 1 and 2.
2. Restatement (Second) of Judgments § 28(5) (1982).
3. Restatement (First) of Judgments § 83 (1942).
4. *See generally* Robert G. Bone, *Rethinking the "Day in Court" Ideal and Nonparty Preclusion*, 67 N.Y.U. L. Rev. 193, 232–88 (1992) (arguing for a less rigid approach to nonparty preclusion).

5. *See, e.g.*, Aerojet-Gen. Corp. v. Askew, 511 F.2d 710, 719 (5th Cir. 1975).
6. Different courts of appeals employed different variations of virtual representation. *See infra* notes 37–42 and accompanying text.
7. *See* Perry v. Globe Auto Recycling, Inc., 227 F.3d 950, 953 (7th Cir. 2000); Tice v. Am. Airlines, Inc., 162 F.3d 966, 970–73 (7th Cir. 1998).
8. 128 S. Ct. 2161 (2008).
9. *Id.* at 2171, 2173–74.
10. *Id.* at 2169–70, 2175.
11. *See* sections 4.3–4.4, *infra*.
12. *See* Fed. R. Civ. P. 23(b)(1)(A) committee note.
13. 255 U.S. 356 (1921).
14. *Id.* at 357–59.
15. Fed. R. Civ. P. 23(b)(1)(A).
16. *See, e.g.*, Green v. Occidental Petrol. Corp., 541 F.2d 1335, 1340 & n.9 (9th Cir. 1976); *see also* Note, *Class Actions for Punitive Damages*, 81 MICH. L. REV. 1787, 1799 n.69 (1983) (citing several district and appellate court cases in which not all plaintiffs were compensated).
17. *See* Mathews v. Eldridge, 424 U.S. 319, 347–49 (1976).
18. *See* section 4.7, *infra*.
19. *See* section 4.6, *infra*.
20. *See* Martin v. Wilks, 490 U.S. 755, 762 n.2 (1989) (recognizing that due process permits preclusion of nonparties when they are "adequately represented by someone with the same interests who is a party" (citing Fed R. Civ. P. 23; Hansberry v. Lee, 311 U.S. 32, 41–42 (1940))).
21. *See* 18 James Wm. Moore et al., Moore's Federal Practice P131.40[3] [a] (3d ed. 2008) ("[Privity] describes those relationships that the courts have already determined will qualify for preclusion.").
22. *See* Aerojet-Gen. Corp. v. Askew, 511 F.2d 710, 719–20 (5th Cir. 1975).
23. *See, e.g.*, In re L & S Indus., Inc., 989 F.2d 929, 934–35 (7th Cir. 1993) (holding that the interests of a principal and a guarantor who are bringing the same claims are not necessarily aligned because the two parties might be seeking different outcomes).
24. 18A CHARLES ALAN WRIGHT ET AL., FEDERAL PRACTICE AND PROCEDURE § 4457, at 532 n.33 (2d ed. 2002 & Supp. 2008).
25. Pollard v. Cockrell, 578 F.2d 1002, 1008–10 (5th Cir. 1978); Sw. Airlines Co. v. Tex. Int'l Airlines, 546 F.2d 84, 97–101 (5th Cir. 1977); Aerojet, 511 F.2d at 719–20.
26. 128 S. Ct. 2161, 2178 (2008).
27. *Id.* at 2176, 2178.
28. *See* 18A WRIGHT ET AL., *supra* note 24, §4557, at 513.
29. *See* cases cited *supra* note 25.
30. *See Pollard*, 578 F.2d at 1005; Sw. Airlines Co., 546 F.2d at 102; Aerojet, 511 F.2d at 715, 719–20; 18A WRIGHT ET AL., *supra* note 24, §4557, at 513 n.2.
31. *See Taylor*, 128 S. Ct. at 2170 (describing the D.C. Circuit's balancing test for virtual representation).
32. *Id.* at 2161, 2167–71.

33. *Id.* at 2167–68.
34. *Id.* at 2168.
35. *Id.*
36. *Id.* at 2169.
37. *Id.*
38. *Id.*; *see also* Tyus v. Schoemehl, 93 F.3d 449, 454–56 (8th Cir. 1996) (establishing the seven-factor test).
39. *Taylor*, 128 S. Ct. at 2169.
40. *Id.*
41. *Id.* at 2169–70.
42. *Id.* at 2170.
43. *Id.*
44. *Id.* at 2171, 2180.
45. *Id.* at 2171.
46. *See id.*
47. *See id.* at 2172–73.
48. *See id.* at 2178.
49. *Id.* at 2173–74.
50. 517 U.S. 793 (1996); *see Taylor*, 128 S. Ct. at 2173–74.
51. *Richards*, 517 U.S. at 794–95.
52. *Id.* at 795.
53. *Id.* at 799–802.
54. 311 U.S. 32 (1940).
55. *Richards*, 517 U.S. at 801.
56. *Id.* at 802 (quoting Hansberry v. Lee, 311 U.S. 32, 46 (1940)).
57. Taylor v. Sturgell, 128 S. Ct. 2161, 2172, 2174 (2008).
58. *Id.* at 2174 (citing S.C. Bell Tel. Co. v. Alabama, 526 U.S. 160, 168 (1999)).
59. *Id.*
60. *Id.* at 2172.
61. *See id.* (quoting Restatement (Second) of Judgments § 40 (1982)).
62. *Id.* at 2172 n.7 (citing Restatement (Second) of Judgments § 62 (1982)).
63. *Id.* at 2175–76.
64. *Id.* at 2176 (quoting Tice v. Am. Airlines, Inc., 162 F.3d 966, 973 (7th Cir. 1998)).
65. *Id.* at 2176–77.
66. *See, e.g.*, Ortiz v. Fibreboard Corp., 527 U.S. 815, 846–47 (1999); Hansberry v. Lee, 311 U.S. 32, 40–41 (1940).
67. *See* Bone, *supra* note 4, at 247–56.
68. *See id.* at 246–47.
69. *Taylor*, 128 S. Ct. at 2171 (quoting Richards v. Jefferson County, 517 U.S. 793, 798 (1996)).
70. In an article presenting a theory of acceptable virtual representation very different from the one developed here, Professor Robert Bone rejects the value (and existence) of a day-in-court ideal. *See* Bone, *supra* note 4, at 283–89. His argument for rejecting the ideal, fashioned prior to *Taylor*, is seemingly based on the conclusion that the

ideal and virtual representation are mutually exclusive: the day-in-court ideal and virtual representation cannot both exist; virtual representation exists; therefore, the day-in-court ideal does not exist. *See id.* at 288–90. This argument presumes that the day-in-court ideal is absolute and in doing so fails to recognize the balancing of interests inherent in any due process calculus. More accurately, the day-in-court ideal, while not absolute, nevertheless does carry a very high value in the due process balance that may be overcome only by the showing of truly compelling competing interests.

71. *See* Rock v. Arkansas, 483 U.S. 44, 51 (1987) (stating that the right to a day in court is a "necessary ingredient[]" of due process (citing *In re* Oliver, 333 U.S. 257, 273 (1948))).
72. *See, e.g.*, Connecticut v. Doehr, 501 U.S. 1, 10–11 (1991).
73. *See* Robert G. Bone, *Agreeing to Fair Process: The Problem with Contractarian Theories of Procedural Fairness*, 83 B.U. L. REV. 485, 509 n.10 (2003).
74. *Id.* at 509.
75. *See generally* Chapters 1 and 2.
76. 311 U.S. 32 (1940).
77. *Id.* at 40.
78. *Id.* at 42.
79. *See* Martin H. Redish & Clifford W. Berlow, *The Class Action as Political Theory*, 85 WASH. U. L. REV. 753, 764–70 (2007).
80. There exist numerous versions of democracy other than its liberal or individualist form. *See generally* JANE J. MANSBRIDGE, BEYOND ADVERSARY DEMOCRACY 8–22 (1980) (contrasting "adversary democracy," democracy based on the theory that democracy should weigh various selfish competing interests and where the individual is protected through equal distribution of voting power, with "unitary democracy," democracy where decisions are made in face-to-face meetings by individuals with equal power through consensus). *See generally* Chapters 1 and 2.
81. *See* Martin H. Redish & Nathan D. Larsen, *Class Actions, Litigant Autonomy, and the Foundations of Procedural Due Process*, 95 CAL. L. REV. 1573, 1581 (2007).
82. *Id.* at 1581–82.
83. *See* U.S. CONST. amend. I; *see also* Wooley v. Maynard, 430 U.S. 705, 714–15 (1977) ("[T]he right of freedom of thought protected by the First Amendment . . . includes both the right to speak freely and the right to refrain from speaking at all.").
84. Redish & Larsen, *supra* note 81, at 1582 ("Consistent with the premises of both autonomy and self-determination, government may not control the minds of its citizens. The First Amendment prohibits government from suppressing private expression on the grounds that it would lead society to make unwise policy choices. These are decisions we leave to the individual citizens to make for themselves. They are not to be made for the individual by external forces, ultimately unaccountable to the electorate, who have paternalistically decided what is and is not good for both the individual and the populace. Nor, under the First Amendment, may government require that individuals utter political messages with which they disagree." (footnotes omitted)).
85. *See, e.g.*, Cohen v. California, 403 U.S. 15, 18–25 (1971).

86. *See generally* JOHN STUART MILL, ON LIBERTY 139–75 (David Bromwich & George Kateb eds. 2003) (1859) (explaining libertarian theory's broad view of individual autonomy); ROBERT NOZICK, ANARCHY, STATE, AND UTOPIA 26–120, 268–71 (1974) (same).
87. *See* Redish & Berlow, *supra* note 79, at 765–70.
88. A notable alternative theory of participation has been developed by Professor Jerry Mashaw in the administrative law context. Mashaw builds his theory on a normative commitment to the second formulation of the Kantian moral command that each person be treated as an end and not merely a means. *See* JERRY L. MASHAW, DUE PROCESS IN THE ADMINISTRATIVE STATE 189–99 (1985). From this commitment, he derives certain fundamental due process values including equality and comprehensibility. Mashaw also derives certain prudential values, including participation, that are thought to further these fundamental values. *Id.* at 204. Mashaw recognizes that participation and indeed all of his prudential values cannot be absolute, but rather "present prima facie constitutional claims for realization." *Id.* He believes that an individual's participation has value "not only because he might contribute to accurate determinations, but also because a lack of personal participation causes alienation and a loss of that dignity and self-respect that society properly deems independently valuable." Jerry L. Mashaw, *The Supreme Court's Due Process Calculus for Administrative Adjudication in* Mathews v. Eldridge: *Three Factors in Search of a Theory of Value*, 44 U. CHI. L. REV. 28, 50 (1976).
89. Redish & Berlow, *supra* note 79, at 769.
90. Martin H. Redish & Andrianna D. Kastanek, *Settlement Class Actions, the Case-or-Controversy Requirement, and the Nature of the Adjudicatory Process*, 73 U. CHI. L. REV. 545, 576 (2006).
91. *See* section 4.2, *supra*.
92. For a more detailed discussion of procedural due process doctrine, *see* Chapter 2.
93. This is not to suggest that some due process floor must be recognized. *See* Martin H. Redish & Lawrence C. Marshall, *Adjudicatory Independence and the Values of Procedural Due Process*, 95 YALE L.J. 455, 468–75 (1986) (explaining that the modern Supreme Court has abandoned its former approach to due process—with certain procedures integral to English common law as a floor—and has adopted a balancing approach to procedural due process where there may no longer be a floor).
94. Taylor v. Sturgell, 128 S. Ct. 2161, 2175–77 (2008).
95. 546 F.2d 84 (5th Cir. 1977).
96. 578 F. 1002 (5th Cir. 1978).
97. City of Dallas v. Sw. Airlines Co., 371 F. Supp. 1015 (N.D. Tex. 1973), *aff'd*, 494 F.2d 773 (5th Cir. 1974).
98. Sw. Airlines Co. v. Tex. Int'l Airlines, Inc., 396 F. Supp. 678 (N.D. Tex. 1975), *aff'd*, 546 F.2d 84 (5th Cir. 1977).
99. Sw. Airlines Co., 546 F.2d at 87–88.
100. *Id.* at 88.
101. *Id.* at 88–89.

102. *Id.* at 89 (" 'This is [not] an effort to undermine the federal decision [in the first case]. This is a frontal attack on it. The word undermined implies something covert about it. We come in with flags flying.' " (first alteration in original) (quoting an attorney at oral argument for Continental Airlines)).
103. Sw. Airlines Co., 396 F. Supp. at 683–86.
104. Sw. Airlines Co., 546 F.2d at 100.
105. *Id.* at 97.
106. *Id.* at 97–98.
107. *Id.* at 97.
108. *Id.*
109. *Id.* at 100.
110. 371 F. Supp. 1015 (N.D. Tex. 1973), *aff'd*, 494 F.2d 773 (5th Cir. 1974).
111. *Sw. Airlines Co.*, 546 F.2d at 100.
112. *See* Freeman v. Lester Coggins Trucking, Inc., 771 F.2d 860, 864 (5th Cir. 1985). There the court stated:

> [B]oth from Southwest Airlines itself and the succeeding decisions of this circuit, the concept of "adequate representation" does not refer to apparently competent litigation of an issue in a prior suit by a party holding parallel interests; rather, it refers to the concept of virtual representation, by which a nonparty may be bound because the party to the first suit "is so closely aligned with his [the nonparty's] interests as to be his virtual representative."

> *Id.* (second alteration in original) (footnotes omitted) (quoting Aerojet-Gen. Corp. v. Askew, 511 F.2d 710, 719 (5th Cir. 1975)).

113. *Sw. Airlines Co.*, 546 F.2d at 101 ("If courts could second guess another court each time a new litigant, dissatisfied with the previous judgment, filed a new complaint, the respect of the previous parties or of the public toward the courts would inevitably decrease. Southwest and subsequent litigants would suffer the harassment and expense of still later lawsuits, as well as the possibility of numerous conflicting judgments.").
114. *Id.* at 102 (footnote omitted).
115. Pollard v. Cockrell, 578 F.2d 1002, 1004–05 (5th. Cir. 1978).
116. *Id.* at 1005.
117. *Id.*
118. *Id.*
119. *Id.*
120. *Id.*
121. *Id.* at 1006–08.
122. 511 F.2d 710 (5th Cir. 1975); *see Pollard*, 578 F.2d at 1008.
123. *Pollard*, 578 F.2d at 1008.
124. *Id.* at 1008–09.
125. *Id.* at 1008.
126. For a complete discussion of the problems that arise from indivisible relief, *see* section 4.7, *infra*. For present purposes, it should be noted only that the relief in both *Aerojet* and *Southwest Airlines* was indivisible whereas the relief in *Pollard* was not.

127. *See* Fed. R. Civ. P. 23(b)(1)(A) (permitting class action when maintenance of individual suits could subject the party opposing the class to a risk of incompatible standards of conduct).
128. BLACK'S LAW DICTIONARY 1440 (8th ed. 2004).
129. It is, of course, conceivable that the danger of double liability could have been avoided in federal court either through the stakeholder's use of interpleader, *see* 28 U.S.C. § 1335 (2006); Fed. R. Civ. P. 22; B's intervention into the first suit, *see* Fed. R. Civ. P. 24; or the stakeholder's invocation of Rule 19 in the first suit to have B declared a necessary or indispensible party, *see* Fed. R. Civ. P. 19. However, under certain circumstances these devices may not be legally available, and since they are not compulsory, they may not have been employed.
130. W. Union Tel. Co. v. Pennsylvania, 368 U.S. 71, 75 (1961) (citing Anderson Nat'l Bank v. Luckett, 321 U.S. 233, 242–43 (1944)).
131. *See* section 4.2, *supra*.
132. *See* section 4.2, *supra*.
133. *See* 511 F.2d 710, 713–14 (5th Cir. 1975) (citing Aerojet-Gen. Corp. v. Kirk, 318 F. Supp. 55 (N.D. Fla. 1970)).
134. *Id*. at 713–14.
135. *See* Société Internationale v. Rogers, 357 U.S. 197, 209–12 (1958).
136. LON L. FULLER, THE MORALITY OF LAW 66 (rev. ed. 1964).
137. Henry M. Hart, Jr., *The Relations Between State and Federal Law*, 54 COLUM. L. REV. 489, 489 (1954); *see also* Martin H. Redish & Carter G. Phillips, *Erie and the Rules of Decision Act: In Search of the Appropriate Dilemma*, 91 HARV. L. REV. 356, 381 (1977) (discussing the difficulties that arise under the Erie doctrine when actors do not know which set of rules will govern their actions).
138. *See* section 4.2, *supra*.
139. City of Dallas v. Sw. Airlines Co., 371 F. Supp. 1015, 1019 (N.D. Tex. 1973), *aff'd*, 494 F.2d 773 (5th Cir. 1974).
140. Sw. Airlines Co. v. Tex. Int'l Airlines, Inc., 546 F.2d 84, 87–89 (5th Cir. 1977).
141. *See* Redish & Larsen, *supra* note 81, at 1606.
142. *See* section 4.3, *supra*.
143. *See* Chapters 1 and 2.
144. For an examination of what constitutes adequate representation, *see supra* text accompanying notes 49–65.
145. There are, however, a variety of ways to prophylactically avoid such situations from arising in the first place. *See* section 4.7, *infra*.
146. *See* Shaffer v. Heitner, 433 U.S. 186, 199 n.17 (1977) (noting that while "'[a] judgment in rem affects the interests of all persons in designated property,'" an action in the nature of rem "'seek[s] to secure a pre-existing claim in the subject property and to extinguish or establish the nonexistence of similar interests of particular persons'" (second emphasis added) (quoting Hanson v. Denckla, 357 U.S. 235, 246 n.12 (1938))).
147. *See* Fed. R. Civ. P. 23(a)(4) (requiring fair and adequate protection of the interests of the class by the representative party as a prerequisite to class action); Taylor

v. Sturgell, 128 S. Ct. 2161, 2173–74 (2008) (discussing adequate representation in the context of nonparty preclusion); Richards v. Jefferson County., 517 U.S. 793, 798 (1996) (same).
148. Fed. R. Civ. P. 23(a)(4).
149. 7A CHARLES ALAN WRIGHT ET AL., FEDERAL PRACTICE AND PROCEDURE § 1769 (3d ed. 2005).
150. *Id.* § 1766.
151. *Id.* § 1767.
152. *See id.* § 1769.
153. *See supra* text accompanying notes 98–115.
154. *See* Sw. Airlines Co. v. Tex. Int'l Airlines, Inc., 546 F.2d 84, 87–88 (5th Cir. 1977). While the chapter points to *Southwest Airlines* as an example in determining adequate representation, we should emphasize that as a case of inconsistent relief, rather than a double or contradictory liability, the issue of adequate representation would not arise. Under our stratification of the three categories, the danger of inconsistent relief would be insufficient to overcome the competing interest in litigant autonomy.
155. *See* 13A CHARLES ALAN WRIGHT ET AL., FEDERAL PRACTICE AND PROCEDURE § 3531.4 (3d ed. 2008). Although the injury-in-fact requirement of standing is designed to promote vigorous litigation, it is not sufficient for ensuring vigorous litigation. *See* MARTIN H. REDISH, THE FEDERAL COURTS IN THE POLITICAL ORDER 101–02 (1991). One can easily imagine a situation in which a plaintiff has suffered an injury-in-fact so small that he is not motivated to expend the resources necessary to vigorously litigate a lawsuit. *Id.* Thus, requiring an adequate representative to have sufficient incentive to litigate vigorously goes beyond the traditional injury-in-fact calculus.
156. Because I have concluded that inconsistent liability does not permit virtual representation, it is not necessary to consider how it interacts with the adequate representation requirement.
157. *See* sources cited *supra* notes 130, 148–49.
158. *See* section 4.10, *supra*.
159. *See* section 4.1, *supra*.
160. *See* 7 CHARLES ALAN WRIGHT ET AL., FEDERAL PRACTICE AND PROCEDURE § 1704 (3d ed. 2001).
161. Fed. R. Civ. P. 19(a).
162. 198 U.S. 215 (1905). *Harris* is cited as an illustrative example of the rationale behind assigning burdens based on information and not as binding authority. The dispute in *Harris* arose from a now antiquated personal jurisdiction issue involving the discredited quasi in rem concept. *See id.* at 226; *see also* Shaffer v. Heitner, 433 U.S. 186, 200–01 (1977) (summarizing the facts and holding of *Harris*).
163. *Harris* 198 U.S. at 216, 228.
164. *Id.* at 216.
165. *Id.*
166. *Id.*
167. *Id.* at 226.

252 NOTES

168. *Id.* at 227.
169. *Id.*
170. *Id.*
171. *Id.*
172. Where absent parties are too numerous for simple joinder, the party may resort to a Rule 23(b)(1)(A) class action, provided that all of the other prerequisites are met. Fed. R. Civ. P. 23(b)(1)(A).
173. 490 U.S. 755 (1989). Section 108 of the Civil Rights Act of 1991, 42 U.S.C. 2000e-2(n)(1) (2000), overrode the holding in *Martin* as it applied to the underlying civil rights claim. However, the court's reasoning as applied to mandatory intervention is still generally instructive.
174. *Martin*, 490 U.S. at 758.
175. *Id.* at 762.
176. *Id.* at 765.
177. *Id.* at 767.
178. *See* 42 U.S.C. § 2000e-2(n)(1).
179. As with double liability, situations may arise in which virtual representation or other measures will be unable to prevent contradictory liability. As already noted, this creates serious due process problems. This chapter does not attempt to solve these remaining problems. Instead, it has shown how virtual representation and other mechanisms could be used to minimize the threat of indivisible relief.

CHAPTER 5

1. *See generally* section 5.4, *infra*.
2. For a detailed elaboration of the point, *see generally* Martin H. Redish & Nathan D. Larsen, *Class Actions, Litigant Autonomy, and the Foundations of Procedural Due Process*, 95 CAL. L REV. 1573 (2007). *See also* Martin H. Redish & Clifford W. Berlow, *The Class Action as Political Theory*, 85 WASH. U. L. REV. 753 (2007).
3. U.S. CONST. amend XIV, § 1 (limiting its restrictions to the "state"). In contrast, the Thirteenth Amendment, prohibiting slavery, imposes its restrictions on all private individuals. U.S. CONST. amend XIII.
4. It should be emphasized that the mere fact that the Constitution does not itself impose these restrictions in no way means that democratically authorized bodies may not impose them under certain circumstances. Indeed, both Title II and Title VII of the 1964 Civil Rights Act restrict the ability of private individuals to discriminate on a number of grounds. 42 U.S.C. §§ 2000(a), 2000(e). When the discrimination concerns issues of ideological or political association, however, the First Amendment right of free expression often insulates the private activity from governmental regulation. *See, e.g.*, Boy Scouts of America v. Dale, 530 U.S. 640 (2000).
5. The extent to which this ideal may be attained in reality is the subject of debate. *See* section 5.4, *infra*.

6. *See* Bruce A. Green, *Must Government Lawyers "Seek Justice" in Civil Litigation?*, 9 WIDENER J. PUB. L. 235, 269 (2000) (footnote omitted) ("Whether one views the client as the government, a government agency or a government official, the client is distinctive in at least this respect: the client owes fiduciary duties to the public").
7. *See, e.g.,* U.S. CONST. art. III, § 1 (federal judges possess prophylactic protections of their neutrality and independence from the federal government by means of protections of their salary and tenure).
8. *See, e.g.,* Adam Liptak, *A Deal for the Public: If You Win. You Lose*, N.Y. TIMES (July 9, 2007).
9. *See* section 5.4, *infra*.
10. *See* section 5.5, *infra*.
11. *See* section 5.4.5, *infra*.
12. U.S. CONST. amend XTV, § 1, cl.
13. Connecticut v. Doehr, 501 U.S. 1 (1991); Phillips Petroleum Co. v. Shutts, 472 U.S. 797 (1985); Mathews v. Eldridge, 424 U.S. 319 (1976).
14. *Mathews*, 424 U.S. 319.
15. *See* section 5.4, *infra*.
16. Liptak, *supra* note 8. According to one commentator, "[t]he contingency fee arrangement has long been regarded as the means by which individuals who lack the economic resources to hire private attorneys may be granted access to the legal system and a legal advocate." Leah Godesky, Note, *State Attorneys General and Contingency Fee Arrangements: An Affront to the Neutrality Doctrine?*, 42 COLUM. J.L. & SOC. PROBS. 587, 587–88 (2009).
17. *See* David A. Dana, *Public Interest and Private Lawyers: Toward a Normative Evaluation of Parens Patriae Litigation by Contingency Fee*, 51 DEPAUL L. REV. 315, 315 (2001).
18. Liptak, *supra* note 8. President Bush, however, signed an executive order prohibiting the use of private contingent fee arrangements by the federal government. Its use in the states began in the 1980s when Massachusetts decided to hire private lawyers to pursue state asbestos claims. "The innovation quickly spread to other states and issues, most notably the late 1990s tobacco-Medicaid crusade which resulted in multibillion dollar payouts to both the states and their lawyers." Walter Olson, *Tort Travesty* (June 4, 2007), online at http://www.pointoflaw.com/columns/archives/003943.php (visited Apr. 16, 2010).
19. Liptak, *supra* note 8.
20. *Id. See also* Godesky, *supra* note 16, at 588 (footnote omitted): "State attorneys general justify their use of private attorneys on the grounds that they are able to bring suits on behalf of the citizens of their states that would otherwise be impossible due to a lack of personnel resources, expertise, and money."
21. Dana, *supra* note 17, at 319.
22. *Id.* at 319–20.
23. *See, e.g.,* Phillip Morris, Inc. v. Glendening, 709 A.2d 1230 (1998); Meredeit v. Ieyoub, 700 So.2d 478 (La. 1997); *Lynch v. Lead Ind*, 2005 RI Super LEXIS, *7 (1998).

24. *See, e.g.*, Va. Code Ann. § 2.2-510.1; Tex. Govt Code § 2254.103; Colo. Rev. Stat. §§13-17-301 to 17-304.
25. John C. Coffee, Jr., *"When Smoke Gets in Your Eyes": Myth and Reality About the Synthesis of Private Counsel and Public Client*, 51 DePaul L. Rev. 241 (2001).
26. Dana, *supra* note 17, at 320 n.8.
27. *Id.* at 323.
28. *Id.*
29. I have discussed the theoretical rationale underlying the values of individual pluralism in two prior works: Redish & Larsen, *supra* note 2; Martin H. Redish & Andrew L. Mathews, *Why Punitive Damages Are Unconstitutional*, 53 Emory L.J. 1, 21–25 (2004). *See also* Martin H. Redish, *The Value of Free Speech*, 130 U. Pa. L. Rev. 591 (1982).
30. Martin H. Redish, *The Adversary System, Democratic Theory, and the Constitutional Role of Self-interest: The Tobacco Wars, 1953–1971*, 51 DePaul L. Rev. 379 (2001). *See* Chapter 2.
31. Boy Scouts of America v. Dale, 530 U.S. 640 (2000).
32. *See, e.g.*, Branti v. Frankel, 445 U.S. 507 (1980); United States v. Robel, 389 U.S. 258 (1967) (in most situations government may not refuse to hire individuals because of their ideological associations).
33. It should be emphasized, however, that the mere fact that the Constitution does not, in and of itself, restrict the discriminatory practices of private individuals or entities does not necessarily mean that the majoritarian branches of government may not legislatively limit those practices. The question in each instance will be whether the Constitution vests the private individual or entity with protection against such governmental interference. *See* Boy Scouts of America, 530 U.S. 640 (First Amendment right of non-association). However, even in those instances in which private discriminatory practices may be legislatively restricted, it is of course only when such behavior is collectively deemed sufficiently repugnant to lead to such governmental action that such restrictions result.
34. *See, e.g.*, Morton Horwitz, The Transformation of American Law, 1780–1860 (1977); Cass R. Sunstein, *State Action Is Always Present*, 3 Chi J. Int'l L. 465 (2002).
35. Frank I. Goodman, *Professor Brest on State Action and Liberal Theory, and a Postscript on Professor Stone*, 130 U. Pa. L. Rev. 1331, 1338 (1982).
36. *See* section 5.4, *supra*.
37. For an excellent explication of the considerations of normative liberal theory underlying the state action requirement, *see generally* Maimon Scharwschild, *Value Pluralism and the Constitution: In Defense of the State Action Doctrine*, 1988 Sup. Ct. Rev. 129.
38. *See* New York Times Co. v. Sullivan, 376 U.S. 254, 265 (1964) (state common law, developed in the course of the litigation of private claims, constitutes state action).
39. *See* Redish, *supra* note 30, at 376–77 (arguing that "[o]nce it is recognized that an individual, even though a member of a community, remains an integral and mentally autonomous entity deserving of dignity and respect, it logically follows that the

individual should be encouraged and expected to employ her personal resources to determine the choices and courses of action that will maximize the welfare of both her and her family.").
40. *See* John C. Coffee, Jr., U*nderstanding the Plaintiff's Attorney: The Implications of Economic Theory for Private Enforcement of Law Through Class and Derivative Actions*, 86 COLUM. L. REV. 669, 669 (1986) ("Probably to a unique degree, American law relies upon private litigants to enforce substantive provisions of law that in other legal systems are left largely to the discretion of public enforcement agencies.").
41. Because the motivations are not mutually exclusive, it is of course conceivable that an attorney representing a private client could simultaneously be motivated by the goal of enforcing public values. The point, however, is that this need not be the case, and to the extent the two interests conflict it is the ethical obligation of the attorney (consistent with the limits of the law) to give preference to the interests of his client.
42. *See* Edmonson v. Leesville Concrete Co., 500 U.S. 614 (1991) (private attorney's use of peremptory challenges on racial basis held to constitute state actions).
43. *See generally* Redish & Larsen, *supra* note 2.
44. In one sense, a contingency fee arrangement appropriately cabins private attorneys' incentives, since if they billed by the hour and would be owed the full amount of their bill win or lose, they arguably would be spurred to stretch out litigation and be less concerned with maximizing recovery. In another sense, however, the two are probably a wash, since any attorney unconcerned with controlling costs or maximizing clients' recoveries is unlikely to obtain continuing business.
45. 295 U.S. 78, 88 (1935).
46. In the following section, 5.4.2, I will argue further that such an arrangement involving private attorneys is not only inconsistent with ethical and political restraints imposed on government attorneys, but in addition violates the Fourteenth Amendment's Due Process Clause.
47. *See, e.g.*, Frank Easterbrook, *The State of Madison's Vision of the State: A Public Choice Perspective*, 107 HARV. L. REV. 1328, 1339 (1994). *See also* Cass R. Sunstein, *Interest Groups in American Public Law*, 38 STAN. L. REV. 29 (1985).
48. *See generally* FEDERALIST NO. 10 (James Madison).
49. *See generally* Joseph H. Carens, *Possessive Individualism and Democratic Theory: Macpherson's Legacy*, in DEMOCRACY AND POSSESSIVE INDIVIDUALISM: THE INTELLECTUAL LEGACY OF C.B. MACPHERSON 2 (Joseph H. Carens ed. 1993).
50. As one unsympathetic commentator described the position, "public choice theory rejects the notion of an overriding public interest. Individual interests are not viewed as being amenable to aggregation in any fair sense." Steven K. Berenson, *Public Lawyers, Private Values: Can, Should, and Will Government Lawyers Serve the Public Interest?*, 41 B.C. L. REV. 789, 804 (2000) (footnote omitted).
51. *See* Green, *supra* note 6, at 256: "Judicial decisions and other professional writings take the view that, even outside the context of criminal prosecutions, government litigators have a different role and different ethical responsibilities from lawyers representing private litigants." *See also id.* at 239 (describing this position as "the conventional view.").

52. Berenson, *supra* note 50, at 789.
53. *Id.* at 813 (footnote omitted).
54. *Id.* at 814.
55. Green, *supra* note 6, at 263 (footnote omitted).
56. *Id.* at 269.
57. Sanford Levinson, *Identifying the Compelling State Interest. On "Due Process of Lawmaking" and the Professional Responsibility of the Public Lawyer*, 45 HASTINGS L.J. 1035, 1050–58 (1994). Note that Professor Levinson was writing exclusively in the context of the state's fashioning of *constitutional* arguments. However, I consider it reasonable to apply his reasoning more broadly to all legal arguments.
58. Freeport-McMoran Oil & Gas Co v. Fed. Energy Reg. Comm'n, 962 F.2d 45, 47 (D.C. Cir. 1992) (quoting Berger v. United States, 295 U.S. 78 (1935)). *See also* United States v. Witmer, 835 F. Supp. 208, 214–15 (MD Pa. 1993); EEOC v. New Enter Stone & Lime Co., 74 FRD 628, 632–33 (WD Pa. 1977); EEOC v. Los Alamos Constructors, Inc., 382 F. Supp. 1373, 1383 (D.N.M. 1974).
59. Brown v. Bd. of Educ., 347 U.S. 453 (1954).
60. *See, e.g.*, Allen v. County School Bd. of Prince Edward County, 198 F. Supp. 497, 503 (ED Va. 1961).
61. West v. Atkins, 487 U.S. 42 (1998).
62. *Id. See also* Lugar v. Edmondson Oil Co., 457 U.S. 922 (1982) (persons for whose actions the state is responsible are to be treated as state actors).
63. *See* section 5.4, *supra*.
64. Michael Dorf, *Dorf on Law: Contingent Fees Do Not Violate Separation of Powers, Period* (July 10, 2007), online at http://michaeldorf.org/2007_07_01_ archive.html (visited Apr. 15, 2010).
65. 31 U.S.C. §§ 3729, 3730(h). *See* Dorf, *supra* note 64; Martin H. Redish, *Class Actions and the Democratic Difficulty: Rethinking the Intersection of Private Litigation and Public Goals*, 2003 U. CHI. L. FORUM 71, 91–92.
66. Gretchen L. Forney, Note, *Qui tam Suits: Defining the Rights and Roles of the Government and the Relator Under the False Claims Act*, 82 MINN. L. REV. 1357, 1364 (1998). *See also* Marc S. Raspanti & David M. Laigaie, *Current Practice and Procedure Under the Whistleblower Provisions of the Federal False Claims Act*, 71 TEMPLE L. REV. 23 (1998).
67. Dorf, *supra* note 64.
68. Vermont Agency of Natural Resources v. United States, 529 U.S. 765 (2000).
69. *Id.* at 773 (footnote omitted): "The [False Claims Act] can reasonably be regarded as effecting a partial assignment of the Government's damages claim." The Court expressly rejected the notion that the relator's financial interest in the suit, created by statute, in and of itself provided the requisite injury in fact: "A *qui tam* relator has suffered no such invasion [of a legally protected right]—indeed, the 'right' he seeks to vindicate does not even fully materialize until the litigation is completed and the relator prevails." It noted that "an interest that is merely a 'byproduct' of the suit itself cannot give rise to a cognizable injury in fact for Article III standing purposes." *Id.*
70. *Id.*

71. *Id.* at 772 (emphasis in original): "It would perhaps suffice to say that the relator here is simply the statutorily designated agent of the United States, *in whose name* . . . the suit is brought—and that the relator's bounty is simply the fee he receives *out of the United States' recovery* for filing and/or prosecuting a successful action on behalf of the Government. This analysis is precluded, however, by the fact that the statute gives the relator himself an interest *in the lawsuit*, and not merely the right to retain a fee out of the recovery."
72. *Id.* at 769–70; 31 U.S.C. §§ 3730(d)(1)–(2).
73. The issue under Article II concerns the extent to which Congress may vest executive power in someone other than the president, in whom the provision vests the executive power. The Court left it issue open in *Vermont Agency*. 529 U.S. at 778 n.8.
74. *Id.* at 774.
75. *Id.*
76. *Id.* at 776.
77. For my prior criticism of the relevance of tradition to modern constitutional analysis, *see generally* Martin H. Redish, *Tradition, Fairness, and Personal Jurisdiction: Due Process and Constitutional Theory After* Burnham v. Superior Court, 22 RUTGERS L.J. 675 (1991).
78. *See, e.g., Michael H. & Victoria D. v. Gerald D.*, 491 U.S. 110 (1989).
79. *See* Dorf, *supra* note 64.
80. *See text supra* at notes 68–73.
81. It should be noted that in any event, the modern form of the *qui tam* action has never been subjected to scrutiny under the analysis by which I have found the private contingency fee action improper.
82. One might reasonably question whether even private attorneys who bill by the hour, rather than operate on a contingent fee arrangement, unwisely insert a personal financial incentive into public decision-making. Alter all, these attorneys possess a personal financial incentive to keep litigation active, regardless of the needs of the state. There seems to be some truth to this reasoning, but I make no judgment about it here.
83. *See* section 5.4, *supra*.
84. *See* section 5.4.5, *supra*.
85. *See generally* Martin H. Redish & Lawrence C. Marshall, *Adjudicatory Independence and the Values of Procedural Due Process*, 95 YALE L.J. 455 (1986).
86. *Dr. Bonham's Case*, 77 Eng. Rep. 646, 8 Coke 114a (CP 1610).
87. Tumey v. Ohio, 273 U.S. 510, 522 (1927); *see also* Aetna Life Ins. Co. v. Lavoie, 475 U.S. 813 (1985); Ward v. Monroeville, 409 U.S. 57, 60 (1972). The Supreme Court has reiterated the primacy of the due process requirement of adjudicatory neutrality in holding that a state appellate judge was constitutionally required to recuse himself from a case involving a person who had made a very substantial contribution to the judge's campaign at a time when it was clear that the case would come to the court to which the judge sought election. Caperton v. A.T. Massey Coal Co., 129 S. Ct. 2252 (2009).
88. *Tumey*, 273 U.S. at 532.

89. *See* section 5.4, *supra*.
90. Redish & Mathews, *supra* note 29.
91. *See* sources cited in note 87, *supra*.
92. *See, e.g.*, sources cited in note 13, *supra*.
93. *Id.*
94. *See* section 5.4.5, *supra*.
95. *See, e.g.*, Santa Clara v. Superior Court, 74 Cal. Rptr. 3d 842, 842 (Ct. App. 2008); Kinder v. Nixon, 2000 WL 684860 (Mo. Ct. App. May 30, 2000). *See also* Godesky, *supra* note 16.
96. *Id.*

CHAPTER 6

1. Malinski v. New York, 324 U.S. 401, 414 (1945) (separate opinion).
2. *See* Henry P. Monaghan, *First Amendment "Due Process,"* 83 Harv. L. Rev. 518, 518 (1970).
3. What those requisite procedures actually are will be discussed in detail subsequently. *See* section 6.3.4, *infra*.
4. *See* Withrow v. Larkin, 421 U.S. 35 (1975).
5. *See, e.g.*, Mathews v. Eldridge, 424 U.S. 319, 348–49 (1976).
6. *See* Coleen Klasmeier & Martin H. Redish, *Off-Label Prescription Advertising, the FDA and the First Amendment: A Study in the Values of Commercial Speech Protection*, 37 Am. J.L. & Med. 315, 315 (2011).
7. *Cf.* United States v. Caronia, 703 F.3d 149, 168–69 (2d Cir. 2012) (concluding that the government cannot prosecute pharmaceutical companies "for speech promoting the lawful, off-label use of an FDA-approved drug," but limiting its holding to those FDA-approved drugs for which off-label use is *not* prohibited).
8. *See, e.g.*, Valentine v. Chrestensen, 316 U.S. 52, 54 (1942).
9. *See* Martin H. Redish, Money Talks: Speech, Economic Power, and the Values of Democracy 16–18 (2001) (describing steady increase in Supreme Court protection of commercial speech post-1986).
10. *See, e.g.*, Greater New Orleans Broad. Ass'n v. United States, 527 U.S. 173 (1999); 44 Liquormart, Inc. v. Rhode Island, 517 U.S. 484 (1996); Rubin v. Coors Brewing Co., 514 U.S. 476 (1995).
11. *See* section 6.3, *infra*.
12. *See* section 6.2, *infra*.
13. *See* section 6.3, *infra*.
14. *See* section 6.5, *infra*.
15. *See* section 6.1, *infra*.
16. *See* section 6.2, *infra*.
17. *See* section 6.4, *infra*.
18. *See* section 6.5, *infra*.

19. *See* Jerry L. Mashaw, *Administrative Due Process: The Quest for a Dignitary Theory*, 61 B.U. L. Rev. 885, 886 (1981).
20. *See* Connecticut v. Doehr, 501 U.S. 1, 10–11 (1991); Mathews v. Eldridge, 424 U.S. 319, 348–49 (1976).
21. *See* Chapters 1 and 2.
22. (1610) 77 Eng. Rep. 646; 8 Co. Rep. 113b.
23. As will be seen, the Court has—rather mysteriously—been much more trusting of administrative adjudicators than of judicial ones. *See* section 6.3, *infra*.
24. 273 U.S. 510 (1927).
25. *Id.* at 519.
26. *Id.* at 532 ("Every procedure which would offer a possible temptation to the average man as a judge to forget the burden of proof required to convict the defendant, or which might lead him not to hold the balance nice, clear and true between the State and the accused, denies the latter due process of law.").
27. Martin H. Redish & Lawrence C. Marshall, *Adjudicatory Independence and the Values of Procedural Due Process*, 95 Yale L.J. 455, 495 (1986).
28. *See, e.g.*, Aetna Life Ins. Co. v. Lavoie, 475 U.S. 813, 825 (1986); Ward v. Village of Monroeville, 409 U.S. 57, 60 (1972).
29. *See* section 6.3, *infra*.
30. 638 F.3d 384 (2d Cir. 2011).
31. *Id.* at 390.
32. Claimants' Notice of Arbitration ¶ 38, Chevron Corp. v. Republic of Ecuador, Uncitral, Pca Case No. 2009-23, http://www.chevron.com/documents/pdf/EcuadorBITEn.pdf (last accessed July 5, 2023).
33. *See* Tumey v. Ohio, 273 U.S. 510, 520 (1927).
34. *See* Aetna Life Ins. Co. v. Lavoie, 475 U.S. 813, 822–24 (1986).
35. *See* Ward v. Village of Monroeville, 409 U.S. 57, 58 (1972).
36. *See In re* Murchison, 349 U.S. 133 (1955).
37. *See id.* at 135, 139.
38. *Id.* at 137.
39. Motivated reasoning also applies to a lesser extent to incentivized decision-making and coercive interference. In both situations, a judge may perceive facts in a light most favorable to the outcome they subconsciously desire based on the potential benefit or the coercion. However, it seems more likely that a judge may be more conscious of the bias in these situations, in which case motivated reasoning would no longer apply because the judge would be consciously searching for a way to reach the desired outcome.
40. Ziva Kunda, *The Case for Motivated Reasoning*, 108 Psychol. Bull. 480, 495 (1990).
41. Dan M. Kahan, *Foreword: Neutral Principles, Motivated Cognition, and Some Problems for Constitutional Law*, 125 Harv. L. Rev. 1, 7 (2011).
42. *See id.*
43. *See id.* at 21.
44. *See id.*
45. *See id.*

260 NOTES

46. *See* Eileen Braman & Thomas E. Nelson, *Mechanism of Motivated Reasoning? Analogical Perception in Discrimination Disputes*, 51 AM. J. POL. SCI. 940, 940–41 (2007).
47. *See* Richardson v. Perales, 402 U.S. 389 (1971); Goldberg v. Kelly, 397 U.S. 254 (1970).
48. *See* Mathews v. Eldridge, 424 U.S. 319, 348–49 (1976).
49. *See Goldberg*, 397 U.S. at 271 ("And, of course, an impartial decision maker is essential.").
50. *See In re* Murchison, 349 U.S. 133, 137 (1955) ("Having been a part of [the accusatory] process a judge cannot be, in the very nature of things, wholly disinterested in the conviction or acquittal of those accused."); Tumey v. Ohio, 273 U.S. 510, 534 (1927) ("A situation in which an official perforce occupies two practically and seriously inconsistent positions, one partisan and the other judicial, necessarily involves a lack of due process of law in the trial of defendants charged with crimes before him.").
51. *See, e.g.*, 5 U.S.C. § 556(b) (2012) (stating that the heads of an agency can adjudicate hearings).
52. *See* ALFRED C. AMAN, JR. & WILLIAM T. MAYTON, ADMINISTRATIVE LAW § 8.1, at 200–02 (1998).
53. *Id.* § 8.2, at 202–03.
54. 5 U.S.C. § 554(d).
55. *Id.*
56. 16 C.F.R. § 2.1 (2018). The "Commission," which is composed of five members, refers to the commissioners of the FTC. *See id.* § 0.1.
57. *See id.* § 3.11.
58. *See A Brief Overview of the Federal Trade Commission's Investigative and Law Enforcement Authority*, Fed. Trade Comm'n, http://www.ftc.gov/about-ftc/what-we-do/enforcement-authority (last modified July 2008).
59. *See About the Division of Enforcement*, U.S. Sec. & Exchange Comm'n, https://www.sec.gov/enforce/Article/enforce-about.html (last modified Aug. 2, 2007).
60. *See How Investigations Work*, U.S. Sec. & Exchange Comm'n, http://www.sec.gov/News/Article/Detail/Article/1356125787012#.VEcMQT7wIhE (last modified Jan. 27, 2017). The "Commission" refers to the five commissioners of the Sec. *See* 17 C.F.R. § 200.10 (2018).
61. *See Office of Administrative Law Judges*, U.S. Sec. & Exchange Comm'n, http://www.sec.gov/alj#.VEcLBD7wIhF (last modified Jan. 26, 2017).
62. *See How Investigations Work*, *supra* note 60.
63. *See About the Division of Enforcement*, *supra* note 59.
64. *Id.*
65. 5 U.S.C. §§ 556(b), 557(b) (2012).
66. *See id.* § 557(b).
67. *A Brief Overview of the Federal Trade Commission's Investigative and Law Enforcement Authority*, *supra* note 58.
68. *Id.*
69. *Id.*

70. 3 West's Federal Administrative Practice § 3352 (2018) (quoting 16 C.F.R. § 3.54(c) (2018)).
71. *See id.* § 3354 (citing 15 U.S.C. § 45(c) (2012)).
72. *Id.* (quoting 15 U.S.C. § 45(c)) (citing 5 U.S.C. § 706(2)(E) (2012)).
73. *See Office of Administrative Law Judges, supra* note 61.
74. *See id.*
75. *Id.*
76. 21 C.F.R. §§ 17.3, 17.19, 17.45 (2018) (although an ALJ will be the adjudicator for all Civil Money Penalty hearings before the FDA, other types of hearings may implicate the Commissioner of the FDA directly).
77. *Id.* § 17.47.
78. *DAB Divisions*, U.S. Dep't Health & Hum. Servs., https://www.hhs.gov/about/agencies/dab/about-dab/divisions/index.html (last updated Sept. 13, 2016). The Department Appeals Board consists of five board members, most of whom have worked for the DHHS or the Board prior to serving as board members. None of the current board members worked for the FDA. *See Who Are the Board Members & Judges?*, U.S. Dep't Health & Hum. Servs., http://www.hhs.gov/dab/about/members/judges.html#board (last updated Aug. 10, 2018).
79. *See* 21 C.F.R. § 17.47(k).
80. *See, e.g.*, Richardson v. Perales, 402 U.S. 389 (1971); Goldberg v. Kelly, 397 U.S. 254 (1970).
81. *Goldberg*, 397 U.S. at 271 ("And, of course, an impartial decision maker is essential.").
82. *See, e.g.*, Ward v. Village of Monroeville, 409 U.S. 57 (1972); *In re* Murchison, 349 U.S. 133 (1955); Tumey v. Ohio, 273 U.S. 510 (1927).
83. *Tumey*, 273 U.S. at 534 (citing City of Boston v. Baldwin, 1 N.E. 417 (Mass. 1885); State *ex rel.* Colcord v. Young, 12 So. 673 (Fla. 1893)).
84. *Murchison*, 349 U.S. at 137.
85. *See* section 6.3.1, *supra*.
86. *Cf.* Williams v. Pennsylvania, 136 S. Ct. 1899 (2016) (concluding that due process was violated when a state supreme court justice refused to recuse himself in an appeal from a murder conviction, even though he had been the district attorney at the time the prosecution was filed).
87. Martin H. Redish, *The Proper Role of the Prior Restraint Doctrine in First Amendment Theory*, 70 Va. L. Rev. 53, 76–77 (1984).
88. Thomas I. Emerson, *The Doctrine of Prior Restraint*, 20 Law & Contemp. Probs. 648, 659 (1955).
89. *See* Caperton v. A.T. Massey Coal Co., 556 U.S. 868, 881 (2009) ("The Court asks not whether the judge is actually, subjectively biased, but whether the average judge in his position is 'likely' to be neutral, or whether there is an unconstitutional 'potential for bias.'").
90. *See, e.g.*, Tumey v. Ohio, 273 U.S. 510, 532 (1927) ("Every procedure which would offer a possible temptation to the average man as a judge . . . not to hold the balance nice, clear, and true between the State and the accused, denies the latter due process of law.").

91. *See* Withrow v. Larkin, 421 U.S. 35, 37–41 (1975).
92. *Id.* at 38–39.
93. *Id.* at 39–40.
94. *Id.* at 40–41, 40 n.4.
95. *Id.* at 41–42.
96. *Id.* at 37–38.
97. *Id.* at 37–41.
98. Larkin v. Withrow, 368 F. Supp. 796, 797 (E.D. Wis. 1973), *rev'd*, 421 U.S. 35 (1975).
99. *Id.* The district court based its decision on two Supreme Court cases—*Gagnon v. Scarpelli* and *Morrissey v. Brewer*—which held that one of the minimum requirements of due process is an independent decision maker. *See* Gagnon v. Scarpelli, 411 U.S. 778, 786 (1973); Morrissey v. Brewer, 408 U.S. 471, 488–89 (1972).
100. *Withrow*, 421 U.S. at 58.
101. *Id.* at 47.
102. *Id.*
103. *Id.* at 56.
104. *Id.*
105. *Id.* at 57.
106. *Id.* at 52.
107. *Id.* at 51–52 (quoting 5 U.S.C. § 554(d) (1970)).
108. Marshall v. Jerrico, Inc., 446 U.S. 238, 242 (1980).
109. *Id.*
110. *Withrow*, 421 U.S. at 47.
111. Tumey v. Ohio, 273 U.S. 510, 532 (1927).
112. *Withrow*, 421 U.S. at 53.
113. *See* section 6.4, *infra*.
114. *Withrow*, 421 U.S. at 53.
115. In some instances, agencies may enforce their awards only through resort to the judicial process. However, the enforcing courts are required to give significant deference to agency findings of fact.
116. *See, e.g., Office of Administrative Law Judges, supra* note 61.
117. *Withrow*, 421 U.S. at 56.
118. *Id.*
119. *See* section 6.3.3, *supra*.
120. *See* note 121, *infra*.
121. Since fiscal year 2006, the SEC's budget has nearly doubled, from a budget of $888,117,000 in fiscal year 2006, to a budget of $1,652,000,000 in fiscal year 2018. *Budget History—BA vs. Actual Obligations*, U.S. Sec. & Exchange Comm'n, https://www.sec.gov/foia/docs/budgetact.htm (last modified June 9, 2017).
122. Tumey v. Ohio, 273 U.S. 510, 532 (1927).

123. For a thorough discussion of the serious problems currently plaguing administrative law judges because of their lack of independence, *see* Kent Barnett, *Against Administrative Judges*, 49 U.C. DAVIS L. REV. 1643, 1648 (2016) [hereinafter Barnett, *Against Administrative Judges*], and Kent Barnett, *Resolving the ALJ Quandary*, 66 VAND. L. REV. 797 (2013). In Professor Barnett's words, "[t]he key problem with all agency hearings . . . is that they create inherent partiality concerns. The adjudicator's employing agency is often a party and controls the adjudicator's budget and perhaps salary. Indeed, the agency may even present expert witnesses who are the adjudicator's own co-workers." Barnett, *Against Administrative Judges, supra* at 1648.

124. It should be emphasized that I do so while simultaneously adhering to the position that the entire administrative process, as currently structured, is constitutionally tainted, requiring significant revision to satisfy the requirements of procedural due process.

125. *See* section 6.5, *infra*.

126. The doctrine finds its modern origins in the Supreme Court's decision in *Ohio Valley Water Co. v. Ben Avon Borough*, 253 U.S. 287 (1920), concerning a constitutional challenge to a rate set by a state regulatory commission. The decision most closely associated with it is *Crowell v. Benson*, 285 U.S. 22, 65 (1932), where the Court held that factual determinations related to factual issues that determined the constitutionality of federal legislation had to be decided de novo by the courts. It has been incorrectly suggested that the doctrine no longer exists, *see* MARTIN H. REDISH ET AL., FEDERAL COURTS: CASES, COMMENTS AND QUESTIONS 213 (7th ed. 2012) (compiling authorities), but that is for the most part because the specific constitutional issues on which *Crowell* turned are for the most part no longer viable. *See* MARTIN H. REDISH, FEDERAL JURISDICTION: TENSIONS IN THE ALLOCATION OF JUDICIAL POWER 51–52, 138–47 (2d ed. 1990); *id.* at 51–52, 138–47 (2d ed. 1990). Something akin to the doctrine was invoked as recently as the Court's decision in *Hamdi v. Rumsfeld*, 542 U.S. 507, 509 (2004). For a discussion of the general issue, see Martin H. Redish & William D. Gohl, *The Wandering Doctrine of Constitutional Fact*, 59 ARIZ. L. REV. 289 (2017).

127. *See* section 6.3.2, *supra*.

128. *See, e.g., In re* Murchison, 349 U.S. 133 (1955).

129. *See generally* Redish & Gohl, *supra* note 126.

130. Monaghan, *supra* note 2.

131. 380 U.S. 51 (1965).

132. *Id.* at 58.

133. *Id.*

134. Monaghan, *supra* note 2, at 523.

135. *Freedman*, 380 U.S. at 60.

136. *Id.* at 59.

137. *Id.* (emphasis added).

138. It is true that on its face, this sentence could also be construed to refer solely to judicially imposed interim restraints. In context, however, it is more likely that Justice Brennan was referring to administratively imposed interim restraints.

139. ALEXANDER MEIKLEJOHN, POLITICAL FREEDOM 27 (1960).

140. *See* Martin H. Redish, *The First Amendment in the Marketplace: Commercial Speech and the Values of Free Expression*, 39 GEO. WASH. L. REV. 429 (1971) (recognizing concept of "private" self-government as justification for extending First Amendment protection to commercial speech).

141. *See, e.g.*, N. Y. Times Co. v. Sullivan, 376 U.S. 254 (1964) (expressing concern about possible chilling effect as partial justification for adoption of "actual malice" test as a First Amendment protection for defamation of public officials).

142. The *Freedman* Court noted that a prompt judicial decision was needed "to minimize the deterrent effect of an interim and possibly erroneous denial" of free speech rights. *Freedman*, 380 U.S. at 59. It has been suggested that the concern about the chilling effect has no place in the regulation of commercial speech, since the profit motive will always incentivize the speaker, regardless of the fears of regulation. *See, e.g.*, Robert Post & Amanda Shanor, *Adam Smith's First Amendment*, 128 HARV. L. REV. F. 165, 169–70 (2015) (relying on the decision in *Central Hudson Gas & Electric Corp. v. Public Service Commission*, 447 U.S. 557 (1980)). In reality, the exact opposite is likely to be true; for the very reason of the profit incentive, commercial speakers may well behave in a risk-averse manner in an attempt to avoid liability or regulatory penalty. The issue is not *whether* the commercial speaker will speak, but whether it will be deterred from communicating what might well prove to be valuable information out of fear of regulatory liability.

143. *See* section 6.3.3, *supra*.

144. On this one point, it should be noted, First Amendment challenges do not differ from other constitutional challenges.

145. *See, e.g.*, Va. State Bd. of Pharmacy v. Va. Citizens Consumer Council, Inc., 425 U.S. 748, 771 n.24 (1976) ("[T]here is little likelihood of [commercial speech] being chilled by proper regulation"); Post & Shanor, *supra* note 142, at 169.

146. *See Freedman*, 380 U.S. at 59.

147. 894 F. Supp. 2d 40 (D.D.C. 2012).

148. *See id.* at 45.

149. 50 F.3d 555, 559 (8th Cir. 1995).

150. *POM Wonderful*, 894 F. Supp. 2d at 45.

151. *Id.*

152. *See id.* at 44–45.

153. *Id.* at 45.

154. A litigant who raises a frivolous First Amendment claim for purposes of delay is subject to sanctions pursuant to Rule 11 of the Federal Rules of Civil Procedure. Fed. R. Civ. P. 11.

155. 143 S. Ct. 890 (2023).

156. 510 U.S. 200 (1994).

157. Charles E. Clark, *The Handmaid of Justice*, 23 WASH. U. L.Q. 297 (1938).

158. *See* Freedman v. Maryland, 380 U.S. 51 (1965); discussion *supra* notes 143–46 and accompanying text.

CHAPTER 7

1. 28 U.S.C. § 1651(a) ("The Supreme Court and all courts established by Act of Congress may issue all writs necessary or appropriate in aid of their respective jurisdictions and agreeable to the usages and principles of law.").
2. *See* Samuel I. Ferenc, Note, *Clear Rights and Worthy Claimants: Judicial Intervention in Administrative Action Under the All Writs Act*, 118 Colum. L. Rev. 127, 136–40 (2018) (describing the adoption of the All Writs Act and explaining how courts have used it to derive authority to issue forms of equitable relief).
3. *See* U.S. Const. art. III (making no mention of the judiciary's power to issue remedies).
4. *See* Tarble's Case, 80 U.S. (13 Wall.) 397, 407–08, 411–12 (1871) (denying state courts authority to issue writs of habeas corpus to federal officers); *see also* McClung v. Silliman, 19 U.S. (6 Wheat.) 598, 603–04 (1821) (holding that a state court lacked the authority to issue a writ of mandamus to a federal officer); Kennedy v. Bruce, 298 F.2d 860, 862–63 (5th Cir. 1962) (holding that state courts may not enjoin federal officers). For a detailed discussion of the issue of state courts' authority to issue writs to federal officers, *see* Martin H. Redish, *Constitutional Limitations on Congressional Power to Control Federal Jurisdiction: A Reaction to Professor Sager*, 77 Nw. U. L. Rev. 143, 157–61 (1982).
5. *See* section 7.2, *infra* (discussing popular scholarly theory regarding constitutional remedies as subconstitutional).
6. *See* section 7.10, *infra* (discussing the Supreme Court's hesitance to build upon the doctrine of implied constitutional damage remedies based on its deferential attitude toward Congress).
7. *See* section 7.10, *infra* (identifying popular scholarly theories that posit that constitutional remedies are a legislative power).
8. *See* section 7.9, *infra* (laying out more sympathetic but still deferential theories of constitutional remedies).
9. *See* section 7.10, *infra* (critiquing the existing scholarship surrounding constitutional remedies).
10. *See infra* notes 11–321 and accompanying text.
11. 5 U.S. (1 Cranch) 137, 177 (1803). *Marbury v. Madison* espouses the powers of the judiciary and explicitly states that it is the role of the judiciary "to say what the law is," expound upon it, and interpret it. *Id.*
12. U.S. Const. amends. I–VIII.
13. *Id.* amends. XIII–XV.
14. *See id.* amends. I–VIII (mentioning no enforcement mechanisms). One exception, contained in the body of the Constitution, is the provision for habeas corpus. *Id.* art. I, § 9, cl. 2.

15. *Id.* art. III, § 1 (providing that judges shall hold their office during good behavior and be compensated); THE FEDERALIST NO. 78, at 465 (Alexander Hamilton) (Clinton Rossiter ed., 2003) ("[N]othing can contribute so much to [the judiciary's] firmness and independence as permanency in office"); *id.* at 468 ("This independence of the judges is equally requisite to Guard The Constitution And The Rights of individuals from serious oppressions of the minor party in the community.").
16. *See* section 7.2, *infra*.
17. Both the Thirteenth and Fourteenth Amendments explicitly authorize Congress to enforce the provisions' substantive directives through legislative action. U.S. CONST. amend. XIII, § 2; *id.* amend. XIV, § 5. Nevertheless, this surely does not mean that, absent the enactment of such legislation, the amendments lack any constitutional floor to be enforced by the judiciary.
18. *See* section 7.2, *infra*.
19. *See* sections 7.7–7.8, *infra*.
20. *See* section 7.13, *infra*.
21. U.S. CONST. art. V (requiring that amendment to the Constitution, as written, can only be accomplished through proposal by two-thirds of both the House and Senate or two-thirds of the state legislatures, and subsequent ratification by three-fourths of state legislatures); *see* Bivens v. Six Unknown Named Agents of Fed. Bureau of Narcotics, 403 U.S. 388, 399 (1971).
22. U.S. CONST. amends. I, II, III, IV, V, VI, VII, VIII, IX, X.
23. 5 U.S. (1 Cranch) 137, 176 (1803) ("To what purpose are powers limited, and to what purpose is that limitation committed to writing, if these limits may, at any time, be passed by those intended to be restrained?").
24. (1610) 77 Eng. Rep. 646, 652; 8 Co. Rep. 113 b, 118 a.
25. *See* MARTIN H. REDISH, JUDICIAL INDEPENDENCE AND THE AMERICAN CONSTITUTION: A DEMOCRATIC PARADOX 16 (2017) ("*The Federalist* paints a picture of a Founding Era obsession with the dangers of tyranny; Hamilton and Madison saw it lurking behind every corner and under every bed. Each measure the Founders took in the course of building the new federal government was aimed at safeguarding the young nation and future generations of Americans from oppression in any form" (footnote omitted)).
26. Randy E. Barnett & Evan D. Bernick, *The Letter and the Spirit: A Unified Theory of Originalism*, 107 GEO. L.J. 1, 22 (2018).
27. *See* U.S. CONST. art. III, § 1 (providing that judges "shall hold their Offices during good behaviour," during which they should receive continuous, undisturbed compensation).
28. THE FEDERALIST NO. 78, *supra* note 15, at 468 (Alexander Hamilton).
29. *Id.* at 464.
30. *Id.* at 466.
31. Barnett & Bernick, *supra* note 26, at 23 (discussing the guardian role of the courts).
32. *See, e.g.*, THE FEDERALIST NO. 48, *supra* note 15, at 306–07 (James Madison) ("The legislative department is everywhere extending the sphere of its activity, and drawing all power into its impetuous vortex. Its constitutional powers being at once more

extensive, and less susceptible of precise limits, it can, with the greater facility, mask, under complicated and indirect measures, the encroachments which it makes on the co-ordinate departments.").

33. *See* Barnett & Bernick, *supra* note 26, at 22 (noting that the principal threats to liberty were likely to come from the majoritarian branches like state legislatures); *see also* Steven G. Calabresi, *The President, the Supreme Court, and the Founding Fathers: A Reply to Professor Ackerman*, 73 U. CHI. L. REV. 469, 479 n.44 (2006) ("With one exception, that of New York, [state constitutions] included almost every conceivable provision for reducing the executive to a position of complete subordination." (quoting CHARLES C. THACH, JR., THE CREATION OF THE PRESIDENCY 1775–1789: A STUDY IN CONSTITUTIONAL HISTORY 28 (1969))).

34. *See* Marbury v. Madison, 5 U.S. (1 Cranch) 137, 176–79 (1803) (explaining the rationale for and establishing the power of judicial review); THE FEDERALIST NO. 78, *supra* note 15, at 463–69 (Alexander Hamilton) (describing the structure and function of the judiciary as a constraint on unconstitutional legislative action).

35. In 1793, Thomas Jefferson, then-Secretary of State in the Washington administration, wrote to the Supreme Court requesting answers to a set of discrete legal questions arising out of the United States' intention to remain neutral in the wars of the French Revolution. On behalf of a unanimous Court, Chief Justice John Jay declined Jefferson's request, emphasizing that the legal questions did not arise in judicial proceedings, and further noting that the Constitution permitted the president to require advisory opinions only from officers in the executive branch. *See* 3 THE CORRESPONDENCE AND PUBLIC PAPERS OF JOHN JAY 488–89 (Henry P. Johnston ed. 1891).

36. It is beyond the scope of this chapter to argue the merits of constitutional theories rejecting the power of ultimate judicial review. It should suffice for present purposes to describe all such theories as "fringe." Prominent alternatives include departmentalism and popular constitutionalism. Departmentalism contends that judicial supremacy is unconstitutional and that each of the three branches is equally endowed with the authority to interpret the Constitution. Redish, *supra* note 25, at 37 (describing alternatives to judicial review). Popular constitutionalism accepts that the Constitution permits judicial supremacy but also makes a normative argument that interpretive authority should rest in "the People" rather than the undemocratic judiciary because the text of the Constitution does not explicitly provide for judicial review. *Id.*

37. *Id.* at 17. Article III, Section 1 of the Constitution insulates the judiciary from majoritarian political pressures with salary and tenure protections. *See* U.S. CONST. art. III, § 1 ("The Judges, both of the supreme and inferior Courts, shall hold their Offices during good Behaviour, and shall, at stated Times, receive for their Services, a Compensation, which shall not be diminished during their Continuance in Office.").

38. Cooper v. Aaron, 358 U.S. 1, 18 (1958).

39. *See discussion* at section 7.11, *infra* (discussing the Supreme Court's deferential constitutional remedy jurisprudence).

40. *See* John Harrison, *Jurisdiction, Congressional Power, and Constitutional Remedies*, 86 GEO. L.J. 2513, 2513 (1998) (arguing that Congress controls constitutional remedies); Henry P. Monaghan, *The Supreme Court 1974 Term—Foreword: Constitutional Common Law*, 89 HARV. L. REV. 1, 3 (1975) (arguing that constitutional remedies are a matter of constitutional common law and thus ultimately controlled by Congress).

41. *See, e.g.*, Korematsu v. United States, 323 U.S. 214, 223–24 (1944) (upholding the constitutionality of the internment of Japanese prisoners in camps during World War II); Plessy v. Ferguson, 163 U.S. 537, 557–58 (1896) (upholding state racial segregation laws).

42. HC Deb (11 Nov. 1947) (444) col. 207 ("Indeed, it has been said that democracy is the worst form of Government except all those other forms that have been tried from time to time").

43. THE FEDERALIST NO. 78, *supra* note 15, at 464 (Alexander Hamilton); *see* U.S. CONST. art. III (stating the powers of the judiciary).

44. Redish, *supra* note 25, at 19; *see* U.S. CONST. art. III, § 1 (stating the salary and tenure protections of the judiciary that insulate it from political pressures).

45. 31 U.S. 515, 594–95 (1832) (holding unconstitutional a Georgia statute prohibiting non-Native Americans from being present on Native American lands without a license from the State of Georgia). In the aftermath of the decision, President Andrew Jackson reportedly said: "Well: John Marshall has made his decision: now let him enforce it!" Edwin A. Miles, *After John Marshall's Decision:* Worcester v. Georgia *and the Nullification Crisis*, 39 J.S. HIST. 519, 519 (1973) (emphasis omitted).

46. *See* 17 F. Cas. 144, 152–53 (C.C.D. Md. 1861) (holding that the president lacked authority to unilaterally suspend the privilege of the writ of habeas corpus).

47. David L. Shapiro, *Habeas Corpus, Suspension, and Detention: Another View*, 82 NOTRE DAME L. REV. 59, 60–61 (2006) (arguing that the Suspension Clause of the Constitution can be used to modify underlying constitutional rights); Amanda L. Tyler, *Suspension as an Emergency Power*, 118 YALE L.J. 600, 602–07 (2009) (discussing the Suspension Clause and its application to modern problems posed by the war on terrorism); Amanda L. Tyler, *The Forgotten Core Meaning of the Suspension Clause*, 125 HARV. L. REV. 901, 902 (2012) (exploring the historical record surrounding the Suspension Clause and arguing that only under a valid suspension could citizens be detained without criminal charges); *cf.* Martin H. Redish & Colleen McNamara, *Habeas Corpus, Due Process and the Suspension Clause: A Study in the Foundations of American Constitutionalism*, 96 VA. L. REV. 1361 (2010) (arguing that the Fifth Amendment's Due Process Clause must be construed to supersede the Suspension Clause).

48. *See, e.g.*, U.S. CONST. art. I, § 9, cl. 2 (habeas corpus guarantee).

49. *Id.* amends. XIII, XIV, XV (expressly giving Congress the power to enforce each respective amendment by appropriate legislation).

50. *See, e.g.*, Thomas C. Grey, *Origins of the Unwritten Constitution: Fundamental Law in American Revolutionary Thought*, 30 STAN. L. REV. 843, 848–49 (1978) (examining and reviewing noninterpretive judicial review, which the author refers to as "unwritten law").

51. *See generally* Martin H. Redish & Matthew B. Arnould, *Judicial Review, Constitutional Interpretation, and the Democratic Dilemma: Proposing a "Controlled Activism" Alternative*, 64 FLA. L. REV. 1485, 1493 (2012) (illustrating the author's view of textualism).
52. I have already proposed a detailed textualist theory of constitutional interpretation. *See id.* (departing from nontextualism and demanding that interpretation be confined to the linguistic reaches of the actual constitutional text).
53. 198 U.S. 45, 64 (1905) (recognizing a constitutional right to contract in the Fourteenth Amendment's Due Process Clause, despite no textual basis for such a right).
54. 410 U.S. 113, 166–67 (1973) (finding a woman's right to abortion under the Due Process Clause, despite no textual basis for such a right); *see also* Griswold v. Connecticut, 381 U.S. 479, 485–86 (1965) (recognizing a general constitutional right to privacy).
55. ANTONIN SCALIA & BRYAN A. GARNER, READING LAW: THE INTERPRETATION OF LEGAL TEXTS 16 (2012).
56. *Id.*
57. *See id.* at 17 (admitting that they do not consider themselves "pure" textualists).
58. 17 U.S. (4 Wheat.) 316, 413, 421 (1819) (rejecting that "necessary" meant "absolute physical necessity" and stating,
"[l]et the end be legitimate, let it be within the scope of the constitution, and all means which are appropriate, which are plainly adapted to that end, which are not prohibited, but consist with the letter and spirit of the constitution, are constitutional").
59. Scalia & Garner, *supra* note 55, at 355.
60. *Id.* at 355–56 (alteration in original) (quoting Martin v. Hunter's Lessee, 14 U.S. (1 Wheat.) 304, 326 (1816) (opinion of Story, J.)).
61. *Id.* at 355 (quoting Utah Junk Co. v. Porter, 328 U.S. 39, 44 (1946) (Frankfurter, J., majority opinion)).
62. *Id.*
63. *Id.* at 356.
64. *Id.*
65. ANTONIN SCALIA, A MATTER OF INTERPRETATION: FEDERAL COURTS AND THE LAW 24 (1997).
66. *See id.*
67. *Id.* at 25 (referring to canons of construction, which are often used and associated with textualism).
68. *See, e.g., infra* notes 83–89 and accompanying text (illustrating how the Court used facilitative textualism to find rights to freedom of thought, association, and expressive anonymity through the First Amendment's protection of free speech).
69. Scalia & Garner, *supra* note 55, at 63.
70. *Id.*
71. This can be intuited from the fact that the countermajoritarian judiciary has the power of judicial review to ensure that the acts of its majoritarian counterparts comply with the Constitution and the fact that the Constitution explicitly provides

for guarantees of specific individual rights. *See* U.S. CONST. amends. I, II, III, IV, V, VI, VII, VIII (providing for the protection of individual rights); Marbury v. Madison, 5 U.S. (1 Cranch) 137, 176–79 (1803) (establishing the Court's power of judicial review).

72. *See* section 7.8, *infra*.
73. The aforementioned article refers to these as "internal" and "external" implicit directives. Redish & Arnould, *supra* note 51, at 1519 (encouraging the acceptance and use of "internal" implicit directives while warning of the use of "external" implicit directives).
74. *Id.*
75. *Id.* at 1486.
76. 381 U.S. 479, 484–86 (1965) (finding a right to privacy "emanat[ing]" from several explicit constitutional guarantees).
77. *Id.* at 484.
78. *Compare id.* at 484–86 (finding a general right to privacy), *with* U.S. CONST. amends. III, IV (prohibiting, respectively and explicitly, the quartering of soldiers during peacetime and unreasonable searches and seizures).
79. Redish & Arnould, *supra* note 51, at 1486.
80. *Id.*
81. *Id.* at 1493.
82. *Id.* at 1519.
83. U.S. CONST. amend. I (referring to the freedoms of religion, speech, press, petition, and assembly).
84. *See* NAACP v. Alabama *ex rel.* Patterson, 357 U.S. 449, 460 (1958) ("Effective advocacy of both public and private points of view, particularly controversial ones, is undeniably enhanced by group association").
85. *See, e.g.*, McIntyre v. Ohio Elections Comm'n, 514 U.S. 334, 357 (1995) (Stevens, J., majority opinion) (holding unconstitutional an Ohio statute prohibiting the distribution of anonymous campaign literature because "anonymous pamphleteering is . . . a shield from the tyranny of the majority . . . thus examplif[ying] the purpose behind the Bill of Rights, and of the First Amendment in particular: to protect unpopular individuals from retaliation—and their ideas from suppression—at the hand of an intolerant society." (citations omitted)); Talley v. California, 362 U.S. 60, 64 (1960) (Black, J., majority opinion) (striking down a Los Angeles ordinance that required the inclusion of authors' personal information on any publicly distributed handbills, and noting "[t]here can be no doubt that such an identification requirement would tend to restrict freedom to distribute information and thereby freedom of expression").
86. 357 U.S. at 460. In *Griswold v. Connecticut*, Justice William Douglas uses this case as an example to justify the right to privacy, stating that "the First Amendment has a penumbra where privacy is protected from governmental intrusion." 381 U.S. 479, 483 (1965). But as this Article has explained, this application is unsound because the so-called right to privacy does not facilitate the effectuation of the rights listed in the First Amendment—or any of the other rights listed in the Bill of Rights

relied upon by Justice Douglas—whereas the freedom of association facilitates individuals' ability to practice the freedom of speech explicitly provided in the First Amendment. *See NAACP*, 357 U.S. at 460 (making this observation); *supra* notes 72–80 and accompanying text (highlighting the important distinction between facilitative nontextualism and supplemental nontextualism).

87. *NAACP*, 357 U.S. at 462–63.
88. MARTIN H. REDISH, THE ADVERSARY FIRST AMENDMENT: FREE EXPRESSION AND THE FOUNDATIONS OF AMERICAN DEMOCRACY 162 (2013).
89. Redish & Arnould, *supra* note 51, at 1519.
90. *See* 5 U.S. (1 Cranch) 137, 176–78 (1803) (exposing the judiciary's power of judicial review through adjudication).
91. *See* U.S. CONST. art. II, § 1, cl. 1.
92. *Id.* art. II, § 3.
93. United States v. Nixon, 418 U.S. 683, 708 (1974) (footnote omitted) (explaining the rationale for a presumptive privilege for presidential communications).
94. *See infra* notes 95–141 and accompanying text (critiquing the existing scholarship surrounding constitutional remedies).
95. Henry M. Hart, Jr., *The Power of Congress to Limit the Jurisdiction of Federal Courts: An Exercise in Dialectic*, 66 HARV. L. REV. 1362, 1366 (1953).
96. *Id.* at 1366.
97. *See Constitutional*, BLACK'S LAW DICTIONARY (11th ed. 2019) (defining as "[o]f, relating to, or involving a constitution"); *id.* at *Statutory* (defining as "[o]f, relating to, or involving legislation, or legislatively created").
98. *See* sections 7.2–7.4, *supra* (arguing that fundamental principles of the Constitution demand judicial control of constitutional remedies).
99. U.S. CONST. art. I, § 1 (vesting all legislative powers in Congress); *id.* art. III, § 1 (vesting all judicial power in the courts).
100. Harrison, *supra* note 40, at 2513 (arguing that Congress controls constitutional remedies).
101. *Id.* at 2514–15 (arguing that Congress has both substantive and structural powers). Substantive powers refer to Congress's ability to create causes of action to be heard in federal courts, whereas structural powers refer to Congress's ability to determine what kind of decrees the federal courts can issue. *Id.*
102. *See id.* at 2518–19 (explaining this concept through an example using the Due Process Clause).
103. *See* U.S. CONST. art. I, § 1 (vesting all legislative powers in Congress).
104. *See* section 7.2, *supra*.
105. *See* text at note 106, *infra* (discussing Meltzer's support for the theory of constitutional common law, that I argue is incoherent and cedes far too much power to Congress and unconstitutionally permits the legislature to reverse or modify the judiciary's interpretation of the Constitution).
106. Daniel J. Meltzer, *Congress, Courts, and Constitutional Remedies*, 86 GEO. L.J. 2537, 2551 (1998) (footnote omitted).

107. *Id.* These premises are: "(1) in the nineteenth century, officer suits based on claims of private right were the predominant, indeed perhaps the virtually exclusive, form of relief against unconstitutional action; (2) in court, the Constitution's principal effect was to nullify statutes or other claims of official defense; and (3) most constitutional litigation involved the validity of statutes rather than of nonlegislative governmental actions." *Id.* (footnotes omitted).

108. *Id.* at 2553; *see supra* note 107 and accompanying text (listing the practices upon which Harrison based his conclusion).

109. Meltzer, *supra* note 106, at 2553–54.

110. *Id.* at 2554 (alteration in original) (quoting Marbury v. Madison, 5 U.S. (1 Cranch) 137, 163 (1803)).

111. *See id.* at 2551 (summarizing the implication of Harrison's theory: that the federal courts acting on their own lack the authority to institute constitutional remedies without the congressional issuance of such power).

112. *See generally* Richard H. Fallon, Jr. & Daniel J. Meltzer, *New Law, Non-retroactivity, and Constitutional Remedies*, 104 HARV. L. REV. 1731 (1991) (developing a general theory of constitutional remedies that keeps government within the bounds of the Constitution, but in some cases denies relief).

113. Meltzer, *supra* note 106, at 2559 (summarizing his work with Fallon).

114. Fallon & Meltzer, *supra* note 112, at 1778–79.

115. *Id.* (addressing the criticism that the Constitution does not explicitly address the subject of remedies).

116. *Id.* at 1787.

117. *Id.* at 1788.

118. *Id.* at 1789.

119. Walter E. Dellinger, *Of Rights and Remedies: The Constitution as a Sword*, 85 HARV. L. REV. 1532, 1548 (1972).

120. *Id.* at 1549 (arguing that, with respect to constitutional remedies, the court should usually defer in advance to Congress). Dellinger comments in a footnote that "[t]he ultimate determination of whether a remedial scheme appropriately effectuates the mandate of the Constitution is, of course, to be made by the Court as an exercise of constitutional judicial review." *Id.* at 1548 n.89.

121. *Id.* at 1549 ("Certainly, given the wider range of remedial techniques available to the legislature, the Court should often defer to the ability of Congress to effectuate a more precise compromise of competing interests.").

122. *Id.* at 1541 (referring to the fact that this power could be found in the granting of the judicial power).

123. *Id.* at 1549.

124. *Id.* at 1541.

125. *Id.* at 1550 (quoting Bivens v. Six Unknown Named Agents of Fed. Bureau of Narcotics, 403 U.S. 388, 399 (1971)).

126. *Id.* at 1552–53.

127. Richard H. Fallon, Jr., *Jurisdiction-Stripping Reconsidered*, 96 VA. L. REV. 1043, 1104–15 (2010) (arguing that the stripping of state and federal jurisdiction would preclude the award of constitutionally necessary remedies, thus violating the Constitution).
128. *Id.* at 1100 & n.264.
129. *Id.* at 1107–08.
130. *Id.* at 1107.
131. *See* section 7.2, *supra* (detailing how the countermajoritarian nature of the Constitution and role of the courts demands that constitutional remedies be constitutional law).
132. *See* Dellinger, *supra* note 119, at 1541 (arguing that, according to the language of Article III, some remedies may solely be in the province of the judiciary); Fallon, *supra* note 127, at 1100 & n.264 (articulating that to not allow federal courts to control remedies for conditional violations would run afoul of Article III); Fallon & Meltzer, *supra* note 112, at 1788 (recognizing that the Constitution designs the judiciary to serve as the protector of the people's individual rights from the majoritarian branches).
133. *See* Dellinger, *supra* note 119, at 1548–49 (arguing that Congress can substitute a remedial scheme for the one created by the courts, and that in most cases the courts should defer); Fallon, *supra* note 127, at 1107–08 (contending that the Constitution does not always require an individual effective remedy in every case); Fallon & Meltzer, *supra* note 112, at 1789 (viewing the countermajoritarian view of the judiciary as an "aspiration[al]" not "unqualified command").
134. Bivens v. Six Unknown Named Agents of Fed. Bureau of Narcotics, 403 U.S. 388, 397 (1971) (finding an implied damages remedy for violations of the Fourth Amendment by federal agents).
135. *See* section 7.13, *infra* (discussing the origin, expansion, and subsequent limitation of the *Bivens* doctrine of implied constitutional remedies).
136. Susan Bandes, *Reinventing* Bivens: *The Self-executing Constitution*, 68 S. CAL. L. REV. 289, 291–92 (1995).
137. *Id.* at 293.
138. *Id.* at 294 (arguing that the ultimate responsibility to enforce the Constitution lays with the courts by being able provide any adequate remedies against constitutional violations).
139. *See id.* at 307 (arguing that if Congress were given authority over the existence, nature, and extent of constitutional remedies "[t]he structural limits on the powers of government would exist only in the unlikely event that those with governmental power did not seek to aggrandize it").
140. *See id.* at 324 ("In a sense, I am arguing that deference to Congress in this area is inappropriate. However, I do not mean to argue that the Court must determine the proper means for effectuating constitutional guarantees.").
141. *Id.*
142. *See* section 7.5, *supra* (outlining and critiquing popular scholarship regarding constitutional remedies that reject the theory developed in this chapter).
143. *See* section 7.1, *supra*.

144. *See* sections 7.7–7.8, *supra*.
145. *See generally* Monaghan, *supra* note 40 (expressing his theory of constitutional common law).
146. *Id.* at 2–3.
147. *See* City of Boerne v. Flores, 521 U.S. 507, 508 (1997) (holding that Congress's enactment of the Religious Freedom Restoration Act of 1998 was inappropriate "because it contradicts vital principles necessary to maintain separation of powers").
148. Monaghan, *supra* note 40, at 3, 10–11 (quoting Henry J. Friendly, *In Praise of* Erie— *And of the New Federal Common Law*, 39 N.Y.U. L. REV. 383, 405 (1964)) (lauding *Erie R.R. v. Tompkins*, 304 U.S. 64, 78 (1938), for enabling the development of a limited, but "predictable and useful," federal common law). The federal common law that Monaghan refers to is the decisional law created by federal courts when adjudicating federal questions. *Common Law*, BLACK'S LAW DICTIONARY, *supra* note 97.
149. Monaghan, *supra* note 40, at 3–10 (exemplifying the theory of constitutional common law through the development of the exclusionary rule); *see Exclusionary Rule*, BLACK'S LAW DICTIONARY, *supra* note 97.
150. *See* Monaghan, *supra* note 40, at 17 (explaining the Court's constitutional common-lawmaking power in the context of its dormant commerce clause jurisprudence).
151. *Id.* at 13–19 (arguing that the authority to create federal common law in different situations derives from the structure of the Constitution and that protection of individual liberties has become and should remain the central function of judicial review).
152. *See id.* at 3, 27–29.
153. *Id.* at 34. Monaghan views this as only "*limited* judicial lawmaking to vindicate existing constitutional rights." *Id.* at 35.
154. *Id.* at 24, 29 (recognizing that when dealing with matters of constitutional common law, Congress provides a safety valve, but one that is not available when dealing with constitutional interpretation and constitutional rights).
155. *Id.* at 24 (differentiating the boundary between constitutional common law, in which Congress has a role to play, and constitutional interpretation, in which separation of powers mandates that Congress has no role).
156. *Id.* at 22.
157. *Id.* at 32–33.
158. *See id.* at 24 (arguing that if an action is not constitutional interpretation then it is common law).
159. *Id.* at 15.
160. *See id.* at 15–17 (providing potential answers to the posed question but subsequently critiquing them). In the context of the Commerce Clause, Monaghan contends that the Supreme Court is not actually engaged in constitutional interpretation but in "fashioning federal common law on the authority of the commerce clause." *Id.* at 17.
161. *See id.* at 9, 24 (advocating for a theory of quasi-constitutional law of constitutional remedies that functionally resembles the common law but for situations when the remedies are indispensable to underlying constitutional rights).

162. *See* Daniel J. Meltzer, *Harmless Error and Constitutional Remedies*, 61 U. CHI. L. REV. 1, 27 (1994) (voicing his support for the importance and validity of Professor Monaghan's constitutional common law); Daniel J. Meltzer, *State Court Forfeitures of Federal Rights*, 99 HARV. L. REV. 1128, 1172–76 (1986) (explaining his support for Monaghan's constitutional common law).
163. Meltzer, *State Court Forfeitures*, *supra* note 162, at 1173–74.
164. *Id.* at 1174 (internal quotation marks omitted).
165. *Id.*; *see infra* notes 166–79 and accompanying text (critiquing Monaghan's theory).
166. *See generally* Thomas S. Schrock and Robert C. Welsh, *Reconsidering the Constitutional Common Law*, 91 HARV. L. REV. 1117 (1978) (arguing that Monaghan's theory of constitutional common law is illegitimate).
167. *Id.* at 1127–29 (objecting to the view that the Court can have subconstitutional power on three grounds).
168. *Id.* at 1127 (articulating the *Marbury v. Madison*-style judicial review objection).
169. *Id.* at 1127–28 (making the separation-of-powers objection).
170. *Id.*
171. *Id.* at 1128.
172. *Id.* (quoting Monaghan, *supra* note 40, at 35) (addressing the encroachment on the executive that would result from judicial power to pass judgment on area of executive law).
173. *Id.* at 1130 (quoting Monaghan, *supra* note 40, at 35) (addressing the federalism objection). Schrock and Welsh argue that the scope of Monaghan's constitutional common law is so great that it could easily claim aspects of criminal procedure once thought to be the autonomy of states. *Id.*
174. *Id.* at 1131; *see* Monaghan, *supra* note 40, at 23 ("I suggest that such legislative rules can be adequately rationalized as constitutional common law. For example, the utility of providing the police with guidance . . . should be self-evident").
175. *See* Schrock & Welsh, *supra* note 166, at 1131–45 (arguing that there is no constitutional source of authority for the constitutional common law). They summarize their findings on the lack of authority for constitutional common law as follows: "While general supervisory powers may allow the Court in limited circumstances to impose rules upon the federal executive department, authority is lacking for similar impositions upon the states. Thus, the constitutional common law runs seriously afoul of federalism and, less seriously, of separation of powers." *Id.* at 1145.
176. *See id.* at 1131 (noting that there is no constitutional source for this authority). Schrock and Welsh also note that *Bivens* is properly understood as "a constitutional (not common law) decision . . . prevent[ing] the fourth amendment from being rendered a 'mere form of words.'" *Id.* at 1135–36 (quoting Bivens v. Six Unknown Named Agents of Fed. Bureau of Narcotics, 403 U.S. 388, 399 (1971) (Harlan, J., concurring)).
177. Monaghan, *supra* note 40, at 12–13 (analogizing the constitutional common law to federal common law).
178. *See id.* at 27–29, 34–35 (explaining that there is a coordinate role for Congress to play in the process of defining and enforcing constitutional rights, and that Congress,

therefore, has the right to revise and reverse the Supreme Court's constitutional common law).
179. Martin H. Redish & Shane V. Nugent, *The Dormant Commerce Clause and the Constitutional Balance of Federalism*, 1987 Duke L.J. 569, 603.
180. The Federalist No. 78, *supra* note 15, at 468 (Alexander Hamilton).
181. *Id.* at 466.
182. Dellinger, *supra* note 119, at 1549.
183. *See* Hart, *supra* note 95, at 1366 (posing the possibility that Congress's power to regulate federal court jurisdiction in effect gives it the power to control federal court remedies).
184. *See* U.S. Const. art. III, § 1 ("The judicial Power of the United States, shall be vested in one supreme Court, and in such inferior Courts as the Congress may from time to time ordain and establish.").
185. 303 U.S. 323, 327 (1938) (remarking that the authority of the Court to issue the remedy was dependent on the jurisdiction provided in the statute).
186. *See* discussion *supra*, text at note 184.
187. *See* section 7.9, *infra*.
188. 303 U.S. at 329–30 (discussing issues regarding the prerequisites to exercise jurisdiction to enforce the Norris-LaGuardia Act).
189. Hart, *supra* note 95, at 1366.
190. *Id.*
191. 303 U.S. at 327.
192. *Id.* at 325.
193. *Id.*
194. *Id.* at 327–29 (analyzing the definition of "labor dispute" in both the Wisconsin Labor Code and the Norris-LaGuardia Act). Under the Norris-LaGuardia Act, a labor dispute "includes any controversy concerning terms or conditions of employment, or concerning the association or representation of persons in ... changing, or seeking to arrange terms or conditions of employment." 29 U.S.C. § 113(c).
195. *Lauf*, 303 U.S. at 329 (quoting Pub. L. No. 72-65, § 7, 47 Stat. 70, 71 (1932)).
196. *Id.* at 330.
197. *Id.* at 327.
198. *Id.* at 330.
199. *See id.* at 329 (describing the conditions that must be met for a court to issue an injunction under the Norris-LaGuardia Act); *see also* 29 U.S.C. § 107 (explicitly setting out the procedure a court must follow and the findings that a court must make to issue an injunction).
200. Steel Co. v. Citizens for a Better Env't, 523 U.S. 83, 90 (1998) (quoting United States v. Vanness, 85 F.3d 661, 663 n.2 (D.C. Cir. 1996)).
201. Compare *Jurisdiction*, Black's Law Dictionary, *supra* note 97, *with Authority*, Black's Law Dictionary, *supra* note 97.
202. U.S. Const. art. I, § 1 (granting legislative powers to Congress); *id.* art. III, § 1 (granting judicial power to the courts).

203. 80 U.S. (13 Wall.) 128, 147 (1871). This case was ostensibly about Congress's Article III, Section 2 power over the Supreme Court's appellate jurisdiction, but it also implicated Congress's authority to control the jurisdiction of lower federal courts, as Congress supplied a new rule of decision for lower federal courts to apply as well. See id. at 141–42 (noting that Congress repealed a law related to presidential pardons that instructed lower federal courts to use proof of presidential pardons to presume disloyalty, in direct contradiction with Supreme Court precedent).
204. Id. at 130–31 (describing the statute).
205. Id. at 141–46 (holding that such action only intends to withhold appellate jurisdiction as a means to an end of controlling the meaning of a presidential pardon).
206. MARTIN H. REDISH, FEDERAL JURISDICTION: TENSIONS IN THE ALLOCATION OF JUDICIAL POWER 48 (2d ed. 1990).
207. Id.
208. Pennsylvania v. Wheeling & Belmont Bridge Co., 59 U.S. (18 How.) 421 (1855).
209. Id. at 421–27 (stating the facts of the case and the original nuisance injunction).
210. See Martin H. Redish & Christopher R. Pudelski, *Legislative Deception, Separation of Powers, and the Democratic Process: Harnessing the Political Theory of* United States v. Klein, 100 NW. U. L. REV. 437, 446–47 (2006) (differentiating between the holdings in *Pennsylvania v. Wheeling & Belmont Bridge Co.* and *United States v. Klein*).
211. Compare Lauf v. E.G. Shinner & Co., 303 U.S. 323, 327–30 (1938) (withholding jurisdiction because the court did not make the required statutory findings), *and Wheeling Bridge*, 59 U.S. (18 How.) at 435 (concluding that because congressional act legalized the bridge, the bridge was no longer a nuisance), *with* United States v. Klein, 80 U.S. (13 Wall.) 128, 141–46 (1871) (holding that although the congressional act appeared only to withhold jurisdiction, it was in fact a means to an end of interpreting the presidential pardon clause of the Constitution and thus unconstitutional).
212. Redish & Pudelski, *supra* note 210, at 447.
213. Id. at 447–49 (explaining how *Klein* supports the larger countermajoritarian constitutional structure).
214. See U.S. CONST. art. III, § 1 (articulating explicitly that Congress can create lower federal courts); id. art. III, § 2, cl. 2 (authorizing Congress to regulate the Supreme Court's appellate jurisdiction).
215. Id. art. III, § 2, cl. 2 (emphasis added).
216. See, e.g., Ex parte Yerger, 75 U.S. (8 Wall.) 85, 94–106 (1868) (examining the Supreme Court's appellate jurisdiction in habeas corpus cases); Ex parte McCardle, 74 U.S. (7 Wall.) 506, 512–15 (1868) (examining the jurisdiction of the Supreme Court to review lower courts' determinations under federal statutory law). If one reads *Ex parte McCardle* "for all it might be worth," it appears that the Supreme Court gives Congress broad, if not plenary, power to control the Court's appellate jurisdiction. Hart, *supra* note 95, at 1364. The Court also cited Chief Justice Marshall for the contention that the Supreme Court can only exercise the appellate jurisdiction that Congress has given it. *McCardle*, 74 U.S. (7 Wall.) at 513 (citing Durousseau v. United States, 10 U.S. (6 Cranch) 307 (1810)). In *Ex parte Yerger*, the Court took a much narrower view of Congress's power over the Court's appellate jurisdiction,

reading the language of *McCardle* to be far from conclusive of what that case indicated to be a plenary congressional power. 75 U.S. (8 Wall.) at 103–06 (discussing *McCardle*).
217. RAOUL BERGER, CONGRESS V. THE SUPREME COURT 285–96 (1969) (arguing for a narrower view of the Exceptions Clause); Henry J. Merry, *Scope of the Supreme Court's Appellate Jurisdiction: Historical Basis*, 47 MINN. L. REV. 53, 57 (1962) (interpreting the Exceptions Clause narrowly to regulate the treatment of fact issues).
218. *See, e.g.*, Redish, *supra* note 206, at 30–41 (discussing jurists, such as Justice Joseph Story, and scholars who question whether Congress has any discretion to refuse to establish lower federal courts).
219. U.S. CONST. art. III, § 1 (emphasis added).
220. Redish, *supra* note 206, at 29. For the leading Supreme Court case articulating this view of Congress's power to control the jurisdiction of lower federal courts, *see Sheldon v. Sill*, 49 U.S. (8 How.) 441 (1850).
221. *See* 80 U.S. (13 Wall.) 128, 141–46 (1871) (holding that congressional attempt to withhold jurisdiction was unconstitutional because it only served as a means to an end of controlling the interpretation of a presidential pardon).
222. For another example of the limitations on Congress's power to control federal jurisdiction, *see Bank Markazi v. Peterson*, 136 S. Ct. 1310, 1324–29 (2016). Although the Supreme Court held that Congress did not exceed its authority in this case because it merely changed the substantive law while litigation was pending, it did make clear that Congress cannot use its power to dictate how the Court should rule in specific cases. *See id.*
223. Redish, *supra* note 206, at 51.
224. U.S. CONST. art. I, § 1 ("All legislative Powers herein granted . . ."); *see id.* art. I, § 8 (enumerating specific legislative powers).
225. *Id.* art. III ("The judicial Power of the United States, shall be vested . . .").
226. *See* section 7.4, *supra* (illustrating the concept of facilitative textualism and arguing that it supports the constitutionality of constitutional remedies); sections 7.7–7.8, *supra* (explaining why Congress's power to create and limit the jurisdiction of lower federal courts does not arrogate to itself ultimate authority to interpret the Constitution).
227. 377 U.S. 426, 432 (1964) (implying a statutory damage remedy based on the purpose of the statute).
228. *See Cort v. Ash*, 422 U.S. 66 (1975) (declining to imply a statutory remedy but laying out factors it would consider in such cases); *see also Cannon v. Univ. of Chi.*, 441 U.S. 677 (1979) (refusing to imply a statutory remedy after the application of the *Cort* factors).
229. 403 U.S. 388, 392, 397 (1971) (holding that an implied cause of action exists for an individual whose Fourth Amendment right to freedom from unreasonable search and seizure has been violated).
230. *Id.* at 390–93.
231. *Davis v. Passman*, 442 U.S. 228, 245–49 (1979).

NOTES 279

232. Carlson v. Green, 446 U.S. 14, 18–25 (1980).
233. *See* section 7.13, *infra* (discussing the expansion and development of the doctrine of implied constitutional remedies).
234. *See id.*
235. *Bivens*, 403 U.S. at 397 (citing J.I. Case Co. v. Borak, 377 U.S. 426, 433 (1964)).
236. Professor Susan Bandes has completed extensive work on the greater constitutional implications of *Bivens* and constitutional remedies. *See generally* Bandes, *supra* note 136 (analyzing the judicial power to create remedies and explaining that the courts, not Congress, are and should be ultimately responsible for providing remedies for violations).
237. 377 U.S. at 433 (finding that "it is the duty of the courts to be alert to provide such remedies as are necessary to make effective the congressional purpose" of the statute).
238. *Id.* at 427. The civil action arose from Section 14(a) of the Securities Exchange Act of 1934, which makes it unlawful to utilize interstate commerce to violate Securities Exchange Commission (SEC) proxy rules and regulations. 15 U.S.C. § 78n(a).
239. *J.I. Case Co.*, 377 U.S. at 427–28.
240. *Id.* at 432 (noting that "among [the statute's] chief purposes is 'the protection of investors,' which certainly implies the availability of judicial relief where necessary to achieve that result.").
241. *Id.* at 431 (stating that "[t]he purpose of section 14(a) [was] to prevent management or others from obtaining authorization for corporate action by means of deceptive or inadequate disclosure in proxy solicitation"). The Court relied on three things primarily: (1) H.R. Rep. No. 73-1383, at 13–14 (1934), which demonstrated the "congressional belief that '[f]air corporate suffrage is an important right that should attach to every equity security bought on a public exchange'" and that the act "was intended to 'control the conditions under which proxies may be solicited with a view to preventing the recurrence of abuses which . . . [had] frustrated the free exercise of the voting rights of stockholders'"; (2) S. Rep. No. 73-792, at 12 (1934), which stated that "[t]oo often proxies are solicited without explanation to the stockholder of the real nature of the questions for which authority to cast his vote is sought"; and (3) the text of Section 14(a), "which makes it 'unlawful for any person . . . to solicit or to permit the use of his name to solicit any proxy or consent or authorization in respect of any security . . . registered on any national securities exchange in contravention of such rules and regulations as the [SEC] may prescribe as necessary or appropriate in the public interest *or for the protection of investors.*'" *Id.* at 431–32 (first and second alterations in original).
242. *Borak*, 377 U.S. at 433 (quoting Bell v. Hood, 327 U.S. 678, 684 (1946)).
243. 422 U.S. 66, 69, 85 (1975).
244. *Id.* at 68.
245. *Id.* at 78.
246. *See* Stoneridge Inv. Partners, LLC v. Scientific-Atlanta, Inc., 552 U.S. 148, 166–67 (2008) (limiting the extent of the private right of action the Court had previously implied in Section 10(b) of the Securities Exchange Act of 1934, 15 U.S.C. § 8j, and

SEC Rule 10b-5, 17 C.F.R. § 240.10b-5 (2020)); Cannon v. Univ. of Chi., 441 U.S. 677, 709 (1979) (finding all four of the *Cort v. Ash* factors satisfied by Title IX of the Education Amendments of 1972).
247. 552 U.S. at 165.
248. *Id.* at 164.
249. U.S. CONST. amend. IV ("The right of the people to be secure in their persons, houses, papers, and effects, against unreasonable searches and seizures, shall not be violated, and no Warrants shall issue, but upon probable cause, supported by Oath or affirmation, and particularly describing the place to be searched, and the persons or things to be seized.").
250. 232 U.S. 383, 398–99 (1914).
251. Silverthorne Lumber Co. v. United States, 251 U.S. 385, 392 (1920). The Court later extended the Fourth Amendment exclusionary rule to apply to state criminal trials. Mapp v. Ohio, 367 U.S. 643, 659–60 (1961).
252. Bivens v. Six Unknown Named Agents of Fed. Bureau of Narcotics, 403 U.S. 388, 389 (1971). The Court had reserved this question twenty-five years earlier in *Bell v. Hood*. 327 U.S. 678, 683–84 (1946).
253. 403 U.S. at 389.
254. *Id.*
255. *Id.* at 390–91.
256. *Id.* at 392.
257. *Id.* at 392–93.
258. *Id.* at 392 (quoting Bell v. Hood, 327 U.S. 678, 684 (1946)).
259. *Id.* at 396.
260. *Id.* These special factors included "question[s] of 'federal fiscal policy'" or whether "to impose liability upon a congressional employee for actions contrary to no constitutional prohibition, but merely said to be in excess of the authority delegated to him by the Congress." *Id.* at 396–97 (quoting United States v. Standard Oil Co., 332 U.S. 301, 311 (1954)) (citing Wheeldin v. Wheeler, 373 U.S. 647 (1963)).
261. *Id.* at 397.
262. *Id.*
263. *Id.* at 407 (Harlan, J., concurring). Justice Harlan also relied on *J.I. Case Co. v. Borak*, 377 U.S. 426 (1964), noting that "in suits for damages based on violations of federal statutes lacking any express authorization of a damage remedy, this Court has authorized such relief where, in its view, damages are necessary to effectuate the congressional policy underpinning the substantive provisions of the statute." *Id.* at 402.
264. *Id.* at 407.
265. *Id.* (quoting Mo., Kan. & Tex. Ry. Co. v. May, 194 U.S. 267, 270 (1904)).
266. 442 U.S. 228, 230–31 (1979).
267. *Id.* at 231.
268. *Id.* at 230.
269. *Id.* at 247.
270. *Id.* at 230.
271. *Id.* at 241.

272. *Id.* at 252 (Powell, J., dissenting) (explaining that "the judiciary is clearly discernable as the primary means through which [constitutional] rights may be enforced" (alteration in original)). For this proposition, the Court quoted James Madison, who when presenting the Bill of Rights to Congress, declared, "[i]f [these rights] are incorporated into the Constitution, independent tribunals of justice will consider themselves in a peculiar manner the guardians of those rights; they will be an impenetrable bulwark against every assumption of power in the Legislative or Executive." *Id.* at 241–42 (majority opinion) (second alteration in original) (quoting 1 Annals of Cong. 439 (1789) (Joseph Gales ed., 1834)).
273. *Id.* at 246 (majority opinion) (hypothesizing factors that may counsel hesitation). The special concern was suing a "Congressman for putatively unconstitutional actions taken in the course of his official conduct." *Id.* But the Court dispensed with this concern as "coextensive with the protections afforded by the Speech or Debate Clause," though not protected by that Clause, and "the principle that 'legislators ought ... generally to be bound by [the law] as are ordinary persons.'" *Id.* (alteration in original) (citing Gravel v. United States, 408 U.S. 606, 615 (1972)).
274. *Id.* at 246–47 (quoting Bivens v. Six Unknown Named Agents of Fed. Bureau of Narcotics, 403 U.S. 388, 397 (1971)).
275. Silverthorne Lumber Co. v. United States, 251 U.S. 385, 392 (1920) (holding that without a constitutionally mandated remedy, i.e., the exclusionary rule, the Fourth Amendment would practically be worth nothing).
276. Carlson v. Green, 446 U.S. 14, 18–25 (1980).
277. *Id.* at 16 (reporting the facts of the case).
278. *Id.* at 18–19 (first citing *Bivens*, 403 U.S. at 396–97: and then citing *Davis*, 442 U.S. at 245–47). The Court also considered the question whether the allegations supported a suit under the Federal Tort Claims Act. *Id.* at 19–24.
279. *Id.* at 19.
280. *Id.* at 19–20 (explaining that Congress exercised "the practice of explicitly stating when it means to make FTCA an exclusive remedy").
281. *See* Bandes, *supra* note 136, at 337–38 (explaining how the Court in *Carlson v. Green* codified the judiciary's deference to Congress in *Bivens* actions).
282. *See infra* notes 283–307 and accompanying text (discussing the Court's limitation of the *Bivens* doctrine in subsequent cases).
283. Bandes, *supra* note 136, at 338.
284. 462 U.S. 367, 368 (1983).
285. *Id.* at 369–71 (reporting the facts of the case).
286. *Id.* at 372 (footnote omitted).
287. *Id.* at 373 (stating that Congress had provided a less than complete remedy). Congress had made available to federal employees like Bush a number of civil service remedies, including through the Federal Employee Appeals Authority and the Civil Service Commission's Appeals Review Board. *Id.* at 369–71 (walking through the different administrative remedial proceedings available to and attempted by Bush).
288. *Id.* at 385–86.
289. *Id.* at 389.

290. *Id.* at 388.
291. *Id.* at 389.
292. *Id.* at 378.
293. *Id.* at 377–78 (summarizing the *Carlson* holding and emphasizing the two factors); *see* Bandes, *supra* note 136, at 297 ("[T]he *Bivens* Court was willing to defer either where a congressional remedy, which was meant to be exclusive *and* was found equally effective, existed, or, even where no such remedy existed where there were factors counseling judicial hesitation.").
294. Bandes, *supra* note 136, at 297.
295. *Id.*
296. *See generally* 487 U.S. 412 (1988) (refusing to apply a *Bivens* remedy to a violation of the Fifth Amendment).
297. *Id.* at 414–20.
298. *Id.* at 437 (Brennan, J., dissenting). It "did not even purport to redress the constitutional injuries claimed." Bandes, *supra* note 136, at 297. Justice O'Connor stated, "Whether or not we believe that its response was the best response, Congress is the body charged with making the inevitable compromises required in the design of a massive and complex welfare benefits program. Congress has discharged that responsibility to the extent that it affects the case before us, and we see no legal basis that would allow us to revise its decision." *Schweiker*, 487 U.S. at 429 (majority opinion) (citation omitted).
299. *Schweiker*, 487 U.S. at 423 (emphasis added).
300. *Id.* at 427 (quoting Bush v. Lucas, 462 U.S. 367, 390 (1983)).
301. Ziglar v. Abbasi, 137 S. Ct. 1843 (2017).
302. *Id.* at 1853–54. Subjects of these 9/11 detention policies were subjected to twenty-four hours of light, little to no opportunity to be outside of their cells, no access to communication outside, no access to basic hygiene products, and faced constant strip searches any time they were moved. *Id.*
303. *Id.* at 1856.
304. *Id.*
305. *Id.* at 1857 (quoting *Bush*, 462 U.S. at 380).
306. *See id.* at 1856–57 (answering that most often Congress should decide whether to provide damage remedies for constitutional violations); Schweiker v. Chilicky, 487 U.S. 412, 423 (1988) (holding that when Congress has provided what it thinks to be an adequate remedy for constitutional violations, the courts should not imply their own damages); *Bush*, 462 U.S. at 377–78 (noting that Congress can provide an alternative remedy in a myriad of ways and making the existence of a remedial statute, regardless of its sufficiency, a factor counseling against the courts' application of a *Bivens* remedy). The Supreme Court denied a *Bivens* remedy in another context in early 2020. *See* Hernandez v. Mesa, 140 S. Ct. 735, 746–49 (2020) (denying the action for alleged violations of Fourth and Fifth Amendment rights when a US Border Patrol Agent shot and killed a Mexican national on Mexican soil partially on the ground that "Congress has repeatedly declined to authorize the award of damages [against federal officials] for injury inflicted outside [US] borders").

307. *See* Michael Coenen, *Right-Remedy Equilibration and the Asymmetric Entrenchment of Legal Entitlements*, 61 B.C. L. Rev. 129, 136–36 (2020) (discussing that today the Court has made the remedy recognized in *Bivens* virtually nonexistent to the rights it attempts to serve).
308. *See* section 7.11, *supra* (discussing the Court's deferential treatment of implied statutory remedies).
309. Thomas W. Merrill, *The Common Law Powers of Federal Courts*, 52 U. Chi. L. Rev. 1, 48–49 (1985). *Contra Bush*, 462 U.S. at 377–78 (developing a deferential attitude toward Congress in the area of implied constitutional remedies).
310. *See* Davis v. Passman, 442 U.S. 228, 241 (1979) (emphasizing that "the question of who may enforce a *statutory* right is fundamentally different from the question of who may enforce a right that is protected by the Constitution"); Bivens v. Six Unknown Named Agents of Fed. Bureau of Narcotics, 403 U.S. 388, 407 (1971) (Harlan, J., concurring) (distinguishing between congressional and judicial roles in vindicating constitutional rights).
311. Bandes, *supra* note 136, at 338.
312. Merrill, *supra* note 309, at 49 n.209.
313. *Id.* (quoting *Bush*, 462 U.S. at 385) (citing Middlesex Cnty. Sewerage Auth. v. Nat'l Sea Clammers Ass'n, 453 U.S. 1, 13–15 (1981)).
314. *See* Ziglar v. Abbasi, 137 S. Ct. 1843, 1857 (2017); Schweiker v. Chilicky, 487 U.S. 413, 423 (1988).
315. Bandes, *supra* note 136, at 303.
316. *Id.* "To uphold the rights of individuals before the Court, the Court must prevent encroachment on those rights by the political branches." *Id.* at 311.
317. Martin H. Redish, The Federal Courts in the Political Order: Judicial Jurisdiction and American Political Theory 39 (1991) (footnote omitted).
318. *See* U.S. Const. art. I, § 7, cl. 2 ("Every Bill which shall have passed the House of Representatives and the Senate, shall, before it become a Law, be presented to the President of the United States; If he approve he shall sign it").
319. Bandes, *supra* note 136, at 313.
320. The Federalist No. 78, *supra* note 15, at 464 (Alexander Hamilton).
321. *Id.* at 469.

INDEX

For the benefit of digital users, indexed terms that span two pages (e.g., 52–53) may, on occasion, appear on only one of those pages.

"actual malice" standard, 264n.141
adequate representation
  alignment of interests, 99
  class actions, in, 21, 23, 99, 100–1, 222n.73, 223–24n.88
  contradictory liability and, 101
  "day-in-court" ideal and, 81–82
    adequate representation and, 20
    preexisting understanding, 81–82
    special procedures, 81–82
  defining, 99–101
  double liability and, 101
  multidistrict litigation, in, 62
  sufficient incentive to litigate, 99–100, 251n.155
  sufficient resources, 100
  virtual representation and, 99–101
adjudicatory bias
  generally, 142–43
  associative prejudice, 144–45, 151
  coercive interference, 143, 259n.39
  disassociative prejudice, 144–45, 151
  incentivized decision-making, 143–44, 259n.39
administrative law
  generally, xxii
  federal adjudicatory process, 146–48
    adjudicatory role of agencies, 147–48
    investigatory role of agencies, 147
    prosecutorial role of agencies, 147
Administrative Law Judges (ALJ), 146, 147, 148, 157
Administrative Procedure Act (APA)
  adjudicatory role of agencies and, 146, 147
  overlapping roles of agencies and, 148, 153–54
  presumption of compliance with due process, 156, 161
  state administrative law, inapplicable to, 155
administrative state
  generally, 164, 214
  administrator integrity, 15–17
    administrative state and, 16–17

    Chevron deference and, 17
    financial incentive and, 16, 220n.45
    misguided faith in, 15–17
    presumption of, 16
  avoiding due process problems in
    generally, 157–58
    adjudicatory neutrality, 158–59
    constitutional challenges to agency authority, 137–38, 140–41, 158–59
  correcting due process problems in, 137–38, 157
  federal adjudicatory process, 146–48
    adjudicatory role of agencies, 147–48
    investigatory role of agencies, 147
    prosecutorial role of agencies, 147
  "First Amendment due process"
    generally, 136–37
  flawed defense of administrative adjudication, 152–56
  neutral adjudication and, 148–52
    adjudicatory role of agencies violating, 148–51, 152–56
    agency employees, 150
    associative prejudice, 151
    cognitive dissonance, 157–58
    constitutional challenges to agency authority, 158–59
    disassociative prejudice, 151
    ex ante rules, 138
    insufficiency of, 211
    motivated reasoning, 151–52, 157–58
    overlapping roles of agencies violating, 149–51, 152–56
    overprotection of, 138
    procedural due process, 139
    punitive authority of administrative agencies, 152–56
  procedural due process and
    generally, 146
    failure of administrative adjudication to satisfy, 139, 152
    neutral adjudication and, 139

administrative state (*cont.*)
  property rights and, 148–49, 150, 160–61
  punitive authority of administrative
    agencies, 152–56
administrator integrity, 15–17
  administrative state and, 16–17
  Chevron deference and, 17
  financial incentive and, 16, 220n.45
  misguided faith in, 15–17
  presumption of, 16
adversary liberal democracy
  generally, 1
  altruism and, 215n.4
  autonomy and, 60
  common interests in, 6
  communitarian democracy versus, 2–3
  competition between interests, role of, 2
  conflict management in, xvi, 5–6
  constitutional remedies and, 167, 206
  "day-in-court" ideal and, 68, 75, 77–78, 86–87
  dignitary theory and, 33
  individual interests in, xvi, xix, 1–2, 18–19
  liberal democracy versus, xx, 2–3
  libertarianism versus, 216n.29
  liberty interest and, 11–12, 23, 27, 39
  mediation of conflict in, 3–4
  meta-liberties in, xvi
  mistrust of authority in, 4
  multidistrict litigation and, 71
  neutral adjudication in, 135–42, 210
  paternalism as incompatible with, 85–86
  pluralism and, 3–4, 209, 215n.8
  possessive individualism and, 3–4
  procedural due process and, xv, xx, xxiii, 209
  scholarship on, 4–5
  selection of counsel in, 110
  self-interest and, 3, 6
  skeptical optimism in, xvi, xx, 6, 18–19
  utilitarianism and, 67–68
advisory opinions, 184, 267n.35
Aerojet, 95
All Writs Act, 165–66, 265n.1, 265n.2
Amendments to Constitution, 266n.21
American Law Institute (ALI), 54
antitrust law, 46–47
APA. *See* Administrative Procedure Act (APA)
appeals. *See* judicial review
appellate jurisdiction, 195, 277n.203, 277–78n.216
Article III standing, 124–25
Articles of Confederation, 170
asbestos litigation, 253n.18

association, freedom of, 115–16
associative prejudice, 144–45, 151
attorney compensation
  common benefit fees, 54–55
  contingent fee attorneys
    governmental use of (*see* contingent fee attorneys, governmental use of)
    private litigation, in, 117–18
  multidistrict litigation, 54–55, 64, 237–38n.148
autonomy
  adversary liberal democracy and, 60
  Bill of Rights and, 87
  class actions and, 44
  "day-in-court" ideal and, 59–61, 86–87
  libertarianism distinguished, 87
  multidistrict litigation and, 44, 71
  paternalism versus, 43–44, 59–61, 85
  procedural due process and, 43–44
  process-based autonomy, 87
  public-private distinction and, 115–16
  selection of counsel and, 62
  substantive autonomy, 87
  utilitarianism versus, 67–68

Bandes, Susan, 185, 279n.236
Barnett, Kent, 263n.123
Bentham, Jeremy, 36–37
Berenson, Steven, 121–22
biased assimilation, 145
biased search, 145
bicameralism, 3
Bill of Rights. *See also specific Amendment*
  generally, 3
  autonomy and, 87
  due process compared, 8
  enforceability of, 167–68
  liberal democracy and, 7–8
  limits on political branches, 169
  unenumerated rights and, 178
Bingham, John, 36
Bivens doctrine
  generally, 168–69
  Congress, deference to, 200–1, 203–4
  construction of, 196–98
  Eighth Amendment and, 197–98
  employment discrimination, extension to, 201–2
  extension of, 201–2
  Fifth Amendment and, 197–98, 203–4
  First Amendment and, 202–3
  Fourth Amendment and, 197–98, 200, 203–4
  freedom of expression and, 202–3

historical background, 197–98
imitations of, 202–4
origins of, 199–201
Blackstone, William, 36
Bone, Robert, 246–47n.70
Border Patrol, 282n.306
Brennan, William J., 160, 200
Breyer, Stephen G., 29
Bureau of Prisons, 123
Bush, George W., 253n.18

censorship, 159–61
Chevron, 143
Chevron deference, 17
"chilling effect," 160–61, 162, 264n.142
choses in action, 19–20, 23, 41, 97
Churchill, Winston, 172
civic republicanism, 120–21
Civil Rights Act of 1964, 201, 252n.4
Civil Rights Act of 1991, 252n.173
Civil Service Commission, 281n.287
Clark, Charles, 164
class actions, 21–23
  adequate representation in, 21, 23, 99, 100–1, 222n.73, 223–24n.88
  autonomy and, 44
  common questions of law or fact, 232n.73
  individual actions versus, 21–23
  indivisible relief and, 21–22
  mandatory class actions, 21
  multidistrict litigation compared, 42–43, 61, 232n.73
  opt-out alternative, 22–23, 42, 61
  paternalism and, 44, 85–86
  "procedural collectivism," as, 41, 72
  relief appropriate for class as whole, 223n.82
  res judicata in, 21
  separate actions not preferred, 76–77, 222n.77, 223n.81
  threat to due process values in, 72
  virtual representation and, 103
Clayton Act, 235n.119
coercive interference, 143, 259n.39
Coffee, John, 113–14
cognitive dissonance, 157–58
Coke, Lord, 36, 128, 169–70
collateral estoppel
  "day-in-court" ideal and, 19–20, 75
  preclusion and, 78
  presumption of fair procedure and, 16–17
Commerce Clause, 274n.160
commercial speech, 138–39
common benefit fees, 54–55

communitarian democracy, adversary liberal democracy versus, 2–3
compulsory counterclaims, 88
compulsory joinder, 103–4, 105
conflicts of interest
  concurrent conflicts of interest, 241n.205
  multidistrict litigation, in, 62–63
Congress
  Bivens doctrine, deference to Congress, 200–1, 203–4
  constitutional common law, Congressional authority over, 186–88, 189–90
  constitutional remedies, Congressional authority over, 165–66, 180–82, 183, 185, 206
  federal jurisdiction, Congressional power to control, 191–92
  Supreme Court, authority regarding, 186–87, 194–95
constitutional common law
  generally, 168–69, 275n.175
  Congressional authority over, 186–88, 189–90
  federalism and, 188–89
  incoherence of, 186–91
  judicial review and, 187, 188–89, 190
  separation of powers and, 188–89
  Supreme Court and, 187
constitutional fact, doctrine of, 158, 159, 163–64, 263n.126
constitutional remedies
  generally, xxii, 165–69, 206–7, 214
  adversary liberal democracy and, 167, 206
  Bivens doctrine (see *Bivens* doctrine)
  Congressional authority over, 165–66, 180–82, 183, 185, 206
  constitutional common law
    generally, 168–69, 275n.175
    Congressional authority over, 186–88, 189–90
    federalism and, 188–89
    incoherence of, 186–91
    judicial review and, 187, 188–89, 190
    separation of powers and, 188–89
    Supreme Court and, 187
  constitutional directives, intersection with, 173–74
  counterarguments, 168–69, 185–86
  countermajoritarian constitutionalism and, 169–73
  generally, 168, 207
  binding nature of constitutional rights, 170–71

constitutional remedies (*cont.*)
    enforceability of constitutional rights, 167–68
        judicial review, 168, 169–70, 171–72, 269–70n.71
        neutral adjudication, 170, 171–72
    existing theory, inadequacy of, 180–85
        generally, 168
        Congressional authority, regarding, 180–82, 183, 185
        enforceability of rights, regarding, 182–83
        federal jurisdiction, regarding, 184
        judicial authority, regarding, 183, 184–85
    federal jurisdiction, Congressional power to control
        generally, 191–92
        appellate jurisdiction, 195, 277n.203, 277–78n.216
        creation of lower courts, 195–96
        judicial power, limitation of, 192–93
        limitations on, 194–96
        remedial authority distinguished, 193
        separation of powers and, 194–96
    implied constitutional remedies
        Bivens doctrine (see *Bivens* doctrine)
        implied statutory remedies versus, 204–6
    injunctive relief and, 185
    judicial review
        generally, 181, 207
        arguments against, 267n.36
        constitutional common law and, 187, 188–89, 190
        countermajoritarian constitutionalism and, 168, 169–70, 171–72, 269–70n.71
        "First Amendment due process" and, 139, 162
    private right of action, 200
    separation of powers and, 185
    state court authority, 165
    status as constitutional law, 166–67, 173, 190, 207
    statutory remedies versus, 180–81, 190, 191, 198
    textualism and, 174–80
        due process, 175
        facilitative nontextualism, 175–77, 178–80
        lack of specific remedial language, 174–75
        presumption against ineffectiveness, 176–77
        supplemental nontextualism, 177
contempt, 144–45, 149–50
contingent fee attorneys, governmental use of
    generally, xxii, 109, 132–33, 213–14
    civil litigation versus criminal prosecution, 112, 121–22, 130–31
    constitutional implications, 127–32
        "adversarial neutrality" and, 129–30
        civil litigation versus criminal prosecution, 130–31
        constitutional argument in perspective, 127–28
        "continued control" alternative, 132
        neutral adjudication, 128–32
        public interest and, 130
    dangers of, 109, 111–12
    ethical limitations, 118–19, 122, 131–32
    formal prohibition against contingent fees, 119–20
    growth of, 113–14
    hourly billing compared, 257n.82
    liberal democracy and, 114–16, 117, 123–24, 127–28
    "libertarian paradox," 126–27
    mass torts, 113, 253n.18
    pluralism and, 120–21
    political limitations, 118–19, 131–32
    political theory of public-private distinction, 115–16
    private litigation compared, 109–10, 111, 112, 117–18
    prophylactic restrictions on prosecutorial motivation, 111–12, 119–20
    public choice theory and, 119–21
    public interest and, 120–21, 122–24, 130
    public policy implications, 114–15
    qui tam actions compared, 124–26
    rationale for, 113–14
        financial advantages, 113
        political advantages, 113
        state legislatures, bypassing, 113–14
    social contract and, 111–12, 114–16, 121–22, 123–24, 129–30
    state action requirement and, 122–24
"continued control," 132
contract non-renewal, 33
contradictory liability
    adequate representation and, 101
    indivisible relief and, 94–96
    injunctive relief and, 94–95
    virtual representation and, 94–96, 105–6, 252n.179
Coordinating Committee for Multidistrict Litigation, 46
Correa, Rafael, 143
cost avoidance, virtual representation and, 82–83

countermajoritarian constitutionalism, 169–73
  generally, 168, 207
  binding nature of constitutional rights and, 170–71
  enforceability of constitutional rights and, 167–68
  judicial review and, 168, 169–70, 171–72, 269–70n.71
  neutral adjudication and, 170, 171–72
cruel and unusual punishment, 202

damages
  implied statutory remedy, as, 198–99
  indivisible relief distinguished, 77
Dana, David, 113–14
"day-in-court" ideal, 18–20
  generally, xx, 12, 18–20, 209–10
  adequate representation and, 81–82
    generally, 20
    preexisting understanding, 81–82
    special procedures, 81–82
  adversary liberal democracy and, 68, 75, 77–78, 86–87
  autonomy and, 59–61, 86–87
  balancing approach, 88
  collateral estoppel and, 19–20, 75
  constitutional theory, in
    generally, 83
    procedural due process, 83–86
  exceptions to, 80–81
  individual interests and, 21
  indivisible relief and, 92
  limitations on, 88
  multidistrict litigation undermining, 57–58, 61–66
  paternalism and, 59–61, 209–10
  political theory, in
    generally, 83
    procedural due process, 83–86
  preclusion and, 19–20
  privity and, 78
  res judicata and, 19–20, 75
  rights entailed by, 57–58
  virtual representation versus, 76, 82–83
Declaratory Judgment Act, 162–63
declaratory relief, 162–63, 185, 198
defamation, 264n.141
Dellinger, Walter, 183, 184, 272n.120
departmentalism, 267n.36
dignity theory of due process, 32–34
  adversary liberal democracy and, 33
  contract non-renewal and, 33
  equality in, 32–33

noninstrumental rationale, 141
  participation in, 32
  privacy in, 32–33
  thin rationality in, 32–34
  utilitarianism versus, 58–59
disassociative prejudice, 144–45, 151
discovery in multidistrict litigation, 71–72
Dorf, Michael, 124, 126
double liability
  adequate representation and, 101
  indivisible relief and, 93–94
  interpleader and, 250n.129
  virtual representation and, 93–94, 103–5
Douglas, William O., 178, 270–71n.86
Due Process Clauses. *See specific topic*

Ecuador, coercive interference in, 143
Eighth Amendment
  Bivens doctrine and, 197–98
  cruel and unusual punishment, 202
elected state judges, 17–18
employment discrimination, 106, 201–2
Equal Protection Clause, 115–16
evidentiary rules, altering substantive law through, 24
Exceptions Clause, 195, 196
exclusionary rule, 187, 199–200, 228n.182, 280n.251, 281n.275
executive power, 180, 257n.73
expression, freedom of. *See* freedom of expression

facilitative nontextualism, 175–77, 178–80
factions, xvi, 5–6, 119–20, 215n.7
Fallon, Richard H., 53–54, 182–83, 184
false advertising, 138–39, 162–64
False Claims Act, 124, 256n.69
Federal Aviation Administration (FAA), 79–80
federal common law, 187, 274n.148, 274n.151
Federal Employee Appeals Authority, 281n.287
federalism
  generally, 3
  constitutional common law and, 188–89
The Federalist Papers
  factions and, xvi, 5–6, 215n.7
  judicial power and, 267n.34
  legislative power and, 266–67n.32
  neutral adjudication and, 266n.15
  tyranny and, 170, 171, 266n.25
federal jurisdiction
  Congressional power to control
    generally, 191–92

federal jurisdiction (*cont.*)
  appellate jurisdiction, 195, 277n.203, 277–78n.216
  creation of lower courts, 195–96
  judicial power, limitation of, 192–93
  limitations on, 194–96
  remedial authority distinguished, 193
  separation of powers and, 194–96
  constitutional remedies and, 184
  federal question jurisdiction, 163–64
  injunctive relief and, 193
  original jurisdiction, 195
federal question jurisdiction, 163–64
Federal Rules of Civil Procedure
  generally, 164
  adequate representation under, 62, 99, 241n.201
  class actions and
    adequate representation, 222n.73, 223–24n.88
    common questions of law or fact, 232n.73
    opt-out alternative, 42, 61
    relief appropriate for class as whole, 223n.82
    separate actions not preferred, 76–77, 222n.77, 223n.81
  compulsory joinder, 103–4, 105
  indivisible relief and, 92–93
  interpleader, 103, 250n.129
  intervention, 103, 105
Federal Tort Claims Act (FTCA), 202, 281n.278
Federal Trade Commission (FTC)
  adjudicatory role of, 147–48
  danger of bias in, 152–53
  false advertising and, 138–39, 162–64
  overlapping roles of, 147, 150–51
Fifth Amendment
  Bivens doctrine and, 197–98, 203–4
  Due Process Clause (*see specific topic*)
  exclusionary rule, 187
  false advertising and, 162–63
  privacy and, 178
First Amendment
  Bivens doctrine and, 202–3
  defamation and, 264n.141
  "First Amendment due process" (*see* "First Amendment due process")
  freedom of association, 115–16
  freedom of expression (*see* freedom of expression)
  privacy and, 178
  self-determination and, 86–87, 247n.84

"First Amendment due process"
  generally, 136, 159, 164
  administrative procedure and, 161–64
    constitutionality, inability of agencies to determine, 161–62
    deterrence and, 162
    judicial review, insufficiency of, 162
  administrative state generally, 136–37
  censorship and, 159–61
  "chilling effect" and, 160–61, 162, 264n.142
  constitutional challenges to agency authority, 140–41
  failure of administrative adjudication to satisfy, 140
  false advertising and, 138–39, 162–64
  federal question jurisdiction and, 163–64
  judicial review and, 139, 162
  motivated reasoning and, 151–52
  origins of, 159–61
  preliminary restraint on administrative adjudication and, 140–41
  prior restraint and, 159–61
  protection in addition to procedural due process, 138
  special status of freedom of expression and, 160–61
Food and Drug Administration (FDA), 138–39, 148, 258n.7
Fourteenth Amendment
  Due Process Clause (*see specific topic*)
  Equal Protection Clause, 115–16
Fourth Amendment
  Bivens doctrine and, 197–98, 200, 203–4
  exclusionary rule, 187, 199–200, 228n.182, 280n.251, 281n.275
  privacy and, 178
  unreasonable searches and seizures, 197–98, 199, 280n.249
Frankfurter, Felix, 135, 175–76
freedom of association, 115–16
freedom of expression
  Bivens doctrine and, 202–3
  commercial speech, 138–39
  content-based restrictions, 219n.25, 224n.105
  facilitative nontextualism and, 178–79
  "First Amendment due process" (*see* "First Amendment due process")
  incitement to violence and, 224n.105
  procedural due process compared, 8–9, 10–11, 26
  self-realization and, 7–8
  skeptical optimism and, 7–8
  strict scrutiny and, 26

Freedom of Information Act (FOIA), 79–80
freezing assets
   presumption of fair procedure and, 28–29
   probable cause and, 28–29
Friendly, Henry, 187
front-to-back constitutionalism, 10–11
FTC. *See* Federal Trade Commission (FTC)
FTC Act, 148
Fuller, Lon, 95

Garner, Bryan, 175–76
Ginsburg, Ruth Bader, 80–81
Green, Bruce, 121–22

habeas corpus, 173, 268n.47
Hamilton, Alexander
   constitutional remedies, on, 206
   due process, on, 36
   judicial power, on, 267n.34
   neutral adjudication, on, 14, 170, 266n.15
   tyranny, on, 170, 171, 266n.25
Hand, Learned, 227n.173
Harlan, John Marshall, 200–1, 280n.263
Harrick, Greg, 79–80
Harrison, John, 181–82
Hart, Henry, 95, 180–82, 192
Health and Human Services Department (DHHS), 148, 261n.78
Heyburn, John G. II, 241–42n.210
historical approach to due process, 34–36
   infrequency of use, 34–35
   personal jurisdiction and, 34–35
   problems with, 34–36
   Seventh Amendment and, 35–36
Hobbes, Thomas
   pluralism and, 3–4
   possessive individualism and, 3–4
Holderman, James F., 69–70

implied constitutional remedies
   Bivens doctrine (see *Bivens* doctrine)
   implied statutory remedies versus, 204–6
implied statutory remedies
   generally, 198–99
   damages as, 198–99
   factors considered, 199
   implied constitutional remedies versus, 204–6
incentivized decision-making, 143–44, 259n.39
incitement to violence, 224n.105
inconsistent liability
   indivisible relief and, 96–98
   injunctive relief and, 96
   virtual representation and, 96–98, 251n.154

indivisible relief
   class actions and, 21–22
   damages distinguished, 77
   "day-in-court" ideal and, 92
   defined, 88–89
   injunctive relief and, 88–89
   problems with
      generally, 92–93
      contradictory liability, 94–96
      double liability, 93–94
      inconsistent liability, 96–98
   virtual representation and, 88–92
      generally, 76–78
      alignment of interests, 90
      legal relationship between parties, 91–92
      res judicata, 90
injunctive relief
   constitutional remedies and, 185
   contradictory liability and, 94–95
   federal jurisdiction and, 193
   inconsistent liability and, 96
   indivisible relief and, 88–89
   property rights and, 97–98
interpleader, 103, 250n.129
intervention, 103, 105

Jackson, Andrew, 173, 268n.45
Jay, John, 267n.35
Jefferson, Thomas, 267n.35
judicial independence. *See* neutral adjudication
Judicial Panel on Multidistrict Litigation, 46–49, 53–54, 55–56, 61, 70, 241–42n.210
judicial review
   generally, 181, 207
   arguments against, 267n.36
   constitutional common law and, 187, 188–89, 190
   countermajoritarian constitutionalism and, 168, 169–70, 171–72, 269–70n.71
   "First Amendment due process" and, 139, 162
jurisdiction
   federal jurisdiction (*see* federal jurisdiction)
   original jurisdiction, 195
   personal jurisdiction and, 34–35
   "tag jurisdiction," 34–35, 226n.150

Kagan, Elena, 28
Kant, Immanuel, 115–16, 248n.88

labor disputes, 192–93, 276n.194
legislative deception, 23–25
   defined, 218–19n.19

legislative deception (*cont.*)
　evidentiary rules, altering substantive law through, 24
　legitimacy of democracy and, 11, 12
　paternity actions and, 24–25
　procedural rules, altering substantive law through, 24–25
　rule-obedience principle and, 23–24
legitimacy of democracy, 10–11
Levinson, Sanford, 122, 256n.57
liberal democracy
　adversary liberal democracy versus, xx, 2–3
　Bill of Rights and, 7–8
　consensus in, 5–6
　contingent fee attorneys, governmental use of, 114–16, 117, 123–24, 127–28
　goals of, 4
libertarianism
　adversary liberal democracy versus, 216n.29
　autonomy distinguished, 87
　contingent fee attorneys, governmental use of, 126–27
"libertarian paradox," 126–27
liberty interest
　adversary liberal democracy and, 11–12, 23, 27, 39
　criminal prosecution and, 121–22, 130–31
　meta-liberties, xvi
　participation in democratic process, xvi, 43–44
　utilitarianism and, 84–85
Lincoln, Abraham, 173
"litigation capitalism," 68–69
lower courts, 195–96

Madison, James
　factions, on, xvi, 5–6, 119–20, 215n.7
　judicial review, on, 281n.272
　legislative power, on, 266–67n.32
　tyranny, on, 170, 266n.25
Magna Carta, 36
Mansbridge, Jane, 4–5
Manual for Complex Litigation, 233n.83, 234–35n.104
Marquess of Queensberry Rules, 2
Marshall, John, 169, 171, 173, 175–76, 179, 277–78n.216
Marshall, Lawrence, 128
Mashaw, Jerry, 32–33, 248n.88
massage parlors, 91–92
mass torts
　contingent fee attorneys, governmental use of, 113, 253n.18
　multidistrict litigation, 46–47

MDL. *See* multidistrict litigation
Meltzer, Daniel, 181–83, 184, 188
meta-liberties, xvi
Mikva, Abner, 122
Mill, John Stuart, 3
Model Rules of Professional Conduct, 62–63
Monaghan, Henry, 159–60, 168–69, 186–91, 274n.148, 274n.160
motivated reasoning, 145, 151–52, 157–58, 259n.39
Mott, Rodney, 227n.173
multidistrict litigation
　generally, xxi, 41–46, 72–73, 211–12
　adequate representation in, 62
　adversary liberal democracy and, 71
　attorney compensation in, 54–55, 64, 237–38n.148
　autonomy and, 44, 71
　bellwether trials, 52–53, 64–65, 69, 235–36n.120, 236n.126, 236n.127
　class actions compared, 42–43, 61, 232n.73
　committees of counsel, 50
　common benefit fees, 54–55
　conflicts of interest in, 62–63
　consolidation of cases, 48, 49, 55–56
　constitutional baseline, 57–58
　constitutional challenges to, lack of, 73
　constitutional problems with, 45–46
　constitutional salvageability of, 70–72
　"day-in-court" ideal, undermining, 57–58, 61–66
　discovery in, 71–72
　due process difficulties in
　　generally, 55–56
　　attorney-client relationship lacking, 63–64
　　attorney compensation and, 64
　　individual interests diminished, 64–65
　　selection of counsel limited, 62–64
　foundations of due process theory and, 58–61
　historical background, 46–47
　individual interests diminished in, 43, 55–56, 64–65, 70
　initiating, 48–49
　lead counsel in, 50, 63–64, 69, 71
　liaison counsel in, 50
　management of, 49–52, 71
　mass torts, 46–47
　mechanics generally, 47–48
　opt-out alternative, 45
　paternalism and, 61, 62–63, 71
　pretrial proceedings, transfer of cases limited to, 42–43, 45, 46–48, 51–52, 55–56, 61, 64–65, 69, 213

prevalence of use, 46–47, 236n.133
"procedural collectivism," as, 41, 72
property rights and, 43, 56
selection of counsel in, 62–64, 212
settlement in, 53–54, 213, 238n.151
steering committees in, 47, 49–52, 62, 69, 71
structure of, 46–47
"tag-along" cases, 49, 51, 233n.87
threat to due process values in, 72
transfer of cases, 46–49, 55–56, 65
trial counsel in, 50
trial packages, 52–53
utilitarianism and
  generally, 45–46, 66
  accurate decision-making, 68–69
  autonomy versus, 67–68
  government interest in reducing litigation, 69–70
  Mathews-Doehr test, 66–70
Multidistrict Litigation Statute, 46
Multidistrict Rules of Procedure, 48–49

Necessary and Proper Clause, 175–76
neutral adjudication
  administrative state and, 148–52 (*see also* administrative state)
  adversary liberal democracy, in, 135–42, 210
  associative prejudice and, 144–45
  coercive interference and, 143
  contingent fee attorneys, governmental use of, 128–32
    generally, 128
    civil litigation versus criminal prosecution, 130–31
    constitutional argument in perspective, 127–28
    judge and jury, neutrality of not sufficient, 129
    public interest and, 130
  countermajoritarian constitutionalism and, 170, 171–72
  disassociative prejudice and, 144–45
  financial interest and, 141–42, 143–44
  historical background, 141–42
  importance of, 135–36
  incentivized decision-making and, 143–44
  overprotection of judicial independence, 210–11
  procedural due process and, 13–15
    generally, 12, 13
    administrative state, 139
    Article III protections, 14–15, 120, 168, 170, 210, 267n.37
    salary protection, 14, 120, 168, 170, 210, 267n.37
    structural independence as constitutional minimum, 13–15
    tenure protection, 14, 120, 168, 170, 210, 267n.37
    term limits, 219n.29
  recusal and, 257n.87, 261n.89
9/11 attacks, detention policies, 203–4, 282n.302
Norris-LaGuardia Act, 193, 276n.194

obscenity, 138–39
O'Connor, Sandra Day, 203, 282n.298
"off-label" advertising, 138–39
originalist approach to due process, 34–36
  infrequency of use, 34–35
  personal jurisdiction and, 34–35
  problems with, 34–36
  Seventh Amendment and, 35–36
original jurisdiction, 195

pardons, 194
participation in democratic process, xvi, 43–44, 87, 248n.88
paternalism
  adversary liberal democracy, as incompatible with, 85–86
  autonomy versus, 43–44, 59–61, 85
  class actions and, 44, 85–86
  "day-in-court" ideal and, 59–61, 209–10
  multidistrict litigation and, 61, 62–63, 71
  procedural due process and, 19, 43–44
paternity actions, 24–25
personal jurisdiction, 34–35
picketing, 192
pluralism
  adversary liberal democracy and, 3–4, 209, 215n.8
  contingent fee attorneys, governmental use of, 120–21
  public-private distinction and, 115–16
popular constitutionalism, 267n.36
possessive individualism, 3–4
preclusion
  collateral estoppel and, 78
  "day-in-court" ideal and, 19–20
  procedural due process and, 19–20
  res judicata and, 78
  virtual representation (*see* virtual representation)
prejudgment attachment, 67

presumption of fair procedure, 27–31
    generally, 26
    balancing test, 28
    collateral estoppel and, 16–17
    deprivation of constitutionally protected
        interests of others, 29–31
    freezing assets and, 28–29
    lack of alternatives, 27–29
    litigant autonomy and, 30–31
    rebutting, 26–31
    urgency, 27–29
Principles of the Law of Aggregate Litigation
    (ALI), 54
prior restraint, 159–61
privacy, 178, 270–71n.86
privity, 78
probable cause, freezing assets and, 28–29
"procedural collectivism," 41, 72–73. *See also*
    class actions; multidistrict litigation
procedural due process
    generally, 7, 38–39
    adequate representation and, 20
    administrative state and
        generally, 146
        failure of administrative adjudication to
            satisfy, 139, 152
        neutral adjudication and, 139
    administrator integrity and, 15–17
        administrative state and, 16–17
        Chevron deference and, 17
        financial incentive and, 16, 220n.45
        misguided faith in, 15–17
        presumption of, 16
    adversary liberal democracy and, xv, xx,
        xxiii, 209
    alternative models of
        generally, 32
        dignitary theory, 32–34 (*see also* dignitary
            theory of due process)
        historical approach, 34–36 (*see also*
            historical approach to due process)
        originalism, 34–36 (*see also* originalist
            approach to due process)
        utilitarianism, 36–38 (*see also*
            utilitarianism)
    application of, 11–12
    autonomy and, 43–44
    balancing test, 31–32
    class actions and, 21–23 (*see also* class
        actions)
    collateral estoppel and, 19–20
    collectivist perspective on, 9
    conditional protection, as, 135
    "day-in-court" ideal, 18–20 (*see also* "day-in-
        court" ideal)
    elected state judges and, 17–18
    "First Amendment due process" offering
        protection in addition to, 138
    freedom of expression compared, 8–9, 10–
        11, 26
    front-to-back constitutionalism and, 10–11
    functionalist perspective on, 9
    individual rights and, 12
    instrumental rationale, 141
    law of judgments and, 18–20
    legislative deception and, 23–25
        defined, 218–19n.19
        evidentiary rules, altering substantive law
            through, 24
        legitimacy of democracy and, 11, 12
        paternity actions and, 24–25
        procedural rules, altering substantive law
            through, 24–25
        rule-obedience principle and, 23–24
    legitimacy of democracy and, 10–11
    necessity of, 9
    neutral adjudication and, 13–15 (*see also*
        neutral adjudication)
    noninstrumental rationale, 141
    outcome-based theories, 84
    paternalism and, 19, 43–44
    preclusion and, 19–20
    presumption of fair procedure and, 27–31
        (*see also* presumption of fair procedure)
    process-based theories, 84–85
    res judicata and, 19–20
    skeptical optimism and, 7–10
    social contract and, 11, 135
    utilitarian approach to, 36–38 (*see also*
        utilitarianism)
procedural rules, altering substantive law
    through, 24–25
process-based autonomy, 87
property rights
    administrative state and, 148–49, 150, 160–61
    choses in action as, 19–20, 23, 41, 97
    freezing assets
        presumption of fair procedure and, 28–29
        probable cause and, 28–29
    injunctive relief and, 97–98
    multidistrict litigation and, 43, 56
prosecutors
    contingent fee attorneys as (*see* contingent fee
        attorneys, governmental use of)
    ethical limitations on, 118–19, 131–32
    political limitations on, 118–19, 131–32

prophylactic restrictions on prosecutorial motivation, 111–12, 119–20
public choice theory, 119–21

qui tam actions
  defined, 124
  financial interest in, 125, 257n.71
  governmental use of contingent fee attorneys compared, 124–26
  separation of powers and, 125–26
  tradition and, 125–26

recusal, 257n.87, 261n.89
relators. See *qui tam* actions
Religious Freedom Restoration Act of 1998, 274n.147
representational standing, 124–25
res judicata
  class actions, in, 21
  "day-in-court" ideal and, 19–20, 75
  defined, 222n.71
  preclusion and, 78
  virtual representation and, 90
Roberts, John G., 29
Rubin, Edward, 23
rule-obedience principle, 23–24

Scalia, Antonin, 34–35, 175–76
Schrock, Thomas, 188–90, 275n.173, 275n.176
Securities and Exchange Commission (SEC)
  adjudicatory role of, 148
  danger of bias in, 152–53
  funding of, 156
  overlapping roles of, 147, 150–51
Securities Exchange Act of 1934, 279n.238, 279n.241, 279–80n.246
Securities Litigation Reform Act of 1995, 224n.104
self-determination, 86–87, 247n.84
self-realization, 7–8
separation of powers
  generally, 3
  Congressional power to control federal jurisdiction and, 194–96
  constitutional common law and, 188–89
  constitutional remedies and, 185
  qui tam actions and, 125–26
September 11th Victims Compensation Fund, 237n.138
settlement in multidistrict litigation, 53–54, 213, 238n.151
Seventh Amendment, 35–36, 227n.163
Sixth Amendment, 187

skeptical optimism
  adversary liberal democracy, in, xvi, xx, 6, 18–19
  freedom of expression and, 7–8
  procedural due process and, 7–10
Smith, Adam, 120
social contract
  contingent fee attorneys, governmental use of, 111–12, 114–16, 121–22, 123–24, 129–30
  procedural due process and, 11, 135
Social Security benefits, 66–67, 203
Sotomayor, Sonia, 29
Southwest Airlines, 89–90, 92, 96–97, 99
"specialized" federal common law, 187
speech, freedom of. *See* freedom of expression
Speech or Debate Clause, 281n.273
state action requirement
  generally, 110–11
  avoidance by delegating authority to private actors precluded, 123
  contingent fee attorneys, governmental use of, 122–24
  private actors suing on behalf of state and, 123–24
  private litigation and, 117
  public-private distinction and, 116
Story, Joseph, 175–76, 278n.218
strict constructionism, 175–76
strict scrutiny, freedom of expression and, 26
substantive autonomy, 87
substantive due process, 217n.2
supplemental nontextualism, 177
Supreme Court. *See also specific topic*
  appellate jurisdiction, 195–96
  Congressional authority regarding, 186–87, 194–95
  constitutional basis for, 197, 276n.184
  constitutional common law and, 187
  original jurisdiction, 195
Suspension Clause, 268n.47

"tag jurisdiction," 34–35, 226n.150
Taney, Roger, 173
Taylor, Brent, 80
textualism, 174–80
  due process and, 175
  facilitative nontextualism, 175–77, 178–80
  lack of specific remedial language, 174–75
  presumption against ineffectiveness, 176–77
  supplemental nontextualism, 177
Third Amendment, 178
Thirteenth Amendment, 252n.3

Thomas, Clarence, 227n.162
tobacco litigation, 113, 253n.18
tradition, *qui tam* actions and, 125–26
Treasury General Fund, 156
tyranny, danger of, 170, 171, 173–74, 266n.25

unenumerated rights, 178
unitary democracy, 247n.80
unreasonable searches and seizures, 197–98, 199, 280n.249
utilitarianism
   adversary liberal democracy and, 67–68
   liberty interest and, 84–85
   multidistrict litigation and
      generally, 45–46, 66
      accurate decision-making, 68–69
      autonomy versus, 67–68
      government interest in reducing litigation, 69–70
      Mathews-Doehr test, 66–70
   outcome-based theory, as, 84
   procedural due process, utilitarian approach to, 36–38
      generally, 209
      cost-balancing and, 36, 37, 38
      difficulty in quantifying utility, 37
      dignitary theory versus, 58–59
      "greatest happiness" principle, 36–37
      individual interests, subjugation to government interests, 37–38
      instrumental rationale, 141
      problems with, 37
      procedural due process
         generally, 31–32
      welfare consequentialist framework, 36–37

virtual representation
   generally, xxi, 75–78, 106–7, 211–12
   adequate representation and, 99–101
   binding effect of judgments, 78–79
   class actions and, 103
   compulsory joinder and, 103–4, 105
   contradictory liability and, 94–96, 105–6, 252n.179
   cost avoidance and, 82–83
   "day-in-court" ideal versus, 76, 82–83
   defined, 75–76
   double liability and, 93–94, 103–5
   incentivizing avoidance of problems
      generally, 103
      contradictory liability, 105–6
      double liability, 103–5
   inconsistent liability and, 96–98, 251n.154
   indivisible relief and, 88–92
      generally, 76–78
      alignment of interests, 90
      legal relationship between parties, 91–92
      res judicata, 90
   interpleader and, 103
   intervention and, 103, 105
   modern development of, 79
   procedural devices to avoid problems, 78, 102–3
   prophylactic measures to avoid problems, 78, 102–3
   resolution of problems, 101–2
   Taylor v. Sturgell, 79–82

Warren, Earl, 46
Welsh, Robert, 188–90, 275n.173, 275n.176
Wisconsin Medical Examining Board, 152–53

zoning, 138–39